All for a Few
Perfect Waves

All for a Few Perfect Waves

Waves The Audacious Life and Legend of Rebel Surfer Miki Dora

DAVID RENSIN

ENTERTAINMENT

An Imprint of HarperCollinsPublishers

HarperCollins books may be purchased for educational, business, or sales promotional use. For information please write: Special Markets Department, HarperCollins Publishers, 10 East 53rd Street, New York, NY 10022.

FIRST EDITION

Designed by Renato Stanisic

Library of Congress Cataloging-in-Publication Data has been applied for.

ISBN 978-0-06-077331-1

08 09 10 11 12 COMCOM/RRD 10 9 8 7 6 5 4 3 2 1

For Miki and his family: in salt water, in secret, and in blood

For Ernest, Gerda, Joe, Sarah, Elizabeth, and Adam Rensin
For Helen, Pete, Gary, and Paul Peterson
For Suzie and Emmett, for always . . . as always

Whoso would be a man, must be a nonconformist. He who would gather immortal palms must not be hindered by the name of goodness, but must explore if it be goodness. Nothing is at last sacred but the integrity of your own mind. Absolve you to yourself, and you shall have the suffrage of the world.

—Ralph Waldo Emerson, "Self-Reliance"

I do not recognize anyone's right to pilfer one minute of my life, nor to any achievement of mine, no matter who makes the claim, how large their number, or how great their need.

— Ayn Rand, *The Fountainhead*

He who is a legend in his own time is ruled by that legend. It may begin in absolute innocence but to cover up flaws and maintain the myth of divine power, one has to employ desperate measures.

— Victor Hugo

Contents

Foreword

The journey to the "book of record" on Miki Dora has been a long one. It was about twenty years ago that Bob Simpson, Miki's good friend and lawyer, and I began discussions with Miki about such a project. We would play our weekly game of tennis at the Château de Brindos in Biarritz, followed by a sumptuous lunch. As often as not, the subject would get around to his biography. Sometimes Miki was enthusiastic, other times he was reluctant. He always wanted to know who should do the book on him. We offered many suggestions. For reasons you will discover here, none worked out.

Once you read *All for a Few Perfect Waves* you will also understand that—with great respect to Miki and his family—an autobiography or biography of Miki Dora, with his authorization and cooperation, the book he often seemed to want to do, was virtually impossible while he was alive.

My friendship with Miki started back in the late 1970s. We met in France, at Lafiténia, when I was making the surf film *Band on the Run*. It was a strange relationship in many respects, not the least being that within a few years I was the entrepreneurial businessman running Quiksilver in Europe, and Miki was the rebel/maverick surfer who defied the establishment and was known to shun not only any commercialization of his name, but of surfing as well. Well, most of the time.

The cynics said that Miki was my "friend" because of what he could get from me and what I could do for him. That was probably true in the beginning. But as the years passed it became apparent our rapport was genuine. For me real friendship is unconditional, so the nuances of one with Miki never fazed me, and I think Miki appreciated that I did not try and hold him to a set of standards he couldn't honor.

On December 29, 2001, as Miki neared death, he signed a note in front of two witnesses, leaving all his "personal effects, including film, photographs, and memorabilia to my father, Myklos [*sic*] K. Dora, in conjunction with Harry Hodge, to protect and non-commercialize my life in any manner . . . Go in peace."

After Miki died, as executive administrator of his estate, my challenge was how to reconcile an authorized biography—or any book—with his wishes. Were they inevitably opposed? I thought I knew, from our many conversations, that he *wanted* a book and, more than that, a legacy. Indeed, he had at various times sat with a number of collaborators, even if each project never produced more than big plans and a couple erratic interview tapes before they fell apart.

I felt then, as I do now, that the mystique of Miki's life was ripe for and vulnerable to bottom-feeders who would try to cash in on his myth and legend, his light side and dark, trashing reality with sound bites and speculation and hearsay that would become "fact" while the truth became a casualty. Anyone could do that book and the estate could not stop it—only refuse to cooperate. And someone would, inevitably, do it. Miki was unique in the surfing world and too tempting a target. Could I let that happen, or should I be proactive? I thought about it for a long time. In the end, I believed, and still do, that a credible book, based on the available facts of Miki's life, and told through interviews with hundreds of people who knew him—really, the only approach to a subject who had since passed away, and about whom such a diversity of opinion exists—was the better of the two choices.

In the many discussions we had about a book, Miki made one thing clear: he wanted a biographer who saw a bigger picture and would acknowledge him as more than just a surfer from Malibu. He was never keen on attending reunions and get-togethers where everyone sat around reminiscing about the old days. Miki was relentlessly drawn to the new, whether it be people, current events, even salsa dancing. Miki said he wanted an author who would respect what he was about and respect the facts and truths of his life. The problem, of course, was getting him to reveal all of that to anyone.

When David Rensin, a highly respected interviewer and author, contacted me in 2003, I remembered him from a story he had written about Miki in *California* magazine in 1983. Miki had ranted to some that he hated the piece, and he had even threatened legal action to stop it before publication—typical of Miki. But, in fact, he carried it with him most everywhere he went and on occasion mentioned to me that it was well written and that he liked the author.

David and I arranged to meet in Beverly Hills for breakfast. At our first get-together, David made it clear that he could not give anyone right of approval on the content of the book, as Miki would have demanded. However, David did say he'd remain open to the family's and my suggestions, and he promised me that even though, as we both agreed, to be worthy of respect the book had to be warts and all, he would not stomp all over Miki's grave. "I'm not here to trash or whitewash," he said. "I just want to hear what people have to say and leave judgment to the reader." After we met a few more times, I felt Miki's legacy would be in good hands. I recommended David to Miklos Sr., and after they met Miki's father also agreed.

Almost four years later, when I read the manuscript, I was gratified to see that David had kept his promise and produced a sober and truly compelling oral and narrative biography on one of surfing's greats.

I want to add that I hope that Miklos Dora Sr. is very proud of his son. He should be. When I met Miklos a few years ago, it was apparent that the love he had for his son was profound. It was also apparent that Miklos Sr. was mystified as to why his son lived the way he did. Even though Miki led a very different life than most of us could have imagined, or lived ourselves, he made a difference. He also made mistakes. But Miki never apologized for his lifestyle. He is a surfing legend who was probably the most committed surfer of all time given what he sacrificed so he could travel the globe in search of waves.

I visited Miki in November 2001 at the invitation of Miklos Sr. and his wife, Christine. It was very difficult for both Miki and me. He was so weak he couldn't come to the table for lunch with the family. However, later we went outside to the bench in a corner of the yard where the sun streamed in. I asked Miki if he spent much time here. He replied: "Gotta die with a suntan."

Driving back along Highway 1 that day from Montecito to L.A., I watched the ocean swells along the coast. I stopped at Malibu and reflected on Miki Dora and this magical wave spot he'd dominated for so long. "Dora Rules" was still painted on the Malibu wall. Even though Malibu can still produce great surf, it is now—and

inevitably—a treasure lost. Like it or not, the innocence of surfing's youth has been replaced by something different. For all his
complaining about paradise lost, Miki knew that. He always said he
never wanted to go back and that for him Malibu was "The Point
of No Return."

In fact, that's what he suggested for the title of his book. But I think
David Rensin also got it right when he wrote that Miki Dora had really lived "All for a Few Perfect Waves."

Harry Hodge
Australia, 2008

Miki, State Beach, 1966. Johnny Fain said, "Dora died for our sins. He was the Messiah then."
Photo: Pat Darrin.

DoraWorld

What we call fame is nothing but the sum of all mistakes circulating about one individual. —**Rainer Maria Rilke**

I'm a freak of nature and don't fit in with anybody. —**Miki Dora**

On December 29, 2001, shipwrecked on his sickbed at his father's home in Montecito, California, his withering, jaundiced body still remarkably tan from the sun in whose sustaining grace he had spent nearly every day of his life, Miki Dora slowly dictated two brief paragraphs as a female friend printed the words on a small sheet of lined note paper. They began: "I, Myklos [*sic*] Sandor Dora, under the circumstances I find myself, I have no alternative but to leave all my personal effects to . . ."

Four days later, the undisputed king of Malibu in its glory days, whose beyond-graceful feline self-possession and uncanny wave artistry had earned him the nickname "Da Cat," and the accolade then that "At the perfect surfing spot, on the perfect day, Miki Dora is probably the best surfer in the world," was dead at sixty-seven of pancreatic cancer.

Had Dora been just another top surfer from a bygone era he might have washed quietly into the back pages of *Sports Illustrated* or *Surfer* magazine years ago. Instead, in his heyday and Malibu's—before and for a short time after the 1959 movie *Gidget* explosively popularized an edge-dwelling sport enjoyed by a rugged and eccentric few and changed it (many say for the worse) forever—Dora not only dominated surfing style and soul, but unlike his contemporaries, many of them break-the-mold wave-masters in their own right, transcended both. Dora's God-given gifts in the water coupled with the living theater of his complicated, comic, nonconformist personality, both on and off the beach, made him what they could never be: a legend in his own time.

And yet . . . in a flawed and restive life framed against the backdrop of a sport and postwar America coping with radical social change in the '50s and '60s, and later, after he abandoned Malibu and California in the mid-'70s to roam a world enduring its own growing pains caused by what he saw as First World corruption, ecological disaster, and the death of the individual, Dora found himself trapped in a black hole of celebrity between the soul-sucking consequences of his iconic talent, charm, and mystique, and his hermetic instinct to reject the spotlight because he believed that nothing in life was more valuable than total personal freedom—no matter what the cost to himself, and often others.

Many desire personal freedom; few actually seize it. Dora did and hung on with all his might, to his betterment and detriment.

If it meant never having a real job, never marrying, never having children (at least that he knew or acknowledged; there are rumors), finding love with an assortment of enraptured women and true love mostly late in life with the loyal canine companion he considered his "child"—he embraced it. If it meant using forged passports and fraudulent credit cards, for a time, to sustain his world travels, or simply scamming you out of a few bucks or a free lunch—he'd risk it. If it meant lamenting environmental ruin, seeing conspiracy and Big Brother everywhere, and pining out loud for the good old days he knew could never return, while predicting the imminent Apocalypse—he'd broadcast it. If it meant dodging the FBI, doing prison time, going expatriate, trusting few and revealing himself to fewer—he'd keep that secret. If it meant flexing his irresistible star quality and rapier wit to live on the kindness, gullibility, or fan worship of strangers, and be reached Poste Restante in odd corners of the world—he'd work it. If it meant avoiding the press, fiercely protecting his public image as someone who never "sold out," leaving a string of breathless movie producers and publishers at the altar, and writing audacious semifictional travelogues for surf magazines that added an ego-boosting literary dimension to his artistic canon and put a few dollars in his pocket—he'd string them along. If it meant being a Rorschach test incarnate that inspired obsessive projection and trans-ference like a sacred text demands constant re-interpretation—he'd be it without even breaking a sweat. If it meant being a delightful dinner companion, courteous guest, friendly to friends' children who could immediately sense his own childlike nature—he'd enjoy the moment. If it meant being estranged from his parents yet unable to cut the cord, befriending the occasional odd or interesting younger man or woman and treating them in embryo as he wished he'd been treated (then test-ing them to make sure they wanted nothing from him), forever reject-ing authority, and seeing most human interaction as a competition to be won—he'd endure the consequences. If it meant speaking out against the commodification of surfing, the tidal wave of corporate groupthink, the sell-out mentality of surfing peers poised to profit from their sudden "careers" or celebrity—he'd bite the hand. If it meant forever baptizing himself in the most intimate communion with the ocean itself, a mysti-cal congruence that he couldn't and wouldn't explain to just anyone no matter how hard they pressed—then let the ritual begin.

Reclusive and gregarious, cocksure and cryptic, primitive and urbane, solemn and witty, canny and reckless, uncompromising and mercurial, contradictory and unequivocal, Dora was surfing's most outspoken practitioner, charismatic prince, chief antihero, committed loner, and enduring mystery.

He wanted it that way. Except, of course, when he didn't.

This much is certain: Miki Dora's is the greatest surf story never told. It's all about surfing, and it's not about surfing at all.

Loner. Rebel. Outlaw. Wanderer. Legend.

Those who knew Miki Dora, those who wished they had or never had, all agree: there will never be another character in surfing like Miki Dora. No one. Not even close.

Which is not to suggest that anyone ever *really* knew him.

"The minute someone says, 'Oh yeah, I was friends with Miki,' you can pretty well count on that being bullshit," says Greg "Da Bull" Noll, the most celebrated of classic-era big-wave conquerors, recently featured in Stacy Peralta's 2004 documentary *Riding Giants*. Noll's relationship with Dora endured for fifty choppy years. "Miki did not have friends as most people think of the word *friend*. Miki went through life—and it was just his style—using people, whether he liked them or didn't, like little stepping-stones to get from one place to another. With Miki it was always about Miki. But he was an absolutely incredible individual, the most different person that I've ever come across. Since he passed away there isn't a day that I don't think about the sonofabitch."

For years, anyone who'd seen Dora surf in person, watched his rare appearances on film, or stared at magazine pictures of him in the perfect position on the perfect wave (or pushing other surfers off so he could have the wave to himself), could not deny his world-class abilities. The late *Surf Guide* magazine editor Bill Cleary—a prime surf culture mythologizer who could spend hours deconstructing Dora—once wrote, "Miki was born with an invisible organ, some mysterious faculty analogous to a radio tuned to higher frequencies. The 'sounds' that reached Miki . . . were more like a swirl of color that contained information Miki's brain hungered for, which enabled him to surf in ways beyond our imaginings."

Author and surf historian Matt Warshaw, in his *Encyclopedia of Surfing*, described Dora's style as, "bebopping to a complex rhythm no other surfer heard."

Surf pundits and pals have called Dora "the Muhammad Ali of surfing," and not just because he rope-a-doped surf media and surf culture with relentless zest.

In Hollywood-speak, think of Dora's life as *The Endless Summer* meets *Breathless* meets *Catch Me If You Can*: part soulful, wandering wave addict; part hyperkinetic thrill seeker; part surf grifter always a few steps ahead of the plebeian beach hordes and "the man." See: It takes three films to describe Dora's life, not the usual two.

His psyche was a Rubik's Cube that no one could solve. Many tried.

In Dora's obituary, the *London Times* described him as "A surfing hedonist who became a hero to a generation of beach bums before turning his back on the waves. (He) was everything that a surfer ought to be: He was tanned, he was good-looking, and he was trouble. West Coast archetype and antihero, he became the incarnation of surfing for the postwar generation . . . indeed he was so much a rebel that he rebelled, in the end, against surfing. . . . Dora was a Kerouac in board shorts, the soulmate of Jack Nicholson in *One Flew Over the Cuckoo's Nest*: A subversive, restless wild man."

The description is almost accurate: Dora rebelled against inorganic surfing culture and its inevitable absorption into the mainstream, but he never turned his back on the waves.

Artist and cultural iconist John Van Hamersveld, who created the original *Endless Summer* poster, as well as the Beatles' *Magical Mystery Tour* and the Rolling Stones' *Exile on Main Street* album covers, sees an artistic kinship between Dora and Andy Warhol, both of whom Van Hamersveld knew. "Like Andy, Miki fed—and made most of his life's work—off of his unconscious behavior, of which he never had to become conscious."

Drew Kampion, the lyrical surf writer who rode his first wave at Dora's home break, Malibu, in 1962, adds a dimension of folklore: Dora as a self-created literary figure, "The Bob Dylan of surf culture."

To the haute-culture-inclined Dora painted a worldview as skewed and dazzling as Picasso's in his cubist period. Or he was Nureyev on a wave.

Surfer magazine, in its book *Perfect Day*, called him "surfing's dark prophet, the enigmatic, nonconformist, slightly nefarious counterpart to the sunny, Beach Boys image of California . . . surfing's rebel without a pause."

To the masses Dora was Elvis—and remains so, even though he has left the ocean.

But Derek Hynd, the noted Australian surfer/writer, who spent much time with Dora when they both lived in Jeffreys Bay, home of a fast, world-class wave at the southern tip of South Africa, cautions against these comparisons. "It's almost as though any twentieth-century American icon would do better comparing himself or herself to Dora rather than the other way around. He was an American original. Every genius surely had a mentor, but Dora perhaps less than other geniuses. If anything, he was, at heart, more like the last great Indian chiefs, refusing to bow before overwhelming force, before they were shunted into the reservations. To me he's beyond. He's not in the mold of."

Hawaii-based oceanographer, professor, and surfer Ricky Grigg, who knew Dora during the early Malibu years, agrees. "People sometimes compare him to James Dean or Brando, but that's backward. They were him."

Dora was in many ways to surfing what John Cassavetes was to filmmaking. Both were groundbreaking independents. Neither catered to the crowd, but practiced their art for themselves. Both created in others raw and uncomfortable emotions. Both wanted bigger questions about life answered, or at least explored. Cassavetes's movies were often quasi-documentaries, focused on real-time, moment-by-moment details. Dora lived moment to moment, truly. Cassavetes learned to play the show business game, when necessary, in order to pursue his muse. Dora did the same by taking money to act in beach party flicks, and creating his own surfboard line. They lived at the intersection of art and commerce with an ambidexterity that allowed them to take either route in order to persevere—no matter what the purists said. And both Cassavetes and Dora are immensely influential even though the masses under their influence aren't necessarily clued in, and know less than they should about either. But filmmakers know, and true surfers know, that these pioneers, however unacknowledged by the mainstream, are arguably far more important than those who later adopted their ideas, donned their guises, and followed in their footsteps.

Even online, the battle to define Dora rages: "Funny how culture takes an asshole rebel and beach drifter and makes him a cult hero by virtue of just being around a long time," one poster wrote. "Love him, hate him or refuse to acknowledge him. One thing is for certain—you could never ignore him," wrote another.

The analogies and allusions could go on and on, and for years they have in an attempt to define why someone so undefinable was so important: Dora was Sid Vicious meets Cary Grant, in board shorts. Dora was a force of nature who rode through life the way he rode the wave: aggressively, poetically, memorably, and totally on his own terms. Dora was a quantum personality: a human uncertainty principle, a question, not an answer. In the circus of surf, he was part ringmaster, part tightrope walker, part Flying Wallenda, part clown in the burning house.

"The late 20th century would have been sculpted differently without Miki Dora," Derek Hynd wrote in a posthumous elegy to Dora, in *Surfer*, in 2002. "Suave and erudite . . . alternately disheveled and subversive, Dora was foremost a deconstructor of the American Dream, a savage prankster whose orchestrations through the mid-'50s to mid-'60s went beyond revolution at the beach. His surfing genius and flamboyance as both a real life and popularized Moondoggie character launched an international subculture whose influence quickly went mainstream. He foresaw Wall Street opening its lips in the mid-'60s and railed against it. He corrupted himself on Hollywood stunt work and royalties from signature (surfboard) models bearing his Da Cat moniker, yet with his sense of black irony, enhanced an unclassifiable image in the process. Hero to the disaffected purist, villain to the crass profiteer, he wore the guise of an arch chameleon. In a mastery of movement in and out of the Malibu lineup, he was a Beat poet without needing to open his mouth, an effortless performance artist without needing to walk the board. His oft-shocking mystique ran parallel lines to that of Cassius Clay in the early '60s. Hundreds of thousands of new surfers and fans clambered to the worldwide post-*Gidget* explosion, and he held those who hungered to know him on a string."

Dora, it seemed, could be anything to anybody, and he was willing to let those on the perimeter imagine what they wanted, especially if it suited his purpose, which is why this dashing, shamanistic wave rider remains so memorable to multiple surfing generations and continues to exert both an esoteric and very real influence today. "If you had to pick one surfer that epitomized California surfing in the twentieth century, it would be Miki Dora," *Surfer's Journal* cofounder/publisher Steve Pezman told the *Los Angeles Times* in Dora's obituary. "Everything that's wrong with it and everything that's right with it."

But leave it to Dale Velzy, the late, crusty shaper and surf cowboy emeritus who was the first to put a brand on a surfboard, for a typically blunt reckoning: "Of all the surfers I knew"—and he knew them all—"Miki Dora was the greatest."

What makes a surfer great?

"A great surfer is like a great anything," says Drew Kampion. "He or she has prowess, knowledge, style, courage, can make it look easy, has a complex skill set, a spirit of adventure, and so on—all these but with something added. A truly great surfer has an artist's sensibility, an empath's intuition. His or her relationship with the ocean and its waves takes place largely in a subtle, morphic field . . . where the engagement is on a soul level . . . and the relationship is very much a cosmic dance."

More than a few surfers possess these basic qualities in abundance, but in the end, it's always that "something added," that ineffable poetry of motion, that unbearable lightness of being, that differentiates the savant from the swarm. Like a greatest anything, you know it when you see it.

Miki Dora wasn't the best surfer in every wave condition. He didn't much prefer short boards when longboards drifted out of style—or more accurately, although he'd use shorter boards and experimented endlessly with concept and design throughout his life, ordering boards to his specifications from shapers around the world, he didn't give up his graceful, down-the-line approach to do acrobatics like he was skateboarding on a wave.

Some say he wasn't even the best at Malibu in his time and cite as proof his rare participation in contests and his failure to win any. But that argument will rage and nuance without resolution forever. In any case, contests weren't his thing.

"He thought it was a fucking joke that surfing could be considered a competitive sport," says surfing champion, Australian native, and Dora pal Nat Young. "He got me drunk the night we met in Hawaii in 1968, in a Waikiki hotel room—we were roommates at a surf contest—and he told me the whole thing was a farce, and to never take it seriously because it meant absolutely nothing. He competed because they invited him and they gave him a free place to stay. He was in there for the game."

Dora played the game as only a natural can. Soul surfing—surfing for the sheer art and pleasure of it—was his church long before the term was coined, and his passion for worship was equaled only by his drive to create and sustain a lifestyle that gave him the liberty to live free to seek thrills, spontaneous adventure, waves, and wonder, wherever he could find them.

"Surfing was his sanctuary, the only place he could be at peace," says C.C., a girlfriend he met in 1985 and stayed in contact with until the end. "You have to be completely focused. You can't think about stuff that happened in the past like an unhappy childhood, and you're not able to worry about where your next meal or bed will be. You have to be in the now. Surfing did for Miki what some people actually pay psychiatrists to help them with."

Dora also played the game in life. A sensitive and artistic child, he had great difficulty handling his parents' divorce (and their subsequent remarriages and divorces), his time in military and other boarding schools, his aversion to rules and to those he thought less clear-minded than he, and his all-too-human need for love and inclusion while rejecting the traditional ball and chain of both. Dora not only learned early to manipulate people and situations to get what he wanted, but he realized how easy it was to get away with his shenanigans.

When on rare occasion he was caught or confronted, he resorted to creating a obfuscatory haze of rationalization and ersatz philosophy to justify his actions, and he delivered it with uncommon charm and a rhetorical manner—always questioning the questioner. He also possessed an obstinate unwillingness to work for a living, less as a rebellion against surfing's commercialization, and more as a way of life to counter society's loss of direction and inevitable rot. And leave him free to surf.

He was the victim—always. Eventually he really believed it. Maybe.

The Zen of surfing may have helped Dora's head, but it never eliminated the demons that plagued him.

To Dora, surfing was more art than sport, and he wanted a clean canvas on which to express his personal connection with the ocean and waves. No wonder he never got over his frustration, resentment, and desire for revenge on the "muscle-headed beach jocks" and landlocked kids who mobbed his beloved once-empty waves at Malibu and elsewhere after the movie *Gidget* debuted. When the beach party exploitation flicks that followed set off a youthquake that popularized a fun-in-the-sun lifestyle and its distractions for a new generation of Southern California kids, he watched as a golden era of natural balance between waves and riders was consigned to the commercial slag heap of new market trends. Now and then, in the years to come, he even regretted having worked in those quickie flicks as an extra, stunt double, and technical adviser.

Almost overnight the waves once enjoyed by a handful were fair game for everyone, specifically the crassly exploited and exploiting young who hunted for the best rides wherever they could be found, no matter whose backyard they had to cut through to get to the beach. Dora did it, too, but as he would remind you, he was there first.

However, since the young make the market, the promise of catering to surfing's fortuitously timed popularity glittered with financial reward. And if you lived beyond the sea, in the land of no surf, no matter: you could still wear the clothes, the hairstyles, use the lingo, listen to the music, dream.

The overcrowding of his sanctuary was a condition Dora could never control, only fight against in a losing guerrilla war. It was the perfect setup for a life spent searching for safe harbor.

For Dora, popularity broke the heart of surfing.

It broke his heart, too—but he'd be damned if he'd just take it. Although Dora notoriously disliked "surf music," the Beach Boys' song "Caroline, No," from their seminal postsurf masterwork, *Pet Sounds*, can help one imagine the—I have to invent a word here: sentimelancholia—Dora and other purists felt at the inexorable expansion of the surfing universe after the Big Bang of *Gidget*.

Just imagine "Caroline" as a metaphor for California.

> *Where did your long hair go? Where is the girl I used to know? What made you lose that happy glow. Caroline, no. Who took that look away? I remember when you used to say you'd never change but that's not true . . . Will I ever find in you again, things that made me love you so much then? Can we ever bring them back once they have gone?*

The song is a perfect lament for the rise and demise of not only the uncorrupted surfing life of the '30s through the mid-'50s, but the innocence of pre– and early post–World War II Southern California. This paradise lost was to Dora the heart of the matter, the wellspring of an enduring disappointment and discontent that eventually flooded other parts of his life, whether it had happened at Malibu or anywhere else in the world that an uncluttered existence and virgin waves were defiled by progress.

If, as some say, Dora's achievement was to stay relatively true to avoiding dull-witted conformity and prosaic obligation, then the take-no-prisoners behavior that liberated him ironically caged him.

In the '50s and '60s, the times were a-changing. Cultural unrest and transformation filled the air. But when that rebellion evolved, for better or worse, into the Me Decade, Dora was left holding the bag as a standard-bearer for the small-time outlaw life. Was that a good thing? Heroic? Noble? Or just an inability or unwillingness to redefine himself?

At the outset, his misdeeds were those of youth, and the consequences ignored—until they added up and he had to pay up. But worse than spending almost a year behind bars—a circumstance totally anathema to the free-roaming Cat—he was also confronted with the contradictions of his outsider philosophy because he never stopped wanting to be able to enter at will the society he claimed to reject, and enjoy its benefits. (Some say he took revenge for the spoiled California dream by exploiting the spoilers in their own backyards.) He warned against the insidious effect of chasing the dollar, but didn't mind enjoying what money could buy, or investing in the very capitalist system he abhorred, to make a few bucks.

Still, prison convinced Dora that anything was better than a life inside, so on release he eschewed the reckless and illegal and moved on, searching for sanctuary. Intimacy. People he could trust. A family of sorts. "He could have had it," says his friend C.C., "if only he was willing to compromise. But he always had to be in control. . . ."

Even though Dora sometimes wanted to come in from the cold, sooner or later he came to know himself well enough to understand that his intimate longings aside, a safe place would never be more than a briefly realized dream. His "families" would be forever adoptive and worldwide, providing only temporary shelter, leaving him at last alone again and waiting for the next wave of opportunity.

Dora was always on the move, in the water and out. The game, as all surfers know, is to be in the best position. But sometimes that position meant living in dilapidated rooms, surrounded by scrapbooks full of family pictures, photos of waves and old-time surfers he admired, as well as wine labels, magazine clippings, yellowing letters from surf magazine editors and lovers, and ads for his signature surfboard. His companions were boards and wet suits, boxes of correspondence, books and CDs and videotapes, memorabilia and wonderous trinkets collected on his world travels. Sometimes a woman shared his home. In his later years, his beloved dog, Scooter Boy, did. It's the price Miki paid for being Miki. To his credit—and this is one reason why he's lionized—he never defaulted.

My fascination with Dora began in the early 1960s when I surfed the California coast, and poorly, I confess. Foremost, I respected Dora's surfing ability and—the proof was in watching him on a wave—his almost ethereal connection to the ocean. I also followed Dora in surf films and magazines, and loved his bylined accounts of improbable international adventures, elliptical and audacious tracts about the true nature of surfing and life, and the rare Dora interviews, all typically sardonic, aggressive, ominous. And totally entertaining. But just underneath the provocations, there seemed to lay a cynical sadness and a wounded innocence. For Dora, who'd had nearly fifteen years of beautiful waves without crowds, the Golden Age was gone and the Apocalypse he so often predicted was surely at hand.

And if it wasn't, it sounded good.

Dora's pronouncements were also a talisman against which I and my surfing friends could privately compare our own budding personal philosophies. We had other surf heroes, but Dora was unique; like the *I Ching*, you saw in him what you needed to see. We would never surf as well or risk as much, but his envelope-pushing example made us ask ourselves important questions about what we wanted in life, and what we might be settling for.

Still, to Dora we were just in the way. Even if we'd hated *Gidget* or the beach party movies, as come-lately surfers we were by definition poseurs and scene-makers whose migration to the beach had to have come from a book or film and not naturally, from living near the ocean. We were, he said, "pollywogs" polluting his purview. Would it have surprised Dora to know that we also really loved the indescribable experience of sliding down a wave face and a lucky few seconds in the tube; that we, too, saw some sense in his complaints about the merchandisers, the silly Hollywood movies, and the lemming-like march off the deep end and into the trench of trendiness? So what if some of us lived in the San Fernando Valley, a once semiarid wasteland of fruit trees and tumbleweeds just over the hills inland from Malibu, that personified for him and others all the hated interlopers. (If the movie *Chinatown* revealed the corruption that brought water to the S.F. Valley, a surf-*Chinatown* might focus on the hollow Hollywood entertainments and entrepreneurial zeal that caused landlocked kids everywhere to flood the pristine waves.) Nothing we could do about it but enjoy ourselves and ride the "wave" in the direction it was breaking. I admired Dora, considered him an inspiration to a young man who didn't want to lead a commonplace life, but I still wasn't about to get out of the water until I was ready.

That came soon enough. Soon I began my own mini-rebellion against the establishment by becoming a writer who, like a surfer looking for ever-different waves, wanted only to forage here and there in search of new stories and experiences.

After doing a piece about Dora in 1983 for *California* magazine and spending some time with him before and after publication, I thought about him now and then for twenty years, while doing countless magazine interviews and eleven books. With his passing in 2002, I began to seriously consider exploring his untold story in more depth. I called Dora's father, Miklos K. Dora. He was traveling, but his wife, Christine, directed me to Miki's longtime patron and estate administrator, Harry Hodge, then a France- and Australia-based top executive at the huge beach and board lifestyle apparel company Quiksilver.

Over the next few months, Harry and I met for long conversations each time he came to Los Angeles. He told me of his history with Dora, and of his difficulties getting his friend of two decades to actually sit down and write the book he'd often told Harry he wanted to write. He also told me of Dora's wish that (with all due respect to the many "surf" writers whose genre expertise leaves me in the shore break—and yet who still gave generously to this project: thank you) a nonsurf (but not necessarily nonsurfing) journalist do the job should he or she have the energy. We agreed that the book would be warts and all, and that although I wouldn't dance on Dora's grave simply to sensationalize, my first loyalty had to be to the story—whatever I found.

We hit it off, and he passed me to Miklos Sr.

At our first meeting, I gave Dora's dad some of my earlier books to read and he liked them. He was also very up front in saying he thought my *California* magazine piece had captured Miki's essence, but had been a bit hard on his son. Still, we got along, and in early 2003, with his and Christine's encouragement and support, I began three years of traveling the globe from California to France to South Africa—and phoning everywhere else—to interview more than three hundred people and gather over a million words of testimony, plus research, on Dora's life.

Although I worked independent of any official family control, Miklos and I agreed at the outset that the idea was to bring together in one place more about his son than ever before. I knew he was both reluctant and curious about what I might find. His only wish: "Be honest, fair, and creditable.

"I am an adult," he said to me. "I expect to have pro and con. Miki had two sides of his life, I know that. Nobody's liked by everybody. I just want you to do a good book."

To find the story required that I travel deep into DoraWorld, navigating narrow channels both personal and political, to speak to his many friends, acquaintances, and otherwise. Most had never talked publicly about him while he was alive and in a possibly retributive mood. Dora's disapprovals were legendary. One person I interviewed for the *California* magazine story—former *Surfer* editor/publisher Jim Kempton—told me that Dora had taken a dump in a box and mailed it to him, as thanks. And he wasn't the only one.

"Basically it was the accusation of 'Everything you said was all made up,'" says Kempton, years later. "Of course the next time I saw him, a year later in France, it's all love and kisses and 'Let's go to dinner and have a big feast in San Sebastian.' Here's the most important point: you have to understand that he sent me the box so that we would have this conversation now. Understand? Whether Miki understood or whether it was unconscious, Miki was always building that legacy."

I heard—and asked—this question more than most: How complicit was Dora in strategically creating and directing the grand play of his life?

"That's the huge mystery," says Jim Kempton. "That's the seminal question."

Who knows what Dora dreamt, what thoughts scattered through his head when he awoke each morning, what he mulled as he showered, ate his breakfast, drove to the beach, trimmed on a wave. What fantasies lay down with him at night? Did he spin schemes or were his musings as mundane and ordinary as our own?

Having lived his life, as Dora sometimes claimed, with attention to every move, he is of course on one level totally responsible. He did it. He is it. But as an eponymous literary character composing a novel of self . . . well, one has to leave some room for inspiration and serendipity, for the character to wrest control of the story from the author, as is common.

John Van Hamersveld's earlier observation that Dora instinctively fed off his unrestrained unconscious is instructive. It's most likely that Dora's studied deadpan and watchful, sometimes paranoid ambiguity simply created in those he encountered a tension that left them wondering what was real and what wasn't. He instinctively knew that once the audience was off balance, all possibilities were in play. Anything could be true or false, and the brilliance of this pose was that there was usually enough truth involved to make deciphering his intentions and motivations impossible. No wonder the *Surfer's Journal*'s Steve Pezman said that writing about Dora can be a fool's game—surf journalist quicksand. Instead of just enjoying the performance, too many were left trying to figure out how the trick was done.

Dora always said he just wanted to be left alone. But during my research it became clear that while he didn't want to be gossiped about, and always cautioned acquaintances, "Don't sell me out," the dictum was hardly inviolable. In fact, the whispers were necessary to the mystery and the life of unaccountability it sustained. As much as this might disappoint the faithful, Dora lived by few absolutes. Instead, he was intuitively connected to life's dialectic, the ceaseless pendulum of existence between poles of meaning and behavior. A true flow to go with. His needs, ethics, and moral floor were situational.

Dora relied on his reputation and legend to help him get by, to the waves, to navigate the chore of living day to day. After all, how could someone who didn't work pay the bills? How could a "nobody" be everybody's guest? Acquaintances around the world didn't put him up just because he surfed, but because he was Miki Dora. And he knew it. And he used it.

Dora was self-aware enough to know that it was better to appear in control even when he wasn't, however it meant playing the game. Reality is perception. Reality is deception. Reality is up for discussion. All of it worked to Dora's advantage, particularly because of his self-appointed and subtly encouraged acolyte network that, having read his interviews and screeds, and having occasionally been dazzled by a personal encounter, found their fantasies of self-reliance and rebellion inflamed. Others simply wanted to suck up and get his approval, and spread the truth and illusion of his legend far and wide.

Someone told me of a group of hard-core Dora-freaks who have Pat Darrin's picture of their hero on the crossed surfboards tattooed on their bodies. "Miki would have laughed and thought they were pathetic," he added.

All this made his mythos, but Dora being Dora, he claimed he didn't want to be a legend; he said it to me himself, sort of: "I've never considered myself a legend." But a careful parsing reveals that he's only absolved himself of the responsibility, not the fact, and not to using it to his advantage. The rest is up to us.

Another question I heard often was, why should anyone care about a ne'er-do-well surfer, or any surfer for that matter? Aren't surfers Jeff Spicoli–like dudes who would just as soon use a book for a bonfire than read it?

Whoa, bro! Not so fast. In its February 28, 2006, obituary of former *Los Angeles Times* publisher and founding family scion Otis Chandler, the newspaper began their memorial this way: "At his apex as publisher of the *Los Angeles Times*, Otis Chandler received a message one morning from a fellow surfer. Waves were cresting at 12 to 15 feet off Dana Point, 'the largest Southern California surf of my lifetime,' he would later recall. Chandler was a busy man, in the midst of catapulting the *Times* from mediocrity into the front ranks of American journalism. He was probably the most successful newspaper publisher in the country . . . 'Within an hour,' he said, 'I had gathered things up in my briefcase, told my secretary, "Well, we can shine those afternoon meetings off," and headed for Dana Point.'"

Why the hurry? Easy. Waves are here and gone. You never want to hear, "You should have been here an hour ago."

Forget the "sport"; this is what sets apart the art of surfing. Even though it may be preserved in photos and on film, and certainly in memories, a wave ride is created by the artist, for him- or herself, with no stopwatch and nothing left behind to analyze. Southern California's fine new Surfing Heritage Museum can exhibit boards, artifacts, and oral and visual histories, but it can't ride a wave for you. And how can one really capture on a page the glistening sun, the refreshing chill of the dawn mist, the taste of saltwater and seaweed, the rush of the drop-in, the Zen of the glide?

Surfing is even more transitory than climbing up or skiing down a mountain. At least when you're done, the mountain is still there.

Waves have always been a spiritual force. Glenn Hening, founder of the Surfrider Foundation and cofounder of the Groundswell Society, likes to tell stories about how, "as far back as 3,000 years ago, the Peruvians venerated waves. They considered them the most tangible reference point for divine power on the planet. Miki Dora, among others, was transfixed by the mystery of riding waves. To understand him you have to understand what it is about a wave and the peak moments of surfing that have nothing to do with BUDWEISER written across a surfboard on a freeway billboard."

"I once heard that had Miki grown up in Japan, he would be considered a national icon, a hero," says *Riding Giants* director Stacy Peralta. "But in this country you have to be the star of an accepted sport. The problem was that Miki had nothing to show for his art. As soon as the wave is gone, it's done. All the beautiful 'wave paintings' he did have disappeared."

Surfing, then, is either one of the most courageous art forms, or the laziest; the ultimate in humility or narcissism. Likely all of the above. And it's still uncertain how well the world will ever appreciate surfing beyond the bodies, bikinis, acrobatics, and commercial appeal, because, as any surfer will tell you, the act is indescribable. You're so in the moment it's like dreaming; you act on instinct. And the dream-state pleasure-producing endorphins are so powerful that when you pull out of the wave you can't wait to catch another and prolong the dream. Talk about addictive.

Okay, then; so surfing is either an indolent, self-aggrandizing pastime or artful solipsism on a board. It's fine for summer, but then it's back to work or school. Surfing isn't something you pursue your whole life, or, as in Dora's case, toss over real life to do, is it?

But what is real life anyway?

That was Dora's question.

Most people don't think of their lives as their own, as something they can spend as they choose. That's what made Miki different. He did. Adamantly.

"Ultimately, Miki does nothing but go surfing," says director/ screenwriter John Milius. "He's the ultimate hedonist. It's the question in *Riding Giants*: Is this hedonism worth it? In that movie, the answer is yes, it's worth it as much as any other endeavor."

Part of our limitations is lifelong conditioning; we've bought into the social routine and, like most everyone else, wear the mantle of restraint and resignation without really knowing it's there. It's not so hard to understand why: To break away from family and responsibility is tough. Tougher still is to actually come face-to-face with your own fear-producing and awe-inspiring power to be who and what you want to be. You have to be willing to accept the costs and rewards involved. Try it. Walk out the front door, turn left, keep going . . . keep going. Don't look back. Don't come back. You're free. Now what?

Writing about Neal Cassady in his 2005 *Los Angeles Times* review of *Neal Cassady: Collected Letters 1944–1967*, author Gerald Nicosia opens with a story that could easily apply to Dora. "Hidden in an otherwise joking, high-on-pot, mocking letter to Allen Ginsberg in 1947, Neal Cassady offhandedly gives the key to his life: '[S]ee how I write on several confused levels at once, so do I think, so do I live, so what, so let me act out my part at the same time I'm straightening it out, so as to reach an authentic destiny.'"

Dora in a nutshell.

"The Beats were all about authenticity," explained author Kem Nunn (*Tapping the Source, Dogs of Winter, Tijuana Straits*), whose surf-noir novels resonate with pervasive authenticity. "What does our culture give us? Our culture gives us what Henry Miller called 'the air-conditioned nightmare.' It closes us off from experience. That was part of the whole trip for Ginsberg and Kerouac and the rest that ultimately led into the hippies and the '60s. Kerouac and Ginsberg were writers and poets, and got discovered by the media. Dora didn't, and for reasons particular to the perception of surfing, even though he had just as significant an effect on the surfing culture and ethos. But in both cases, the question was: How do you stop living an inauthentic life? How do you break down some of these doors? For surfers it was riding waves and the beach life, and even though surfing was always a little bit off the radar, eventually the media found it, too—though they didn't exactly portray it correctly. Today we talk about soul surfers—surfing for the sheer love of it—versus competitive surfers, and Dora was the poster boy."

While the Beats were howling non sequiturs and staccato poetry in smoky basement cafés from Manhattan to San Francisco about all that was wrong with the gray flannel suits and the military-industrial mentality, and the attractions of just being real, Dora and a small coterie of like-minded radicals were actualizing those desires on the translucent swells of Southern California—and getting a tan at the same time. Robust, trim, and athletic, they just seemed to be having more fun.

Dora took the royal aspects of surfing's Hawaiian origins, the individualistic bravado of pre–World War II watermen/surfers, the Beat era/free speech/free love/tune in–turn on–drop out rebelliousness of the 1950s and 1960s, and the me-ism of the 1970s (way before the '70s), and, combined with his natural ability and riveting persona, wrapped it into one tantalizing package that at some point, while he was still alive, slipped beyond even Dora's ability to control.

Did the myth transcend the man? You will always find those who think Dora should have made more of his potential, who say "if only" he'd been more honest, less self-indulgent, more focused, less willful, willing to have a job. "He could have been anything, done anything."

Dora would have enthusiastically agreed.

In fact, that's just what he did: *anything*. That was the whole point.

These days Dora's predictions of corporate and commercial infiltration have come true in surfing and beyond. All board sports—skateboarding, snowboarding—are so popular that genre apparel and equipment companies rake in multibillions a year and sponsor most competitions. Board sports are worldwide, snowboarding is in the Winter Olympics—and the revolution is televised. Take surfing alone: Its image is now de rigueur in Madison Avenue campaigns to sell everything from financial advice for aging baby boomers, to health food, to video equipment, to cars, to cell phones, to antacid. They wouldn't use surf images if they didn't think it would excite young consumers and make older ones hark back to something heartfelt.

Many of these companies have done much for the sport and are environmentally minded. It's not necessarily a bad thing, unless you like to surf on empty waves.

"Surfing's a lot more important than people think, and has a lot deeper meaning to society than people are willing to admit," says surfing veteran and diving entrepreneur Bev Morgan. "The whole goddamn *Gidget* thing and *Beach Blanket Bingo* thing, that was the wrong path. Bruce Brown came along with *Endless Summer* and set that straight. That doesn't necessarily mean it will emerge victorious or even have any lasting influence on the world, but I think it's had a hell of an influence already."

Guy Trebay, writing on June 1, 2006, in the *New York Times* agrees. "Lately, the octopus grasp of surf culture has become so inescapable that it is hard to contemplate a time, just over a half-century ago, when surfers were legitimate counterculture types, a wave-riding minority of oddballs, semi-sociopaths, dropouts, athletically gifted isolates with the occasional drug or messiah problem, or just all-around good-time freaks. . . . It is possible that no sport practiced by fewer people has ever had the influence of surfing on American style."

Finally, I was asked, if one *must* write about surfers, "Why Miki Dora?" A riddle waiting to be unraveled, sure, but aren't there other worthy candidates with less esoteric stories, whose triumphs and tragedies lead to clear and perhaps prescriptive conclusions? After all, we still can't decide if Dora was some kind of hero or a misanthrope. Was he just a surf grifter with antisocial tendencies, or a visionary whose life held layers of as yet unrealized wisdom?

The answer: Love him or hate him, Dora's life is a looking glass and kaleidoscope all in one. He is the beckoning rabbit hole. The Yellow Brick Road. According to Steve Pezman, Dora was a "romantic Robin Hood of surfing (who) became so important to all of us who were living traditional, canned, commodified lives because he was a larger-than-life figure who somehow lived our dream for us. He expressed everything—athletically, politically, emotionally—that we couldn't express ourselves. He was the rebel spirit who flipped-off society and went his own way."

America loves a rebel. Eventually.

~

Since Dora was such an elusive and attractive figure, a desire exists among those he rubbed up against to somehow be included in his story. Though few would speak on the record while he was alive—and gave every indication that they would never talk—an unexpected and unprecedented parade of his associates, friends, family, and foes were finally willing to go on the record for this book. Similarly, many breathless rumors and guilt-by-association stories, usually inimical and unverifiable, poured in as I wrote. "This will be explosive" was a common refrain. Often I heard four or five versions of the same tale, with the "facts" slightly twisted to amp the sensational, or aggrandize the source. Often the facts were simply wrong. I've tried to spare readers the need to endlessly compare and contrast, choosing for inclusion those stories and scenes that match other accounts, or the event with multiple witnesses.

But remember this: When it comes to Dora, acts have been laid at his feet that he didn't do; some of what he did do has been inflated, even by himself; much that he actually did remains hidden—both the negative and positive. In this book you have to learn to live with a measure of uncertainty, and ineffability. Read in the spirit Miki lived his life: It's a magical mystery tour.

Of course, one or two sources still balked at contributing here and decided to guard their experiences with Dora. In each case I felt it was less a matter of them jealously saying, "I know, and you never will," and more that they simply identified with the facet of Dora's philosophy that had moved them most: his insistence on privacy. I could respect that, especially when they told me so, and didn't just ignore my e-mails.

Another important point: According to Dora's friend C. R. Stecyk, who, with writer Drew Kampion, created *Dora Lives*, a photo and essay tribute published in 2005, Dora, contemplating the eventual unveiling of his story in book form, "banned research interviews with alcoholic surf stars or old girlfriends."

All for a Few Perfect Waves does not honor that ban—I believe to its benefit—particularly with respect to Dora's paramours. I couldn't possibly speak to them all, but those in this book were all intense relationships, whatever the duration. These women bring to the biography an emotional resonance and insight crucial to a complete picture. Dora let his guard down with women. He wanted to be close even though he didn't trust them, or at least saw them as nesting creatures incongruent with his restless ways. I understand why he wanted to limit their participation: They saw him, if only briefly, as no others did, as he would allow no others to. It's a valuable perspective.

Given the acute awareness of the factual whirlpool of Dora's life, there were—understandably—many days when I felt I'd hardly penetrated his personal proscenium. It seemed that Dora was just a ghost in the machine. Sometimes it still feels that way. It can make your head spin, and it has. But with Dora this is as it should be.

"There's two questions I get asked at this stage of my life," says Greg Noll, who was among the most gracious in helping me reveal the Dora DNA. "One is, 'What was it like to ride a big wave?' and the other is 'What was Miki Dora really like?' Both put me in the snore mode. You got a week to talk about it—and then you don't even scratch the surface. The answer to the first is that you don't know unless you do it/been there, and then what's there to really talk about? Once I told a guy, 'Frankly I feel sorry for all the poor bastards who didn't have the experience because they're never going to know.' And it's that way with Miki Dora, as well. If you try to figure him out, all you'll end up doing is chasing your tail and wasting energy because he was a master at fucking with people's minds."

My approach: I didn't want to "figure out" Dora because then, by definition, he wouldn't be Dora. The mystery is organic to the man and must remain so. One can allude and speculate and gather the facts, such as they are, but to set him in stone is a dead end and a disservice. Does that defeat a biography's purpose? Not if the idea is to both inform and make the reader experience what others felt when they were with Dora. In and out of the water Dora was synonymous with the unexpected, the unexplored, and the unresolved. His story and influence contain all the elements of complex chemistry and classic myth. He can be best described in paragraphs that end not with periods, but with . . .

So: Better to present his life as an oral history told by the eyewitnesses, the philosophers, the storytellers, the contextualizers, the confused, the historians, even the liars, and let the story find its own level.

There is also interstitial writing, paragraphs to move the story along, or short chapters to set the scene and provide context.

What I discovered is that many possess a piece of Dora's complex saga, holographic bits that suggest the whole. But, always the master compartmentalizer, he wanted no one to have it all. By collecting recollections and experiences and letters and other artifacts in *All for a Few Perfect Waves*, my belief is that a fresh and deeper portrait of Dora will appear.

What might that portrait look like?

John Milius, who, among his many credits, wrote and directed the classic surf-themed studio film *Big Wednesday*, makes an intriguing suggestion: "The more I once thought about how to tell Miki's story, the more I saw that it had to be like *Citizen Kane*, which is based on people's opinions of Kane. It's probably the only movie that's ever been done like that, where you really examine the life of someone not good, not bad, but big and colorful and misunderstood. And the deeper you get into it the less you understand him. In fact, you understand as much about Kane from the newsreel at the beginning of the movie, as you do at the end."

Paul Reader, a former surfer who was on hand when Dora ruled Malibu, echoed that insight. "Both Kane and Dora were plucked from a comforting familial environment and sent away at very early ages; both, in their own ways, spent the better part of their lives trying to recapture happiness; Miki through his search for a place that resembled the paradisical attributes of Southern California before the hordes and the development; and Kane, while initially imbued with high ideals regarding his fellow man and American society, sought escape through accumulation of an increasing cascade of coveted and treasurelike possessions.

"Both were complex individuals who, in their quests, sacrificed relationships, damaged reputations, and were ultimately unable to control the flow of events (and in some cases helped to accelerate unintended negatives). Both were disdainful and cynical about their fellow bread-and-butter Americans. But most important, Kane and

Dora were in large part a manifestation of what went on in America and in particular in the Southern California of their times."

"And yet," says Milius, "the story is terrifically compelling all the way through because there is no easy answer. Life doesn't have an answer. In *Citizen Kane*, Welles throws out these huge symbols: the girl, the sled, Xanadu, the snow globe falling on the floor, Rosebud. And none of it leads anywhere. The same can be said of Miki's life, but the journey is fascinating."

The story begins just before Dora's birth in Budapest, on August 11, 1934, to his American mother, Ramona Stancliff, and his Hungarian father, Miklos K. Dora. It continues from a teetering, troubled childhood in the military schools and on the unspoiled beaches of Southern California, to his reign as Malibu's best when Malibu was the cynosure of surfing. When, midway through the '70s, Dora—also known as "The King of Malibu," "The Black Knight," and "The Malibu Gypsy"—abandoned America for decades, for what can only be termed bluer pastures, even his whereabouts were unknown.

In Dora's absence, his legend only intensified.

Word of his death in 2002 left many in denial. It had long been assumed that Dora, who'd had the dignity (or smarts) to pull his vanishing act as both his and Malibu's star declined in the early '70s—only to be sighted here and there like a Yeti in board shorts and flip-flops—would forever circumnavigate the globe like some Heathcliff in search of breaks that echoed the lost love of his now-overcrowded California. Then he'd carve up those empty, perfect waves long before anyone else arrived.

Thus, when, in 2001, whispers of his illness leaked, not many believed it. In *H₂O* magazine, writer Bob Feigel, who knew and was inspired by Dora in the early '60s, wrote: "I dismissed the news as just another rumor in a colorful life plagued by rumor. Besides, it seemed unlikely that a man who had always radiated such vibrant health could now be fighting for his life."

Until his death, Dora continued to challenge the ocean with the youthful panache and energy of men half his age. To some, his greatest ride didn't come until he was sixty-three.

Neil Young sang, "It's better to burn out than fade away."

Miki Dora burned.

Loner. Rebel. Outlaw. Wanderer. Legend. Man.

LONER

In school damn near everything was concocted around the buddy system. They never left you alone. But with surfing I could go to the beach and not have to depend on anybody. I could take a wave and forget about it.

—Miki, *Surf Guide*, 1963

CHAPTER **ONE**

Same Son of Different Fathers

1

7.31.1934 [Letter from Ramona Stancliff to her best friend]
Dear Yolande—Undoubtedly you will drop in a dead faint when you
see the Budapest postmark, as I am supposed to be in China by now, no?
But I fear you really will get a shock when you read why I am here—so
prepare yourself . . .

MIKLOS DORA SR.: I was nineteen, a second lieutenant in the Hungarian Hussars, the same regiment as my father's. I was also a law student at the university. Every six months I had to take examinations. Mine were scheduled for September 1933. After summering with my mother in Vienna, going to the opera, appreciating the arts, I took a passenger boat on the Danube back to Budapest to take my tests. That's when I met Ramona.

JUANITA KUHN: Miklos was in uniform and he flirted with my sister, who took after our father: very dark skin, black eyes, lovely, curly dark hair. Ramona looked Italian or Latino. She was a free spirit and blossomed early, and by the time she was fourteen she had already turned men's heads. I was a little pip-squeak blonde. I was always a little jealous because she was much more artistic, imaginative, and glamorous. When Ramona graduated from Beverly Hills High, our mother had figured I didn't need any more education either, and in 1933 she took us, and our younger brother Elwood, on a two-year trip around the world. I thought it was neat because I didn't have to study.

MIKLOS DORA SR.: I was elated to meet an American family, especially one with good-looking girls. Ramona was seventeen and quite mature. Can you picture a young Dolores Del Rio? Suddenly I was thinking about an affair with an American girl, if I got lucky. In the old days, in Hungary, you courted girls from nice families, but to get in their pants was very difficult. All the girls wanted to get married as a virgin, so you played around. I hoped that maybe the American girl would be different. The trip took seven or eight hours and I spoke English, so I talked to Ramona and Juanita, and their mother, Mildred Stancliff. Ramona said they'd been in Germany, Holland, France, and elsewhere and were coming to Budapest to stay at one of the best hotels, the St. Gellert. We hit it off and I offered to show them the city.

JUANITA KUHN: After we met Miklos, Mother wasn't at all sure about Ramona going out with him unless I also went along, so Miklos had to dig up a friend for me. I was fifteen and thrilled. The young men would take us to the theater, or dancing at afternoon tea at the hotel. Sometimes we snuck out at night, but I chaperoned Ramona and it was all very proper.

We stayed in Budapest about five months, in part because Ramona had gotten involved with Miklos. The idea that they might get married was even in the air, but she was headstrong, and, of course, too young. We left Budapest and continued traveling.

[Ramona's letter, continued]

Do you remember last December I wrote to you from Zagreb saying that I had something to tell you, only you'd have to wait until I got home because I couldn't write it? Then I wrote again from Capri and said that my sister Juanita had discovered by accident, but that my mother didn't know? Well, she knows now. (I told her when we reached Egypt.) So now I can tell you.

Darling, Miklos Dora and I were married when I was here in Budapest last November. We didn't tell anybody (the ceremony was performed secretly), because I wanted him to finish his university studies and become established first. He's studying for a diplomatic career in the Royal Hungarian Ministry. It would take him about two years and then he was coming to America to fetch me. Meanwhile I intended to travel with my dear mother and sister and see the rest of the world. . . .

Of course, when I told my mother last May in Egypt, she was very much surprised, but she is very fond of Miklos and was pleased that I had chosen him rather than somebody else. Of course, as soon as I told

*her she turned around and came right back to Budapest. I was very
foolish to think that I could leave my husband for an uncertain amount
of time—too many things could happen. Miklos says now he will never
let me be separated from him again. If I go back to California to live,
which I am sure I shall do, he is coming, too. . . . Love, love and write
soon.   Ramona.*

*ps: Miklos is a Hungarian Cavalry Hussar of the first regiment and
he looks grand in his uniform.*

pps: Young lady, I am Ramona Dora now!!

MIKLOS DORA SR.: That's a wonderful story. Amusing. Glamorized. A young girl's fantasy. Ramona's mother did discover a secret in Egypt, but not that we'd been secretly married.

I had just come back from a trip and they called me. I met them the next day and they told me Ramona was pregnant. Her mother said, "What can we do about it?" I was surprised. I was very fond of Ramona, and definitely still interested, but I hadn't planned to marry her. Anyway, I said, "Look, I will marry you. I told your mother, too." I accepted what had happened. I said I would do my duty. Her mother, a very nice lady, wasn't angry; in fact, she was very helpful.

My father, Kornel, was furious. He said, "I spent all my money and time to give you a good education and now you're getting married? You have nothing!" He wouldn't even meet Ramona. In Hungary you became "of age" when you were twenty-four. Until then you couldn't do anything officially. To get married I had to get permission from my parents. My father wouldn't give it to me. He and my mother, Nadina, had been divorced when I was eight or nine. I went to Vienna to ask her. She was shocked, naturally, but she said, "Of course." She came to Budapest and met Ramona and her mother.

We married in 1934. That summer, on August 11, twelve days after Ramona wrote the letter to Yolande, never mentioning the truth of her situation, our son, Miklos Sandor Dora, was born in Budapest's Baba Intezet Hospital.

PHIL JARRATT: To celebrate the arrival Miklos presented his wife with an exquisite photo album, "In the Beginning," published by Paul Elder & Co. of San Francisco in 1911. In the rather gushing style of the times, the album begins with a prose poem entitled "Mother to Baby: First Letter": "Dear little one, may the days depicted here be those of a bright and happy childhood, and may I be given wisdom to do my part in making them a fitting prelude to the after years of a beautiful and useful life." Some might say that Miki's strange and sometimes lonely life was neither beautiful nor useful, but he kept that album with his most treasured possessions through decades of country hopping.

MIKLOS DORA SR.: The Dora family is from Hungary. We could be described as patrician. My mother, Nadina Nezvanova, was Russian, born in Georgia— Tiblis, Stalin's home—but her parents died early and she was raised by her aunt in St. Petersburg. When she was very young, she went to Berlin to study piano with the same man who taught Arthur Rubenstein.

My father, Kornel, was in the Hungarian army. He went to Berlin for military study and there met my mother. They were young, fell in love, and despite being two very different characters, married. My mother was very artistic, very genteel, and very beautiful then. My father was a rough and tough character. The marriage didn't last.

I was an only child, born in Budapest. After the divorce my mother married Arturo DeSanctis, a famous voice coach for the Vienna Opera. I stayed with my father. He loved life, but left alone with me he said, "I can't take care of you." So he put me into a Catholic school.

After one year, and then until I was eighteen, I went to a Jesuit boarding school. The fathers gave me a good foundation, good discipline, so I could always control my life. Today I am still a Catholic, but a bad Catholic, because when you grow up you start thinking for yourself.

After graduation I went into the military. In Hungary, if you had a high school education you were automatically accepted into officers' school. Our outlook on life then was completely different than it is today. We were nationalistic and we felt it was an honor to serve.

JUANITA KUHN: My father, Edwin Radeker Stancliff's family was from Elmira, in upstate New York, and well-to-do. Ramona, our younger brother, Elwood, and I grew up in Southern California. Ramona was born in 1916; I came two years later in New York; Elwood in 1920. Our father died in 1923, when I was five. He was an alcoholic but tried to straighten out. He had a job in San Pedro and was building us a house there, on a hill. One Sunday morning he told Mother he had left a tool on the roof. The house was on a slope and the top was more than one story up. Mother, protecting me, later told us that his hat blew away and when he reached for it he fell off, landed on his head, and died. But the autopsy showed there was alcohol in his system. I don't know if he was chasing his hat or was just drunk, or both.

DOUGLAS STANCLIFF: My grandmother Mildred never remarried. She had a life insurance policy from the Auto Club and got money from the trust set up

ABOVE LEFT: Miklos and Ramona, Budapest, 1933. Courtesy Gard Chapin Jr.

ABOVE: Miki and Miklos, 1940/41. Courtesy Dora Estate.

LEFT: Miki and Ramona, 1936. Courtesy Dora Estate.

by my grandfather's aunt and uncle. I think the original distribution in the 1950s was about $150,000 per person. That was a lot of money back then.

JUANITA KUHN: After Miki was born, Miklos and Ramona went to Vienna to stay with Nadina because Miklos was still in law school and had a problem coping with all that had happened. Eventually they moved to America.

MIKLOS DORA SR.: We arrived in the United States in January 1935. Ramona had got fed up with Europe. She told me she missed the drugstore soda counter and the malted milks. I didn't understand exactly what she wanted, but I agreed. I became an American citizen in '38 or '39.

When my mother took us to the railroad station in Vienna, I cried like a baby. My father remained behind. He lived through all the Nazi turmoil and the Communist occupation.

In 1968, I took Miki to visit him in Hungary. I remember telling my father, "You opposed my marriage to Ramona and yet this was the greatest thing that ever happened to me. If I wouldn't have gone with her to the United States, I could have been dead, because my regiment was sent to the Russian front. Out of my year of young officers, only two of us are alive. See? I wouldn't even be able to sit with you here."

He hemmed and hawed, but what could he say?

I also told Miki: "You saved my life." Miki just shrugged.

In America, I had some connections with the wine business as the representative for Royal Hungarian Wine Cellars. Through them I met some people in the restaurant business—Billy Wilkerson, who owned the *Hollywood Reporter*, owned the Trocadero, and the manager, John Steinberg—and I got the idea to open up a Hungarian restaurant in Los Angeles. To learn the trade, I went to work with a friend who ran a very elegant place called Victor Hugo's, in Beverly Hills. A couple years later I had some money, and my mother-in-law gave me some, and I opened my own place, Little Hungary, on the Sunset Strip, a few doors west of the bank on the corner of Sunset and Clark, which later became the Whisky A Go Go.

When Arturo DeSanctis died of a brain tumor in 1937, I brought my mother to America. Ramona and I had lived with her mother for maybe two years; she had a nice home in Silverlake, off Micheltorena, on Murray Drive. I still remember the number: 1551. Silverlake was a very nice district then. When my mother came, she lived in West Hollywood, on Larrabee. Later, we moved to the top of Hilldale, renting a house owned by Frank of Musso & Frank's restaurant. This way there was always someone to take care of Miki. Ramona dined often at Little Hungary. Miki, too. Ramona didn't like to cook. Fortunately, even as a child, Miki liked Hungarian food.

We worked like dogs at Little Hungary, but it paid off. We were very popular, especially with the European film community: Gottfried Rheinhardt, George Cukor, Andre de Toth, Paul Lukas, Charlie Vidor, Marlene Dietrich, Sam Spiegel, Michael Curtis, Billy Wilder, Paul and Frederick Kohner, Vincent Korda. There were many refugees during the war, mostly Jewish. Fortunately, I speak four languages: German, Hungarian, Spanish, and English. French a little, but not so well.

I made many friends in the motion picture business, and with some I became close. Errol Flynn was a very good friend. Sometimes we double-dated. When Miki was ten or eleven, Errol would sometimes come for breakfast or brunch. Miki had seen him in *Captain Blood* and, since Errol was a very friendly man, they'd sword fight together. You never know what a child picks up. Errol impressed him; the other actors and actress I knew, I think not.

JUANITA KUHN: My sister adored going to the restaurant in the evening to be part of the social scene. She just glowed in it. She imagined herself as a movie star. I don't think she felt any responsibility toward anything. Ramona stayed up late. She was lazy. She just wanted to be pampered. This is a kindly way of putting it, but she wasn't meant to be a mother, to wash and iron and cook. In fact, she was a lousy mother. Ramona was very proud of Miki, but once the responsibility faced her, she was too immature to make the necessary sacrifices to dedicate herself to raising him. Miklos was hurt that Ramona didn't do a better job, but he was too busy to stop everything in his life to do anything about it.

MIKLOS DORA SR.: When Miki got a little older, he attended a Catholic kindergarten and elementary school at St. Victor's, a church on Holloway Drive, just below the Sunset Strip. That's where he took his Holy Communion. [May 17, 1942.] At the time, Miki had some difficulty with reading and writing. I put him into a summer school. Then Ramona got the idea that he should go to a special place, the Fernauld School, which was part of UCLA. They helped children with learning disabilities. He went for a couple years. To be closer, we moved to Wilshire Boulevard in Westwood where today the big condominiums stand.

By the time Miki was five or six, it was obvious that I wasn't happy with Ramona and that Ramona wasn't happy with me. Ramona had once enjoyed my company; I suppose she loved me for a few minutes. But that's life.

Eventually, on a sailboat trip with her sister, Ramona met a young man who worked for the studios. She came back and said she was finished with me. Just like that, out of the clear sky. I said, "Is it really final?" She said, "Yes." I said, "That's fine. If you feel that way, I can't do anything about it. But since Miki's involved I want to meet the fellow." She agreed. He came to Little Hungary and then we went to my apartment. I asked, "Are you seriously interested in Ramona?" and he said he was. "The only reason I'm asking you is because I have a son and I want to be protective if his mother is divorcing me and marrying somebody else." We talked quite a bit. He was very pleasant. After our conversation, he broke off with Ramona. What happened I couldn't say, but eventually she went to Las Vegas and in 1939 filed for divorce anyway. The split was mostly friendly and we got on with our lives. But soon, Ramona made a big mistake and married a man who, in my opinion, was a bum: a surfer named Gard Chapin.

2

In the 1930s, before WW II, surfers were not considered counter cultural icons. Early surfers were known as "watermen," or people who had a multidimensional relationship with the ocean: swimming, diving, fishing, boating, and beach combing. "Watermen" lived by the ocean and had an intimate knowledge of tides, currents, and weather patterns because their livelihoods usually depended upon it. Before the era of wetsuits and the surfboard industry, this generation surfed in cutoff Levi's and handcrafted their own surfboards. It was only during the post World War II period that surfers came to symbolize a "laid-back" style of life that contrasted with the affluence, anxiety, and consumer contentment of the early Cold War era.
—Carin Crawford, San Diego State University head coach of women's water polo, from her Internet thesis "Waves of Transformation"

GLENN HENING: Waves are for free. To surf all you need to do is take off your clothes, go naked into the water, find a log, and ride. The simplicity is fundamental.

JOHN MILIUS: You get out there, wait all day, jockey around until you finally get the wave. You run up to the nose, side-slip, make a couple flashy cutbacks, and come through a section that no one thinks you can make. You blast out of the white-water finish with a beautiful kickout—and all of this is for nothing because when it's done, it's gone.

Surfing produces nothing. You can't take it home. Nobody has any piece of it left. No one even remembers what you did because here comes another hot guy on another wave and everyone's watching *him*. Surfing is sort of a Zen exercise, the *philosophy of action* being everything and results nothing. *That's* the joy of surfing. If you really love it, you begin to understand being in the moment, and you begin to surf for the sheer pleasure—not for someone telling you you're good, not for winning a contest, not for anything but the experience.

STEVE PEZMAN: Take it a step further: You are as a surfer as you are as a person. People surf the way they dance, the way they act. Personality is revealed. When you're young and you're surfing, you can't imagine how anyone ever leaves it. You're there early and you stay late, and the fire in your belly is geared around being there for the perfect moment. In truth, you're there for *all the moments*, and you get the perfect ones and take full advantage only because you've been training through all the imperfect moments. Eventually you begin to master the wave—and yourself a little bit. Although surfing is an escapist, detached activity, as you gain chops you gain maturity as a human being. Unlike other sports, it's very personal and not particularly social, even if you're in the water with twenty other guys. To the uninformed, surfing appears to be a nonproductive act, but it's also nondepletive. It's just a dance unto itself. In surviving the wave circumstance you learn lessons that you can use to survive the life circumstance.

Before World War II, surfing was an eccentric pastime practiced by just a few hundred distinct individuals. You could tell who was in the water by their style, without even seeing their face. "A surfer was a nonconformist," says renowned Santa Barbara–based board builder Reynolds Yater. "He'd sleep in his car at the beach and didn't mind being considered odd. It wasn't yet an attractive culture that made lots of people think, 'I wanna do that.' It wasn't even big enough then to be a subculture. A lot of guys senior to me went to their jobs all week and then bailed out at the beach on the weekend. I was younger, part of a new generation; I wasn't going to surf only on weekends. Instead, I'd go *during* the week when no one else was there. Meanwhile, those who made it home from the war used their GI bill for an education, got jobs—and went right back into the water."

"When the war ended . . . boom, we were back in the environment," surfer Dave Rochlen told *Surf Guide* magazine in its November 1964 "Malibu" issue. "It was devotion, like seeing a girl again . . . like, I'm never gonna leave! We plunged into this thing . . . gave ourselves over to it entirely. I think it was because we had spent four or five years in the war; it was all bad and we had survived. Now there was no question about what had us by the throat. It was the ocean. Everything else was secondary."

"It was pretty golden in the early days," says Miki's friend Bob Beadle, "driving into a gas station in Huntington Beach and some Okie filling up your tank, asking, 'What are them things sittin' on top of your car there? Them glider wings or somethin'?' They didn't know. Or driving down the highway you'd see a car you hadn't seen before, with boards on it, coming your way. You'd both stop, somebody would do a U-turn and ask why you were going that way."

Everyone agrees: Surfing was a special fraternity.

"But nowadays," says longtime Malibu regular Mysto George, "if you see somebody with a surfboard on their car, you hope they get in a wreck before they get to the beach.

STEVE PEZMAN: Surfing's fertile crescent in Southern California lay between the Tigris and Euphrates of Manhattan Beach and the Palos Verdes Cove area just south. In 1934, clubs like the Manhattan Beach Surf Cub and the Palos Verdes Cove Surfing Club formed and blossomed.

LEROY GRANNIS: The Palos Verdes club members were just regular guys. We worked or went to school, and were pretty much on our own. We were all like little animals. Nobody had much or *any* money, so there was no incentive to go looking for places to spend money and have fun. We just stayed on the beach and everybody was happy. I was an apprentice carpenter for my dad, building houses along the oceanfront in Hermosa. If the surf was good and my friend Hoppy Swarts came by, ready to go, and my dad wasn't there, it was really hard for me to stay on the job. Three days later I'd come back and my dad would be madder than hell.

JOHN ELWELL: We were never bored and we were always in pretty good shape. And of course there was always partying, alcohol, and women. Sometimes, about five in the morning, the beach looked like a gypsy encampment: bodies in the sand, bottles of booze, women with sand in their hair and all rumpled up in blankets. A couple people making coffee and frying eggs over a fire.

There was also a group at Coronado, a group at Sunset Cliffs, and a group at La Jolla. The most important thing about the San Diego area is that Duke Kahanamoku came down here during World War I, when there were no Olympics, and did surfing exhibitions like he'd done on the East Coast after winning gold medals swimming in the 1912 Games. The Red Cross sent the Duke on a tour. It was probably 1917.

STEVE PEZMAN: Simultaneous to the Cove era was Corona del Mar, which was good from the '20s into the early '30s. But when they extended the jetty and screwed the break, the whole culture migrated south to San Onofre. Guys from San Diego would also come north to converge there.

DORIAN "DOC" PASKOWITZ: Between 1935 and 1940, San Onofre was The Place. You could lie on the beach and sleep. You could fall down on the beach dead drunk and wake up the next day, and nobody would roust you. I stayed on the beach for a whole week naked. That's gone now.

San Onofre was as popular and rideable a spot to us as Malibu would later be to Miki. San Onofre is the greatest wave of its kind in the continental United States. Between the Shack, where people surfed, to a point a mile north on the other side of the Marine base, is a gigantic, primordial river mouth like you find on the northwest coast of the United States. During the centuries that river flowed, it would move fast into the deep water and the eddies would swirl off rocks. Most of the rocks would settle close to the shore, and less so and less so as you went farther out. Over the rocks grew eel grass. It was such a beautiful green and would wave back and forth. That eel grass and the rocks have held that plateau solid, from millions of years ago to this very day. That created a magnificent, gentle incline, and a feathering wave. Unlike the wave at, say, the Pipeline in Hawaii, which just jumps right up and crashes in shallow water, as the San Onofre wave got really big it would tipple off the top and you'd have white water coming off all the way down the slope, with the slope as high as ten feet.

STEVE PEZMAN: The San Onofre guys, however, were generally disinterested in advancing the surfboard, and they clung to the old, heavy, awkward craft. The waves were gentle, they rode them straight in. The whole deal was pretty sleepy and kind of cruisy, and more about scoring chicks and drinking wine and playing music—which is all good. Joe Quigg and all the hot-rod guys who later tried to make boards lighter and from different materials, and were really into surfing hotter and better, rode at Malibu and thought of San Onofre as a disease. You went by it at fifty miles an hour and hoped that it didn't catch you.

3

DOUGLAS STANCLIFF: Gard and Ramona were a god and goddess, stunning to look at. Gard was 6'1" or so. Extremely muscular. Kind of an Aryan blond. He was also a chauvinist, intolerant, maybe racist, and loud. He drank too much. Ramona did, too.

KIT HORN: Gard was an unbelievable surfer. I remember him at Malibu, coming across a seven- or an eight-foot wave. He did this fabulous cutback on a ninety-pound redwood surfboard. He drop-kneed this thing and came back into it so hard, I just thought, Who was that?!

JIM "BURRHEAD" DREVER: I first saw Gard surf at the Palos Verdes Cove. He would howl while he rode, and his voice would echo off the Cove walls.

LEROY GRANNIS: The yelling was exuberance and wanting to have people watch him. Most of us then felt it wasn't necessary to draw attention to yourself surfing. If you were good enough, we'd watch anyway.

WOODY EKSTROM: Sometimes Gard would use guys paddling out to get over his wave as a slalom course. He'd go around one, then around the other, and yell, "We'll all be killed!"

JOE QUIGG: Gard was a member of the Palos Verdes Surf Club, and the best surfer then. He ran circles around most guys up and down the California coast because most surfers in his generation were laid-back. To them, surfing was like going fishing. Then here's this wild, radical guy tearing up the ocean. No wonder some guys didn't like him that much. I think they were jealous. All those tricks that Miki did later, Gard did first: going over people, under them, around them, behind them, pushing them off waves—and they had the same audacious, wry humor doing it.

E. J. OSHIER: The rest of us believed nobody had any claim to the wave they were on. We'd have five or six guys on one wave and the more we had, the more fun it was. We'd holler back and forth, talk and ride in together. It was pretty square and orchestrated but it worked for us. But guys like Gard would go under you and shove your board out. It's not that he was trying to perform and needed room; he just wanted to do what he wanted to do, and if you were in the way he wanted you out of the way.

JIM "BURRHEAD" DREVER: Gard also used to pick on a Jewish family of surfers down at the Flood Control in Long Beach. He called them kikes all the time. I don't know why he did that, because any one of those guys could have beat him up.

GARDNER CHAPIN JR.: When I was in first grade, there was this kid who only brought oranges for lunch. I thought it was really weird. I went home and told my parents about it. I also mentioned that he was Jewish, and my dad said, "What!? The guy's a Jew?"

On the other hand, my father had a good friend who was Jewish, a guy named Perry, who used to come over and drink with Gard on the weekends. Gard said that if anything happened to my mother and him, Perry and his wife, Alice, were going to adopt me. So, was Gard anti-Semitic? Hard to say.

DORIAN "DOC" PASKOWITZ: Gard Chapin had two sisters, Nancy and Martha. Nancy was penultimately beautiful; Martha was penultimately not beautiful. Nancy took a fancy to a guy named Bill Van Dorn, a freewheeling intellect who went to Stanford University. He was brilliant; his father invented the modern streamlined train. Bill became a big shot oceanographer at Scripps Institute in La Jolla and married Nancy.

BILL VAN DORN: The Chapin place was run-down and didn't look like anybody lived there. Chunks of cars rusted in the yard, and surfboards leaned up against the eaves. Inside the front door, immediately to the right, was a piano in an alcove, but it had been completely covered with skis. Books, mostly Martha's, were piled everywhere. The kids' mother, Louise, had pretty advanced cerebral palsy. Nancy and I didn't socialize much with Gard. He came to visit a few times, once with Ramona, twice without. While I was in the service, she left him a couple times. I saw him at the beach when I got back. I remember once he got in a big fight with Martha.

Nancy supported the whole family working for an advertising agency in Hollywood. Martha did bit parts, wrote scripts, and contributed to a few books now and then. Gard did nothing much.

JIM "BURRHEAD" DREVER: Gard went to Douglas Aircraft right out of high school and worked in a tool crib making twenty dollars a week. He wasn't an engineer, but in the late '30s that was still a lot of money.

WOODY EKSTROM: He just couldn't go into the service. Because of his ulcers he was 4-F and had to rest a lot. But as soon as he'd get them healed up, he'd go on a drunk binge and be right back to crackers and milk again.

Eventually Chapin started a cabinet and overhead door building business when he and Ramona lived at Elwood Stancliff's Studio City home, in the garage apartment. He also began building surfboards. Later, when he had his own shop, Chapin hired a helper named Bob Simmons, whom he had met while both were in the hospital recovering from accidents. Chapin told Simmons about surfing as a way to exercise and strengthen a shattered elbow and arm.

Simmons took the short-lived job building garage doors with Chapin because it taught him woodworking skills. Gard also sold him a board. It was about 150 pounds and obviously no good. "He just suckered Bob," says John Elwell. "Even Velzy said, 'I can't believe Chapin did that to him.' But from that board, Bob recognized there was something wrong. You couldn't carry it, you couldn't turn it. Simmons had read a book called *The Naval Architecture of Planing Hulls*, written by Lindsey Lord, Ph.D., an MIT professor who'd been hired by the navy and who had also designed fast rum boats for the Mafia. He started talking about hydrodynamic planing hulls, then worked the ideas into boards as part of the new revolution in surfboard design.

4

MIKLOS DORA SR.: After Ramona and I divorced, I lived with my mother, and Miki lived with us. In 1944, I got married again, to Lorraine. Miki was a very nice boy, a sweet kid, and I enjoyed spending time with him. I took Miki to see the cowboy pictures every Saturday at a small cinema across from the Pantages Theater on Hollywood Boulevard. We went rollerskating at the big rollerdrome at Sunset and Gower. I also liked to go to the beach. Miki came with me to Paddleboard Cove, off Palos Verdes. The first time, he couldn't have been more than three years old. Ramona had come as well. I heard people talking about this thing, surfing. I tried it, but I was a lousy surfer. I had a board, though, and the next year I bought Miki a little one, too. I took him surfing his first time, in 1938, when he was four.

But mostly I focused on establishing my business. In 1942, I even had to change the name of my restaurant from Little Hungary to the Little Gypsy, just because Hungary was with the Axis in the war.

As Miki got older I told Ramona that I couldn't properly take care of him, and that like any child, he needed more supervision. I'd been very happy at boarding school and I believed not only that the experience would be good for him, but that like me, he'd be happy, too. Gard Chapin was very much against this. He told Miki, "It's no good for you. You should go to public school." Ramona was influenced by Gard. We argued and argued, but in the end we did it my way. With me at the restaurant at night, Ramona being an ineffective mother, and Gard off doing who knew what, there was no other choice. When Miki was ten, we put him in St. John's Military Academy.

PETER WOOLEY: I worked at St. John's from 1956 to 1957—years after Miki was there—as assistant headmaster. But it hadn't changed much. Half of the students were day students who came in from the neighborhood, and the other half were boarders. They lived in dormitories run exclusively by the Sisters of Mercy. The school went from the second to the ninth grade, so I'd say there were maybe 250 students.

GEORGE GEORGE: Miki and I were in the same class at St. John's, and I made it a point to befriend everybody. He showed up for part of the fifth grade, the sixth, and part of the seventh. 1944, 1945, and part of 1946. Miki and I were both rebels without a justifiable cause.

The school was part of a Catholic church, run by the Sisters of Mercy. Very religious. We were required to be at chapel every morning at 6:00 A.M. The nuns bathed you, fed you, taught you to eat everything on your plate.

One nun taught the first and second grade, and a different nun taught each of the rest. In the sixth grade Miki and I had a tough, heavyset Irish lady. I think her name was Sister Evangeline. She would knock you around if she had to.

I remember there being some kind of mystery about Miki's parents—though everyone, it seemed, had a mysterious deal. I recall him being proud of his dad, something to do with Hollywood, and we were long on Hollywood. Gregory Peck had gone there almost twenty years before. Lash Larue. Bing Crosby's kids. Barbara Hutton's.

The school itself was three stories, of really old brick, like a dungeon. We drilled on the football field. They gave us a rifle in the first grade and taught us how to do shoulder arms. We wore uniforms. They were gray with a black stripe down the side of the pants. We had to wear them at all times. The dress uniform had lapels and a little insignia with a cross in the middle. A jacket and white shirt with a black tie. The officers had what they called a "Sam Brown" leather suspender coming crossways. They'd sometimes have sabers. We had hats with bills, like the police.

To get promoted you had to behave yourself and not be a pest. You were given demerits for pushing or shoving in line, talking in line, general disruption. You were allowed 44 demerits a week and I'd get 650.

Even so, Miki didn't really stand out. Those of us in the Goon Squad antagonized the teachers on a steady basis; he tried to stay out of the limelight. Miki was actually quiet and withdrawn. Passive-aggressive and hidden. A guy

ABOVE: Gard Chapin, early 1940s. Courtesy Bill Van Dorn.

ABOVE RIGHT: Miki, midteens, with Gard and friend. Courtesy Dora Estate/ Refrigerator Collection.

RIGHT: Miki in St. John's Military Academy uniform. Courtesy Dora Estate.

with a brain who was bored, sort of like he was later in life, but before the outgoing, charismatic, movie-star-looks side emerged. I thought he was insecure and unloved—like all of us.

DENNY AABERG: Miki told me he put fiberglass dust from sanding a surfboard in a nun's Kotex box. The next day in class she stood there sweating, with no idea what was going on.

MIKLOS DORA SR.: Miki was a good kid except he didn't like to study, and he just didn't shape up. Perhaps he was unhappy, but I couldn't tell you.

One weekend I went to pick him up and the principal, a nun, said, "Mr. Dora, Miki is not doing well. He's not trying. You should discipline him somehow."

I asked what she suggested. She said, "If he doesn't do well next week, why don't we take away his privilege of going home for the weekend."

I said, "Fine."

The next weekend the principal said, "He didn't cooperate. You should keep him here."

Miki came down from his room and I said, "Miki, you didn't shape up and you won't be able to come home."

Miki was very unhappy at the news but didn't cry; he seldom did. He was a stoic young man. But you know how children are: They have a fantastic instinct. They know how they can get away with what they want. Somehow he got hold of his mother. She called me and said, "How dare you restrict Miki!" I explained, but she took him out for the weekend anyway and told me that I had nothing to say about it, that she controlled his life.

I didn't realize it, but she was right. When Ramona and I arranged for the divorce in Las Vegas, we agreed on mutual custody. Ramona had a lawyer, but I was young and immature and didn't get my own. Everything seemed friendly, but when this disagreement about Miki happened, she told me, "You have no rights. I have his custody." I talked with the attorney in Las Vegas and he told me that, yes, she got sole custody. As soon as I found out I should have gone to court then to rectify it, but I was too stupid and I didn't. Because of this Ramona was able to get away with many things that I would never have allowed and we always had friction about Miki in his formative years. Of course, my mother and I took care of Miki about 80 percent of the time anyway. Ramona was always happy to share him with me because of the convenience.

Unfortunately, Ramona also tried to make Miki hate me. Years after we were divorced I received a letter from her accusing me of ruining her life. She said that by impregnating her with Miki I had wrecked her looks, especially her breasts. Maybe she told this to Miki.

Miki never asked me about the divorce until he was in his twenties, when he mentioned certain things that he could have heard only from his mother. Ramona told Miki that she was pregnant with him before we married—which is fine, but she didn't put it in the right way. I tried to be very nice to Miki about his mother. I said, "Yes, we made love and she got pregnant. But we were in love, and I did the correct thing and married her."

PEACHES: When Miki and I dated in the late '6os, he told me about a letter he'd found in which his mother wrote that she had wanted to abort him. He acted as if the way she felt and the circumstances of his conception were the end of the world. He was an unplanned pregnancy—so what? But it was really hard for him to accept. It was as if he believed that maybe he wasn't meant to be here.

MIKLOS DORA SR.: Of course, no matter how poorly she behaved, Ramona loved Miki very much. But it was like a monkey love. An animal love. Not a constructive love. Not thinking, but feeling. To Ramona, Miki couldn't do anything wrong.

5

GARDNER CHAPIN JR.: Sometimes my father would take Miki and me to work with him, usually on Saturday. He taught Miki how to make a board. When Miki wasn't in school, my dad took him to San Onofre just about every weekend. At first we'd take the '37 Ford. At the end of 1950, my dad bought two 1950 Fords, one for my mother and one for himself. He took the backseat out of his and put in some plywood to make a camper bed. Miki and I would sit on the plywood and fall asleep on the way. At San Onofre there'd be twelve or fifteen cars in a semicircle around the campfire. These were regular people, all good friends. I'd sleep in the car with my mother; Gard and Miki would sleep on the beach. We'd spend Friday and Saturday nights and come back Sunday night.

DALE VELZY: Gard had made Miki a good surfboard out of a Swastika board and shaved it down pretty thin. At the time, "swastika" meant plank.[1] Gard

---

[1] According to the Surfing Heritage Foundation's Web-based Board Registry, the Pacific Systems Homes Swastika model was changed in 1942 to the Waikiki model "for obvious reasons."

and Simmons had this planer that could take the meat off a wooden door real quick. What Gard did is knock the V tail out of the back of this plank and flatten it. Gard's planks were all flat, very heavy, no V bottom, no belly.

BILL VAN DORN: By the time Miki was about ten, he was skinny as hell and always in the water. Gard liked Malibu better, but he'd come down to San Onofre, and bring Little Gard and Ramona, too. I got the feeling, though, that Ramona wasn't that enthralled with Gard anymore. She'd begun to have problems with his drinking and stuff.

STEVE PEZMAN: The summer Miki was fourteen, Gard just drove away and left him at the beach, which is consistent with Gard's personality. Maybe Miki was out in the water, wouldn't come in, Gard got pissed and drove off: "Fuck him, let him get back home to L.A." Miki didn't bother. Benny Merrill told me he picked up Miki off the beach at San Onofre and gave him a place to stay.

MARTIN SUGARMAN: When Gard left him alone, Miki would roam around unsupervised, in packs with other children. He became a feral child growing up on the beach at San Onofre. Not that he was antisocial, but he was unsocialized. He didn't really know right from wrong, and he was brought up in a junglelike culture. He lived like a wolf. Or a cat. Anything went. The code was survival.

JIM KEMPTON: Later, Miki never liked to admit to surfing San Onofre. He felt very unappreciated there. They didn't dig his act at all. He was the arrogant latchkey kid who was already getting into trouble, whose parents were pissed off. He was a punk. They called him "Meatball."

MERRITT STANFIELD: When I was a junior at UCLA, I lived on Micheltorena Street in East Hollywood, with my mother. The street goes right up the hill off Sunset, and Miki's mother, Ramona, lived there on Murray Drive. I think she was going through her divorce, because Gard Chapin lived in Long Beach. My friend Leland introduced us, and Miki would walk down to my house because Leland had arranged with Ramona that we'd take care of him.

I was a member of the San Onofre Surfing Club, so during the summer we'd take him there. Miki's mother gave me five dollars a week for food and we'd scrounge the rest. Usually we'd pick up bottles from the beach, take them into San Clemente, and collect the deposit money.

On the way to San Onofre we'd turn off at South Laguna and go to a small market that sold horse meat. We'd buy ten or fifteen pounds and put it in the cooler and have food for two or three days. As long as it had lots of garlic it tasted pretty good.

Miki would surf early in the morning. I was rather in awe of him, to tell you the truth. I loved to watch him. His progress was apparent. He started off on little waves and worked his way up. Sometimes we'd paddle all the way to the Trestles. Miki loved that.

Miki was a very quiet kid. Sometimes on the trip south he wouldn't say a word. He never mentioned Gard Chapin or his mother. He was painless. Just a mellow fellow. Ethereal. At the beach he didn't need any supervision. He was the most mature sixteen-year-old I've ever seen. He kept to himself and didn't bother us. Miki made a few friends, too. One guy was Terry "Tubesteak" Tracy. He was Miki's buddy. Greg Noll and Phil Edwards come to mind as well.

GREG NOLL: Meeting another kid around my age was great. It's not like today, where there are thousands of kids and everybody's pissed off because you can't get a wave for yourself. In those days it was bitchin' to have somebody you could relate to.

Miki and I did things kids did. I'm not very proud of this, but I remember a plan to put out food for the pigeons and, when they came, throw stones at them. When I was maybe thirteen or fourteen, Miki and I also had a really well-thought-out plan to burn down the shack at San Onofre. We wanted to create a huge stir, piss off society, piss off the old San Onofre guys. We were going to crawl over the cliff, watches synchronized and all this crap, and light it up. We never did it, though.

MERRITT STANFIELD: Once, on the way back to Los Angeles, we stopped at a little market in Laguna Beach, right next to the pier. All of us—Leland, myself, Tubesteak, and Miki—went in. After getting what we needed, Leland and I stood around outside, leaning against our car, talking to someone from out of town, waiting for the boys. They came out just as two cops pulled up. Before I knew it, the four of us had been handcuffed and whisked to jail.

Turns out Tubesteak and Miki had loaded their pockets with a quart of milk, apples, oranges—whatever they could put in. The kids were hungry; we never had enough to eat. Leland and I were threatened with contributing to the delinquency of a minor. Not good.

We were at the jail for about fifteen minutes when Kellogg, the chief of police, walked in. He had hired me the year before as a lifeguard in Laguna Beach and he liked me. He gave me a big lecture, then told us to "get out of town. Tubesteak and Miki, I don't ever want to see you again." It's lucky he let us go.

Miki and Tubesteak were panicked and upset, but not nearly as upset as

I was. We may have driven home in silence or I may have lectured them, but I don't remember much except saying, "You don't steal." After that I never let him go into the market. He'd sit in the car.

Capers and mischief notwithstanding, young Miki exercised his adventurous spirit mostly in the water. "He knew there was more to surfing than San Onofre," says Reynolds Yater. Burrhead had once taken Miki to Trestles, north of San Onofre, and he came back a convert. With another young surfer named Phil Edwards the pair started tearing up the place, challenging and pushing each other to improve their skills and have fun at the same time.

JOHN SEVERSON: Miki and Phil used to have these little expression sessions just between themselves. They'd ride these hot little inside waves back and forth. It was a thing of beauty; I wish I'd had a camera then. But it never seemed like they were trying to outdo each other; it seemed more like they were trying to do *for* each other, to perform and surprise the other guy. They were getting off on each other. It seemed more like a sharing or a "How far can we go with this?" than competition.

STEVE PEZMAN: Years ago Phil told me that Miki taught him everything he knew. I've always been fascinated by their relationship and how they stimulated each other. That particular period is so fanciful and romantic and seminal. I envision them inventing modern hotdog surfing at Lower Trestles all by themselves, challenging each other to make the wave.

Although Miki and Phil early on enjoyed a friendly competition, for most of the late '50s to mid-'60s, surfers and the nascent surf media, zeroing in on Phil's golden-boy good looks and Miki's dark charisma, and their reputations as the era's outstanding performance surfers, found it convenient to drum up a little controversy by casting them as the White Knight and Black Knight. It fit neatly, says Bob Cooper, because although it wasn't cast in stone, "for all intents, Phil surfed south and never came up past Laguna Beach, and Miki surfed north, so the kingdom was divided."

Both Miki and Phil rejected these labels.

ABOVE TOP: Bing Copeland, Tubesteak, Greg Noll, Miki clowning around. Courtesy Noll Family Collection.

LEFT: Phil Edwards, Ken Price, Miki, at Trestles, early 1950s. Courtesy Dora Estate.

ABOVE: Miki's 1930 Sedanca Seville Rolls. Courtesy Dora Estate/Refrigerator Collection.

PHIL EDWARDS: That white knight/black knight stuff—we never even thought about it. I don't want to make some special culture out of it because it wasn't. We were just trying to have fun. It was so romantic to be in this wilderness area then and find these perfect waves. I loved being able to goad each other onward, pushing. You'd try and outsurf the guy, but it was fun and it was innocent.

I'm always reluctant to talk about this stuff because everything that I say now gets analyzed and distorted. Remember, this was *fifty* years ago. Okay? I was born in 1938 and the first time I went to San Onofre was in 1949. It could have been in 1950, though, you know? All I remember is that Miki could actually drive a car, so he must have been fifteen or sixteen, a few years older than me, which was a lifetime at that age. He was way more sophisticated than me. I was sort of a country bumpkin. Anyway, Miki was there. I watched him surf and I couldn't believe it. We weren't performance surfers back then. It used to be that wherever we stood up, that's where we stayed. I was just riding beach breaks; we didn't even angle. Then, to see what Miki did was unbelievable. He was so much more original than anybody else. He put on a show. It's like if somebody came from outer space and started surfing in front of you. He was so graceful and beautiful and fluid, and once I saw what was possible, it opened up a whole new world for me.

When Miki and I were young, we cut down planks and made funny boards. Just before the balsa/fiberglass era there were still a lot of redwood planks around. That's how I learned to shape. Miki, too. He had that board with the Japanese rising sun and "Meatball" painted down the side. "Meatball" was his nickname then. He also had a purple board with Japanese characters going down it. Pretty soon we got decent boards; but yeah, we ruined a few planks. Miki and I probably had some really bad equipment there for a couple summers. We were just kind of stumbling.

And honestly, it really wasn't a two-way relationship in the sense that we spent a lot of time together away from the beach. Occasionally he wrote me letters addressed to "Master Phillipe Edwards Jr. the III Esquire," and drew Japanese kamikaze pilots on the envelope corners. Swastikas. Japanese warlords on the back. Once he came to my house and stayed the night and charmed my parents. They thought he was wonderful. Otherwise, he was just fun to surf with in those early days when we were both developing and no one was looking over our shoulders.

Then it became all political; who's who and what's what started to be a big deal. I never cared about that. For instance, when I'd go out at Windansea they'd clear the water. All of a sudden it wasn't the same anymore. I have enjoyed my notoriety at times, but generally it's a pain in the ass. I mean, it has its moments, but a lot of times you attract guys who want to talk to you who are hung up in the wrong stuff. They don't want to get their own life.

Probably the worst thing that ever happened to me was the day that somebody said, "You can surf as good as Miki." From then on we were as good as poisoned. Steve Pezman once quoted me as saying "It was downhill from then on." He got that right. But in my mind—and I'm sure in Miki's—we were never opposite numbers.

Years later Miki would tell filmmaker Bill Delaney about those days: "We rode waves together and we had fun when there were no leg ropes, no motion picture cameras on the beach, and no one gave a damn about anything but pleasure. That's how I remember him and that's how we grew up together." Edwards agreed. "That's exactly the way it was! Exactly. Miki got it right, and I get pissed off at anybody trying to make it into something else." Still, the damage was done. The comparisons are part of surf culture mythology, and even after Edwards sought other pursuits, and Dora disappeared, the bitter taste left behind would foreshadow the coming changes in surfing that alienated each, in their own way, from the culture and the crowd.

6

My own father taught me a gracious manner of living, while my stepfather showed me how to survive when confronted with adversity. Which was the better? Which was the worse? One father showed me how to atone for indiscretions and the other demonstrated how to commit them. I was able to live to tell the tale because of the imbalance inspired by both.

—Miki, from *Dora Lives*

It's fascinating, Miki's two fathers. The Central European pseudo-noble element meets John Fante's worst L.A. urchin. In many ways that is American culture right there.

—Derek Hynd

MIKLOS DORA SR.: Gard Chapin influenced Miki a great deal in petty ways. Gard felt that the laws were made for his protection but that he didn't have to respect them himself. One day I saw him at the beach stealing ice cream from a Good Humor man. One guy did something in front to create a distraction while Gard went in from behind. Unfortunately, I couldn't influence Miki about Gard. I blame myself.

MIKE MCNEILL: Miki once told me that when he was a kid, he and Gard would come back from San Onofre and pull up in front of Miklos's restaurant in shorts and T-shirts. They'd walk through the door and into the kitchen, grab whatever food they wanted to eat, then walk out, get into the car, and drive away.

MIKLOS DORA SR.: Many times Gard got out of hand at the restaurant because he was drinking; and the more he drank, the meaner he got. One night I left the restaurant early and went to a movie. When I came back, my manager said, "Gard came. He walked in and said, 'This place is owned by my wife!' He went in to the kitchen. I had some roast ducks left over from dinner, and he picked up a whole roast duck. He said, 'I'm taking it. It belongs to me!'"

I called Ramona and said, "You tell Gardner that if he comes in again and behaves like he did last night, the police will be here and he will be put in jail." He never came again.

GARDNER CHAPIN JR.: Miki admired Gard—in a way. Gard took him surfing. Gard was one of the guys. Gard spent a fuck of a lot more time with Miki than Mr. Dora ever did. Lots of Miki's personality came from Gard because he was probably the only consistent role model. Military school isn't what Miki wanted, only his father. I don't think Miki ever forgot that.

But I'm also sure Miki thought my father was a complete madman, and he'd have been correct. There are lots of examples. My father liked to shoot buckshot down on the neighbors below us on July Fourth, then wait until the police came. Then he'd show them a shotgun that hadn't been fired. Of course, the trick was that he had two identical guns.

Another time, I guess it was around 1950, as both Miki and my mother told it to me, Gard got the newspaper, read about new parking meters in the city, and completely blew his top. He said, "This is it. Communism is taking over." That would have been it with anyone else, but not with him. He started drinking and he kept ranting and raving. As the day wore on, he got madder and madder, and madder and madder. He finally cracked around midnight. He said, "Miki, let's go."

"Where?"

"To take out the parking meters."

Gard grabbed a baseball bat and they got into the car.

When my dad got to the parking meters, he looked around. There was a little traffic but no cops. He started swinging the bat, and in about two minutes had smashed every meter. He threw the bat on the ground; it was shattered anyway. Then he jumped in the car and took off. Miki said he'd never seen anything like it, that Dad was like a man possessed.

In the book *Dora Lives*, Miki added one more detail: "When we were finished, Gard suddenly became very calm, and he climbed up the sign pole on the corner. 'Here's a souvenir.' He handed me the street sign from Hollywood and Vine. I kept it for years."

According to Gard Jr., his father's temper was not only reserved for parking meters, surfers in his way, and bothersome neighbors. "We had a peach tree in the backyard and when I deserved it my dad used to make me pick my switch from the tree. Then he'd get out his pocket knife and cut the little branch, pull down my pants, and whip the hell out of me."

Miki, too, says LeRoy Grannis. "Miki told my wife and me that Gard used to come home drunk and drag him out of bed and beat the hell out of him."

Then, when Miki was twelve, Gard insisted that his stepson get circumcised.

MIKLOS DORA SR.: Miki told me he didn't understand why Gard had made him do it. He complained that he was always sore. I was shocked and angry. To me, Gard Chapin was a crazy man with strange ideas.

Miki suffered. I tried to act correctly, always. I never lied to him. I always took care of him when he needed something. But so often I couldn't talk to Miki.

As Miki grew up, we often had disagreements. He'd say, "You're not happy with me" and "You're not proud of me." He thought I felt better about my daughter, Miki's younger half-sister, Pauline. I told him, "Miki, I love you but sometimes I have to criticize you. I don't like your outlook on life." His vagabond style wasn't mine. I am very fond of the United States. I like America. I am very thankful that I am here. I try to see the nicest things. Miki criticized everything, from the president to Social Security to the traffic cop. He was always belittling. After he finished high school, instead of staying in college he went surfing. He never wanted to work. But he was my son, and I always loved him very much.

If he were still here, I would ask him, How come we couldn't get together? How come we couldn't talk to each other?

In 1948, Miklos Sr. "got fed up with the restaurant business" and moved to Buenos Aires. He'd been married to Lorraine for four years, but it wasn't working. She took their daughter, Pauline, and her son, Tony, and moved to Port-au-Prince, Haiti. Gard and Ramona also split up.

GARD CHAPIN JR.: Gard was in a car accident. Someone rear-ended him while he waited at a stop sign. It broke his neck. He wore a huge cast for a year. He started in on codeine painkillers and drank more. After the cast came off, he was still in a lot of pain, so he drank even more. His real downfall was the absinthe he smuggled in from Mexico. The stuff made him insane. Everything came unglued. He lost the cabinet shop, he and Ramona split. I was sent to live with my relatives—my uncle Rad Stancliff and his wife, Frances, and their kids, Doug Stancliff and his brothers, in Rialto, California, near San Bernardino. My mother became a secretary someplace near downtown L.A. She took the streetcar to work but said a lot of times she walked so she could save the fifteen cents. She'd come to Rialto about every two weeks and take me back to L.A. to spend the weekend. She lived in hotels. It was different in those days: everybody seemed to know everybody in the hotel and they'd all play cards, plus they had a swimming pool. She had different boyfriends in these places; they seemed nice to her.
C.C.: Miki always thought they took advantage of her, and that after Miklos Sr., it had all gone downhill.

"If anything," says Juanita Kuhn, "Miki got his worldview from those years when he was pushed around between pillar and post." And so, beset by family turmoil, Miki began to rebel. For the ninth grade, difficulty reading landed him, in the Marian Colbert School on La Brea Avenue in Hollywood. Joel Laykin, whose father owned the jewelry store Laykin et Cie, met Miki at the Colbert School.

JOEL LAYKIN: The school was for kids with learning disabilities and other problems. Miki's *real* problem was that he didn't give a shit about what they wanted him to give a shit about. I was attracted primarily to his sense of humor. We enjoyed the same jokes. A couple years later, when *Mad* magazine came out, we collected them. He had the first ten issues. Miki also drew and his work was very much like Harvey Kurtzman and Will Elder. We became friends. It had nothing to do with surfing. Miki told me some great stories. After St. John's he'd gone to a boarding school in the desert, in Perris, California. He said this big bully character who ran the school treated all the kids like they were in a concentration camp. When his father visited, everybody was so nice and so wonderful; but the minute Miklos left. . . . It was just like a movie where the headmaster turns out to be a real monster. We were at Marian Colbert only a short time. That place was a freak show. Afterward I went to Hollywood High for a semester, then changed schools. Miki went to Hollywood High for the whole thing.

ALLAN CARTER: Miki once got suspended from Hollywood High when he got out his wang and urinated on the track team. Another time, in gym class the coach had all the guys lined up like in the army. He said, "Okay, all you total fuckups. I've got the class of total fuckups. Any of you fuckups who want to flunk out right now, two steps forward to save our time." Miki stepped right out, went to Malibu, and went surfing. But Miki was very smart and aware of what was going on. Even then he was interested in the world economy and politics. He was self-educated and probably better read than most UCLA graduates.

Even so, it didn't keep him out of hot water. In an October 28, 1951, letter to Joel Laykin, Miki wrote: "On the matter of the rocks, business is ____ these days. I had two friends working for me, distributing the rocks for me. The principal of Hollywood (High) found out some way. I managed to recover all that I'd given out before the principal saw my friends. Don't worry; they did not squeal. I'm laying low for a few weeks until the heat's off and I can resume business again."

MIKLOS DORA SR.: In 1953, Miki flew to Port-au-Prince and stayed with Lorraine and Pauline. From there he came to Buenos Aires and stayed with me two or three months. Because of the Korean War, the draft board wanted him to come home and register. Miki asked for an extension to stay out of the country. Ultimately the draft board rejected Miki because he was asthmatic. That made him very happy.

When Miki wasn't traveling, he lived with his grandmother Nadina in Hollywood, in a small bungalow house just behind Barney's Beanery.

Cordoba, 2524.
Bunos Aires.
Argentina.
August. 25, 1953.

My Dear Joe Lakin,
        Are you willing to put up $200.00. in a
~~Money~~
MONEY $$$ deal. With your $$200.00 & my $$400.00
which Ishal invest in stock in the Congo Dimond Co.,
French Equatoial Africa. I already 23, shares of
this stock, and I need more. Acording to very
realiable sorceses will be dobbling in a weak or two.
I will give you a good deal __25__75, of all the
profats. I put out all the work, time, expance for
travel, and the ticket to Africa is over $750.00.
alone. For just investing $200.00. you get 25% of all
my stock and 25% of the jack pot, for just siting
on your big ASS.

        If your interested write, and i will
send you the information on the deal.

                        Sincerly,

GREG NOLL: Miki's grandmother totally pampered him. She talked with this goofy Hungarian accent, and at some point he began using his grandmother's accents and phraseology: "What is this all about?" "Where is it that we're going?" It was for fun, but it set him apart.

BOB COOPER: But Miki kowtowed to her. She called the shots. She had a strong deep voice. When she yelled "Mee-kee!" he'd jump, run in, and take care of whatever she wanted.

ALLAN CARTER: He had a single bed that he slept in so much the bed was indented like an animal's lair in a cave. I sat down on it one day and almost fell out the window because it was so uneven. Miki once dug out a hole under his grandmother's house and built a wine cellar in which he kept a huge collection, most of which I think he looted out of the Beverly Hilton.

Miki also had some gold coins—part of a lifelong interest in investing in gold. One day some workmen came to repair the ceiling in his grand-mother's house. Miki had stashed his coins in the attic. When the guys left, the coins were gone. He told his grandmother. Everybody said, "Oh Miki, you're imagining that." Or they figured he was pulling a fast one. Nadina said, "Miki, did this really happen?" He said it had. So she called the president of the company, found out it *was* true—and got all his gold coins back.

MIKLOS DORA SR.: My mother always let him get way with things. She served him hand and foot. Cooked his breakfast. Did all his laundry. Helped him with homework. He could come home whenever he wanted and expect din-ner. I used to say, "Mother, you are waiting from six o'clock until ten o'clock at night with the food. Tell him that he has to be home at a certain time." But she was too good, God rest her soul, and he took advantage of it. But this I know: Miki loved my mother. I believe she was the only person whom he ever *really* loved.

Miki graduated from Hollywood High School on June 18, 1954, just shy of turning twenty. Five months earlier, in February 1954, Miki and his classmates—who included Ozzie and Harriet's son David Nelson, DJ "The Real" Don Steele, Ruta Lee, Sally Kellerman, and future Nevada lieutenant governor Rex Lee—received a form letter from principal Louie F. Foley, asking graduates to kindly keep in touch. Miki didn't.

In fact, one of the few, if not the only high school contact he maintained was with filmmaker Grant Rohloff. According to Rohloff, they'd met in 1953 "on a routine visit to the dean's office. It was my senior year. I was in the vice principal's office, awaiting my turn. I saw this guy next to me talking to a friend of his, setting him up with what they had to say so they could get out of a trouble spot. He talked with his hands a lot." According to writer and Dora pal C. R. Stecyk III, "This was the infamous Miki Dora, also no stranger to the long arm of the Hollywood High administration. Then Miki turned to Grant and asked him if he surfed, to which Grant replied, 'I think there's a south swell in.' The two agreed that Malibu was probably 'firing' that day, took off, and the rest is history."

CHAPTER **TWO**

The Vintage Years

1

If surfing can be seen as a sport of fugitive grace and improbable physics and among the only athletic pursuits undertaken in a medium that itself is always in motion, then there is surely something futile in attempts to pin down its poetry.

—Guy Trebay, *New York Times* 6/1/06

STEVE PEZMAN: By the time Miki got to Malibu, he was looking for a wave that was profound and that could hold his interest. Some waves are too simple: not a drop of water is out of place, it's easy to ride. But the Malibu wave has different modes, and although it's dependable in some ways, it's never the same twice. It has enough complexity and variation to hold one's attention, almost like a human relationship. When you find a wave like that, you invest in it.

MIKE DOYLE: The Malibu wave looks like it's drawn on a drafting table. Every one is perfect. There's no crashing section, it just peels and peels and peels. You can set up a rhythm with your eyes closed and climb and drop, walk the nose, climb and drop, cut back, climb and drop, walk the nose. I've ridden it at night when you can barely see, and it doesn't matter.

PETER DIXON: In the old days, there were cobbles and lots of sea urchins, and kelp out front. At high tide you could surf right to the edge of the beach and into a chain-link fence that went from where the end of the Adamson's concrete block wall is now, out to the beach homes.

LEROY GRANNIS: The first time I surfed Malibu, in 1936, there was no one else out. The water was clear as a bell. When I got out of the service in September 1945, I went up to Malibu again with a friend. I saw eight or ten guys in the water. I turned to my buddy and went, "The place is ruined."

For years Surfrider Beach in Malibu was to surfers what Jerusalem is to the major Western religions: God's country—and eventually a battle-ground. Home to a perfect right-breaking wave, it helped give birth to modern surfing in the late 1940s and early 1950s; was ground zero for its Big Bang after the movie *Gidget* in 1959; and a leading edge of the superinflating wave-riding universe throughout the 1960s. It's not that other indigenous surf cultures didn't exist—they did, from Australia to South Africa to Hawaii to France to New Zealand—or feature excellent waves, but the world was a larger place then. Long-distance travel was difficult, word of great waves spread slowly, and board technology, although ever-evolving, had yet to catch up with the demands of different and more powerful breaks. And so, Malibu became a perfect test site for the board design and surfing style innovators—and the glamour of the adjacent movie-star colony homes didn't hurt a bit.

Soon, even the name "Malibu" took its place in the cultural lexicon, ending up on products from Chevys to Barbie dolls. "Malibu," wrote C. R. Stecyk III (using the pen name Carlos Izan), in a 1976 *Surfer* article, "Curse of the Chumash," "was the first spot to come of age . . . and the first one to go. It's evenly peeling 'machine waves' became the standard against which (in the '50s and '60s) all other waves throughout the world were rated. Now, though swathed in stardust and celebrity and priced-out-of-reach homesteads, it's just another crowded beach."

In that same piece, Stecyk seemed to refer not so obliquely to Miki and the early harbingers of "progress":

> *1952—A young man in his 1938 La Salle, wooden gun besides him. It was obvious to him that time was running out. The ticky tacky tract houses were erupting everywhere. The moronic aircraft workers who had come from Oklahoma or someplace the same, to work in the war effort, now clogged the cities. They were spreading out and he knew there would be no stopping their onslaught . . . (But for now) He was at Malibu, it was six feet and no one was there. He could*

Hollywood High School

Los Angeles City High School District

This Diploma is awarded to **Miklos Sandor Dora** who has been found worthy in Character and Citizenship and has satisfactorily completed a Course of Study as prescribed by the Board of Education

Given at Los Angeles, California, this eighteenth day of June, nineteen hundred and fifty-four

President Board of Education

Principal

Superintendent of Schools

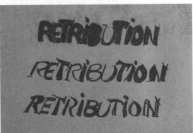

ABOVE TOP: Malibu before the crowds, early 1950s. From Miki's scrapbook left in New Zealand. Courtesy Dora Estate.

ABOVE: Miki's high school diploma. Courtesy Dora Estate/Refrigerator Collection.

RIGHT: Miki's classroom doodlings. Courtesy Dora Estate/Refrigerator Collection.

forget about them for a while. It was obvious they were coming . . .
probably three years at the most.

In the beginning was paradise: four thousand years earlier the
Chumash Indians had called Malibu—their home—Hamaliwu, which
literally means "the surf sounds loudly." Today, the city of Malibu
boasts twenty-one miles of coastline, with many beaches, but the
name refers specifically to Malibu Surfrider Beach, the little stretch of
wave-riding heaven between the Malibu pier and the mouth of Malibu
Creek. Around that point—there are actually three points, closely
spaced—when the conditions are right, wrap the beautiful south swells
of summer, and the imagination of surfers everywhere.

The Rindge family—Frederick and his wife, Rhoda May—were
the last to own Rancho Topanga Malibu Sequit, the vast land tract
that included the Malibu coastline. Purchased for ten dollars an acre,
it was, to them, a country home paradise, or, as Rindge described it:
"A farm near the ocean, under the lee of the mountains, with a trout
brook, wild trees, a lake, good soil, and excellent climate, one not too
hot in summer."

Rindge died in 1905 and his wife, known to many as the Queen of
Malibu, took charge. Until her death in February 1941, Rhoda May's
life was an almost constant struggle to keep the land intact and intrud-
ers out. She spent most of her money battling neighbors, plans for a
lighthouse on Point Dume, the Southern Pacific Railroad—she built
her own private railroad instead—and the state and federal govern-
ments' declaration of eminent domain with plans for constructing the
future Pacific Coast Highway through her property. Rindge put up
fences, employed armed guards on horseback, even used dynamite
to keep out the unwelcome. Perhaps her story later inspired Miki's
protestations against "progress."

"So Malibu became sort of a mystical spot," Stecyk told Peter Day
and Ovidio Salazar, producer and director of the 1996 TV Dora documentary, *In Search of Da Cat*. "Nobody would ride Malibu for years at
a time (because of May Rindge), and so people would develop elaborate strategies and connections, and do anything to get in there and
find work. Pete Peterson's girlfriend worked in the Malibu tile factory,
which in the '30s was a mile south of the pier. He would take her to
work every day, park his car, surf all day, and take her home because

he was a considerate boyfriend. Don James, the photographer, got in through Jackie Coogan's house. He was an actor and surfer, used to live with Betty Grable. . . . Dale Velzy had a merchant seaman's card so he got in during WW II when it was a Coast Guard base. Some people got shot at, like Joe Quigg, who hid behind a rock while they used him for target practice."

Rindge lost her battle, and in 1929 the Roosevelt Highway (now the Pacific Coast Highway) was built from Santa Monica to Oxnard. That same year the public got access to the beach between the Malibu pier and the creek mouth. To stay financially solvent in the 1930s, May Rindge reluctantly sold off parcels of beachfront land north of the Malibu Creek. Since the first lots were offered to movie celebrities, the strand became known as the Malibu Movie Colony.

Imagine only a decade later, Malibu as Camelot, still without posh hamburger joints, exercise salons, coffee boutiques, T-shirt hawkers, celebrity hairdressers, houses scattered through the hillsides and canyons, or tony shopping centers. Clear today's traffic jam. Send most of the sightseers home. Clean up the beach. Open public beach access between the tightly packed private homes. Add some classic old cars, windows down, rolling easily along the highway, past fish restaurants and atmospheric joints, through a tableau of Edward Hopper lighting and the creeping low fog of film noir. And picture the long, sweeping swells wrapping around the first and second points and crashing over the rocks and sand.

Out in the water a young surfer eyes the six-foot combers that have been rolling in since before dawn. He is darkly tanned and his wavy hair is the color of wet mahogany. He waits patiently outside, spots the wave of the day, turns, strokes, breaks through a lip of light mist, and drops to the bottom, carving a white trail through a perfect blue-green wall. He stalls for a moment, then almost imperceptibly using his hips, knees, and ankles to position himself, rises into the curl and trims. He saunters casually forward, looking for all the world as if he is waiting patiently for a bus and not balanced on a foam and fiberglass rocket, hurtling through the water. He moves with the grace of a cat: arrogant, taunting, relaxed, and totally in control.

To Miki Dora, Malibu was home. His place. His palace. Paradise. He said it all once in a letter to a girlfriend: "I am the rightful king of Malibu."

In no time, even as other fine surfers rode Malibu, Miki's name began to appear painted on the wall between the sand and the highway, in various iterations: "DORA," "DORA RULES!," "DA CAT," "DA CAT LIVES."

Every time the Malibu wall was sandblasted, his name inevitably reappeared. It's still there.

2

The vintage years are over. I have my memories and that's it. I want to keep them to myself. I don't want to share them with a bunch of idiots . . .

—Miki Dora, Surf Guide, November 1964

TOM MOREY: Miki had a tremendous sense of self-importance and theatrics on a wave. He was onstage at all times. Muhammad Ali had the same presence and audacity. The first time I watched Miki surf it came off like: I AM RIDING THE WAVES. I AM IT.

JIMMY GANZER: Dude, when he went out, it was like, "Miki's going out, Miki's going out!" Word would spread and the kids on the beach would move close to the water, lie there in the warm sand, and pick up on every single move.

JAN MAYER: Miki was the "King of Malibu" and wore the crown proudly. I remember clearly when the six-foot-plus "wave of the day" would come, Miki would appear out of nowhere and come screaming across the face like a Greek god, with his tanned muscular body, white trunks, the skills of a magician, and the grace of a ballerina.

CYNTHIA APPLEWHITE: And yet, he used to tell me, "There are things that I do out there that I don't know how I do it." It was like the Laurence Olivier story about doing the perfect scene in *Othello* and not knowing how he did it.

DREW KAMPION: For Miki, the ride was a long thought rather than a series of moves. The word *symphonic* might be an exaggeration, but he clearly took it all in and planned ahead. Then, to watch the way he wove together his relationship with the people who dropped in on his ride and how he got around them was stunning. When you took off on a wave in front of him, you were an intrusion not only on a particular maneuver but on the composition he was throwing together extemporaneously. For Miki, the primary way to express his artistic nature was surfing. He realized it as an artistic form and nuanced it with the language of an artist in a way that I don't think anyone prior and hardly anyone since has done. Of course, everyone has their influences.

GREG NOLL: Miki was virtually a dead ringer for a guy named Matt Kivlin, just a younger version. Their surfing styles were also intertwined to some degree. When Miki was trimmed out, sliding across the face of a wave at Malibu, and he gets in that kind of leaned-back pose with one hand up . . . it was Matt. Of course, Matt never grabbed his balls; but Miki's got one hand down, usually on his cashews.

STEVE PEZMAN: When Joe Quigg, Matt Kivlin, and the early guys from Malibu came to Hawaii and saw Rabbit Kekai doing hot stuff on the waves, it just blew their minds. Soon there was a cross-pollination between Hawaiian hot curl surfing in Waikiki, in the '40s, and the Malibu chip board that was a postwar adaptation of Santa Monica aircraft technology, balsa wood covered with fiberglass. The big deal with fiberglass is not that it coated the wood. Fiberglass made it possible to attach the fin to the board. For maneuvering surfboards, the fin was everything, and before fiberglass the torque in the water was too much; the fin would snap off. They even tried bolts but they'd just weaken and break off. But fiberglass worked, and it changed surfing forever.

Hawaiian hot curl boards were pointy and sleek like missiles; the only way to slow them down was to do kick stalls. A rider would move toward the back of the board and lift the nose up all of a sudden, bring the board to a halt and let the wave catch up. Then to get the board going again, he'd move forward on the board while the curl broke over the back. That's when riders realized they could control the board from up front—*and ride on the nose.*

Both Matt Kivlin and Joe Quigg were highly influential in creating what came to be known as the quintessential Malibu board. According to surf historian Malcolm Gault-Williams, "This balsa board would go on to dominate the 1950s surf scene."

"In July 1950 I helped Matt Kivlin build his first all-balsa board," says Joe Quigg. "I sold him the balsa and loaned him my clamps. Then he shaped and glassed it. We were best friends at the time and a lot of the ideas about the new boards and new riding styles were things we came to as a result of endless talks about what to do next. Matt was by far the best rider at the time. I was more the builder. Matt also studied his architecture."

The pair had for a time done piece work gluing boards for Bob Simmons, on designs that included concave bottoms and dual fins, as well as boards with a foam core. While Simmons is often referred to

as the father of the modern surfboard, Quigg says that in 1940, before
going off to war, he had himself already created a twenty-seven-pound
lightboard that was more maneuverable than the Simmons hydrodynamic planks that came later.

After the war, Quigg and Kivlin took these changes even further.

"Board evolution," says Kivlin, was "pretty straightforward. As soon
as new materials like balsa wood came along—and it's not that it was
new; balsa wood was used primarily for life rafts and other things in
World War II, and the movie studios used it, but there wasn't enough
around for a while—it was apparent that heavy redwood boards offered
no advantages. When balsa wood came back, I just built surfboards to
suit what I tried to do."

In July, 1947, Quigg built a light board named the Easy Rider,
though it is more famously known as the Darrylin and is named after
Fox studio head Darryl Zanuck's daughter. Sixty pounds light, made
of balsa and sealed with fiberglass, the board was originally designed
for "novice girls."

A couple of months later at San Onofre, surfer Dave Rochlen,
who was then dating an actress named Norma Jean Baker, borrowed
Darrylin's board. Years later, C. R. Stecyk wrote of its capabilities: "It
is immediately apparent that Rochlen is turning four times faster and
making it into and out of what would previously have been inconceiv-
able situations . . . Kivlin is intrigued and promptly decides to have one
built for his girlfriend."

Just prior to the Darrylin board, Quigg crafted his first pintail,
and other interesting designs followed. The reaction from traditional
quarters was mostly negative, but Quigg persisted even though being
"ridiculed and embarrassed to take the board to the beach." One of
the few to offer support: Gard Chapin, who had himself built boards
with Bob Simmons. Chapin bought a pintail for his stepson that Miki
later considered "his greatest board."

JOE QUIGG: Gard Chapin came to Malibu a couple times in the summer of
1952, when the waves were good. He'd built Miki a small version of one of his
bigger boards. It was okay to learn on, but it really wasn't right. Miki looked
awfully young and skinny for an eighteen-year-old, and the board was too
big for him. Gard saw me riding a pintail, and he bought it for Miki for $50. It

was the fifth one I'd built, and the best one I'd built—an all-balsa, superlight pintail built before anyone else had built a modern pintail. It had a modern shape with a rocker, low rails, and a neat spoon. It was about 9'6", balsa and very light, and at least half the weight of other boards. Miki—we knew him as Chapin then—was still young. He got good later, at the end of the '50s.

Miki had his own design ideas, as well. He made his first surfboard when he was fourteen. He wanted something light. He glued up the wood, sawed it, drilled holes all the way through the surfboard, and stuffed them with Ping-Pong balls. He sealed it all with rice paper and varnish. It took him weeks to make, and left a big mess in his grandmother's garage. Then he took it to the beach.

GREG NOLL: The story Dora told me was that he finally rode this board in a big storm at Malibu. He made it all the way to the pier and he jumped off. The board hit the pier and broke into a thousand pieces, and the beaches were littered with Ping-Pong balls. Or maybe it was Rincon. There's a thread of truth in there somewhere. He could have made a hollow deck board, because that was typical of the time period. And somebody, when they were decking the thing over, might have dropped in a Ping-Pong ball or two.

It's goddamn funny, though, and so typical of almost everything Miki did: out of the ashes of the truth come these incredible stories.

3

Everything under control. Plenty of action and opportunities to be taken . . . Staying at the best hotel in Honolulu, but moving to an apartment this month. My address will be 219 Lilliokalani Way. Plenty of excitement, lots of girls, and a high scale night life. Spend money as soon as I acquire it, but at all times living at a high standard. Hurry on over, and we take over.

—Miki, postcard to Joel Laykin from Waikiki, August 1954

MICKEY MUÑOZ: Because of where I lived—Uplifters Ranch in Santa Monica Canyon—and its proximity to Malibu, when I got my first real surfboard in the early '50s, I quickly ran into Miki. We had mutual respect; at least I think we did because I didn't take much shit from him and I don't think he ever took advantage of me.

We also had this in common: my dad was an opera singer and his grand-mother was an opera coach. He was very proud of her. He took me to visit her, in West Hollywood.

For money I patched balsa boards out of my garage. I wanted to go to Hawaii. I had planned to go two years earlier, with Peter Lawford, but he got an acting job and couldn't take me. Miki helped me patch boards. My grandfather had died and left hundreds of boxes of cigars stacked in the back of our garage. My dad was a gin drinker and had cases of Gordon's. Miki and I learned to open gin bottles and replace the cap so that it looked like it wasn't really open. We drank lemonade and gin, and smoked my grandfa-ther's cigars, listened to Chico Sesna in the afternoon, and worked with the sun streaming into the garage.

I turned Miki on to his first joint. I remember him smoking it in my bath-room, looking in the mirror at himself, and going, "I don't feel a thing. I don't feel a thing."

Dora's attitude, even repairing surfboards, was "Do it half-ass, get it done, get the money, and run." I remember once we did a fill-in on a fin with graham cracker crumbs mixed into the resin. Another time we crumbled dry leaves into the mix.

Eventually, between the money from patching and from a bicycle I sold, I scraped together enough to buy a one-way ticket to Hawaii through a very du-bious character and writer in Santa Monica, named Frank Donahue. We went with Frank's stepson, Mike Donahue—he also called himself Mike Donovan—and another incredible character, Jimmy Fisher, from Santa Cruz. The last time I saw Jimmy, I left him in an alley at three in the morning. He was facedown, beating his fists on the ground and screaming about all of the people he was going to take with him when he met his maker. Luckily, he didn't mention my name. Dora was on the list, though.

The four of us flew to Hawaii in 1954. I had written my mother a note: "Dear Mom, Going to the islands, Love, Mickey. PS: I will write." I landed with six dollars in my pocket; I don't know how much Dora and Fisher and Donovan had. The day we arrived we rented a little apartment in Honolulu, right up from Waikiki, and lived together for four months.

Turned out that Jimmy and Miki were fairly experienced at shoplifting. Fisher was a smart guy—brilliant, even—and several weeks into our stay he put on a sports jacket, slacks, and shoes, the typical tourist in Waikiki, and said, "Follow me and I'll show you how this is done." In a jewelry store he looked around, talked to the jeweler, examined some cuff links. Then he dropped some cuff links into the cuff of his jacket and kept talking, casually put his hands in his pockets so the cuff links dropped in. Following him was like watching three-card monte. I walked out and then he walked out, and I said, "Geez, how do you do that?" He said, "It's the eyes. They don't really see what they see. You ever watch somebody check their watch, and two seconds later you ask what time it is and they look at their watch again? I've got it wired." He did have funny eyes: one was lazy and went up, and that was a little disconcerting. People would look at him but they couldn't really tell whether he was looking at them.

I didn't like it, but I was fascinated by their talent for theft, and we had a couple similar adventures. The attitude was, and I believe the quote came from Dora, "If I don't do it, somebody else will." That was his credo, the rationalization. But in the end it wasn't for me. I didn't have the balls. But those guys kept scamming because they had the *cojones.* I guess there was an adrenaline rush, a certain thrill. It was all about antiauthority. I decided to earn my way instead and got a job at a restaurant and worked as a busboy, and I was happy with that.

BOB COOPER: I heard a great story about that trip: Miki was surfing at Queens, a neat little break at Waikiki, snaking the other surfers, japing them, like he usually did, really pushing things. In those days everybody rode balsa wood boards and they had a slot fin system. The wood board was glassed and then they put two pieces of board that were unglassed into a slot. You jammed the fin in there and when the wood got wet it would swell up and hold in the fin. It wasn't a very successful plan and lasted maybe only a year. Anyway, Miki was in Hawaii with a slot fin board.

After asserting himself for a while, Miki felt a jerk. A Hawaiian had stolen Miki's fin and told him to go in. You can't surf without a fin, so Miki rode in, sliding, ticked off. When he got to the beach, he noticed a crowd of Hawaiians following him. They yelled and swore and Miki began to panic. Miki got to his car, but before he could get away, they grabbed the door and said they don't want no howlie kook pushing them off waves. It's their water, they're very territorial, and they're gonna beat the crap out of him.

This is what Miki told me he did: threw a fake epileptic fit. He sat straight up in the driver's seat, looked straight ahead, and started shaking. All the blood drained out of his head. He turned absolutely white. He opened the glove compartment and tried to jam his head in. He foamed at the mouth. It was an absolutely perfect fit. The Hawaiians knew that it was a put-on, but they had never, ever encountered somebody who had that much ticker that they would actually do something like that to avoid getting beat up. They watched him for a while, called him an asshole, and left.

JIM FISHER: One day in late August 1954, Miki, Mike, and I decided to take the cruise ship *Lurline*, from Oahu to Hilo, on the Big Island. Muñoz didn't go. We put on sports coats and ties and boarded. We figured we'd blend right in—which was important because we hadn't bought tickets.

DR. DON SMALL: I was a surfer, a lifeguard at San Clemente and Doheny, and a student at Occidental College. I'd come for the summer, made friends with some girls in the Islands, and they were going back to Los Angeles on the *Lurline*, which sailed from San Francisco to Oahu, to Hilo, then to Los Angeles. My friends and I came onboard in Oahu, had a good time drinking beer, and before we knew it the ship started to move. A few people jumped off—a long jump—but we stayed on and figured we'd go to Hilo. We had a party going. You could buy a ticket for the cruise to Hilo for, I think, $20. Unfortunately, we didn't, and we all got caught going into the dining room about four or five hours into the cruise. They put us in the brig with others who had hitched a ride, including Miki.

Dora was a tall, dark, thin kid. He was quiet, or pissed and surly, and kept saying he'd been imprisoned unfairly. Some of us made a joke and said we thought we might get caught but could buy our way into a ticket—which it turned out they wouldn't let us do—but not Dora.

In Hilo, they took us ashore, cuffed and photographed us, and made us talk to two FBI agents. The next day the agents took us in handcuffs on a plane to Honolulu. They interviewed us again at the court in Oahu, and we entered our pleas. The newspaper took some pictures. Most of us were in Hawaiian shirts and shorts and flip-flops. I pled guilty and said it was my fault, and most of the others said the same. Only Miki pled not guilty.

MIKLOS DORA SR.: The surfers always used to stow away on the boats. After so many years the shipping line got disgusted with it. They staged raids and the kids were caught. Because they were out past the three-mile limit, it became a federal case and the FBI got into it. The *Los Angeles Times* and the *Herald* had big headlines: "Los Angeles Kids in Jail in Hawaii."

My mother told me the news. She was upset. She said, "What do we do? Miki's in jail."

I said, "Look, he got into it. He has to get out of it."

"You are a cruel father."

"I can't do anything," I said.

I sent Miki a cable: "I heard that you got into it. You better get out of it."

Miki wouldn't plead guilty. He said he was invited onboard by a couple who gave a going-away party. He had a few drinks and fell asleep and didn't notice that the boat had left. This was his defense. They found him guilty anyway and fined him a few dollars.

JIM FISHER: I was the only one they didn't capture. I hid out in the stateroom of a girl from Texas when I saw the authorities scooping up people. The ship's officers went to every cabin on every deck. I hid in the bathroom while they questioned this girl, then walked off the ship in Hilo.

I saw Miki next in Oahu after he entered his plea. He couldn't believe that they didn't get me. He said, "I've got to appear in court again next week. I have to go in front of a judge, and the FBI wants to talk to all of us. I think they rounded up about thirteen people, maybe more."

I decided to help Miki by testifying at his trial. Miki's story would be that he'd wanted to have dinner on the Big Island and fly back the next day, but then he couldn't find a purser quickly enough to pay for his passage. Of course, we'd had no intention of buying any ticket; we just brought enough money to fly back from Hilo to Oahu.

My story would be that I was partying aboard the ship before the last bell rang asking all visitors to go to shore, and that I got off. But the last thing I'd heard Miki saying was, "I'm going to find me a purser."

He said, "You're going to do this for me?"

I said, "Yeah. I'm going to put on a tie and a coat and I'm going to do the 'I can't understand how this happened' routine."

They tried Miki last, in September. After he told his story, the prosecutor said, "All you had to do was ask ship personnel where the purser's office was and buy a ticket." He said he'd had a few drinks and got disoriented, the ship was rocking, and all this other stuff. He was expert at telling a story, making it sound good.

They asked me, "When did you hear the first bell to leave the ship?"

I said, "There was a man walking around with a gong. So I said good-bye to Miki, have a good trip, I'll meet you at the airport when you fly back."

They said, "We have it that you'd stowed away, too."

"Absolutely not! Who said that?" I knew Miki didn't say anything.

"Some of these other people say they saw you on the boat with Miki. In fact, a couple of them testified that you were there."

I said, "Who are these people? I don't know them. They may say anything to get themselves out of trouble! I'm telling you the truth!"

Since they couldn't break down Miki's story or mine, all he got was a $150 fine and they said he couldn't come back for a year. Miki and I walked off together and the prosecutor came up from behind and said, "You got away with that but you're not fooling us at all. You're lucky this time. Where were you hiding?" I stuck to my story. "I wasn't on the ship. Didn't you hear my testimony?" He finally said, "I give up. Good-bye."

4

Miki had a side you couldn't penetrate. I kept wondering, Who are you?
—Kathy "Gidget" Kohner

BOB COOPER: When I started surfing full-time at Malibu, Miki was still known as Mickey Chapin because of his stepfather. He was almost a regular guy, not as eccentric as he would be later. But one trait stayed pretty much the same: he was a loner who was only social when it was to his advantage. He'd never just sit down and talk about the weather. You hardly saw him at parties. He lived a very separate life from the rest of us. At Malibu, or at any break, he was intense and there to pluck whatever he could from the beach and its culture and the people—then he'd disappear.

VICK FLAXMAN: He was like a will-o'-the-wisp, zipping up and down the coast. He never stayed in one spot, even at Malibu, which was his scene. Nobody ever pinned him down. You'd ask him a simple question like, "Where have you been? I haven't seen you in ages," but you'd never get a straight answer. And he got more and more quirky as he got older.

ALLAN CARTER: Miki simply didn't want to know people who would try to pry away his secrets, whatever they were. Sometimes he even registered his cars out of state. He had an aspect of Holden Caulfield—only wilder, heading towards Mars, like a supersonic gypsy. He liked his mystery. He said, "When I go, my secrets go with me."

SUSAN MCNEILL: Miki didn't suffer fools. He was very intuitive. He evaluated people according to his personal rule book. He categorized everybody he knew. Miki drew people in, would hook, line, and sinker them; and then decide where they belonged. Depending on where you fell is what you could get back from him. He could be wrong about someone but it didn't really matter. I don't think you could even switch categories. The stupid people were to be taken advantage of. They got stolen from. Practically all of them, actually. He didn't think taking from the stupid people was wrong. First off was always, "How can I use this person, to my best advantage?" What can this person do for me? Most of them fell under "They'd do anything," so they became the stupid ones. Others would do some things but had to work a deal. Part of his

ABOVE TOP: On the *Lurline,* 1954. Dr. Don Small, second from left. Mike Donovan, fifth from left. Miki, sixth from left. Courtesy Dora Estate/Refrigerator Collection.
ABOVE: "Simmer Down Zeek!" by Miki. Courtesy Dora Estate/Refrigerator Collection.

game was that the deals would always end up destroying the thing itself. Then there's the other end of the scale, the people he actually had respect for. You could have him in your home, give him anything he wanted, and he wouldn't take a damn thing.

ALLAN CARTER: People think Miki was all about surfing, and in a way he was. But here's the surprising key to Miki, which most people seem to miss: the greatest thing in Miki's life, the number one thing he avidly pursued, was personal freedom. Sometimes we'd sit around with a cup of tea in the afternoon and ask ourselves, if we had only one thing in life, what would be most important? And the answer, always: personal freedom. In so many ways during his life he paraded his personal freedom like a banner. Personal freedom made surfing possible, and surfing was the way he could escape this world into a reverie and a euphoria. Surfing suspended all the conflicts in his head. When he got on a good wave, it was like going to a psychiatrist, but cheaper and more beneficial for his health.

GREG NOLL: The trouble was, the more you knew about Dora—stuff that was very hard to come by—the more you realized you didn't know. His whole persona was so inexplicable and complex that I basically gave up. I figured, Okay, our relationship is going to be based around the time we spent in the water and the time we were kids. All this other complex shit I'm not going to even worry about it because I can't figure the guy out anyway.

REBEL

In everyday life you will find that your boss, your lover, or your government often try to manipulate you. They propose a "game" to you in the form of a choice in which one of the alternatives appears definitely preferable. Having chosen this alternative, you are faced with a new game, and very soon you find that your reasonable choices have brought you to something you never wanted: you are trapped. To avoid this, remember that acting a bit erratically may be the best strategy. What you lose by making some sub-optimal choices you make up for by keeping greater freedom.

—David Ruelle, *Chance and Chaos*, 1991

CHAPTER THREE

Portrait of the Artist
as a Young Wave Rider

1

Mike was like a stone; an attractive, magnetic, powerful stone. A stone that was vaguely translucent; that you could see into for a few inches and then it went milky and inscrutable. And around the stone all the little iron filings gathered, people who did not see anything in the stone, but could not resist it. When the stone moved, they rearranged themselves, shifted positions, made an intricate complex maneuver to get closer to the stone.

—Eugene Burdick, *The Ninth Wave*

In his *Los Angeles Times* essay, "Why We Worship the Irrational," Crispin Sartwell wrote, "We love, or at any rate, ogle obsessively, the perversity of famous people and thus encourage and reward that perversity. The more insane the belief system, according to Kierkegaard, the more worthy it is of belief. The more insane the celebrity, the more worthy she is of our attention. This of course has a religious flavor: We worship our crazed demigods by virtue of their beauty, their power, their wealth, and, of course, their craziness . . . you can adore only what challenges your ability to comprehend, only what appears alien or arbitrary, what resists or exceeds your attempt to explain it."

Miki, by virtue of his charm and talent, his eccentricities and humor, his elusive self-containment and burgeoning mystique, began to emerge as Malibu's first bona fide celebrity. "Like a moth to the flame people were transfixed by the man," says Johnny Fain, a Malibu regular who was, for a time, both Miki's sidekick and nemesis. "Miki," says another friend, "was a nondefinable force of nature that pulled you toward him like stars and planets to a black hole." Time and attention would only intensify the effect.

BOB COOPER: Miki definitely had his own style. He would stand in the sand at Malibu dressed in a white shirt, elephant cords, sandals or Florsheims, no socks, and a nice hunting jacket, and assess the whole situation. He'd make sure that he was seen. Then he could leave—unless he wanted to stay and surf. Sometimes he had on tennis shorts and a tennis sweater. He had smoking jackets, an expensive houndstooth tweed. He always dressed up, never down. I never saw Miki in a pair of jeans, deck shoes, an aloha shirt. He never wore any of the surfer uniform, and because Miki lived in Hollywood he could pick up his attire cheaply at the Goodwill store.

Miki also had a unique collection of overcoats, ankle-length stuff that looked like it was from a movie. He had a full-length black leather, authentic Nazi trench coat, and sometimes he'd wear it with his World War I fighter pilot helmet and goggles. A month later people would show up at the beach with their own big coats. His Nazi gear is in a New Zealand museum now.

He'd bring other interesting items to the beach, like a crocodile-skin doctor's bag with phrases written on it in paint, like graffiti: "Life is short, why bother to live it." He had unique toys that he'd reveal only briefly so people could see them and say, "Oh my gosh, where'd he get that!?" It was done to keep himself interesting and to make sure that people watched him. Miki wanted to establish himself as an individual *visually,* using his appearance *and* his gestures. Miki sauntered with confidence and purpose. Everything about him showed his disdain. "Look, I am not part of all of you. You can look at me but you don't know who I am. You don't know what's going on in my head." It's like his persona was scratching its head, asking: "What am I doing down here with all these plebeians? I want to surf and I want to have a good time, but I have to deal with the sand flies."

HENRY FORD: Maybe it sounds weird, but Miki didn't even want to be known as a *surfer.* He hated the word. He loved the sport but he hated the general observation that people would make—that surfers are worthless, uneducated, and unsophisticated—if it somehow included him. Miki probably thought that of *other* surfers, but he always appeared sophisticated. He dressed so differently than the rest of us, he didn't belong at the beach, he belonged in Beverly Hills.

BOB COOPER: He would also ridicule the sacred surfboard by the way he handled them on the beach. He'd pick up his board by the tail and drag it through the sand like it was an accessory that had no meaning. Nobody did that. You put it under your arm or on your head. You treated this weapon with respect; it was going to save your life.

He'd color his boards. One day he came down with an incredibly multicolored wax job that was just vivid. It looked like a tapestry. Up to that point all wax was white. I'm going, "Where'd you get all this different-colored wax?" He looked at me as if to say "You stupid oaf" and then said one word: "Crayon." It was great.

His cars were another symbol. He'd show up in incredible vehicles. Everyone was going for woodies or Plymouths with the backseat out. He would show up with a 1937 Oldsmobile, an absolute collector's item. "Miki, where'd you get that car?" He says, "Oh, the chauffeur found it in the back of a thirty-seven-car garage in a mansion in Beverly Hills and didn't know what to do with it."

At one time or another Miki's autos included an English Alvis that he'd gotten in a trade for showing someone how to game the early computerized airline reservation system, one or more VW camper vans, a VW Bug, an early '50s Ford coupe, a Cadillac convertible, a '50s-era Ford woody with a Chrysler hemi dropped in, and a 1962 Chevy wagon. Miki was also reported to have driven actress Myrna Loy's Cadillac, and actress Sylvia Sidney's Cadillac. According to C. R. Stecyk in *Dora Lives*, "His garage housed such swift examples of the milieu as a 1948 Jaguar XK120, more than one Porsche 356 Speedster, a 1953 Mercedes Benz 300 ille Miglia Sport Leicht, a 1956 Rometsche Beeskow, a 1958 Porsche 350A Spyder, and a 1968 Lotus Coventry Cosworth-powered race car." Allan Carter recalls, "Miki had cars scattered all over, a fluid assemblage, usually parked outside his grandmother's West Hollywood cottage."

According to Mike Doyle, "He used to buy old cars and park them on the most dangerous corner on Chatauqua so they'd get hit on purpose. He'd claim they were classic relics and then he'd demand a real high amount in court for what he should get. Some of them didn't even run."

In 1952, Miki Dora's uncle Rad gifted him with a 1930 Rolls-Royce: a Phantom II Town Car, Cooper Sedanca de Ville. The model has an open front with a convertible roof over the chauffeur and a divider window between him and the passengers.

"The car originally belonged to Sol Wurtzel, who screen-tested Shirley Temple and pretty much saved Fox's ass from going under in the middle of the Depression," says Jim Rapheld, who bought the car in the late '60s and restored it. "Wurtzel used the car until 1940, then brought it to the lot for use in several films. Finally the studio didn't want to store the car anymore, so Wurtzel sold the car to Rad who gave it to Miki, cheap, as a birthday present."

Joel Laykin remembers being co-owner of the car for $300. "Miki played owning a Rolls to the max. He really enjoyed meetings of the Rolls-Royce Club of Los Angeles, and he took me along. We'd sit with these extremely well-to-do people, everyone talking about their odometers and this and that."

"We had a bunch of adventures in that car," says Mickey Muñoz. "One time we put on turbans with jewels and cruised Hollywood."

~

Miki also had a highly stylized way of speaking and gesturing, a carny-intimate bebop jive that could seduce, deflect, or disdain. "Acolytes were struck by his dazzle . . . and his wildly intelligent if disjointed sentences, combined with a lot of blowhard paranoia," Sheila Weller wrote in the August 2006 issue of *Vanity Fair*. "He had his own way of talking: edgy, staccato, wiseguy ("So-so-so what's goin' on, ennhk?") mixed with campy Continental ("Vuht are you doing here, dahlink?"). And he was always gesturing with his hands, with an emotive, bent-elbowed, loose-fingered gusto. . . ."

ED GARNER: You would see Miki talking to a crowd, and his hand gestures were almost like pantomime. He'd have his right hand on his chest and then, as he said something, the hand would start going out. Then he'd point down to the sand, keeping the thumb up, then point the hand back to himself, and then it would go some other direction. And the left hand would do its own thing.

JIM KEMPTON: Miki's method of conversation was always rhetorical. He would answer questions with questions. He'd speak intensely. His words

ABOVE: "He had a beautiful face and body," says Toni Colvin. Miki at Malibu, 1960. Photo: Toni Donovan Colvin.

BELOW: Glamour shot of a lifelong nonsmoker. Photo: Peter Gowland.

ABOVE: Miki in front of Chasen's Restaurant, in a 1964 ad for the Malibu Ltd. board made by Tom Morey. Used also in Miki's SAG composite. Courtesy Dora Estate.

were clipped and conspiratorial. I always felt this clenched-teeth sense of frustration and agony when he spoke—like he couldn't tell you enough. And then he would just stop. Many people do Miki impressions. Denny Aaberg's is fabulous. If you ever get a chance to see John Milius's film *Big Wednesday*, just before the movie ends a guy paddles out and talks to another guy who is talking about selling drugs to the kids. That's Denny doing Miki.

DENNY AABERG: The thing is that *everybody* took up Miki's mannerisms. At Malibu or State Beach in Santa Monica you could see twenty "Mikis" trying to cop his attitude, doing the side step, catlike, hands splayed inside their waistbands, a wry smile, cocky under the sunglasses, not talking straight.

CYNTHIA APPLEWHITE: What's amazing is that people did it in front of him. One guy at Malibu copied him so much that everyone called him Chickey Mapin.

JOHN VAN HAMERSVELD: In those days, the *pose* was everything. You *were* your pose, in the water and out. And because surfing is nonverbal, this becomes even more interesting. The psychological shield of style was wrapped beautifully around this Dora figure: the incandescent smile and white teeth that lit up his tanned face; those dark eyes that you couldn't see into; the mahogany-colored curly hair. We were confronted with a total mystery and asking ourselves, "What is this all about?"

JOHN MILIUS: And yet it embarrassed Miki to be treated like the king. His in-group, the hard-core Malibu surfers, were really the Negroes in his eyes. We were not quite as evolved. I remember talking to him years later about the old surfers and he'd say, "These guys are animals, terrible people, dolts, stupid kids." And I'm sure that from his point of view it looked like they were the scum. Just the idea of all these guys coming up to him, and imitating him, and trying to get in on his scene and be cool, just revolted him. And yet, here's his paradoxical aspect: he was pleased to have everyone so enamored of him. His disciples say that the commercialization and organization of surfing, and the crowds, upset him, but I think that's overly romantic. I don't believe he really mourned the loss of those days. When he was out at Malibu with only four people on a great day, it must have been glorious and great fun, but it was also great fun to be able to get all the girls and have all the people say, "God, Miki, what's the word?"

2

Miki had the looks and the charm of Cary Grant, the hell-raising ability of a Steve McQueen, and something inside akin to Dillinger—

but not quite that far south, of course. He was hypnotic. If he ever
focused on you, he owned you.

—**Bob Morris**

TONI DONOVAN COLVIN: Miki had a beautiful body and a lovely face. He was very, very attractive.

CYNTHIA APPLEWHITE: When we would walk along the street together, women would do double takes just to see him. He never had to compete with other men to get women.

TUBESTEAK: At his grandmother's, he would put on this face cream, put a towel over his head, and steam himself to look young. Imagine a guy in his early twenties trying to look young. He used a lot of hairdo stuff . . . remember Sulfur 8, that straightens hair?

ALLAN CARTER: Miki was only vain in an amusing way. We'd check out our profiles, but it was mostly just a joke. I'm sure he wanted to look good, but we laughed at movie star actors, who are so insecure. He called them stars that shed no light. Whatever Miki was insecure about, it wasn't his personal worth. Miki never acted hungry. Miki liked intelligent women. They were totally different than some cutesy idiot from the beach with the IQ of a rutabaga.

CYNTHIA APPLEWHITE: I went to Malibu one day in 1959. It was a beautiful scene. Surfers in the water—and this one fabulous surfer, head and shoulders better than anyone else. That was Miki. I wanted to meet him and I saw to it that I did. I suggested my husband go over and talk to him. And while they were talking I just joined in the conversation.

We shared a lovely chemistry, a wavelength. I was a little older, and compared to other men I knew, he had a gentleness about him. He liked me and cared about me. I know he didn't trust many people but for some reason he picked me to trust.

I didn't surf. I was writing then and I'd go off under the pier with my notebook and work. Or I'd bring my paints. And on the way home we'd stop at Wil Wrights and get a milk shake. Spending time with Miki was fun and fabulous, but in some ways it was difficult for Miki to have a full relationship with a woman. I knew he would never reveal himself fully to me. It's not that he was closed off, but he liked to call all the shots. If I wanted to see him, I couldn't call up and say come over right now. He had to be in the mood. We only got together when he felt like it.

CYNTHIA GARRIS: Cynthia Applewhite was my mother. She came on the scene just after the movie *Gidget*. According to her, the film was based on a girl who chased Miki, who was the real "Moondoggie."

When I was twelve or thirteen, during summer vacation and on weekends, my mom would drop off me and a girlfriend in Santa Monica and then disappear for hours. One time she picked us up with Miki in the front seat. Remember the Tree-Top apple juice jingle? "It's the pick-pick-pick, the pick of the crop/from the top-top-top, the top of the tree." Nancy and I sat in the backseat and sang it about eight hundred times. I could see Miki's eyes rolling up every time we started again. When we dropped him off at his apartment, he got out, looked at us, and said, "Nice meeting you creeps."

As I got older and the sexual revolution was upon us, my mother got more comfortable talking with me about Miki in intimate detail. She reminisced about the first few years, about his beautiful body. To her he was this golden god. She talked about how his skin had this velvety, deep tone. And it had this beautiful smell—probably from years of layers of suntan lotion.

CYNTHIA APPLEWHITE: I knew Miki also had a girlfriend named Virginia. They used to go to the beach together, but Miki would hardly talk to her all day. When he was through surfing, he'd give her a little sign and they'd leave together. With me it was almost the same thing. What's strange is that I spent almost a year on the same beach with Virginia but never knew who she was because Miki didn't acknowledge her and no one ever introduced us.

CAROLINE BARNETT: Miki always called me Virginia, but I've never cared for the name. In my forties, I started going by my middle name, Caroline. At the beach my nickname was Deetsie. Back then I had long blond hair, was slender and athletic. I loved to go out on a board and paddle around. I went to Malibu, saw Miki surfing, and was taken by his grace and his beauty. I remember saying to my girlfriend, "That's my hero."

At a party, Miki and I sat on the couch and talked. Pretty quickly I was crazy about him. What struck me most were his beautiful hands, his fingers. He was very artistic. Sensitive. A gentle soul. I didn't see any of the posturing. Afterward he said, "Would you be my girlfriend?" I was young and shy, and I probably just giggled, but I was quite excited.

I discovered soon that Miki was a chameleon. He changed depending on what the audience might think. At the beach Miki was paranoid and didn't get close to anyone. I had a Samoyed named Tanya and Miki would leave us in the sand by ourselves when he surfed. Sometimes Miki sat with me for a while, but he was very guarded when there were other people around. They'd talk to him and he'd go into his little act: posturing, speaking in a funny voice, and other nonsense. He complained that he felt on display. He said he was afraid of being exploited and taken advantage of. The theatrical persona was just his way of keeping people at a distance, of maintaining his reputation and protecting himself. I understood his beach persona and I accepted it. Alone, he was quite different—otherwise, I probably wouldn't have had anything to do with him.

Every so often I'd get free tickets to openings and then he'd take me to dinner and buy the steaks. We'd attend the occasional party, stay an hour, and leave. He never seemed to really fit in.

I worked and went to school at night, and I lived with three other women near UCLA. We had a big party one evening. I had all the surfing people over. Miki was there. I don't remember what happened, but we left for some reason to go to his grandmother's. On the way, we had an argument and I got out of the car in Westwood and walked back to my apartment. I was very upset with him. He drove back and forth on Sunset trying to get my attention, but I didn't respond. He had been drinking and I didn't care for drinking that much. In fact, I think he'd been sick in the car. Sometimes I drank, but I always tried to maintain some kind of sobriety.

Another time, we had an argument because while waiting for him at a party, I was innocently talking to another surfer, Jim Fisher, a friend of his. When Miki walked in and saw us, he was instantly furious. He pulled me out of there and into his car, and we drove away. He was jealous, but what he said always stuck with me: "You're just like my mother." He felt betrayed.

SUSAN MCNEILL: Miki adored his mother, but he also had a lot of anger toward her, and it affected his relationships with women. He would say that his mother was a pathetic person who became an alcoholic and was into all that Bible crap on TV, and that his dad had never taken much of an interest in him because he was off fulfilling his own dreams. It depressed him. When Ramona married Gard, he felt excluded because Gard didn't want him around. Sometimes when he told me things about his childhood, he'd have tears in his eyes. I don't think Miki ever lost the feeling of being alone. It was hard for me—and I suppose anyone—to make Miki feel that you really cared, that you were honestly interested in what went on inside of him. He was open as a child and had been let down, so he became very guarded. But the Miki I knew had a big heart. If you really needed him, he'd be there.

3

Work!?!

—**Maynard G. Krebs**

. . . the difference between Maynard's brand of slacker—and with his famous aversion to work, he was certainly among the first of the slackers—and today's acne-ridden layabout is that Maynard, for all his silliness, was inherently wise. His sense of justice arose directly out of his cultural interests, not in spite of them. His character was the result of what he dug rather than what he didn't dig.

—**Meghan Daum,** *Los Angeles Times,* **2005**

KEMP AABERG: In *Gidget,* Cliff Robertson, the Big Kahuna, was the guy living on the beach. At the end someone says, "Summer's over. What are you going to do?"

"Well, I'm just going off to find some waves," says Robertson. "There's waves in South America." That was the first glimpse we got of the *idea* of someone actually being a surf bum, searching for the endless summer—except that in those days no one actually did that. Everyone went back to college and to work. Even in the Hollywood version of Malibu, the Kahuna decided to go straight and get a job. But not Miki. As a kid I used to see Miki hanging around at State Beach in the winter, and I'd think, "Boy, that must be neat to be out of school and at the beach all day." I'd scratch my head and wonder: "How do you do that?"

ROBERT GILBERT: Miki once told me that there were two kinds of surfers: those who had to go home at night and those who didn't."

NAT YOUNG: Miki swore to me that he would never work a day in his life. I said, "Well, what do you do?" He said, "I do nothing. And I don't intend to do anything, ever." It amazed me that someone could be so proud of that. He believed that you could either waste time working or you could live life.

RICKY GRIGG: According to Miki, only the most demented humans worked, troglodytes, the dregs of society. On the other hand, surfing was a unique and liberating experience. Thrilling. It felt so good to do that it made you better than anyone not doing it. That gave Miki a terribly rich aura of superiority that had nothing to do with being handsome and in great shape. He was the superior being because he had discovered how life *should* be lived. They key was to reject all the values of the other world, which was everybody else.

JOHN MILIUS: Daniel Duane, in his book *Caught Inside*, writes about the essential quandary of surfing: If you give your life to this, what are your rewards? Freedom, health, that kind of thing. But the drawbacks are: you're a bum. People will look down on you, say, "What did you do? Did you contribute anything?" To be a real surfer, someone who attains a knightlike prowess and the acknowledgment of his peers, you have to open yourself to some tremendous dangers both in the water and in your psyche—and you may never recover from letting go. You may never have a work ethic again. You may never be able to do anything but be a worthless bum.

LINDA CUY: I don't think Miki wanted to be a lawyer, or an actor, or a wine merchant. Miki was what he was, and that was enough. It's simple: Miki's life was all about a few empty waves. What do you have to do, how do you have to live, to get those few empty waves?

Even for Miki, the answer to Cuy's question included at least a small measure of employment, albeit typically brief.

MIKLOS DORA SR.: In 1955, I got Miki a job at a big wine distributor. They trained him as a salesman, but again, he went surfing instead of selling. He also screwed the boss's wife.

DALE VELZY: One day Dora came into the shop I had with Hap (Jacobs). He said, "I need another board. I have some very important wines here, and fancy imported Scotch." Hap and I went out to his car, and he had a trunk full of Stuart's of Dundee Scotch. He said "How about a case for you and a case for Hap, for an unglassed board?" That was $45. Hap and I were Scotch drinkers at the time, so we said, "Let's do it. Come back tomorrow and you'll have your board." He left, hauled ass, smoked those tires clear down Pacific Avenue in Venice—and the trunk opened and all the wine bottles fell out and broke. The next day he came for his board and told us he got fired because "somebody" stole two cases of Scotch and broke all his wine bottles.

Other brief bouts of employment: Miki's friend George Samama, the maître d' at La Scala in Beverly Hills, took on Miki as a bartender, but he didn't last. At another job he dropped a wine bottle through a glass case and was let go. Miki also worked briefly as a host at Villa Frascati restaurant on Wilshire, parking cars when the Beverly Hilton Hotel opened, and for a short time he was a lifeguard with Jim Fisher at San Clemente. Typically, the two invented a third lifeguard, got him paid, and split the paycheck.

Miki also worked, briefly, as an associate lifeguard at an L.A. city pool, but quit abruptly after tangling with the locals.

TUBESTEAK: To get back at them for stealing a twenty from his wallet, Miki put a rat in a box in his locker and refused to feed it. When, after four days, Miki's tormentors heard the rat's toenails scratching inside the box, they said, "Hey, Ese, what's that noise?"

"Nothing, fellows, only my lunch."

"What do you mean, your lunch? You mean *our* lunch."

"Help yourself," said Miki. A guy reached up and into the box, feeling for what he no doubt thought was going to be a juicy sandwich. When the starved rat chomped down and took a huge bite out of his finger, a bloodcurdling scream filled the locker room. By the time the screaming subsided, Miki had sprinted to the parking lot and speed-shifted away.

Since Miki had no steady job, it's not out of line to ask how *did* he pay the rent, buy food and gasoline, travel and survive? "It always seemed to me that Dora, much like Blanche DuBois, lived on the kindness of strangers," says Wayne Speeds, a young surfer who met Miki in the early '70s.

And family. "When Miki was almost twenty, Ramona inherited some money from her trust, and she told me, 'I am giving Miki $5,000,'" says Miklos Sr. "I said, 'Ramona, don't give it to him. Let him get a job. Put it in trust.'

"'No, no. I will give it to him,' she said. She did, and Miki pissed it away."

Some money-gathering methods would later become obvious: movie work, cadging funds from neophyte surfers and stooges, petty theft, renting surfboards, writing magazine pieces, the largesse of rich friends and whomever else he could charm, investing (Miki had a friend in Santa Monica who sent him good advice and regular financial clippings from the *Los Angeles Times*), and, according to a former girlfriend, more than occasional checks from his father.

Another source of income is probably apocryphal, but the story's existence illustrates the mythic esteem accorded Miki's financial independence. And if it's true, what a scam! A wealthy surfing friend supposedly fronted Miki $150,000. He put it in the bank, using a phony name and identification, and using the account as collateral, he applied for a Gold Amex card. With the card he bought high-ticket items for sixty days. He returned the $150,000 and skipped on the bills. Then he sold the goods and put the proceeds in the bank.

ALLAN CARTER: Miki always had *something* stashed. He loved treasure, and would have died to have been with Sir Francis Drake after he sacked Panama, when they put all the loot out on the deck.

MARCIA MCMARTIN: I have a photo of him holding up a gold bar, and he always traveled with gold coins because he said he needed something negotiable if he got in a jam. Paper money was no good.

MIKE DOYLE: Miki was always generous with financial advice. One day when we were younger and I was collecting Coke bottles on the beach to turn in for money, Dora said, "Buy gold, Doyle. The entire world economy is going to collapse. Buy gold."

DARRYL STOLPER: We went to Tijuana in 1960 and bought 50-peso gold pieces and pure silver dollars. I bought two or three. He bought them by the bagful. He also told me to buy Occidental Petroleum, which turned out to be a good buy.

SKIP ENGBLOM: I ran into Miki at the old lighthouse, north of State Beach, in 1969. I told him I'd been traveling around the world on ships. He said, "Did you bring back any gems?" I said I'd seen some star sapphires in Ceylon, but didn't know much about gems. "Oh listen, man: They're international currency. You can always cash them out. It's very important that you always have some kind of gemstones available. You never know when the government's going to fail and you'll need this stuff." He also said I should always have gold. "No matter what. That's what people worship."

4

In the Kivlin era they had a hard-core clique. After Simmons died and everyone got married, everyone settled down and the Tubesteak era came into being. They sat on the beach and made their surfboard talk. That's when I had my best time, and I had about three or four years there all to myself. As for the group, I wasn't in . . . I wasn't out. I was just accepted there. I was accepted for my wave-riding—not for my personality.

—Miki, *Surf Guide*, the "Malibu" issue, November 1964

TUBESTEAK: In 1956, I had a job at Home Insurance Company at Seventh and Spring in downtown Los Angeles. For some reason Miki said, "Get me a job, too." On his first day he met all these big-shot executives in their forties. One took him into the company library, gave him some instructions, and left. The minute he was alone, Dora started drawing surf cartoons. In "Lil' Abner" Al Capp had characters called schmoos. Dora drew a couple schmoos on the nose of a board going across a wave. Three days later the big shot came in, looked over Dora's shoulder to see his progress, and saw a cartoon instead. They took him upstairs and shit-canned him.

I also got shit-canned, but not for recommending him. I had a whole drawer full of racing forms. It was June 1956. I had a white Ford parked outside, and I went from Home Insurance straight to Malibu and set up headquarters. Headquarters was the Shack.

A couple guys I knew—the mother of one was part owner of the famous Wilson House of Suede in Beverly Hills—hiked up Malibu Creek, got some Phoenix palm fronds, and paddled them down to the beach using our surfboards as barges. Our friend Harold Fred had two by fours. We built a frame for the Shack, put on the fronds, and it lasted all summer.

While a cross-fade of postwar watermen and hot young surfers crunched the waves on ever-better boards, the Shack became the social center of Malibu's beach—as distinct from water—in-crowd.

"People would throw beach parties all around us and give us the leftovers," Tubesteak once told writer/editor Ben Marcus. "For nightlife we would generally go up to Santa Monica or Harold Fred's house to take showers and have parties. There were no showers or hoses on the beach. The nearest fresh water spigot was across the street at Tube's Steak and Lobster House."

Described by Marcus as "Falstaffian," Tubesteak positioned himself as "'the centerpiece' at Malibu during some of the 'Best Years of Their Lives,' when the hotdogging sensation swept the Point. There was a lot of atmosphere . . . the Lieutenants were (Kemp) Aaberg and (Mike) Doyle."

A couple years later, insiders would know Tubesteak as the inspiration for Cliff Robertson's beach-dwelling "Big Kahuna" in *Gidget*, starring Sandra Dee and James Darren, based on the 1957 book by the real Gidget's father, Frederick Kohner.

KEMP AABERG: The Shack was full of donated furniture like old couches, ottomans, coffee tables, and an end table with a phone—connected to nothing. People would go, "Tube, what is that phone for?" And he'd go, "In case my agent calls."

DENNY AABERG: The boards were all up against the fence, Tubesteak stood in front, all suntanned, a bit of a tummy, drinking some Thunderbird wine.

MYSTO GEORGE: It was the start of homelessness. [laughs] A fifth of booze a day and a shack on the beach.

FRAYNE HIGGASON: Of course, we all drank like fish. And then if you had to go, you'd just step to the side of the Shack. By fall it was pretty odiferous.

Miki never really *hung* in the Shack. He'd go out in the water, come in, go out, come in. If there was a fire on the beach, he'd hang around in his trench coat, getting warm, or spend a few minutes in the Shack.

TUBESTEAK: The people in the Shack didn't much like Miki because he didn't want to be accepted by the Malibu regulars. He'd go to a party and start loading surfboards of people he knew into his car. He'd steal booze. You couldn't trust him. But what else was new? He was tolerated because he was a great surfer. He was entertaining. He pulled stunts they probably wanted to, but didn't. I didn't want him to go away. He was funny.

FRAYNE HIGGASON: One day, when driving home from school, I went to Malibu, changed in the Shack, and paddled out to the lineup. Then I noticed that the Shack was on fire. I thought, Jesus Christ, what's going on? I found out that two guys I knew had burned it down. They said, "It's an eyesore."

TUBESTEAK: The next year we built another Shack. When big waves came up, they had broken over the sand berm and gotten into the first Shack, soaking mattresses, sleeping bags, everything. This time Harold Fred got telephone poles and a prefab grass hut from his backyard. We laid the poles in the sand, put the hut on top, and even built a patio and a picket fence. Inside was a bed, pennants, wine bottles, old furniture. We called it the "Uptown Surf Club" and even had membership cards printed.

KEMP AABERG: Tube surrounded the second Shack with circular barbed wire. I asked him, "What's all that for?" He said, "To keep out the riffraff." Tubesteak made it sort of an elite area, a Mecca for Malibu characters. Everyone had a nickname: Mud Hen, Golden Boy, Scooter Boy, The

Bag, The Fencer, Meatball, Mysto, Pork Chop, The Jaw, Turtle, Mongoose, Moondoggie, and many others. We'd hang around and watch people surf. It was like the Roman coliseum: it was either thumbs-up or thumbs-down depending on what kind of ride you got. If you were being observed in the water, you felt this shot of adrenaline to do something spectacular, like a great crash, or a fabulous pullout. Some guys would get out into the shore break and self-destruct. Or get too nervous, or force something that didn't work. But if you could pull off a move that was beautiful and make it look easy, you could become an instant hero. You'd get a round of applause. One good ride got you into the club.

The second Shack lasted a year, until the cops and county leveled it. No one built a third.

5

1953: The Wild Ones
1954: On the Waterfront
1955: Rebel Without a Cause
1957: On the Road
1959: Gidget

If you add up the raw commerce, based on the Gidget *movies and television shows alone, not to mention the rest of the surf industry, which, for the most part, erupted in the 1960s, you've got a multibillion-dollar empire built almost entirely on* Gidget's *back.*
—C. R. Stecyk III to Deanne Stillman, in "The Real Gidget,"
from the book *Surf Culture: The Art History of Surfing*

TONI DONOVAN COLVIN: I married right out of high school and started going to Malibu with my husband, Mike Donovan, in 1955 or 1956. Mike was a lifeguard at Santa Monica, and I felt very cool to be there with him. He drove the woody, had cute freckles, and surfed. I met all these famous surf guys he talked about. The beach was so interesting then because everybody was a character. We'd all go to the Sip and Surf, right on Channel Road. We'd hang out, talk stories, tell lies. I was in heaven.

At Malibu, they did all sorts of crazy stuff. They'd wear swastikas. They'd wrap people in toilet paper and put them out to sea. They'd lock somebody in the portable toilet and roll them down the hill. Tom McBride would scream "Shark!" and everybody would run out of the water. Some days they'd play cards out on their surfboards; skateboarding started. Once, someone put vodka in an aquarium—a bad thing. It was all original stuff.

I just wanted to be part of the whole scene. We didn't have a care in the world. Sun, gorgeous guys, the water, the colors, the sky, the sunset. Tubesteak was in his Shack. Mickey Muñoz, Miki Dora, Johnny Fain, the Aabergs, Lance Carson, Mike Doyle, and occasionally Jimmy Fisher were in the water or in the Pit. It was just magical.

JIM FISHER: The Pit—really just a spot in the sand—was ruled by the best surfers, guys like Muñoz, Dora, Aaberg, Cooper, Doyle, Morey, Patterson, Grigg . . .

JOHN VAN HAMERSVELD: Malibu was iconic. If you sat in the Pit, then you were in and you made commentary on the people passing by. If you weren't in the Pit, then *you* were the controversy walking by.

BILL JENSEN: One day, an incredibly good-looking girl walked by the Pit and of course everybody made comments to each other—not to her. Then somebody looked at Miki and said, "What do you think?" "Sex is for colored people," he said. He was full of stuff like that, so we just let it drop.

KEMP AABERG: That atmosphere was what made Kathy Kohner—Gidget—run home and tell her dad stories about the beach: "Hey, there's a guy on the beach, and he never leaves, and he's building a shack out of palm fronds. God, how can he do that? How does he eat, Dad?" And the next day she'd bring him sandwiches. We didn't know she was telling stories to her dad until the day when Frank Donahue, Toni Donovan's father-in-law, got me and Miki and a few other guys a few miles up the coast to Secos—Leo Carillo Beach—to shoot some film of us surfing. We got a per diem of like fourteen bucks, which was a kick in the ass for me: "Oh boy, I get paid for surfing!"

KATHY KOHNER: I was a fifteen-year-old little wannabe. I lived in Brentwood. I had no weltanschauung. I was fascinated with Tubesteak and his friend Harry Stonelake living in a shack. I thought, Wow, don't they have a mommy and daddy like me and go home? I wanted to surf, I wanted to belong. I had a crush on a surfer named George Bek whom I'd met when I was nine or ten. Very few girls hung around, although there were some.

VICKI FLAXMAN: The girls who started surfing at Malibu around 1950, the guys were happy to have us there. They let us into waves because they wanted us to learn. They wanted us to go on surfing safaris with them. So they were terrific to us. When the younger guys came along, they had no use for us at all. I quit going to Malibu in about 1957, when I had my first child. I got too busy; it got to be too much of a hassle. Besides, one of the last times I was up there, some kid came up to me and said, "Do you have any wax, ma'am?" That just about burned me up.

KATHY KOHNER: I first went to Malibu—the 'Bu—when I was three years old. My parents loved it, and we would go to the beach every weekend with friends. My mother used to take young Matt Kivlin and Buzzy Trent to the beach in her Model-T Ford when they'd hitchhike with their surfboards. My mother liked the men, just like I do.

On June 24, 1956, my parents wanted to visit friends in the Malibu Colony. I didn't want to go, so I asked my dad to drop me at the beach. There were no steps down to the Pit, but there was a path—steeper than they have now—and I took it. That was the day I went down to Malibu myself for the first time.

According to world-champion Australian surfer/author Nat Young's *History of Surfing*—one of many places to find versions of this oft-told story—Tubesteak, Mickey Muñoz, and Miki Dora were supposedly "standing on the incline above Malibu, checking out the waves, when a young surfer in a baby-blue ski parka pulled a new Velzy/Jacobs board from the rear of a Buick convertible and headed off down the path.

"'Hey,' shouted Dora, hassling the new arrival.

"'Go back to the Valley, you kook!' shouted Muñoz.

"The stranger got such a shock he stumbled and the board tumbled to the rocks below. Tubesteak told the others to shut up and went to help, and discovered the new arrival was a girl. A very short girl!

"'For Chrissake,' mumbled Tubesteak, 'It's a midget, a girl midget—a goddamn gidget!'

"The girl was not amused. 'I'm not a gidget,' she yelled. 'My name is Kathryn—and you can keep your filthy hands off me, you creep.'

"Tubesteak laughed. 'Hey, Gidget, see you around.'"

KATHY KOHNER: It wasn't Tubesteak who said, "It's a girl, it's a midget—it's a gidget." If he wants to say he said it, that's wonderful, but Bill Jensen believes it was Golden Boy—Jerry Hurst—and so do I. Unfortunately, I didn't record it in my diary—and I recorded just about everything in my diary. I'm not even sure if Gidget was an original name because I have a vague recollection that somebody said they heard that name somewhere else, at a club. But even so, I became the Gidget. No question about that. I was Gidget, girl midget. I also didn't have a board that day, and didn't until Mike Doyle sold me one for $35 on March 6, 1957. *That's* in my diary.

Kohner is correct. In H_2O magazine, Tubesteak told writer Bill Cleary, "I used to hang out in a bar in downtown Los Angeles, and one day when about six of us were there drinking, a buddy of mine dropped by with his girl, who was about four foot nine, and he introduced her. 'Boys, this is my girlfriend, Gidget.'

"'What's that?' I asked.

"'A Gidget? Why that's a girl-midget.'" We all thought it was very funny."

KATHY KOHNER: The guys liked to tease me. They'd bury my surfboard; they once disconnected my car's distributor. Later I found out it was because I was at the beach with a very attractive girl; she had large . . . she was very well endowed. They called that "the continental shelf." So somebody said, "We just wanted you to hang out a bit, so . . ."

That wasn't Miki, though.

I don't remember when I met Miki Dora, or Miki Chapin—as we all knew him then. But I do remember when I saw Miki surf; it was unbelievable. I could pick him out of any lineup. He had mannerisms that most everyone on the beach copied. I even found myself using the hand gestures.

Here's an entry from my diary:

> *February 12, 1957: Today we didn't have any school so Mike Donahue called me and asked me if I wanted to go to the beach. Of course I did. The weather was so warm it was unbelievable. We went down to State Beach where Miki Dora was. He said the surf was up at Malibu so we drove up there. The surf was pretty good. Tube was there. It really seemed funny to be surfing at Malibu at this time of the year . . .*

I never had a crush on Miki. I was just a little pest, a kid who would bring him sandwiches, or give him a ride home.

Here's something else about Miki in my diary: *Miki came over in the afternoon and we had a big fight, and he left in a huff but I'm sure he'll be back again.*

I remember once I saw Miki at a party in Brentwood and he was with Deetsie. I was like, "Oh, wow." That's the only time I ever saw him with a girl. He was a good-looking man, very well built. But there was a side you couldn't penetrate. I hear that he had a troubled childhood, but I wasn't aware of that kind of stuff then.

Miki was an amazing athlete. We played tennis together at the Barrington courts. He came over to my parents' house a lot and we played Ping-Pong. I remember he lived with his grandmother. He also told me that Mike Wallace the newscaster was his stepfather. [Author's note: Miklos's second wife, Lorraine, subsequently married Wallace.]

When we went skiing he didn't want to pay the chairlift fees so we hiked up the mountain together. Actually, it was kind of cool. At least he didn't try phony lift tickets.

He took me to Rincon once.

March 31, 1957: Everything was beautiful at the beach except the fact that Bill was there and I still love him so much and he can't stand me. I really feel terrible. I think there must be some way to forget him. I'm living now for next Friday afternoon and weekend. I've just got to forget him.

Everyone was down there. I took Miki and Jenny down in the morning but Miki left early because he doesn't get along well with the other surfers.

Miki was the king, so maybe when Miki got on a wave, the others felt intimidated.

DREW KAMPION: Miki was the champion not only of his own life and his own idealized purity, but he defended the pristine pursuit of his sport. There's a lot of verbiage attached to that, which makes it seem so over the top that you tend to throw out the baby with the bathwater on the interpretation. But when you consider what he had at Malibu and what it represented to him psychologically as a place to escape, as a place to manifest, as a place to express, as a place to be appreciated and kind of fit in—and then after three or four years some guy builds a shack and this short girl shows up . . . and her dad writes about it . . .

KATHY KOHNER: I wanted to write the book myself, but my father said, "You tell me what's going on in Malibu and I will write the story for you." Which he did. He started writing in early 1957. It took him six weeks to finish, and he dedicated the book to "the Gidget, with love." It came out in October of 1957. It was immediately on the bestseller list, one above Jack Kerouac's *On the Road*. Other books on the bestseller list then were *By Love Possessed, On the Beach, Atlas Shrugged, The World of Susie Wong,* and *Peyton Place.* They all became movies. I don't think my dad had any concept of the success he would get from this little book.

After the book, and then the story "Gidget Makes the Grade," in *Life* magazine in 1957, I'm not exactly sure what the people at Malibu thought of it. Honestly, I figured that they just didn't care, you know: "Win a few, lose a few—there's another wave coming, just keep moving along."

DARRYL STOLPER: The *Gidget* book may have been a bestseller, but at the beach it had no effect. If anybody read a surfing book, it was *The Ninth Wave*, by Eugene Burdick.

It would have been almost impossible then for the boys of summer to sense the enormous cultural sea change rolling in. Surfers numbered in the low thousands at most. Even when Frank Donahue took test film of Kemp Aaberg, Johnny Fain, and Miki, to analyze how it might come across on the big screen, nothing yet seemed out of place. Surf movies were not uncommon, at least those made by Bud Browne, Bruce Brown, Greg Noll, John Severson, and others, which were more like professional home movies. These films toured high school auditoriums, rented halls, and small movie theaters to enthusiastic crowds eager to see not only hot surfing and their favorite riders (and sometimes themselves), but waves from far-off beaches. For Miki, it was an open invitation to mischief.

TUBESTEAK: I once wrote a story for *The Surfer's Journal* under my nom de plume of Bruce Savage, called "Miki Goes to the Movies." Greg Noll, who used to make surf films, was showing *Search for Surf* at the Pier Ave. Junior High in Redondo Beach. Miki was really pissed at Greg for something, so Miki and Jimmy Fisher and I filled a mayonnaise jar with moths. Then Miki put the jar in a valise. We went in the front door and Miki disappeared to find another way in because lifeguards had been posted to be on the lookout for him. Miki was dressed like Groucho Marx—glasses with eyebrows. Wore a multicolored coat. Fisher and I sat in the back of the auditorium, listening to the surfers scream for the show to start. I saw this "Groucho" guy come up from the bowels of

ABOVE TOP: Johnny Fain, Miki, at Malibu, 1960. Photo: Toni Donovan Colvin.

ABOVE: Always the entrepreneur. Malibu, late 1950s. Photo: Kathy "Gidget" Kohner Zuckerman.

LEFT: Miki and Kathy "Gidget" Kohner at Malibu. Photo: Allan Grant/LIFE, 1957. Courtesy Kathy Kohner.

the stage. Then he snuck behind us and said, "Are you ready to go?" He said, "Stand back," and pulled the jar of moths out of the valise and unscrewed the cap, and up they went, swirling in formation until they saw the projector light and dove right for it. Greg Noll screamed, "I know he's here!" We snuck out right in front of the lifeguards. We went across the street to a bar while Noll shut down the show.

GREG NOLL: The first time he did it with June bugs, those fat bumblebee-like bastards. Generally, he was not crude enough to duplicate a prank; it showed lack of imagination. So when I saw moths I knew damn well they came from Dora.

RICK BECK: He once told me he wanted to make a surf movie called *The Great Rip-Off,* show it at Santa Monica Civic Auditorium, and film the people getting free donuts as they're filing in. Then the film comes on, and it's him loading up a plane full of money bags and flying away. That was Miki's sense of humor.

With the success of Frederick Kohner's book, Hollywood pounced and *Gidget* went into production. A number of prominent surfers were hired as extras and stuntmen, including the diminutive Johnny Fain, who doubled Gidget caught in a kelp bed.

JOHNNY FAIN: They put me in a wig and a one-piece bathing suit and I did the scene. Moviemaking was great fun except a lot of the Malibu guys resented the fact that they weren't hired, too. I got Dora in—he was my mentor. I couldn't leave home without him. I introduced him to the producers as "Moondoggie."

FRAYNE HIGGASON: I don't remember any sharing between them. It was, "I'll keep this secret and then I'll be the god." They'd run around, secretly following each other, trying to figure out where that day's shoot would be. When I'd run into Dora, he'd say, "Seen Fain? I've got to get on the beach where they're making that movie. They've got a good lunch."

DON WILSON: When the first *Gidget* movie was filmed, Miki got hired as an extra. One day the fog came in. Of course, they had all the surfboards, cameras, and other odds and ends on the beach. The fog lasted for about half an hour and when it lifted, all the surfboards and one of the giant cameras were gone. It was simple enough to figure out who did it.

6

Coincidental to the *Gidget* phenomenon, the surfboard teetered yet again on the crest of another design and materials evolution. In 1953–54, board maker emeritus Dave Sweet began experimenting with Styrofoam. Soon he moved on to polyurethane foam, which could be sealed with fiberglass and resin. "I talked Miki into trying out one of my boards. He wasn't supposed to do that because he was getting free boards from Dale and Hap, but he was willing to try it, of course, to see what it was like. I didn't ask anybody else. It was four feet that day at Malibu, a perfect size for proving if a board surfs. He put on a fantastic performance. Of course, he could surf an ironing board. That was the beginning. After that I sold boards on the beach at Malibu, displayed on a tripod."

"Suddenly, foam core boards could be manufactured in less than half the time for less than half the raw-materials cost of wooden boards," wrote Drew Kampion. "Thus (in 1959), with *Gidget* drawing thousands of new enthusiasts to the beach, the board builders were ready for them, and the 'surfboard industry' was born."

Just in the nick of time.

As board makers vying for a piece of the exploding new market grew heated, so did competition between surfers—and the builders who wanted the top riders to promote their product.

"We gave Miki free boards," said Dale Velzy, "but then he'd sell them and get someone else's board for a week. And sell that. But I needed him to ride my boards because he would get me at least five orders a week. So it was good public relations.

"I shaped him a lot of boards, which I didn't mind, except that I also used to have to sit and talk to the bastard while I did it. I listened to his radical design theories because some of them worked, but sometimes he'd want to tell me his problems. Dora would rattle on about 'I can't surf tomorrow because I gotta meet the Frenchman at Frascati's for an appointment for a new movie.' He was always into something to do with the studios because it made him sound important. He'd come into the shop dressed like a wannabe movie star. Or he'd go on about 'that little weasel,' Johnny Fain. 'Make my board thinner. I want to go by and slice his ankles.' Miki wanted stuff on his board for him, and no one else. But Fain used to say, 'Next time you shape one for me make sure my rails are as thin as his because he wants to slice me.' They talked a lot, but pretended like they hated each other.

"I had them in the shop together a couple times. Miki would say, 'I'm going to go behind you so clean I'm going to cut your toes off.'

"Johnny: 'You'll never catch me.'

"It seemed pretty much like an act, but who knows what went on outside of the shop."

"All I know," says Velzy's former partner Hap Jacobs, "is that every time I saw the two of them together on a wave, it was a competition."

JOHNNY FAIN: I was thirteen in 1957. Gas was less than thirty-five cents a gallon. People drove Ford woody station wagons and it was a golden era. We lived in Malibu Colony. I begged my mother to get me my first surfboard and we finally went to Velzy's shop in Playa del Rey, two years before he hooked up with Jacobs. It was a pure balsa wood seven-foot board.

When I got good enough to go to Surfrider Beach, I paddled out and was washed in very quickly—not so much because of the waves, but because the people were merciless. They had no regard for anyone trying to learn; and it's the same today.

Miki Dora ran the place. Even before the *Gidget* movie caused such big crowds, if you could cause accidents or create some kind of mayhem to discourage newcomers from coming back, Miki would pay attention to you and you'd have standing. Miki didn't mess with the Hawaiians, though, because they knew how to punch back and they delivered severe damage. Everyone else was fair game. This was 1958, before lifeguards had any say; Cal Porter was the first and he didn't show up until halfway through 1959, when the county took control of the beach. Even then, some lifeguards turned their heads because they didn't want the guard tower burned down. Some did not turn their heads and the tower got burned down.

Miki Dora, Mike Doyle, Kemp Aaberg, and a terrible person named Tubesteak, who wasn't that good a surfer but created an awful lot of havoc, were on the beach then. Miki didn't trust Tubesteak, but they laughed at each other and pretended they were pals.

I took my licks for about a year. I even got eighteen stitches because of Tubesteak. On my first wave, he took off in front of me and deliberately ran to the nose of his board, submerged it, and held on until I got in range. Then he let it go and the board's tail block hit me in the face. Had it hit my eye instead of my eyebrow I'd have been blinded. I went home and my mother about had a heart attack. A month later I went back. Miki said, "Are you all right now, champ? That was a big blow you took." From then on it was clearly survival of the fittest.

Since I lived at Malibu, I'd come and go alone. I was shy. I tried to make friends but it didn't come that easy—until people discovered where I lived.

One day I told Miki, "Come on over and hang out." When he got to my place, his eyes lit up like he'd discovered a diamond mine. It was lunchtime; luckily we had a full refrigerator. We played Ping-Pong; it was close but he won. Then we went back to the beach. Three or four days later I asked my mother if he could stay in the guesthouse, she said "Yes," and he took me up on it. He didn't have to drive anywhere. My mother fed him three times a day. When the surf was flat, Miki was the master of ceremonies, inviting people over to eat and play croquet on the lawn. It may seem strange or unsavory today, me only fourteen and Miki nearly twenty-five, but my mom did it for my safety. She knew he would look out for me in his own way, and he did—protecting me from Tubesteak and anybody who tried to do me harm. I'd told her, "It's good to be friends with the guy who's the best there is. I could learn from him." That did it.

When we talked, I'd always compliment Miki on how good he was. He loved that. He would encourage me. His favorite expression was "Go for broke." That was his code, how he rode the wave, how he got through life. He didn't just say it; he practiced what he preached. "Slip and slide" was another phrase he used. Also, "Don't hesitate on the wave. As soon as you hesitate, you're lost." That made me more fluid and I could execute. Between Miki Dora and Dewey Weber I formulated my own style. Miki would nose-ride a little better, but Dewey had famous cutbacks.

Miki liked being my mentor. And I, being the protégé, became an extension of him. Whatever he did, I did—like a younger brother. I almost talked the way he did. Unfortunately, you never knew if he was telling the truth or was sincere; he always used double meanings. But we wore the same striped shorts, the same Panama hats. He even had capes. He'd come to the beach in bathrobes, like Gorgeous George. He had coonskin caps, Roaring '20s coats. He was the pacesetter.

You never knew what he was going to do next.

BOB COOPER: Fain and Miki. Yeah, that was Laurel and Hardy. Fain became a bit of a pet, a lonely kid who, when he discovered the beach and what went on there, really glommed onto it. Fain became a very good surfer, and he and Miki had a love-hate relationship. Miki used him, and he'd abuse Miki; then

Miki would disdain him, and Johnny would apologize and bring him a sandwich the next day to get back in his good book. It went back and forth that way—for a while.

7

SURFER MAGAZINE: Why did you drop the name Chapin?
DORA: That is actually a personal family question, but I can tell
you this much: Gard Chapin, a unique surfing frontiersman, either
remembered or not, had a profound influence in my life. His untimely
premeditated murder in Mexico can only be linked with his
individualistic personality. For my own peace of mind I felt it would be
safer to use my given name. However, I sometimes have misgivings on
this decision.

—*Surfer* interview, 1969

GARDNER CHAPIN JR.: My dad had come to see me only twice when I lived in Rialto with the Stancliffs. The first time was really great. We went out to eat, then to see Rad's orange grove. Rad gave him a bunch of oranges. He said he'd be back in two weeks to see me again. I didn't see him for two months. When he came, the oranges were still in the backseat of his car, rotting, and he was drunk as hell, so Frances—Uncle Rad's wife—had him arrested. He'd brought a bunch of Christmas presents for me, so Frances let him give me the presents before she called the cops. That was the last time I saw him.

Not long after, when we had just come back from visiting an aunt in San Juan Capistrano, I got the news that Gard had died.
JUANITA KUHN: He went skindiving in Mexico and drowned. Miki said murdered, but I don't believe it. That's Miki for you; he put a huge glory on everything.
MIKLOS DORA SR.: I heard that he was on a dinghy, was drunk, and collapsed. I thought it was here in California, south of Newport Beach.
JOHN MILIUS: Every time I've heard about Gard's death, even from Miki, it's been a different story. He said that Gard had gone surfing in Mexico and they found him in his car, or on the beach, or in the water—murdered. Okay, maybe. It's possible. But he also said there were political complications. I asked him what he meant, and he said, "You have to understand. There are a lot of really dangerous forces loose in the state." I said, "What would Gard

have to do with any State of California politics at that time? He was a happy-go-lucky surfer."

BILL VAN DORN: Gard was thirty-nine. He was in the dumps over Ramona. He drank. He'd get dried out in the Bay of La Paz with a fisherman who had befriended him, a guy who tried not to let him drink. This time he'd been gone for a month, just before Christmas. One day the guy who owned the boat called me and said he had some bad news. They'd had dinner in La Paz. They'd been drinking a bit; Gard said he had a headache and would take the dinghy back to the boat and go to sleep. When the captain got out to the boat, he found no dinghy, no Gard, no nothing. He thought Gard had gone somewhere else, so he went to bed. In the morning, still no Gard, so they started looking. They found the dinghy way down in the bay, beached. Then they found Gard's body five days later, floating. There was no evidence of injury or foul play. Nothing missing from the boat. We figured he could have just slipped getting out of the dinghy, or getting in. The dinghy was upside down when they found it.

The authorities got in touch with me and Nancy and asked what we'd like to do. Nancy said, "Let's have them bury him down there." They said they could, but it would cost some money. We sent about a thousand bucks. They buried him in La Paz.

We went looking for his grave eventually, and couldn't find it.

GARDNER CHAPIN JR.: My mother and Gard's sister Martha finally talked to the fishing boat captain. He said that one of the two Mexicans in the dinghy hit Gard in the head with an oar and took his money. He didn't say why, or if there had been an argument, but they found his body and his wallet was empty. I don't think the fish took the cash. The captain also told my mother—and of course my mother and Martha knew this very well—that my father was in excellent shape, a great swimmer, and there was no turbulence. The weather had been fine, the harbor very calm. He didn't simply drown.

Eventually my mother got letters from the embassy, and some newspaper articles. I wish I could find them.

In 1978, my then-wife and I went to La Paz to find the grave. I met a guy in a bar there—a supervisor for Hughes Aircraft—and we chartered a fishing boat the next day to catch marlin. We fished all day and that night I told him that my dad had died years ago in La Paz. "There's only one cemetery in the city," he said. "Tomorrow let's get a cab and go there."

The next day, we all went to the cemetery and got the caretaker to look Gard up in the records. Sure enough, we find Gard listed under 1957. The caretaker said, "OK, Gard was buried here May 23." Then he looked some more and said, "We've got that as his birthday, too." Then it hit me, we were there on . . . May 23!

I found the grave. There was an old cross over it. I took a couple pictures.

GREG NOLL: When Gard died, it seemed like Miki made a sharp left turn in his life.

DARRYL STOLPER: He changed his name back to Dora, and if you brought up Chapin he'd say, "That's not me. That's the stepfather I hated." He didn't say why.

BOB COOPER: I don't know if Gard's death put some sort of scare into him, but afterward, I never saw him laugh spontaneously again. Never a belly laugh. An amused laugh or an appropriate laugh or a constructed laugh, but never just a let-it-all-hang-out laugh. He became much more eccentric, and his language affectation intensified.

VICKI FLAXMAN: All of a sudden he was not only kind of a cuckoo, but an angry guy. We all asked, "What's the story?" Of course, we never got a straight answer. The answers we did get were so convoluted you couldn't remember them—and you'd know it wasn't true, anyway.

CHAPTER FOUR

The Angry Young Man of Surfing

1

Malibu is summer. . . . summer is ruined. Now you have to share your summer vacation with everybody—I hate to share my time with working slobs. Summer has had it . . .

—Miki, *Surf Guide***, November 1964**

Call some place Paradise, kiss it good-bye . . .

—The Eagles

After *Gidget*, the brave new surfing world at Malibu and elsewhere had just begun. For Miki Dora and his peers, it was already over—and ruined. *Surfing U.S.A.* had been invented. Gremmies, kooks, hodads, and surfer girls swarmed the waves and sand. Peroxide futures skyrocketed. Woodies were resurrected. The new foam surfboards sold faster than tanning lotion. Magazines like *Surfer*, *Surf Guide*, *International Surfing*, the homemade surf movies, the Hollywood beach party flicks, and spreads in *Life* magazine about the sunny surfing lifestyle helped a California-dream-oriented youth subculture spread nationwide. What could Miki and his peers, now just "characters" on the Malibu stage, do about it except be horribly depressed and maybe fight back.

Sheila Weller, writing about that era's young surfers in *Vanity Fair* in 2006, suggested an answer: "As surf culture was puff-balled into a popular girlish love story, Miki Dora began living out a brazen, swash-buckling, counternarrative."

He didn't realize then that it would forever change his life.

DENNY AABERG: Malibu became a radical place, a lawless, esoteric society with surfing as the entertainment. One wild ride after another. If you weren't a regular, you had to watch your step because there were some pretty tough characters around. When I first got there, Tubesteak was on his last year. Guys like Kivlin were gone. I'd heard stories about him, about Bob Simmons, Joe Quigg, and a black surfer—maybe the first—named Nick Gabaldon, from Santa Monica High, who got killed when he rode a big wave into the pier in 1951 and got crushed to juices.

Now, there was Crazy Kate, a chick who had big tits and whose top would fall off in the water. Big Mike, a huge guy who got in a lot of fights and once screwed a girl on the point, in broad daylight. There was a "Nazi" contingent, people who had swastikas on their boards. Some guys would wear German helmets, old army surplus jackets, or trench coats.

My group were gremmies in our early to mid teens. One kid was a klepto-maniac. If you left your wallet on the beach rolled up in your pants: a big mis-take. He'd crawl underneath the boards and pick all the wallets clean. There was also Mokie Mokini, a Hawaiian with a bum leg and wires in his teeth. He was a nice guy, but always asking for a quarter.

Somehow, Miki, in his own way, led the charge. He was the trendsetter. He set the bar. We'd heard stories of his escapades and maybe that gave license to everybody to be a little bit on the wrong side of the law.

Eventually, the early guys got sour about the crowds. It was always, "Malibu's going to the dogs." When the media came in, the surf magazines, most guys played along, took advantage, tried to parlay their names into free boards, being in surf films, and more. The industry grew. Some guys made boards for a living. But the guys who considered themselves real, pure surfers hated having so many people in the water. Miki was affected the most.

GREG NOLL: The whole Hollywood bullshit deal just brought more assholes over the hill from the Valley. If you're from the Valley, don't take offense, but this is basically what the beach guys thought. When you watch Stacy Peralta's documentary, *Riding Giants*, they ask the guys, "What did you think of the Hollywood movies and the surf music?" Answer: It was just a bunch of shit.

Take the movie *Ride the Wild Surf*; it shows Tab Hunter and his friends sitting in the water, not a hair out of place, water calmer than a fish pond, no surf in the background. Suddenly someone yells, "Surf's up," and they cut to the same guys riding twenty-foot waves. Man, who's gonna believe that? It's one of the biggest laughs in the movie.

KEMP AABERG: Miki called Valley surfers "white kooks." Those people were supposed to go to the beach to sun themselves, not to surf. Now people said, "Boy, doesn't surfing look like fun. Doesn't look *that* hard. I'd like to try it."

TONI DONOVAN COLVIN: It wasn't just our little clique anymore. All these people we didn't know came to Malibu to have a look, to start writing about it and publicizing it. It had been our private thing and now all these outsiders wanted a piece of it. We hated them. We'd yell: "Hodads go home!" They had no right to our deal, our parking places, our waves. Miki felt that Malibu was his beach, and he was the king. When his peers copied him, that was okay. They were part of the in-crowd. Now strangers copied him, held their sunglasses like Miki, tried to imitate how he spoke. They wanted a piece of his glory.

SAM GEORGE: Post–*Gidget*, surfing experienced not only unprecedented growth, but unprecedented exuberance. The Beach Boys introduced the ebullience, and everybody was so happy to be a surfer. Miki Dora was the lone voice of cynicism, going: "This is fucked. These guys are creeps and kooks and Valley fags."

KATHY KOHNER: I spent the summer of 1959 in Hawaii. When I came back to Malibu in 1960, there seemed to be a new group of people. Not even Tubesteak was around. Nineteen sixty was the last time I went surfing for many years. Everybody asks me why. It's kind of hard to go back. Malibu was for me a teenage rite of passage. When I went to college in Oregon, *that* was my first real encounter with the opposite sex. Oh, I was always in love, I always had crushes; I was the makeout queen, excuse the expression. But the actual emergence into the world of adulthood happened in college—not with a surfer. I had grown up, discovered foreign films and the writings of Bernard Malamud. I went to the poetry readings. It was another world. Malibu was just something that I had done, something I *needed* to do then so I could feel I belonged.

Another reason I left Malibu is because of what Hollywood created from the *Gidget* story. It's a fabulous film, always and forever, but the result was that Malibu got crowded. Really crowded. I was a little bit frightened.

The last time I saw Miki was in the early '80s, at the Fashion Island mall in Newport Beach. I was with a girlfriend, and I saw him in the distance. I said,

SURF GUIDE

Published Monthly Volume II, No. 7   OCTOBER, 1963   RM 50 cents

MICKEY DORA

THE ANGRY YOUNG MAN OF SURFING

SPECIAL HOTDOG ISSUE

LEFT: Cover of classic *Surf Guide*, October 1963.

BELOW LEFT: Note from surfer/inventor/drummer Tom Morey to Miki, found in Miki's scrapbook left in New Zealand. Courtesy Tom Morey.

BELOW: Miki's skateboard (underside reads "Property of Mickey Dora" next to a swastika), was discovered, along with a pair of his orange board shorts, in Marcia McMartin's garage. Courtesy Dora Estate/ Refrigerator Collection.

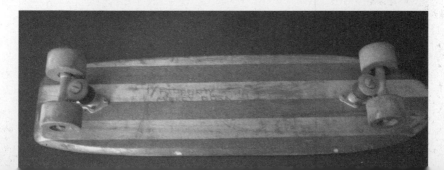

Sept 14, 65

Dear Mickey,

The winner is not the winner. The contest is not the contest. You are the great surfer of this generation. Others prejudice, jealousy, innacuracy and your own unusual personality have denied you your satisfaction.

Tom.

"Oh my God! There's Miki Dora!" I went over and said, "Miki!" He made his hand gestures, cocked his head, and said, "You *remember* me?" I couldn't believe it.

BOB SIMPSON: The truth is that Miki didn't remember those days fondly. Years later, Miki showed me a fax he wanted to send to a writer in California who'd asked him to comment for a story she was doing about the real Gidget. After I read it, I said, "Jesus, Miki!" He said, "Why should I tell her anything? It's part of something I hated. It's part of the beginning of the end."

7.6.99 [Excerpt from letter to writer Deanne Stillman]
Dear Mrs. Stellman, (sic)
    . . . Usually I feel extreme antipathy towards journalists. I never write anything or Rat-out friends . . . However, I'll take the liberty now to thank "TUB-STAKE" for coming out of your closet after 40 years and saying in print that I was never part of their strain of imbeciles . . .
    I've been Vindicated, Liberated and re-born! Thank God all merciful!!!
    Anyhow, I only mumbled a few unpleasantries to her (Gidget) a couple of times . . . Sometimes I would regenerate my strength in the hot sand behind the fence next to the wall, alone, dreaming of some of my best waves. Now, she knew better than to annoy me, (but) once she eclipsed my sun; I looked up from my lair, she was glaring at me . . . She was a hairy little thing for her age. . . She asked me some asinine question. I told her to FUCK-OFF and go back to her Kook, Wine-O-friends! They hated me, I hated them, they got tanked up; I jackrolled waves. . . .
    That's all there was to it. . . .
    Now if you want to know how I helped sabotage that film, that's something else. . . .

2

Q: You've been accused of being ruthless on waves.
A: It's a lie. I'm vicious.
Q: Doesn't this . . . strike you as a selfish attitude in view of how crowded surfing spots have become?
A: Well, it's a selfish world.

Q: Well, what's your solution?
A: We should have had birth control twenty years ago. It's too late now,
send them to Saigon.
   —Interview with Mickey Dora, Surf Stuntman, *Surfer,* **Vol. 6, Number 3, 1965**

BOB COOPER: When Malibu became an incredible zoo and everything began
to go down the gurgler for Miki and the rest of us, it opened the gate for ag-
gression.

   Usually, a couple of good surfers on a wave would trade places: one guy
would come up in front, drop down to the bottom so the other guy could trim
past him higher up. This is called doing go-behinds. Miki invented the mass
go-behind to show his disdain for all these goons. He'd come from the back
and go behind six or eight people and then drop in front of them all. They
wouldn't know what hit 'em. And if he didn't make it, he'd drop in on top of
you and everybody would pile up. Once Miki took this symbolic action, everybody else who had the skill to pull it off tried it, too.
DARRYL STOLPER: Miki was so good he could kick out on somebody and miss
their head by inches. But most of the time he'd get people in the ankles or
the shins.
ANTHONY FRIEDKIN: I saw Miki pull guys off their boards by the hair and the
shoulders, or lift the board from underneath and throw someone over the top
of the wave. He didn't need to run a kid over—but he would.
ROBBIE DICK: I was fourteen. I lost my board on a wave, and it washed in.
Miki was on the beach. He picked up his board and ran into the water and hit
my board full blast, right in the center, with the fin of his board. The result
was a four-inch rail gash. I complained. He looked at me and went, "Oh Jee-
sus. Unbelievable. Sorry about that, old chap." He told me to take it to the
Gomes Glass Shop to get it fixed. "I have a tab there." He rammed my board
on purpose. I knew it and so did he. And so did everyone else because, let's
face it, all eyes were on him at all times. I was pissed, but I couldn't be pissed
because the guy apologized and disarmed me. Finally—maybe it was the look
on my face—he said, ". . . and I'll pay for it!"

Eventually, Los Angeles County got involved at Malibu. All of a
sudden there was a list of rules and lifeguards. According to Kemp
Aaberg, who worked as a lifeguard there in the early and mid-'60s,
"Some days we'd get 125–200 people in the water and I'd have to
stop fights."

Henry Ford also worked the beach. "I was sent to Malibu because some of the other lifeguards couldn't get any respect." As a surfer he was familiar with the mind-set, so instead of calling the cops, Ford told the hard cases to take their mischief up to the Point. But Miki . . . "Miki constantly fucked with people in the water. I used to talk to him off to the side, plead with him to be more realistic about the danger he could create. He'd try to appease me: 'Oh, don't worry, baby, I've got this under control.' If I pressed him to be careful, he'd say, 'Baby! Baby! What are you doing? This is my beach! These guys don't belong here. They're kooks! They're kooks, baby. What are you trying to do with me.' I always got the hand movement and the 'baby' shit."

Miki, of course, didn't like the changes, and he came up with an ambitious plan to keep out the riffraff by starting the Malibu Surfing Club, with membership cards, beach privileges, and exclusive parking. Miki sent letters to various city departments and officials on letterhead listing a luminary board of trustees that included: Buzzy Trent, George Downing, Rabbit Kekai, Renny Yater, Dave Rochlen, Hap Jacobs, Dale Velzy, Cliff Robertson, Reed Templeman, Darrylin Zanuck, and Louis Zamperini. The only problem: Most of these people had no idea they were involved.

Also, in response to news stories like this—"The Board of Supervisors order a new county law drawn up to regulate the sport of surfing at county-owned beaches. Supervisor Burton W. Chace moved for the action. Report his office had received complaints that surfboard riders at many beaches interfered with swimmers and even endangered small children."—Miki petitioned to have the rules changed.

Miki's plans gained some official support, but ultimately went nowhere.

Boxed in, Miki had to deal with his antagonists and objects of scorn. One, a gymnast/surfer nicknamed "the Masochist" for his willingness to take punishment on the waves, came in for special harassment— and the nickname became part of surf history and a character in John Milius's 1978 epic, *Big Wednesday*.

THE MASOCHIST: Once, I was at State Beach, after surfing, smoking a joint. I fell asleep and woke up because of a loud noise. It was my car, a '55 Volkswagen. Miki had opened and dropped the hood down. A few days later my car conked out. I didn't know what the fuck was the matter. When I finally towed it to my mechanic, he told me he'd found sand all through the crank-case. Later on, when I spotted Miki's car in the State Beach parking lot, I did the same to him.

DARRYL STOLPER: I found a case of old dynamite in a mine in Death Valley. I had four sticks left and we decided to frame the Masochist. We put the dynamite sticks on the battery of Miki's car and called the police. The bomb squad took a look and said it could never have gone off. They asked Miki if he had any idea who might have done it. He said, "Well, the only enemy I really have is this guy. . . ."

THE MASOCHIST: They called me into the police department on Purdue Street in Santa Monica. Miki and his buddies were there: Darryl Stolper, and some beautiful chick from the Palisades I used to like. I was just heartbroken to see her. They were giggling and lining up against me. I said, "I don't know anything about this." I'd been working with a friend in Boyle Heights and my friend stuck up for me. The detectives said, "Just stay away from each other."

KEMP AABERG: For someone who got into all sorts of arguments, Miki was afraid of actually fighting. If a big guy yelled or threatened him, Miki's clever reply—and I saw it work on more than one occasion—was, "I'm sorry, I didn't know it was you!" It worked like a charm.

HENRY FORD: Of course, in Miki's mind, no matter what he did, he was always right and the other guy was always wrong. In his defense, I have to say that he was often right.

DUANE KING: One day Miki arrived at my door with a black eye. He said, "I pushed some guy off a wave and he punched me out."

JOHNNY FAIN: This Mexican kid named Oscar, who couldn't have been more than midtwenties, 130 pounds, and maybe 5'7" or 5'8", came to Malibu with his family. He was an average surfer and he made the mistake of taking off in front of Miki. Miki was all alone on the wave. He screamed and tried to wave off Oscar, but the kid still took the wave. Miki kicked out into the guy's body and they both went over.

They both paddled in, Miki still screaming. The kid knew he was semi-wrong, so he let it go and he didn't go back out in the water. Miki went out, finished his surf session. Meanwhile, the guy's on the beach with his kids, eating lunch. Miki comes in, sees at least fifty people around watching the scene, throws down his board, and calls the guy out. He says, "Hey, you want to settle this now, because I'm tired of your little punk ass. Get the hell off the beach right now or else I'm gonna beat the shit out of you."

Oscar did a double take, pushed his family to the side, and stood up. Miki was so much bigger; there must have been at least seven inches and fifty pounds difference.

Miki came in wailing, no jabbing. The kid started to block. Miki couldn't hit him and got frustrated. The kid ducked a roundhouse, and with one punch hit Miki in the jaw and knocked him out. He lay there for two or three seconds, stunned. The whole beach was silent.

Miki didn't know that Oscar had fought Golden Gloves. Oscar said, quietly, "I'm leaving now."

Miki got up. There was blood dripping down his lip. My heart went out to him. He had lost face. It was one of the few times Miki looked foolish.

Miki waited until the kid left, then he left. The buzz was unbelievable. Miki didn't come back for five days until the swelling had gone down. He tried to act as if nothing had happened and that the guy had a lucky punch.

Miki sued Oscar and, according to his lawyer Paul Fegen, got $131.90.

SKIP ENGBLOM: Miki could just as easily stand up for you. When I was fourteen I took off on a wave inside, at Malibu, and this guy, "Porkchop," pushed me off. I recovered my board from the rocks and was really bummed. Paddling back out, I saw Miki go over to Porkchop and say, "Did you really have to do that to that kid? You're really kind of an asshole." I still don't know why he even bothered.

KEMP AABERG: A surfer named Bob Perko told me that in the winter of 1961, at Rincon, Dora pulled out of a wave and hit him on purpose. Perko chewed him out and kind of scared him a little bit, "You ever do that again I'll tear you to shreds." Perko was a muscleman, so Miki took the admonishment to heart and stayed clear. About two weeks later at the Ventura Overhead, which is about six miles south of Rincon and breaks in a huge peak way out in the ocean, Perko took off on a steep ledge and free-fell into the blender. He surfaced with a severe gash on his forehead; blood was all over his face. His board had been ripped away—no one had leashes then—and Perko gagged and floundered and faced a long swim in. Miki saw it happen. He paddled over to Perko, put him on his board and paddled him to shore.

DARRYL STOLPER: Miki, Frenchie, Marty Sugarman, and I had been trying to find someplace to surf all day. Finally Marty convinced us to try #9 Jetty in Ventura, just north of the marina. It was unrideable. But we could see a crowd of people standing on the breakwater watching a small amphibious vehicle about seventy-five yards out. It had lost power and the three passengers were in serious trouble. They had launched in Oxnard but hadn't anticipated the swell at the Marina, which was breaking at about twelve feet and keeping the lifeguard boat from attempting a rescue. Suddenly the three people in the amphib jumped out and started swimming toward the breakwater, running the risk of being smashed to death against the boulders. We screamed at them to stay away, and two listened. Without saying a word, Miki ran back to the car, grabbed his board, and jumped in. When he reached the first swimmer, he pulled him onto the board and took him in. Then he turned around and did it again for the second swimmer. Meanwhile, the third guy was trying to climb the rocks. I tried to help but a wave knocked me flat. Fortunately, it also sent him on top of the breakwater, saving his life. In the car later, Frenchie told Miki he was a hero. Miki said, "It's more dangerous being exposed to the parasites from the Valley."

MARTIN SUGARMAN: As we drove off he said, "Oh shucks! I forgot to get their wallets."

And sometimes, one-on-one, away from the public stare, Miki could completely surprise.

BILL WISE: In 1965, I broke my neck in a surfing accident and was paralyzed. At the time I co-owned a surf shop in Delaware and had written and taken photographs for *Surfer* magazine. I had connections with a lot of the West Coast guys and sold a lot of Hobie surfboards. That day, Mickey Muñoz surfed with me. I almost drowned and he helped pull me out of the surf just as I started sucking water into my lungs. I spent a year in the hospital.

In 1967, when I was still more or less finding my way, Hobie asked if I'd like to go to the Duke contest in Hawaii. I thought he was pulling my leg so I said, "Why, of course, I really would." He said, "Good, because there are some airline tickets on their way to you." Then I started backpedaling. "I don't think we can handle that." He said, "Just get on the plane with your stuff. I'll have people in Hawaii make sure that everything's squared away so that you can handle this."

My hands are paralyzed and my arms are partially paralyzed, but almost the first thing I did was learn to handle a camera again. I had a mount bolted on to my wheelchair with a Nikkomat and a Nikor telephoto lens. With my hands the way they are, I couldn't handle shutter release, so I had a shutter release cord that I held between my teeth and flipped.

I was on the beach taking pictures of the contest, when I noticed a very recognizable figure sitting on his haunches, looking out at the waves. After a bit he looked over and said, "Wow. I'll bet you're the first guy who ever wore fur-lined shoes on the North Shore." We struck up a conversation. He wanted to know where I was from and we gradually got to talking about my accident. I explained to him exactly what had happened. Of course I knew he was Miki.

He didn't talk much about himself. He never made me feel on the spot about what had happened to me, and he was very empathetic. It didn't really surprise me at the time, but over the years his manner was contrary to what I've read about him.

After talking for a few hours, Miki stripped off his contest jacket and threw it in my lap and said, "Here, I want you to have this. You deserve it." I don't think it meant as much to me then, though it was completely unexpected and very gracious, but it means more as time goes by.

3

We were encouraged by the times to wave our cocks in front of the headlights of authority. We weren't encouraged to blend in.
                                                            —Kim Fowley

Every now and then I hear my name associated with something uncomplimentary, and of course it bothers me. We're all in this together. I'm no different than anybody else. . . . But you have to ask yourself what kind of people are they who talk about me, yet have never seen me? It bothers me when small minds and small people talk behind my back. I've been called a lot of things at one time or another . . . you name it. But I've never been in trouble.
           —Miki, "The Angry Young Man of Surfing," *Surf Guide*, **October 1963**

STEVE PEZMAN: Dora's surfing suave was so acute and transcendent that it was excruciatingly delicious. The same extreme inherent in his surfing was also inherent in his looks and personality. His style and body language glued it all together. It added up to something we'd never quite seen before. I don't think it was ever an option for Dora to be a normal person. Unfortunately for Miki, his talent also brought acceptance of his downside.

The list of Miki's antics, mischief, and adventures is long and legendary—and in some cases apocryphal. Over the years, it has come to include: wearing Arab garb and commandeering a sailboat, putting cherry bombs in theater toilets at surf films, firing home-built rockets with disastrous effect at Malibu, firebombing the San Onofre Shack, putting rotgut wine in a high-class bottle and recorking it before serving it to his father, being secretly married, glassing Owsley acid capsules into his board, cowriting a surf movie that inspired *Point Break*, stealing surfboards from movie sets and reselling them, skateboarding as early as 1959 at the Twelfth Street tennis courts in Santa Monica, renting surfboards at Malibu (sometimes borrowing other surfers' boards when they were at lunch) and copying information from the driver's licenses he held for security so he could use the information to later create an alias, traveling with friend Darryl Stolper to Watts during the 1965 riots to buy smoke-damaged television sets, manning an anti–civil rights desk at a 1965 UCLA protest, forging ski lift tickets with a special kit, putting a second set of license plates on his car to avoid getting ticketed when parked in the Malibu red zone, bullshitting a highway patrolman into believing he was waiting for a surf contest so he could sleep all night in his car at Malibu, going to a 1966 Dylan concert at the Santa Monica Civic in a long-haired wig, ratting on his friend Greg Noll to the IRS in order to escape his own troubles, crashing the Academy Awards in 1972, stealing an Oscar-winning screenwriter's statue during a party, five-fingering Ringo Starr's snuffbox at a party, skipping out on restaurant bills by leaving early or climbing out bathroom windows as part of his "tennis shoe act," putting bugs or glass in his food to get a complimentary meal, getting rear-ended in bodily injury insurance scams, driving stoned out of his mind and pulling a 360 on Sunset Boulevard and nearly killing Frank Sinatra, knowing too much about who kidnapped Frank Sinatra Jr., making out with a young Barbra Streisand on the couch at a Beverly Hills party, dating Cher before Sonny, stealing a hand-carved burlwood table from a beach home to use as firewood, snatching various items (like cameras) from unsuspecting naifs at Malibu, writing SOS in the sand and commandeering an unnecessary rescue helicopter ride on Kauai when he and Denny Aaberg—who'd gotten a touch of dysentery—couldn't complete a hike with iron man surfer Joey Cabell, trying to mount a gold prospecting expedition to Bolivia, journeying to the Ivory Coast and bringing a surfboard bag full of his laundry to be done by the locals, causing a punch-up in the early '60s between Dennis

Hopper and some skinhead in the stands at a Tijuana bullfight, smashing a huge Afrikaaner lifeguard in the face with a golf club in Jeffreys Bay, trading phony airline tickets for a rare English Alvis auto, blowing his nose in a lace dinner napkin at a Biarritz hotel and replacing the napkin, fake-choking a photographer when he tried to take his picture at a Biarritz restaurant, impersonating a rabbi when calling *Surfer* magazine, and crashing the Ambassador Hotel reception the night Robert Kennedy was shot and being interrogated afterward.

The list is much, much longer, of course. *Everybody has a Miki Dora story.*

GARD CHAPIN JR.: Miki told me he had these lesbian friends who'd done something to make him mad. When they decided to drive their VW to Palm Springs, he put sugar in their gas tank. Then he showed up at their house the next morning and asked if he could go with them. Miki told me after they'd gone about forty miles the driver turned to him and said, "My car doesn't seem to have as much power as it had." She pushed the gas pedal down further. The car went slower. She floored it. The car stuttered and coughed. Meanwhile, Miki sat in the backseat watching. Finally the car just conked out in the middle of nowhere. That's when he got out and hitched a ride back to Brentwood. He'd just wanted to see it all go down.

ALLAN CARTER: I had to save Miki's life once. He had a 1949 Ford station wagon. I knew these two crazy characters from the marines. Insane buddies, gunnery sergeants on a week's leave. Miki met them and said he had to switch the engine in his car, and they said, "We'll do it." They agreed to a price and dropped in a Chrysler engine. Not long after I showed up at my parents' house in Bel Air. They had a beautiful garden with big trees. I walked through the back gate and there was Miki standing on a chair with a rope around his neck. The Marines were going to swing him because he wrote a bad check for the engine transplant. I had to negotiate and calm them. They were literally ready to kick out the chair—or at least they told Miki they were. I'm sure Miki made the check good.

KEMP AABERG: Miki always wore fashionable surf trunks. As an easily impressed teenager, I asked him, "Hey, where do you get trunks like that?" He said, "Oh, I have a pair for you."

From his car, he got some nice black surf trunks, with stripes on the side. He said, "Seven dollars and they're yours." I didn't carry that kind of cash, so the next day I brought the money and bought the trunks. I went out for a big surf session and sat at the Point waiting for a wave. I happened to look down, and I noticed the water was discolored. I looked closer and could see dye coming out of the trunks. They had turned brown. Miki had totally duped me, sold me an old pair of trunks that he'd dyed black. I was really mad and decided he wasn't going to get away with it. I wanted my money back.

I confronted him the next day, and he said, "I thought they were fine." Miki always denied everything or made heavy excuses. I wouldn't let go, like a dog with a bone. I lashed out with all these profanities. He said, "Stop this, my friend. You can't get all excited. Hmmm, maybe I have something else for you." He looked in his car again—a dark blue Ford sedan—and pulled out a pair of orange, black, and yellow striped trunks made of itchy yarn that fit skintight. "This is just the thing for you," he said.

I said, "You wouldn't wear those to a costume party."

I didn't accept them, and I kept badgering him for my money back. After we filmed those test shots at Secos for *Gidget,* I knew Miki was solvent. I said, "I know you have more than seven bucks. Give me my money back." Instead of the money, he gave me excuses about having to pay the electric bill. He was so cheap.

DARRYL STOLPER: About ten o'clock one Sunday morning, Miki and I were driving along the Coast Highway in his old LaSalle four-door convertible. It had probably burned about twelve quarts of oil between Hacienda Place, where he lived with his grandmother in Hollywood, and Malibu. We were headed south, going down that hill from where Pepperdine College is, to Malibu, when we saw Elvis Presley in a white Cadillac convertible, in a white suit, with a blonde who had almost-white hair. Miki said, "Oh my God, I can't pass up this opportunity."

Miki got the LaSalle going as fast as he could. As we roared down the hill, we passed Elvis cruising in the right lane. Miki turned the engine off, waited, then turned it back on. We laid down a smoke trail like Admiral Nimitz's destroyer escort. The whole thing enveloped Elvis and his girlfriend in a cloud of black, tarry, gunky motor oil smoke. The woman was about ready to kill us, but Elvis was laughing.

GREG NOLL: The guys surfing after the Second World War were really heavy-duty individuals. LeRoy Grannis, Don James, Doc Ball, Burrhead, Opai. Decent guys who, in my mind, went to church and wore white shoes, didn't say nasty words or try to rat-fuck each other to the point of absurdity. They were rebels only to the extent that they shared one thing in common with all surfers: They hated to work. They did, but they also loved to hang out at the beach. They even put surfing before their girlfriends.

To my and Miki's generation, that kind of rebellion was mild. After the war, something snapped and the whole thing went bonkers. The idea of going to college, and then putting your time in a desk job, which once seemed like it was the thing to do, got tossed. The age of the RF'er started, and Miki Dora was probably the guy, like in the Crusades, who rode in holding the banner that read: "Rat Fuckers!"

Today, people hear about the stunts Miki pulled in the old days and don't know what to make of them. Most of the time it was just mischief. He'd lift a pair of trunks, a guy's lunch. And even when it got more serious it was, what . . . bad checks? He didn't have anybody killed. He pulled things that for the most part made his life easier to go surfing.

I have trouble making people understand this because everything has come full circle now, and the way to behave once again is to be a good guy. I don't mean to piss off anyone but it goes hand in hand with the commercialization of everything, and kids lining up like pigs at a trough for endorsements, and the big money from clothing companies. There certainly are exceptions and standouts—Kelly Slater and some of the other better surfers—but you go down to the beach today and there are all these sheep going "Baaaaa." They all surf together. They all wiggle their little asses the same. They all look like whoever the top guy is.

Miki and I came up in a different time period. Yesterday *is not* today. One writer told me, "Well, a thief's a thief. In Baghdad they cut off your hands." I think it's more important to understand that then, from the time you got up to the time you went to bed, was about how to spend the most time in the water and catch the best waves. And any time left over was for how to embarrass or screw up and in every way be a nonconformist. Steal your buddy's lunch? Sure.

I did it, too. I have the trunks Miki wore in the movie *Ride the Wild Surf*. He left them on the mirror to dry and I ripped them off. Just totally RF'ed him. It's a huge trophy. I bet there aren't five times in Dora's life where somebody's ever gotten anything *from* him.

Three or four years later I said, "You know those trunks that went missing that day?" "Yeah." "Who do you think got 'em?" He got this shit-eating grin on his face and called me a sonofabitch. "I always wondered who got my trunks." And I've still got them.

Dora was like the Jesus Christ of put-on. He even had disciples: anyone who tried to surf like him, talk like him, act like him. He lived his fantasy and it became his reality. Dora played the part forever because he got so used to it that he couldn't go back.

JOHN VAN HAMERSVELD: With Miki it was always more than a prank, it was *media*, a visual. A performance. Miki was a supremely conscious person. Like Warhol, he thought of himself as a symbolic piece of the culture. He performed and acted out, created theater and a reputation, and—although unlike Warhol, who created objects—Miki and stories about him have become "collected" in folklore. Miki didn't really talk about or analyze this. The artist doesn't have to be articulate about what he does, because it's intuitive. It's unconscious. What makes the artist who he or she is are the journalists, the curators, the collectors. If one is aware enough artistically to move toward performance, and individualize the performance, then surfing qualifies because it's a three-dimensional theater that the artist, or surfer, performs intuitively.

SKIP ENGBLOM: All artists are outlaws, but not all outlaws are artists. If you're involved in your art, you're forced to be an outlaw because art dictates that you can't follow the rules. Miki's life was his art and his art was his life, so therefore he had to continually be this outlaw in order to maintain that art form. The art form was Miki Dora and the Miki Dora canvas of existence. Miki constantly fine-tuned the business of being Miki Dora. That's the only business he had. He was his product and he wanted to ensure its survival.

CHAPTER FIVE

Throwing a Monkey Wrench into the Works

1

State Beach in Santa Monica was Miki's home away from his Malibu home—and another scene entirely. Although it had a surfable wave until runoff from the deluge of 1969 doubled the sandy acreage between the parking lot and ocean and ruined the break—and sanded in Malibu as well, for a season—State Beach mostly served Miki's social needs. It was less about surfing and more about being a public Mecca for beach volleyball players, gays, card-playing senior citizens, aspiring *Beach Blanket Bingo*–type actors, actresses, models, and hustlers of all stripes.

Classic State Beach starts at the Green Wall of the Beach Club, which was Hearst girlfriend Marion Davies's old house, and runs north to where Entrada Drive, Chatauqua Boulevard, and Channel Road spill out of Santa Monica Canyon onto the Pacific Coast Highway. Unofficial headquarters for the in-crowd was the lifeguard storage building and restroom on the sand opposite the nexus of the three streets. "The 'royalty' sat near the structure, either on a bus bench that Craig Leonard and some others had stolen from across Pacific Coast Highway, or on the sand," says Dora pal Darryl Stolper. "The single pay phone served as the communal call center/office for anyone awaiting callbacks, deals, and logistical intelligence on the latest parties."

Miki held court, entertained, pontificated, conned, spun tales, manipulated quickly assessed opportunities for personal gain, and possibilities for after-hours entertainment at lavish parties in Hollywood, Beverly Hills, Bel Air, at the beach, and in the canyons. "Instead of being apart from the culture," says Terry Lucoff, who once owned Santa Monica's Natural Progression Surfboards and now sells high-end real estate in Malibu, "Miki connected with it and was influenced by it. For someone considered so antisocial, he had the highest level of social insight."

TONI DONOVAN COLVIN: At State, the girls were usually very beautiful teenagers from University High. They didn't go in the water; they would just come and look gorgeous. They were mostly streaky blond from the sun, tanned, in the latest bathing suits, with great bodies. The guys were always handsome surfers and volleyball players. State Beach had all the elements: Hollywood, surfing, beautiful people, parties.

ED GARNER: Often, Miki would be there early, in his trench coat. If there weren't any waves, he'd be in his car, reading. Lots of times he'd read while he walked. This was his alone time. When the beach became more alive, everyone wanted to hang out near the volleyball players. Miki didn't want any part of that, so he was always in front of the restroom, because there was a pay phone.

CRAIG LEONARD: Other regulars included Marty Sugarman, Pat Darrin, Rick "Spider" Josephson—who became a Buddhist monk for a while—Robbie Dick, George Samama, Jimmy Ganzer, Pete Eggers, and Jim Dixon. Peter Gowland, the famous photographer, and his wife, Alice, hung out at State Beach. Also "Uncle" Rudy Tartaglia, a hairdresser who was at one time Barbra Streisand's chauffeur. Miki really enjoyed Uncle Rudy, who would sometimes show up with an anvil and chains and set himself up in a corner where it would reverberate off the walls as he pounded, until people would leave. His father owned Ludwig's, the clothing shop, and Rudy sometimes invited Miki and me to go shopping at midnight in the store—for a reduced rate. Unfortunately, Rudy, who worked for Gene Shakove and did all the stars' hair—and sometimes acted as Miki's bodyguard—wound up blowing his brains out.

DARRYL STOLPER: Once in a while a guy named Terry Hansen showed up. His father, Jack, owned the hip and exclusive Daisy Club in Beverly Hills, and Jack's Shoes. Terry used to drive us around in a silver-gray Rolls-Royce. Miki had his own beautiful Mercedes, which he sold to the Pink Pussycat, a strip

ABOVE TOP: Darryl Stolper, Miki, Pierre Salinger. Fund-raiser for Salinger's 1964 Senate run in Pacific Palisades. Photo: Peter Gowland.

ABOVE: Miki flips off photographer Pat Darrin at State Beach. Seated blonde in left foreground is Mary Hughes. Seated man to her left, in shades, Darryl Stolper. Man in front of Miki, Gypsy Boots. Photo: Pat Darrin.

club on Santa Monica Boulevard. It sat in front of the club for years and years. Most of the time Miki drove an old mid-'50s Ford, dark purple with burnt-off paint. When he sprayed the windows black, he immediately got a ticket. That was his State Beach car. It didn't have a backseat. He had cut the struts out so he could keep his board inside. He would also practice stopping this car and falling out of it in the parking lot so that if his car was ever hit in an accident, he could tumble out onto the street.

Miki also had issues with the State Beach lifeguards, who would put up the black ball flag on the lifeguard towers at 8:00 A.M. each morning and kick the surfers out of the water. One guard, Don Rohrer, came in for Miki's particular disdain even though Rohrer says he talked the city's chief lifeguard into letting him wait until 10:00 A.M. to raise the flag.

"I talked to all the kids about it," says Rohrer. I said, 'We'll let you surf until we think there's enough people on the beach to call you out of the water. Then, we don't want any bullshit. You've got to come out, be courteous to people in the water, and act like a gentleman on the beach. We want this thing to be a winner.'

"All the kids said 'great.' But not Miki. We had commonsense rules, but those were not his rules. I tried to talk to him a few times. His respect for authority didn't exist.

"Finally, there were enough complaints against him that I got the kids together and said that to get a cop to actually witness him making trouble would be almost impossible. But we came up with something else. If Miki did anything untoward in the water, they would just surround him and say, 'Get out of the water.' We'd circle, he'd paddle around and realize he wasn't going to get any waves, so he'd leave."

But Miki didn't just leave. He and Darryl Stolper, an underassistant West Coast promo man type in the music business, with one of the finest blues collection around—"I remember the Rolling Stones showing up at the beach with him on a windy November day, and they were all hanging out making the scene. They bought records from him," says Jim Ganzer—decided to cause some trouble. Stolper purchased five hundred baby chicks really cheap, from the hatcheries out in Anaheim, and put them inside Rohrer's lifeguard tower.

"That morning the beach was pretty empty, except for me and some friends, and a woman right near the tower, with her two kids," Robbie Dick recalls. "Rohrer opened the door and we heard,

'Oh fuuuuuuuuck!!!' These chicks began wobbling out. The place smelled like crap, and it probably was crap. 'Goddammit! Fuck! Who did this!' He started tossing chicks in the trash can. The woman screamed, 'What are you doing with the chicks?'—and hit Don with her purse. 'You can't do that! My kids are here!'"

According to Rohrer, "the incident also made heroes out of us. People came down to get chicks until we ran out."

But Dora and Stolper weren't through with Rohrer. "Miki also came up with the idea to pour butyric acid in the lifeguard tower," says Stolper. "I managed to get a bottle at Santa Monica College, in the chemistry lab. It smelled like a combination of baby barf and monkey shit. We poured it in on the third of July. The next day it smelled so bad the lifeguards wouldn't even go in. State Beach was packed in the mid-'60s, especially on Independence Day. Every time the wind shifted, whole corridors of people got up and moved. It smelled for months.

"At that point, I think Don asked for a transfer."

2

MICKEY MUÑOZ: Even though he'd out and out insult them, Miki had special devotees who would bend over and do anything for him. Miki called them lapdogs and stooges.

MYSTO GEORGE: Bruce Surtees, who's now a well-known cinematographer, used to drive him around in a Mercedes. Miki would sit in the back, cross his legs, open the financial section, and tell Bruce to "Drive on." But he had the paper upside down!

JIM BEST: We knew we were just lapdogs, but basically we didn't give a shit. Dora was a legend. One time he asked me, "Hey, you want to go to Point Zero? I'll get us in if you drive."

To drive Dora was like, "Are you kidding? Let's go!"

At Zero, he knew somebody at the gate and we got in. Afterward, we went to Malibu. He surfed for a couple of hours and I just watched. You can imagine, just walking around Malibu with him, as his gofer, was pretty awe-inspiring. Afterward I think I bought him a burger.

The next day, down at State Beach, Chuck Lohrman and Darryl Stolper came up and said, "Miki's asking for character references on you." I go, "What do you mean?" They said, "He's missing $100 out of his wallet."

I said I didn't know who took it; I didn't even know he had a hundred dollars. The scam was, he knew I was a lapdog. He'd never lost any money. He figured I'd just give him a hundred dollars to get over the guilt or the shame. Which I never did. I never took him anywhere after that. It pissed me off.

BOB FEIGEL: Miki had an inherent dislike of people, a contempt for the masses. He was uncomfortable, I think, around his admirers. It's almost as if he had to force himself to insult them because he was so uneasy.

One of Miki's biggest admirers was George Samama—Frenchie, the Frenchman. It seemed like they were together all the time. I cringe even now at how Miki sometimes treated him. On the other hand, I thought, That's their relationship. I'm sure if George didn't like it, he was perfectly capable of driving off.

SUSAN SAMAMA: George worked at La Scala in Beverly Hills then. He and the owner used to room together and were good friends. George was a bartender, then the maître d' and manager. George had the idea to open the La Scala in Malibu. Everyone in Beverly Hills and Hollywood knew him, and because La Scala was so successful, George had a following, and other people who wanted to open restaurants would hire him. He'd take a short leave of absence to do it. George also opened the Daisy Club for Jack Hansen, Greenhouse for Jerry Magnin, Harry's Bar in Century City.

When I married George in 1960, he already knew Miki so Miki came along with the package. They met because George used to work in movies. He had been raised in the south of France, right on the Mediterranean, and was a very good swimmer. His agent, who was also French, thought George would be perfect for this surfing part. Of course, my husband did not surf. He had to learn. That's how Miki came into the picture—to teach him how to surf. Miki found George interesting because he had been in the French resistance during World War II.

JIMMY GANZER: Because his friend was the maître d', Miki would hang out at La Scala. In those days, he dressed like Cary Grant in *To Catch a Thief*, with the black long-sleeved sweater, black pants, black socks, black loafers, and a great tan; that was his evening wear. We could imagine him with Grace Kelly, driving around the Riviera. Really cool.

George had influence. He was very respected and knew all kinds of very famous people. But George was also a pussycat, quite usable and willing to be used by Miki. George would of course give him everything gratis. Miki groomed him but really had no respect for him except for his power in those circles to which Miki would have loved to belong.

DARRYL STOLPER: What Miki saw in George Samama and Terry Hansen was a free ticket into the Daisy Club. We'd get tips on when there were parties at the club, and if we could come. One night, George sat us with Mia Farrow and Liza Minnelli. They'd both gotten really close-cropped haircuts, so I asked them if they were dykes. They got pretty pissed and got up and left. Then Miki went over and talked to them as they were leaving, but they didn't come back. In fact, they got even madder, so he must have said the same sort of thing.

SUSAN SAMAMA: George was very patient with Miki, and very generous. Because he worked restaurant hours, he and Miki surfed early in the morning. They cruised up and down the coast, from Rincon or the Overhead, down to Swami's. George had the car, George had the gas, George would buy breakfast. That was Miki's M.O. with everybody. Most people could only tolerate Miki to a certain point. George would just say, "Oh, that's Miki."

Sometimes it took only one misstep for Miki to have a change of heart about those who thought they were his "friend." Although Miki and Johnny Fain had been mentor and student, others saw their "battle" as intentional theater, which Fain confirms: "Dora shoved me off waves, dropped down on top of me. My board and I were like scrambled eggs in the soup. I threw a few rocks at him from the beach. But we had the right to do this. There were no rules. We were like gladiators—the more people strewn over the rocks, the more the crowd loved it."

However, in 1962, the relationship actually began to deteriorate.

JOHNNY FAIN: When I was nineteen, Miki, Armand Riza, a kid named Josh Harding—who later committed suicide—and I headed for Mammoth to ski. Josh was transfixed by Miki and would finance these trips. We took Armand's car. Miki rode in the back; Harding rode in the front. I had introduced him to Miki. His mother, Isobel Lennart, wrote *Funny Girl*. They had a big estate and Miki loved that; he could play tennis up by Point Dume.

On this trip, it was my turn to drive on the way to Mammoth. But somehow I missed a ramp and we wound up in Bakersfield at seven in the morning when we were supposed to be on the slopes by eight o'clock.

ARMAND RIZA: When Miki and I woke up and saw a WELCOME TO BAKERSFIELD sign, we realized we were on the wrong side of the Sierras.

JOHNNY FAIN: Miki was so infuriated, he called me a goof and kicked me as hard as he could in the back of my head. I went into a rage, pulled over, flew across the seat at him, and tried to punch him in the head. I never would've done that, but I was so pissed that he had the nerve to think I was incompetent. Armand and Josh broke us apart. They put me in the backseat and Miki drove.

ARMAND RIZA: By the time we got close to Mammoth, the snow was so heavy they'd put up a roadblock. Miki said, "Let's go around the roadblock." Pretty soon the snow became so deep it was impassable. We turned around and went to the closest motel. We were all in one room. Thirty minutes later the Highway Patrol knocked on our door. They'd seen the tracks. They knew somebody tried to run their barrier and figured out who. "Who was driving the car?"

Miki confessed and pulled out his driver's license—from Hawaii.

JOHNNY FAIN: Miki said he didn't know any better. This infuriated the officer. Also his license was expired and he had nothing else to back up who he was. It didn't even have his right name on the license. [12/6/60: Hawaii DL: #375149, issued to Mickel S. Chapin] The cop cuffed Miki and took him to jail. I was ecstatic. My prayers were answered. I begged Josh not to bail him out right away. Josh said, "Hey, come on." I said, "It won't hurt him. Just one night in jail." Josh said, "Look, I can hear him howling from here," but he waited until the next morning. Meanwhile, I got the best night's sleep I've had in my life. The next day Josh paid $200 to get Miki out. Afterward it was pretty tough because Miki and I had four days of tension. It was my first warning that there'd been a breach in our relationship, and I had to watch out.

BOB COOPER: There were stages, I think, where Miki got tired of this yapping pup and would whack him once or twice. Put him in his place. Then that gave Johnny ammunition to attack Miki through whatever avenues were available to him—graffiti, innuendo, the grapevine, in the water. He'd try to undermine Miki's position in any way that he could, trying to get at him rather than lying down and taking it. But he knew he was outclassed all the way and eventually would have to come crawling back to Miki.

JOHNNY FAIN: Some people say that to know Miki was to love him or hate him. I think to know Miki was to love him *and* hate him.

3

DIANE SWANSON OOSTERVEEN: I was a Valley girl and would have graduated from Birmingham High in 1962, but I had just gotten thrown out for hooking up a time stamp machine in my locker—the kind they have at the school office desk. I was also born with a photographic memory, so I was an excellent forger.

I had seen *Gidget,* had a crush on James Darren, and ran away from home to hitchhike to Malibu with friends. It was an absolutely perfect day. I watched the guys in the water, and this one guy pushing them off their boards.

All of a sudden, I saw him walking up to me. He dropped his board on the ground, lay on top of it, looked me in the eyes, and said, "Do you want to go to a party?" I was so shocked, I said no! He absolutely terrified me. The next week, my girlfriend and I went back to Malibu. Sure enough, he was there. When he came over, I invited him to dinner. I'd gotten a sales job and had moved into an apartment with three girls. I didn't mention that I didn't know how to cook. A couple hours later Miki called and said, "You live in the Valley? I can't come to the Valley." I said, "What do you mean? I've got dinner on!" Actually, I had nothing in the refrigerator but hamburger meat. When he showed up, he took one look at the meatball I'd made and said, "We've got to go out," and took me to dinner.

During dinner Miki asked me why I had been thrown out of school. And of course, from the beginning he loved the idea that I was a bad girl. We started dating immediately, but he didn't come to the Valley anymore. He would meet me at Tiny Naylor's, or somewhere off the Sunset Strip. I'd have to get a ride. Then we'd sit in his car and neck.

One day I said, "I want you to be the first one." We'd been dating a few months and he knew I was still a virgin. But the odd thing is that waiting didn't make him anxious or lose interest. He gained interest. I think he realized I was a great asset.

He took my virginity when I was seventeen. He was almost thirty. But he didn't know my age because I still hadn't told him. We had to borrow a friend's apartment. After a wonderful dinner, Miki kept trying to give me alcohol, "Have some wine, have some wine." I didn't drink. I said, "Let me go to the bathroom." The guy who lived there had left me six different birth control foams and gels, and I stood there for half an hour reading the small print. I didn't want to goof up!

Finally, I asked Miki. He said, "What are you worried about? We're already taken care of!" We laughed. He was very gentle, and we fell in love.

Eventually, Miki got tired of meeting me at the Tiny Naylor's parking lot, or getting thrown out of my apartment full of roommates, so he said, "Let's find a place. But it can't be in the Valley."

I found a place we called "Alice's Little House"—because my name then

was Alice—at 824 Gretna Green Way in Brentwood. We had the back apartment in a four-unit building. Inside the front door was a little living room, a
little closet, and a big overstuffed chair. It had a corner hutch where we stored
the wine. From the back porch you could walk into the garage where Miki kept
his Volkswagen. It cost $125 a month.

Miki told almost no one where he lived, and those who knew wondered why he didn't live closer to or on the beach. One day, while
checking out the surf from Bob Feigel's house at Topanga Beach, Miki
explained. There were, according to Feigel, three reasons:

"The first was vintage Dora. He wanted to keep surfing and the
other aspects of his life completely separate. 'If everyone knows where
I live, then everyone will want to come to my house and touch my
things and eat my food. Then they'll come back when I'm out surfing
and steal from me.'

"The second reason I'd never considered, but learned to respect
over the years. He never wanted to take the sea for granted and felt
that people who lived at the beach became so used to being close to
the sea that they forgot how special it was. 'Every time I drive down
Sunset or Channel and see the beach for the first time each day, I want
to fall in love all over again . . . and again.'"

Was the irony lost on Miki that this reason swept away all objec-
tions to Valley surfers? Probably not.

Feigel says that Miki carefully scanned the area before whispering
his final reason: "Saltwater . . . It's in the air. Then you breathe it in
and, after time, your brain rots like a driftwood log . . . That's why so
many surfers we know are so stupid."

"Right," Feigel said. "So . . . what about me?"

"Move," said Miki. "Move before it's too late."

~

"Alice's Little House" was anything but plain inside when Miki got
through with it. And over the years it got even more eclectic and ornate. He liked rich-looking fabrics and carpets. He tacked bedspreads
to the ceiling like a sultan's tent at an oasis. One visitor remembers
"fake cobwebs and plastic spiders, political pamphlets, a swastika or
two. The place was dark and dingy and crammed." Another recalls
trinkets from all over the world.

ABOVE: A hot night in Beverly Hills. Left to right: Paul Fegen; his date; Diane Swanson Oosterveen; Miki, early 1960s. Courtesy Diane Swanson Oosterveen.

RIGHT: Miki and Cynthia Applewhite. Photo: Peter Gowland.

BELOW: Deetsie, Malibu, 1960. Photo: Toni Donovan Colvin.

Peggy Barr, a live-in girlfriend in 1968, recalls the place being "full of papers, books, reference material, and drawings. He was big into making graphs and different time lines of things that were going on in his head. He gave me very explicit instructions not to touch anything, so I didn't. He also must have had a hundred suits jammed into his closet, and he talked about where the suits were made and the fabric. The garage, where he kept his vintage burgundy Porsche—with a mural painted inside on the roof—and his VW van, was crammed with surfboards. Maybe fifty. Maybe one hundred.

"He also had a bear trap set in the bedroom window. I asked, 'Who's after you?' but he never told me."

NAT YOUNG: The first time I stayed there I was with my first wife. She found a gun under the bed. That freaked her out. He also had an incredible setup where he did his forgery: an architect's workbench set at an angle, and great lighting overhead. He had fine writing instruments and cutting tools. He showed me. I guess it was for working on the airline tickets, for example. When I saw the movie *Catch Me If You Can*, I thought of Miki. If he would have posed as a pilot, he could have gotten away with it.

MARCIA MCMARTIN: His place was like a rabbit warren. Dark. He collected things: magazines, surfboards, stuff from trips. I never spent the night there. I didn't want to.

LINDA CUY: (Later, when I was with Miki) you could hardly walk around in the apartment. The coffee table was a big piece of broken glass and the edges stuck out at odd angles. If you snuck in at night, you'd get hurt. The windows were closed and nailed shut. Only the bathroom window was halfway open.

Rumor had it that Miki also had a filing cabinet with one purpose: he would write a little note to himself about anyone who'd slandered him, called him a name behind his back, written about him, or maybe, said Don Wilson, "coughed up wind and it came down on him," and put it into the drawer so he could use it as a reference some time in the future.

"He would *say* he had a list of all the people, even teachers from way back when who had done dirty things to him," said Cynthia Applewhite, "and that he'd one day get back at them. But I think it wasn't in a real file cabinet; it was a mental file."

DIANE SWANSON OOSTERVEEN: On a typical day we woke up and listened to the stock reports first because Miki was investing in Occidental Petroleum. Then we would watch Jack La Lanne and exercise, and take tons of vitamins. Then we'd get in the car and go up and down the coast. It would make me crazy. He'd jump out of the car, make me sit, freezing, drinking coffee from Denny's, while he watched the waves. It wasn't until I lived in Hawaii that I figured out what he was doing: the Hawaiians watch the waves for the currents. It's an art.

After checking out the surf, we'd go home and have a protein drink, I'd get ready for work, and he'd pick out a board to go surfing—and it still wasn't eight in the morning. When he'd come back from surfing, before I got home, he'd take a nap. He used a sleep mask. We also used to listen to talk shows on the radio and he read all the time. He loved James Bond. We lived for each book and movie as it came out. After work, I'd make him dinner. It was always the same: a great steak—or whatever he decided to steal from Gelson's market that day—and a great bottle of wine.

I was naïve and would ask lots of questions. He'd teach me about life. He'd say, "Fuck the world. Watch out for you."

On my eighteenth birthday I told Miki my real age. That shocked him. I'd also lied to him about my name. Between Miki and I, we had numerous names. We'd make up more daily.

About a year after we started living together, we had dinner with his father at some fancy restaurant. His dad was a trip. I couldn't believe anybody could be more gorgeous than Miki, but his father looked like Omar Sharif.

They fought because his dad wanted him to straighten up and get a life. I agreed, because the only other surfers I knew were dumb blond guys. I tried to convince Miki to give up surfing and work for his father. I was more interested in being with a sophisticated, classy guy. Miki thought I was crazy. I knew he'd never give up surfing, though, and every once in a while I'd lose it because we couldn't go someplace I wanted to because the waves were up. I finally said, "Saltwater is going to destroy you. Your brain will get moldy and rot."

CHAPTER SIX

What's in It for Me?

1

ED GARNER: I ran into the director Bill Asher in Malibu. He told me about a movie he was doing called *Beach Party*. We talked about Miki Dora, Johnny Fain, Butch Van Artsdalen, and other surfers, and he asked me to put a group together. I pulled in Brian Wilson from the Wilson House of Suede Wilsons, Duane King, Mike Nader—who I think brought Johnny Fain on board—plus a couple other guys and girls from State Beach. At the audition we had to dance to some beach tune. Asher asked everybody if they were comfortable in the water. Next thing you know, we got the parts.

KEMP AABERG: Miki's an extra. You see him in the background, and he's making a mockery of rock 'n' roll dancing, or partying on the beach. He hated the whole corny mechanism that he claimed was ruining the sport, and he made fun of them behind their back. But he also wanted to get the easy money.

DUANE KING: Miki liked acting because he thought it didn't require work. Maybe he even thought he could be good at it. At Hollywood parties, Miki always tried to meet people who could help him. He could look someone in the eye and convince them that complete bullshit was reality.

MIKE NADER: Johnny Fain was a good little actor, but Miki had no rhythm outside the water. He was a terrible actor. Johnny had the chutzpah and the hunger. Miki might have had the desire for the look-good, but he did not have the ability. In the beach party movies he's in the background jumping up and down, or doing stock A to B to C looks. Funny, but no Hollywood potential. I tried to help him a couple times. I said, "Miki, you can't clown around. You've got to be in the moment. Yeah, sometimes they make us do these stupid things, but you gotta make those things real." He'd say, "C'mon, Mikey, I can't do this stuff. I gotta do my thing." No, he was not preparatory material.

DARRYL STOLPER: Miki had a habit of talking himself into a job, and then right out the other side. He'd oversell himself. He'd go to movie auditions, recommended by Bill Asher. He'd be the surfer they'd want. Miki would ask for too much money and turn off the casting directors.

ED GARNER: One thing Miki loved to do was sit on the beach and if there were a few girls around, he would arrange his trunks so that his dong would be right there in the sand. I guess anyone might do that if their dong made it to the sand. It was such a casual thing that most people thought it was natural. But it was premeditated, believe me.

Most of the guys who were attached to Miki followed him around like he was the court jester. One day we were all waiting in line at the catering truck for lunch. Miki had his trench coat on, like something Cary Grant would wear. He could put his hands through the pockets and grab stuff and stash it at the same time he'd carry on a conversation with the caterer.

Once, Don Rickles was in front of him in the line. Don used to pick on everybody, including Miki, who responded, saying, "I love your humor. I appreciate what you're doing, but it's really not that funny to me." Don just cracked up.

DREW KAMPION: Miki might have thought he was working over these Hollywood guys, but the problem was that while he thought he lived outside the system, as soon as he took the money he was complicit, no matter how he tried to excuse it later.

WILLIE HOUSE: One day Miki said, "I'm just a whore." I couldn't figure out what he was talking about. Then I realized, my god, he's talking about selling out for this movie crap.

Even when the ocean was placid and no surf or movie was to be had, Miki did not go wanting. He simply turned his attention in other directions: he skied, played tennis, went to concerts, tinkered with his car collection, immersed himself in the burgeoning new youth culture. In West Hollywood, Miki's grandmother (who died in 1966) lived close to La Cienega Boulevard, where, south of Santa Monica Boulevard were many art galleries and evening art walks.

"Miki was a very bright kid," surfer Corny Cole remembers. "He was a lot more intellectual than people realize. He was very aware of the art scene. At that time, the scene wasn't so much at Venice as it was at La Cienega, right near Barney's Beanery. Miki spent a lot of time going to those shows. That would be the Ferris Gallery, south of Santa Monica, and Landau, the most prestigious at that time."

C. R. Stecyk also placed Miki at numerous "counterculture rites including the Gas House in Venice to take in poetry and music, to hear jazz at Shelley's Manne Hole . . . to bet the ponies at Santa Anita with Charles Bukowski; to see Lightning Hopkins at Xanadu; to the Sunset Strip riots at Pandora's Box . . . to Topanga (photographer) Edmund Teske's . . . to the Avalon Ballroom in San Francisco with Rick Griffin as a guest of Bill Graham . . . to greasy spoon breakfasts including one at Olivia's Place in Ocean Park with Admiral Morrison's son, Jim," and more.

"I remember when we used to hang out and talk to Henry Miller at State Beach," says Barbara Sievers, a former Playboy Bunny and girl-friend. "He wasn't that social, but Miki would always tease out some conversation. They'd get into philosophical exchanges. Miki usually did most of the talking, expounding on his 'Tennis shoe philosophy of life.' Henry was really old at that point and kind of cranky, but Miki made him smile. Henry even gave Miki a watercolor he'd done."

JOHN MILIUS: Miki played perfectly into the changing world of the '50s and '60s, when the emergence of *Playboy* magazine redefined the term "playboy" from the old money, golden sportsman who owned polo ponies, drove motor-boats for world's records, climbed mountains, screwed the finest women, and shot skeet, to a regular guy who could have everything the aristocracy tradi-tionally had—all he had to do was buy the dream presented in the magazine: a new stereo with round speakers. A round bed. The right clothes. The Porsche.

But the secret, at least in Los Angeles, was that you *didn't* have to own all the trappings; you just had to appear to. If you had a few things, it could look like you had it all. To be a movie producer you only needed an office, a bunch of posters, and to *say* you were a movie producer. Why? Because there were no qualifications whatsoever for that job. Everything about Miki gave the impression that he *knew* he could be anyone he wanted to be—and everyone followed him.

The bottom line is that Miki loved fraud. He was fascinated with the concept of deceit. He would come to the beach with a couple faggots and have the word pass around that Miki was gay. Three days later he'd show up with the most extraordinary girl on his arm. It was quite funny. I am convinced that most of this was studied and rehearsed and that he loved starting the rumors among the natives. The "untermenschen" at the beach all looked up to "Über-Miki" and said, "My God, look what he's doing. He just showed up in this fancy car."

He assumed the poses. He was *Playboy* come to life.

ED GARNER: Miki surfed during the day and crashed Hollywood and Beverly Hills parties at night. I had dated Dean Martin's daughter, Deana. All of a sudden, at a party at Dean's house, I saw Miki serving hors d'oeuvres. Thirty minutes later he was wandering around in a suit and tie. I guess he went in under the pretense of being there on behalf of La Scala, then joined the party as a guest. I also saw him at Janet Leigh's house.

ARMAND RIZA: I was Miki's party connection. I'd find out from friends who were valet parkers where to show up. We all had party kits in the car so we could change to suit the occasion. The whole idea was to be dressed right and be able to drift in like everybody else. We would drive by, see what was going on, park somewhere, and pick our clothes. We had everything from a suit to a Hawaiian shirt. Tuxedo. Tie. Bartender's jackets. Even a glass with ice cubes.

CYNTHIA GARRIS: According to my mom, Miki always kept a champagne glass and some bubbly water in his car. He'd park down the street from the party, pour the bubbly, and slowly walk in backward.

DON WILSON: He'd bring a plastic bag with him and when people weren't looking he would fill it with food so that he could have something to eat the next morning.

DARRYL STOLPER: The *Los Angeles Times* on Thursdays used to publish a society page, so that was our menu for the weekend. The party group was Jerry Goldman, Armand, Johnny Fain sometimes, Mike Nader on occasion, myself, Miki, and a couple others. Goldman also made some fake press credentials for us. They looked like driver's licenses and just said PRESS. They worked pretty well. We went to a Natalie Wood party. Then we tried to get into a Herman's Hermits party in Laurel Canyon. We flashed the press cards but the cop said, "That doesn't look like an official LAPD press pass."

We said, "No, this is for the studios."

He said, "Oh, go on in, then."

Miki was also a big James Bond fan. I created a briefcase modeled after the one with the hidden knife, in *From Russia, with Love*, only mine held different drinking glasses, a bow tie, and other odds and ends. Miki went crazy for it. He called it my SMERSH kit.

When the Beatles had a party at Alan Livingston's house in Beverly Hills, we both crashed. We walked in wearing ascots, holding a drink. We were dandies. I stood around watching John Lennon and Groucho Marx talk. Miki just wandered. Later, he held Ringo's coat while he went to the bathroom, and he took Ringo's cigarette case. That was his big souvenir.

I recall only one party in Beverly Hills where we had trouble. We got in but the host caught us immediately and told us to leave. At the next party that night we met Armand. We told him, "We just went to the absolutely greatest party." Armand went and they called the cops. He never suspected we had set him up.

JOHNNY FAIN: One night I'll never forget: myself, Duane King, and Miki Dora, in my Falcon station wagon, coming back from a party at the Hollywood Hills Hotel. There were bungalows, gardens, ponds, a great view. Very, very exclusive. If Miki gave you the party lead, you drove the car. No gas money.

We were a little drunk. Miki said, "Hey, let's crash the Daisy." But we got there just as it was closing. Outside, we saw a guy locked in an embrace with this beautiful blond girl, standing in front of a car, her ass against the hood. She was radiant; he was like Rock Hudson. They were the embodiment of Hollywood showbiz.

Miki grabbed the wheel, stepped on the gas, honked the horn—and before I knew it my car was headed directly into them from at least a block away. I said, "What are you doing?" He said, "Don't worry, we'll turn the wheel." Well, we didn't turn the wheel; we kept going. I yelled, "Miki, we're going to crash!" At the last moment, this dashing, daring guy, this handsome, gallant fellow, reacted. He must have thought, "This is it; we're going to be killed." He spun the girl around, pushed her toward my car to absorb the impact, then dove over the hood to the sidewalk, and ran down the street, leaving her at the mercy of whatever fate might befall her. She stood there like a deer in the headlights. Of course, Miki swerved at the last moment to avoid hitting her. Then he rolled down the window and said, "Boy, did we save you a lot of problems"—and we kept going.

2

In a town of creamy opportunism, the thefts by which he supported himself were so small-time, high risk, and potentially humiliating, that they bespoke a cockeyed integrity. He made the patently tacky petty theft a symbol of bravado and status envy.

—Sheila Weller, *Vanity Fair*

DUANE KING: On the set of one of the beach party movies, I saw Miki come out of the guitarist Dick Dale's trailer. He wore a shit-eating grin. About half an hour later Dale freaked out. "Oh my God, my jewels are gone!" I looked at Miki and he still wore this grin. It's circumstantial, but if I had to bet, I'd bet he took them.

DARRYL STOLPER: He told me he took Dick Dale's diamond ring. He said he hid it in a Greyhound locker until things cooled off.

JOHNNY FAIN: He saw me as he came out of the trailer. "You didn't see me here at all," he said. "If you open your mouth, you're dead." Miki knew some jeweler in Beverly Hills. He could bring jewels to them and they would ask no questions.

I'm sure he did it because after he'd lived with me and my mother for about three weeks, *her* diamond ring went missing. We put two and two together. Miki was a kleptomaniac. He couldn't help himself. Did Greg Noll tell the story of the time he had to take a dump and he took his suitcase and personal belongings into the bathroom with him so that Miki couldn't go through them? When he came for dinner, you put out paper plates.

RICK HODGSON: There were so many poses, stories within stories, all for appearances and style. I ran into an old girlfriend recently. Miki once dated her sister. He picked her up at the house in a brand-new Ferrari and they drove all over, had dinner. Then he took the car to the Valley and left it in front of a house and they took a cab back to the girl's place. She asked what was going on and Miki said, "Oh, the car was stolen." Of course it wasn't. He'd borrowed it from a friend and staged a bit of theater to make her think he was running on the edge with the dangerous crowd, something of a pirate.

Miki had another girlfriend in Santa Monica. My friend Chuck Lohrman, who sells real estate in Cabo now, drove to Miki's house to pick him up to play tennis. He went in and saw Miki in an argument with this girl, so Chuck walked out to wait in the car. When Miki came out, he sat in the car and went, "Women!"

Chuck said, "What's up?"

Miki said, "She called me a common thief."

Chuck said, "Oh, that's really terrible."

Miki smiled and said, "Oh no. It took her a whole year to find out."

SKIP ENGBLOM: Miki was honest about his dishonesty. He'd always let you know you were a rube. People try to use deductive logic on Miki, like if this means this, then this means that. But in reality, only Miki knew what he thought, and why he did what he did. He was like a diamond. We usually focus on a facet, the brilliance, the light. But no one ever sees the entire stone. And once it's set, there's always a hidden part underneath.

BOB COOPER: Miki had figured out how to work the beach, and he did constantly, whether he tried to pick up dumb girls or eat somebody else's lunch. Later, it became more sinister, when he'd pick up girls not with amorous intentions, but to fleece them. He'd take it as far as he could and try to go through their purse. He was good at assessing character, and he could spot the dumb chicks, the bush pigs, and the fat ones coming down the trail. They'd lay out their towels and pretty soon he'd saunter over. You could tell from his posture, even at a distance, that he'd started to throw them the line about, "Oh, do you girls surf? . . . I'll give you a few lessons. . . . Interesting. . . . Where you from?"

Once upon a time, but not so long ago, in the land of credit, cards were not made of plastic, they didn't have magnetic strips. You signed on the front, showed the card, and they trusted you. If a card was bad, there were no computers to immediately track it. Merchants depended on a list of missing or stolen cards published weekly—that is, if they bothered to check the list at all.

DIANE SWANSON OOSTERVEEN: Miki and I used to dress up and walk into parties looking fabulous. I'd go to the bedroom, where the coats were piled, to put down my purse, but in fact I'd be fishing through someone else's purse. By the time our drinks came, I'd have three credit cards. We had that down to a beautiful art. There was nothing Miki loved more than me walking out of a bedroom with a big smile on my face and a Diners Club card in my pocket. It's not something I'm particularly proud of now, but it was a lot of fun for a short time. We started this whole credit card thing of his. We were Bonnie and Clyde. We didn't want to hurt anyone. We didn't steal to make ourselves rich. This was revenge, releasing anger at the corporate world. This was the '60s. We didn't need the money, just the excitement. I made a salary. He made money in the stock market. But I worked in a shop; I had the stolen credit card list. If I confiscated a card, I knew how long we could still use it. In those pre-computer days, you could use a card for about $50 before they would call in to verify anything. We knew the routine, so we'd go shopping. We'd spend the money on good wine, fine dinners, a new outfit to wear to the next party, or to fill the gas tank. That was the life.

BARBARA SIEVERS: Some of the wildest parties were thrown by very rich, spoiled, vulnerable young heiresses whose parents went out of town for a weekend and either left the girls alone or with the trusted help. The parties would be suggested to the girls by any number of cute guys who, once they gained the girl's confidence, would put the word out over the human party line, and hundreds of partygoers would descend like vultures. Kegs of beer were ordered, probably charged, and all kinds of booze poured from the parents' unlocked bar. All this time the "cute" guy would make sure the girl whose home it was felt like a queen, but by the time the party ended, appliances, silverware, art, even small pieces of furniture would go out the door.

On our first date, Miki had a long list of parties to go to, with the goal, I soon found out, to train me to "rifle hookers' purses." I don't know if they actually were hookers, but he had a crazy rationalization for why this was okay, and of course I went for it. I grew up a very spoiled, willful child, and I always tested the boundaries. Besides, there was no point going to a dozen parties a night unless you were going to do something like that. I guess I liked the challenge and the danger, and there was the incentive of splitting the money at the end of the evening. It was like having a part-time job.

But for Miki it was never about the money. It was about testing one's intelligence, trying to find out where the limits were and how far he could go. It was about creating the danger, living on the edge of that danger, and riding that adrenaline wave with his physiological electricity cranked all the way up, using every measure of his agile capacity to turn it all on in whatever moment he was in.

CRAIG LEONARD: There used to be homes on the coast at Topanga before they were all torn down to make it a public beach. At a party, Miki said, "Twin! Twin! Come here." (I have a twin brother, Keith.) He took me into the bathroom and said, "Look what I got." Showed me a wallet. Then he said, "I want to show you a trick." He removed the cash, lifted the toilet tank cover, put the wallet in the tank. Suddenly some guy banged on the door: "Okay, Dora! We know you're in there! We got you this time!" Miki opened the door and said, "What's the problem?"

"We know you swiped that wallet. Where is it?"

Miki emptied his pockets. He had some cash, but no wallet, and we just walked out.

DIANE SWANSON OOSTERVEEN: I think if I had stayed with Miki I would have ended up in jail. Our Robin Hood thing would have escalated. I could see the direction we were going in was not going to be good for us. But in the end, as complicated as he was, it was always the simplicity of life that gave Miki the most joy. A good glass of wine, a great wave, a beautiful day. There was nothing more exciting to him than jumping on a wave, a force of nature totally out of his control, and—not mastering it—achieving a harmony and balance. I respected that but it eventually tore us apart. Surfing was Miki. Nobody could be on the water the way he could. He was totally dedicated. And he was *somebody* out there, you see. When he was on the water, he was king of the world.

3

On one picture we went to Hawaii and lived on the North Shore for two and a half months. We did something that had never been done before. Big-wave riding was filmed in 35 mm. They were good people and really wanted to understand surfing . . . to capture the atmosphere surrounding the many surfers who make the annual winter trip to the Islands to ride big waves. I had faith. I wanted to make this thing a success, not only for them but for me, also. . . . It was murder. . . . I was psyched out! My hair began to fall out. I got stomach ulcers. The Pipeline was a little scary but Waimea had the biggest waves I've ever seen in my life . . . Like it was Judgment Day. I'm paddling, trying to get going, and these guys are in it even before it stands up on the reef. They're driving and I'm just getting into it . . . by choice, I'm a four feet and under man!
—Miki, from "Surfing's Angry Young Man," Surf Guide, October 1963

LOUIS ZAMPERINI: Miki had been a stuntman in some of the beach party movies, so my wife, Cynthia, and I got him a job with Art and Jo Napoleon who were in Hawaii making a movie called *Ride the Wild Surf.*
MICK MCMAHON: When the big swell started, LeRoy Grannis, Bruce Brown, and Bud Browne arrived with big telephoto lens cameras. Then came Art Napoleon with a lens twice their size. He had a story line for *Ride the Wild Surf*, a base, but not enough money to actually do the film. His plan was to shoot a half hour of surf footage, then take it back to the States and pull the film together.
CYNTHIA APPLEWHITE: The Napoleons took Miki to Hawaii at the end of 1962 and rented a house on the North Shore. He lived with them. They had a fourteen-year-old son and Miki was his hero. In order to save money they

put the kid in the same cabin on the beach with Miki. I heard he constantly hounded Miki.

According to writer Leonard Lueras, the movie, which came out in 1964, "starred *Turn Me Loose* pop singing star Fabian Forte as big wave rider Jody Wallis. Also cast into this cinematic backwater were blond heartbreaker Tab Hunter (as the surfer Steamer Lane) and pop star Shelley Fabares (as the foxy surfer girl Brie Matthews). Splashing about in supporting roles were Barbara Eden (as Augie Poole), Peter Brown (as Chase Colton), Susan Hart (as Lily Kilua), and James Mitchum (as the surfer Eskimo)."

Randy Rarick, now a collector and event organizer in Hawaii, was fourteen when Miki came over, and repaired dinged boards at a Hobie shop in Honolulu. "The board that Fabian actually used had a big metal plate on the bottom, with a welded loop. They'd tie a rope onto that and anchor it, so when they filmed him in the water he wouldn't drift away. Fabian was a kook, you know; he didn't know how to surf at all."

When Miki's board came in for repairs, Rarick said, "Hey, I'll fix this! It was browny-purpley and had a bunch of dings on the bottom of the rails. I fixed the dings and then had to match this super-hard color. I matched it almost perfectly. Back in those days everything was taped off with pigment and you had to put a clear coat of resin over it, then you polished it. I did the whole repair deal and it came out pretty well, and I was proud of myself. Wow, I fixed Miki Dora's board.

"He came in person to get it. I stuck the board out and went, 'Mr. Dora, here's your board. I've repaired all the dings.' He just looked at me, said, 'Fuck you, kid,' grabbed the board and walked away. I didn't know what to do. I was blown away because I'd put my heart and soul into fixing the board because it was his, and instead of saying 'Thanks' or 'Good job,' he said 'Fuck you.' The guy I worked with said, 'What did he say?' I said, 'Well, he didn't really thank me.'"

During his stay, Miki wrote to Joel Laykin:

Hey Big Shot,
The picture is going slow. Junked the first script. Looks like another three weeks at this morgue. This ocean has been out of control for weeks. Yesterday I almost drowned a half dozen times. Believe me, I'm

working my brains loose. I'm stuck out here in the country on the Sunset side of the island. These show biz creeps have me a prisoner. They're really getting their shekels worth. I'm on a starvation diet: Metracal, Metracal, Metracal. My head alone has lost 15 pounds.

The natives are restless and so are the mosquitoes, flies, moths, and wasps. I feel like I'm in Baja, Mississippi. My total kingdom for those four o'clock naps, Wil Wright splurges, and Steve Allen nightcaps. Believe me, there's nothing out here except big, bad waves. It looks like judgment day out there.

MICK MCMAHON: Miki came in late October. Surfers like Pat Curren, Mike Diffenderfer, and Mike Hynson were there, living in a Quonset hut right on the beach, shaping boards in the back. You've never seen such appalling conditions. Most of the surfers I knew at that time lived in hovels, were dirty, were drinkers. Miki came walking along Sunset Beach. He wore a white shirt, sports coat, and his red and yellow board shorts. He looked like Mr. Movie Actor. He dressed that way every day.

We made $25 a day and lunch. We also worked at the poi factory, jumping waist-deep into the mud to pull up the poi and put it in bags. You got like five cents a plant. It was really horrible work. Mosquitoes everywhere. The Portuguese workers got really pissed at us. But we needed the money to stay longer. Miki hung out with me and my friends because we were Australians and we didn't care who the shit he was. He could do or be whatever he wanted. He asked our impression of Australia, what went on there. I said, "What do you mean, what's going on?" He said, "Well, is there any marijuana down there?" I said no. We were beer drinkers.

Miki told everybody he was going to play the number one part when the production returned to film the actual movie. No women had been cast yet, so my friend Barry Carter and I dressed in muumuus during a crowd scene. I wore the red dress, he wore the blue. A guy up on the rock photographed all the people below. We accidentally moved a couple of times. Miki yelled, "Someone's moved out of synchro!" He was a mite pissy; maybe he thought he was the director.

In another scene, a guy dove off Waimea Falls; the superstition, in the story, was that it would bring up the surf. They offered one guy $50 to jump. He declined. Bob Beadle said, "You give me $50, and I'll *dive* off it." It was eighty feet down, and no one knew how deep the water was, only that you supposedly couldn't touch bottom.

BOB BEADLE: Fifty bucks? No. Twenty-five. That was big money then. In 1962–63, I took a leave of absence before finishing at UCLA and went to the North Shore. That's when I met Miki. Miki had never ridden really big waves. He asked me one time, "Are you, uh, afraid?" I said, "Well, I'm afraid to be afraid."

JIM FISHER: Big waves scared Miki because he couldn't swim that well. To be honest, it took all his guts to go out. But he liked the thrill and he knew he had the skill. He just didn't want to have a really bad day where people said, "You can't handle it after all." You know how guys are. He was concerned about his rep.

PAUL STRAUCH: I was really surprised Miki went out there. Big surf is a whole different environment. You have to deal with more elements—undertows, rip-tides, the wind factor. Especially in Hawaii: The waves don't even break all the time in the same spot. You've got to be able to adjust. Sneaker sets come all the time and you have to be constantly on the watch. In contests I told him, "Watch the guys you have to compete against. As long as you're next to them, you're going to be in the right position."

RICKY GRIGG: To me, the best surfers at the time were Phil Edwards and then Paul Strauch. Miki had a beautiful style and he was lovely to watch; he could trim his board and he had a nice cutback. But he didn't have a real charging, motivating energy like you needed to surf the bigger waves on Hawaii's North Shore. His arrival was a nonevent. I hate to say this, but it's because he didn't have the heart, the power, the lust. On the other hand, had he stuck around I'm sure that would have changed.

DUKE BOYD: No one would have given Miki a nickel in a tin cup if he hadn't been a good surfer. The fact that a Malibu nose-rider was able to, on call, never having done it in his entire life, go out and ride the wild surf at twenty-foot Waimea—Christ almighty!

GREG NOLL: If the wave gets steep enough and it's a late enough takeoff, the board just goes airborne and you're hanging there. A lot of that was due to the equipment then. Guys nowadays are better surfers and better athletes. They'll even mess a little with the wave. Watch Laird Hamilton: On a thirty-five-foot wave he's perfectly at ease, screwing with it. In the old days, you'd make the drop and pray for daylight.

Miki didn't know the rest of the guys like he knew me, and he knew that I liked Waimea the same way he liked Malibu. So he followed me around. He used me for the lineup—where to sit in the water. He watched when I paddled. Not that I'm any great surfer, but it was a smart move. He sat a bit on my outside, playing it a little safe.

To my ol' friend
mick?
Greg Noll

ABOVE TOP: Miki and Greg Noll at Waimea. Signed by Noll. Photo: Laura Noll. Courtesy Noll Family Collection.

ABOVE: Miki at Sunset Beach, Hawaii, 1966. Photo: Tim McCullough.

We got three or four big-ass twenty-footers together. He was stiff, but he made the transition from the king of small surf to twenty-foot Waimea like nobody I'd ever seen or can think of even now. Miki did it in just one day.

On one pretty good-sized wave he dropped in, in front of me, hunched over just as tight as a knot, while this monster kept grinding behind me. I could see the writing on the wall: I was gonna eat it. I was used to the whole deal so I stayed pretty loose and slid right up underneath Miki, almost like him in that famous picture at Malibu where he's underneath Johnny Fain's board, giving Fain a heave-ho. I reached over and put my hand on the small of his back. He probably thought I was going to push him off his board, like he'd done to a thousand people at Malibu. Meanwhile, this monster wave is going *RARRRRR!* behind us. Just at the point when it was ready to dump on me, I shoved him. That gave Miki enough forward energy to make the wave. I got eaten. I had to swim in for my board.

Half an hour later I paddled back out, and I'd never seen Miki so happy. He said, "That's the nicest thing anybody has ever done for me. Why did you do that?" As we waited for a set he went on and on and on. For a few years, every time I saw him he would mention that. Even though we went way back to when we were kids, our relationship changed after that. That's how odd the guy was. He was less confrontational. His knee-jerk distrust of everyone was less deep-rooted for me.

MICK MCMAHON: Miki stayed in Hawaii until he was driven out by the underclothes. Originally, the film contained a story line where Miki took this young guy under his wing and showed him how to surf. But after Miki started playing games with Napoleon's wife—they started getting pissed off at each other because Miki played the spoiled actor—everything changed. Plus, Miki had started punking the Napoleons, with whom he lived. He wanted his own area in the bathroom. His shaver, his comb, his face flannel, his towel, all had to be in the same spot. Very finicky guy. Always spotsy clean.

One day, while waiting for a surfing bit, he said, "These people are pissing me off."

"What are you talking about?"

"I came out today and she had her underwear on my shaver," he says.

"Why didn't you just pick it up and throw it away?"

"It was UNDERWEAR!"

He wound tighter and tighter about this underwear shit. He told me she was playing with his toiletries, *using* his toiletries.

Miki had already told everyone that the Napoleons had a contract with him saying that if he'd ride the big waves and finish the time in Hawaii, he would be in the lead part. Art Napoleon had sucked him right in, saying, "You're going to be the winner here."

One night at a barbecue, I said, "Where's Miki?" Jo Napoleon told me he had hopped on a plane without telling anyone where he was going.

I know he wanted that part. He kept talking about how *Ride the Wild Surf* was his big break. But Jo had tried to get rid of him, and it worked. She'd bugged him so much that he just disappeared, and they gave the part to Fabian.

4

Surfing is about position and Dora knew that best. The (surf) media gave him a new stage and he took to it as naturally as he took to being in perfect trim on the perfect day at Malibu . . . . He realized quickly, intuitively, that this was yet another way to get along without having to sell out to the man—at least obviously. His reputation grew and so did his social options and his ability to twist the surf culture to his purposes.

—Drew Kampion, *Dora Lives*

Surf filmmaker, artist, photographer (and former high school teacher) John Severson had started *Surfer* in 1960—then called *The Surfer*—as a one-off companion to his film *Surf Fever*. "The 36-page, black and white marketing tool sold 5,000 copies, enough," Matt Warshaw wrote in his *Encyclopedia of Surfing*, "to convince Severson to produce *The Surfer Quarterly* in 1961. The magazine went bi-monthly in 1962, and was renamed *Surfer* in 1964." For all intents, *Surfer* is the *Playboy* or *Rolling Stone* of its genre.

Surfer still publishes, even as many competitors tried to catch the same wave only to wipe out quickly. The most intriguing casualty was *Surf Guide*, published by former Los Angeles County lifeguard R. L. Stevenson, who also developed and manufactured the legendary Makaha Skateboard line.

Bill Cleary, a surfer, ex-marine, and writer often called the Hemingway of the beach—a moniker that says more about his relationship to his subject matter than his sentence structure—lived at Topanga and edited *Surf Guide*. "Cleary"—who died in 2002, leaving behind a treasure trove of unpublished material—"wrote books, stories, and captured the gestalt of surfing from an intellectual, literary perspective," says Jimmy Fitzpatrick, whose father, in 1963, published the indispensable *Surfing Guide to Southern California*, a handbook co-authored by Cleary and David H. Stern and well thumbed then by every surfer.

Cleary and the other Topanga residents knew Miki because when Malibu got too crowded he'd show up a few miles south, at Topanga. "Living on the beach in Topanga was marvelous because it was a world in which everyone was accepted," Bob Beadle recalls. "There was the golfing drunk next door who had dry heaves late at night, the gay guys, the grandmothers, the little kids, the cats and dogs. It was a community. And when Miki showed up he was like a ghost, drifting in and drifting out at the unlikeliest moments."

Fitzpatrick, then a teenager, recalls the scene: "In 1960, we lived in a long, narrow hallway of a house, with no beach access. Just to the east was the old Los Angeles Athletic Club House, and a weird pedestrian tunnel under the Coast Highway. People stored stuff in this tunnel, and even slept there occasionally. And there was a stairwell down to the beach. At the bottom of the side stairs of our house was the hot-water shower. No one could use the shower unless you were a Cleary or a Fitzpatrick.

"In 1960, Miki used this stairwell, slinking very quietly like a cat, along the side of the house, over the bulkhead, onto the sand, and into the water. He didn't want to be paid any attention. He just wanted to get to the waves.

"Eventually, our entire family moved from 18664 PCH to 18658. We lived upstairs. Cleary lived downstairs in the 'artist's area' with Willie Hunter Jr., a naturalist. My mother, Dodie, was one of the few housewives always at home. One day, after I got back from school, she said, 'Some jerk came through the house today. He was really rude to me and wouldn't respond.' I didn't know who she meant. That weekend, the swell was still up, and here comes Miki. She says, "There's that jerk who ignored me." I said, "That's not a jerk, that's Miki," and told my mom that if anyone would have the privilege to come through the house, it was he."

From this communal sensibility sprang *Surf Guide*, which debuted in January 1963, on newsprint. It was, according to Matt Warshaw, "wholly unexceptional until October 1963 when Cleary ran a cover story on Miki (then spelled Mickey), called "The Angry Young Man of Surfing." This was Miki's first full-length interview, and his introduction to a new generation of surfers.

"The Angry Young Man of Surfing" begins: "Mickey Dora is too strong a personality for many people to admire or approve of. To say the least, he's controversial . . . he's a purist . . . He loves the sport intelligently and lives his own life . . . He's not locked in . . . He's grown more with the sport than most, but in a slightly different direction."

Cleary questioned him about surfing, but also did his utmost to put Miki's personality on display. The result was a wake-up call to Miki's peers who, familiar with Miki's edgy antics and opinions, were either horrified or bemused to actually—and finally—read about them in print.

"Whenever a magazine wanted an interview, Miki called me," says Darryl Stolper. "He wouldn't do them in person, only in letter form. We'd sit together and hash out the answers. Miki always wanted to sound like Mort Sahl. We'd try to come up with things that made him look controversial but not criminal. But a lot of his stuff was so over the top that it wasn't believable, so it had to be watered down."

The Q&A's tone is actually less unrelentingly angry than wryly contentious, unforgiving and hyperbolic. In fact, if one rereads all of Dora's early magazine appearances, he now comes off much less defensive and guarded than myth has it. Despite the pungent hipster slang, his answers were generally honest, and cast his disdain for crowds and a new generation of Malibu wannabes into sharper relief. "Get yourself a photographer and your picture in a few magazines and you're known," he said. "But it's a lazy way of becoming famous."

Doraphiles today still argue about whether or not Miki himself wanted to be famous—or chuck it all in disgust for a Pacific paradise with perfect waves. But that's asking the wrong question. Miki wanted both, and with the advent of full-time surf media, he had to manage perceptions on a wider, public stage, according to his need and often shrouded purpose. He claimed it was repugnant, but Miki required the exposure in order to compete—not only as a surfer, but as a media figure—on a burgeoning new playing field. He had to be able to conjure his spotlight, and he sought only to control its focus and intensity. This established a sometimes tense, sometimes playful dialectic that lasted his entire life.

"In fact," says Jim Kempton, "much of Miki's mystique today would have been impossible without the surf media responding to him the way they did. Miki understood how to get attention. He knew the press loved that character. He knew that being mysterious and saying less was far, far more interesting to people than saying too much."

Miki knew he was into a good thing. "Print media is different. . . ." Drew Kampion wrote in *Dora Lives*. "The implications were not lost on Miki. The fates had dealt him a forked temptation. He suddenly had media to magnify his impact, to explain himself, to tell his version of the story, to enlarge his message (whatever that was) and his stage . . . Miki was uniquely groomed for celebrity; like no other surfer he was there to optimize the situation. He was in position, and being in position, as every surfer knows, is the most important thing in surfing."

According to Steve Pezman, the surf media's original interest in Miki was based largely on his being the epitome of the California point stylist. But the focus quickly became his personality. "He styled himself as evil incarnate while everyone else wanted to be perceived as good. We reveled in him being that dark side of human nature, even though it was as much an act as not.

"He had a certain fractured integrity in that he lived the role by his rules and wouldn't compromise those twisted values for a buck—unless there were enough of them. There's no way to reconcile those aspects, and yet they exist in this one person. That alone makes him unique and interesting."

The result? Think of irradiated insects in cheapo sci-fi movies. Suddenly they're giant and wreaking havoc.

Miki being Miki, he soon began to do interviews while simultaneously bad-mouthing the magazine running it. He cast himself as a humorist and humanist of high intelligence, a brave white truth hunter, who was, if not selfless enough, at least generous enough to perform a distasteful but necessary public service for his fellow surfers by reporting back on all the shit he'd endured or imagined in order to warn everyone to avoid the shit. It only encouraged his fans.

Yet however ardently Miki claimed to wish the return of empty waves and the vintage years, he was no fool. He knew you couldn't ride the same wave twice. Gone were the good old days. *Today* was the good old days. Whatever nostalgia Miki actually felt for the past, or indulged in publicly, for whatever effect or angle, he never revealed how much of his act was based on an authentic belief that time would move in reverse if only this damn surf fever would die. He never allowed himself to be seen sincerely wallowing in maudlin sentimentalism. As a savvy investor, Miki simply adjusted to the new market reality and aggressively expanded his business in his own personality quirks.

If anything actually surprised Miki, it must have been how strongly his dissonant tones resonated with the anti-establishment tenor of the times, and the beat of surfing's rebel heart. Miki now had fans who marveled at his public willingness to criticize and cross the line of sportsmanlike, gentlemanly behavior. If he hadn't planned or at least hoped for this reaction in the first place, he quickly realized its value. As a result, his mystique began to morph into mythology, the real Miki receded into mystery and an Über-Miki took center stage.

~

In Hawaii to attend the first Duke Kahanamoku Surf Classic in late 1965, Bill Cleary, as he often did, tried to write about Miki in the context of a larger, fictional work. His ruminations showcase the vexing frustrations Miki could have on even the most soulful and poetic of surf culture analysts. Though Cleary's observations remained largely part of his unpublished material, what did leak out over the years was substantial and resilient enough to shape the memes, themes, and root ideas that infiltrated almost every recollection and deconstruction of Miki that followed.

Among the most telling observations:

> *Conversation with Mickey Dora is never dull. His wit is as lightning quick as it is acerbic. But compassion, empathy, sympathy, humility, self-deprecation—these words do not hold a great deal of meaning to his life. They are perhaps even missing in his emotional vocabulary . . .*
>
> *There is more than a little gypsy to him with the dark, feral cast to those eyes of his which are always roving, reflecting a mind that is never still. When he is in one of his moods, conversation is a good deal like having your pocket picked . . . In surfing as in his life, Mickey Dora has made up his own game, plays it by his own rules, harvests his own rewards. Nobody understands him. Even those intelligent enough to relate seldom grasp what he is saying and doing—because the Cat never lets anyone get too close. He is good at what he does, and he does it with grace and style. That's enough for me. People like*

him should be granted special status. Maybe they should be turned into national parks. At the very least they should be left alone.

~

Gidget and the beach party flicks had augured the first phase of surfing's commercial transformation, surf magazines the second—hand in hand with better boards, surf-influenced clothing styles, "surf music." (You couldn't surf in Kansas City, but you could still assume the identity and yearn for what was being sold as a clean and liberating adolescent lifestyle.) Surf movies by surfers was the third phase.

In response to the Hollywood bastardization of surfing, the community began ambitious counterprogramming like *The Endless Summer* (1964), directed by Bruce Brown, with financial seed money and encouragement from a far-sighted Dale Velzy.

In "Waves of Transformation," San Diego State University women's water polo coach Carin Crawford's unpublished master's thesis that found a home on the Internet, Crawford noted that the film "was the first to elevate surfing into the search for the perfect wave. In this film, which purports to be a documentary, surfing takes on transcendental meanings that work against the notion of surfing as a professional career or a summer lark . . . it is a spiritual pilgrimage to find the ultimate experience."

The Endless Summer was also the first film produced by a surfer to reach a wide national audience. "It chronicles the 35,000 mile around-the-world travels of two surfers, Mike Hynson and Robert August, who, on a quest for the perfect wave, become the first modern day people to surf such locations as Ghana, Senegal, and South Africa. (They) become international surfing apostles moving from country to country, beach to beach, using surfing as a language to teach a new awareness of how the ocean connects people throughout the world to a common experience."

"The idea was to create what would be a fantasy for surfers," Bruce Brown has said. "You travel slowly around the world and stay right in the middle of summer for the rest of your life. But, you know, when I first came up with the title and idea, people thought, What? That's stupid. But it worked out. I just loved the ocean and I wanted to make other people appreciate it."

Wrote Crawford: "Operating on a shoestring budget, Brown, who was 28 years old at the time, spent more on producing *The Endless Summer* than all of his first five films together had grossed. In the summer of 1964 the film debuted at the two-thousand-seat Santa

Monica Civic and sold out seven nights in a row. By 1966, Brown sought to distribute the film in regular movie theaters across the county; however, according to Brown, the film distributors he contacted replied, 'Look, there's no Frankie, no bikinis, no bongos on the beach. Let's face it, it's a documentary.' After this rejection Brown got a friend to take *The Endless Summer* to Wichita, Kansas, because, according to Brown, 'it was as far inland as you could get.' The film showed for two weeks and broke the theater's attendance record, making more money than the two other premiere films, *The Great Race* and *My Fair Lady*.

"Brown, working independently, spent all the money he had made so far blowing up the film to 35 mm and renting Kips Bay Theater in Manhattan. *The Endless Summer* ran at Kips for a year and generated significant attention from movie critics who published favorable reviews. These reviews indicate the ways in which non-surfing audiences perceived surfing, and also show how *The Endless Summer* served to help redefine surfing outside the cultural and commercial constraints of Hollywood. Vincent Canby wrote: 'Surfing is a sport which in California has become a way of life, if not actually a religion.' In addition, *Time* pointed out 'Brown . . . demonstrates quite spiritedly that some of the brave souls mistaken for Beachniks are, in fact converts to a difficult, dangerous and dazzling sport.' *The Endless Summer* was the surfing community's first filmic attempt to represent itself during negotiations over the cultural meaning of surfing. The film also proved to be a big financial success."

Endless Summer's 1966 wide re-release spread the word and defined the soul of a surfing generation. The Sandals' score is still instantly recognizable, and the iconic one-sheet poster designed by John van Hamersveld is a collector's item today.

Miki claimed to hate it. He even complained to Bruce Brown about having been portrayed early in the film. However, some suggest that maybe Miki was just pissed that he'd signed his rights away for a reported $1,500, while Brown went on to make millions.

5

I go into contests once or twice a year for the pleasure of shaking up the status quo . . . the more restrictive they can make a contest's (rules), the

*less (the judges) have to think or know about what you're accomplishing
in the water, thus making an easy job easier at our expense. What do
these people care about your subtle split-second maneuvers, years of
perfecting your talents?*

—from "Miki on Malibu," *Surfer*

Contests of a fraternal and convivial sort had long been a part of
surfing, starting in Southern California even before the "modern
era" began, and in 1954 with the Makaha International in Hawaii,
on Oahu's west shore. The West Coast Surfing Championships debuted in 1959 at Huntington Beach, California, and morphed into
the United States Surfing Championships in 1964, when the sport's
popularity demanded a bigger imprimatur. (Since 1973 the contest is
held at a rotating series of American breaks.) And because of its reputation, according to Matt Warshaw, as "the ultimate high-performance
wave" and its position as "Surfing Mecca," Malibu hosted the Malibu
Invitational from 1962 to 1967.

Today it would be tough to find a major break that hasn't hosted
a competition.

Miki disdained not only contests, but contest-sponsoring organizations like the then-new United States Surfing Association. He especially
hated their public relations attempts to clean up the sport's image for
mass consumption, to make it safe for financial investment.

"For a while there was a heavy reform movement going on via the
Association: Let's clean up surfing," recalls Corky Carroll, a three-time
international and five-time U.S. surfing champion, who met Miki in
1961. "The general public was supposed to have this incorrect image
of surfers as Bohemians, hanging out at the beach with drugs and wild
parties. The new idea was, Let's make them think that everyone's a
cub scout, real good guys and athletes. But the first version was the
real color of surfing. I used to go on a lot of TV shows and be asked
questions like, 'Is it really true that most surfers are a bunch of drug-
crazed hippies?' I'd just say, 'Yeah! Sure is! So go ahead; send your
young daughters down here. They'll be safe.'"

In 1989, Miki shared his philosophy with filmmaker Bill Delaney
for *Surfers: The Movie*: "The competitive part of it all is a whole different ballgame. . . . I don't want to think about it because it destroys
the whole purpose of riding waves. I don't like noises, I don't like
crowds, I don't like bullhorns and people giving me orders how to

ride and certain maneuvers. All this is beyond my comprehension of pleasure. . . . But something inspires these guys. [laughs] Whether it's power, fame, fortune, ego—it's probably a combination of them all. But that's their direction, and let them go. . . . Who's the best in the world? Who's the worst in the world? I don't give a damn. If people want to think I'm good, fine. If they don't think I'm any good, I don't give a shit."

"His competitive arena was Malibu, but that was competing for waves, not prestige and trophies and money, which is what I had to do," recalled Nat Young. "So it's very easy for him to say it was all garbage. I had this discussion with him pretty heavily at one point. I said, 'Competition is the only fucking yardstick we've got. It's no good having a bloody expression session, you've got to have a winner. The world needs winners. They need somebody to cross the line first.' He told me that he thought I was wrong."

Even when the contest was sponsored by surfers for surfers, Miki usually didn't participate. In his 1993 autobiography, *Morning Glass*, Mike Doyle wrote, "One of his favorite tricks was to sign up to compete in a surf contest just to get everybody talking—'Is Dora really gonna show?'—then he would never appear. That always got him lots of publicity. Or else he'd show up at the contest with an 11' 6" tandem board and just goof around on it while everybody else was competing, making a mockery of the whole thing."

One small example: Miki signed up for Tom Morey's July 4, 1965, nose-riding contest at California Street in Ventura and paid the $10 entry fee. He never participated. And his check bounced.

When asked by *International Surfing* magazine why he didn't enter contests more often, Miki said, "First of all, it has to be an invitational. Second, I need a little gold to make it worth my while. Next there has to be decent wave conditions. Up to now, California has little or none of these factors, especially waves."

"Only the Duke has the class and the elements needed for success," he said.

~

The Duke Kahanamoku Invitational held from 1965 to 1984 at Sunset Beach on Oahu, Hawaii, was Miki's kind of event. Only the top of the top were invited. The promoters even sent out gilded invitations—now worth megabucks on the nostalgia market. Says Greg Noll, "This was the most prestigious contest of the time period.

There was nothing like it. To just even get a goddamn invitation was a huge deal."

As usual, Miki also obtained side benefits from attending. "He got a free ticket to go to the Islands, and free meals," says Noll. "The painful part of it was that he had to get up in front of everyone and accept the little trophy everyone got."

On the other hand, he also got to show his stuff on the challenging waves of Sunset Beach and impress the locals who thought he was only a small point break surfer, as well as hang with the Duke himself, for Miki a long-cherished memory.

Miki liked Hawaii because another facet of his personality emerged in the face of big waves and locals devoid of hometown Hollywood artifice. He felt safer as a little fish in a big pond. Miki thought highly of Hawaiian surfers, and how the sport was dignified by having been practiced by Hawaiian kings. "He admired how it had been handed down," says Harry Hodge. "He respected the Keaulana family—Buffalo, Rusty, Brian—and many others."

Miki and twenty-three of the world's best surfers showed up at the first "Duke" from December 13–17, 1965. Fifteen-year-old Jeff Hakman, from Hawaii, was the surprise winner. Dora didn't place, and apparently didn't spend much time trying to. However, that didn't stop him from attending the contest in the future, whenever invited—and not primarily for the surfing.

"Miki was my roommate at the fourth Duke contest in 1968," Nat Young recalls. "I walked into my hotel room and he was sitting on the end of the bed. I thought it was bizarre that Miki Dora could be in the same room with me. He wasn't dressed like a surfer. He had a trench coat—in Hawaii not a lot of people wear a big fucking coat—and the facial stubble. I had a great deal of respect for him as a surfer, and because I'd been reading *Surfer* magazine, I figured that whatever he said I'd listen and gobble up.

"That first evening, he asked if I wanted to go out for a nightcap. I said sure, and he took me out to a gay bar. It was pretty bizarre. I was pretty young and coming from Australia was reasonably naïve. I don't know what he took me there for, other than it was an out-on-the-town bit of a turn-on. He asked if I'd ever been out in Waikiki? No, I hadn't. Did I know where Honolulu was? No, I didn't. Okay, well let me show you.

"To be quite honest, I always found him a bit like my surfing big brother. Even with some of the games we got into later in our lives that were fucking bizarre, I had total faith in him."

~

Although he had six stitches in his foot from a skateboard injury, Miki did compete in the 1964 Malibu Invitational and managed to win his heat. Then he decided to blow it all by riding a twelve-foot tandem board in the semifinals. When Miki entered again in 1965, his battle for supremacy with Johnny Fain finally brought to a head the former friends' conflict, and turned it into an indelible day in early surf contest history.

JOHNNY FAIN: Miki forced himself into the contest to show everyone that no one was better than he was. We both ended up in the finals, with Andy Newman, Dewey Weber, Butch Linden, and Buzz Sutphin. To win a heat you had to catch a certain amount of waves in thirty minutes and do as much on them as you could. What made this contest so different is there were no rules, no holds barred. It was a gladiator sport.

I was coming down a wave as Dewey paddled out. He knew it was the wave of the day and I could win this hands down. He got off his board and kicked it into my board. Unbelievable. My fin hit it and catapulted me into a somersault. The crowd went nuts. I had fifteen minutes left on the clock. I ran in on the rocks to get my board. I couldn't even feel my feet they're so bloody.

Now I was forced to catch waves with Miki on them. I didn't care what happened. Miki jammed his board underneath mine. So I took off in front of him. We'd get halfway through a wave and I'd do a spinner in front of him. He would time his board on the kickout and just barely hit my head; not hard, but just enough to knock me off and take me out. That was his way of getting back at me for ever having the audacity to think that I could even compare to him.

This is the contest with the famous picture of him behind me and he's got his hand right on me, holding me 'til the last moment, because he knows I'm going to go over backward and hit my head. He held me there for a long time. He could have pushed me off anytime, but he waited until the wave got so frigging critical that it was an elevator dropping out from under me. Later, I threw rocks at him. That's also on film. I knew I couldn't fight him, but I tried to get rid of the rage. A lot of people were afraid of Miki, but I wasn't—maybe because I didn't know any better.

Then, as Fain later told Bill Cleary for his *Surfer* story "The Day War Came to Malibu," they both rode the "Truth Wave."

JOHNNY FAIN: It was close to six feet. Miki and I took off. I started climbing and dropping immediately. Miki was behind and I didn't know what he'd try to do, but he decided to maneuver like me. But of course he couldn't, and when he followed me he caught an edge and fell off, and I had the whole wave to myself all the way to the beach. Afterward, everybody thought I'd won it hands down. They announced sixth, fifth, fourth . . . and then said Miki for third. You could see a maniacal look on his face. Then me second. Sutphin, who was only seventeen, who had stayed out of everyone's way, was first. I was half a point short of winning. Four judges had me first and the fifth judge had me fifth. If Kemp Aaberg, who had been judging, had not gotten sick, I'd have won. Miki was disappointed. I was crushed. And yet, I was also halfway off the ground on a magic carpet.

I had beaten Miki.

When the trophies were awarded, Miki threw his into a trash can. A little kid got the trophy and gave it back to Miki. Miki said, "You keep it," and walked away.

TOM MOREY: I had helped judge the contest. Dora didn't lose because he was less stylish; nor did he have poor wave judgment on that day. It was just how the cards fell. Even so, he did make one major mistake. Upon receiving his third-place trophy he heaved it up the beach in disgust, and arrogance. But it wasn't tossing the trophy that was the mistake. I think it was despair at having entered the stupid contest in the first place. After all, who's to judge the master, for Neptune's sake?!

GREG NOLL: In 1967, Dora entered the Malibu contest again. I think he could have won the thing. But when it finally came time to get serious on the wave that made the difference, he streaked across the inside shore break, dropped his shorts, and did a BA for the judges. As it happened, the contest was broadcast on TV.

GLENN HENING: It was a Saturday morning heat. The day was slightly overcast. The surf was really good—better than in 1965 when he lost to Sutphin and Fain. He surfed with Weber and Mike Ballard. Only two guys would advance out of the heat, and both Weber and Ballard had been shredding. Miki didn't get enough waves and he knew it. He was a little out of position. He finally got a good wave toward the end of the heat, did a bottom turn, and bent over to bring his board around. When he bent over, his trunks split. These were the green nylon trunks with the orange band, and he'd worn them a lot at State Beach.

In other words, this whole thing that been written about in the surf magazines and repeated over and over about him mooning the judges at the Malibu contest—that didn't happen. His trunks were split, and with only a few minutes left in the heat, he realized he couldn't advance. So he got out of the water, wrapped his jersey around his waist, went straight to his car, and left.

CHAPTER **SEVEN**

Da Cat

1

Greg Noll and Miki did love each other. They were both bigger-than-life figures. The fact that the two of them ended up in the surfboard business together was kind of a delicious irony in that they were both the biggest RF'ers on the face of the earth. They were constantly locked in a battle and just trying not to roll over the cliff in each other's clutches.
—Steve Pezman

Once, Miki Dora was just Miki, or Mickey, or Dora, or Chapin, or Meatball, or the Black Knight, or Mr. Malibu, or the Fiasco Kid, or the Malibu Gypsy, or simply, "that fuckin' asshole." Any number of Teflon nicknames—not to mention shadowy aliases—had come and gone, until one day he was simply "Da Cat."

No one really knows who named him. Bill Cleary certainly, in an early iteration. Now, many claim it, but does it matter? The feline metaphor worked—and not only because it perfectly described his graceful, sure-footed surfing style. It also drew energy from his cunning lifestyle. Despite scams and cons and an unpredictable personality, Miki had always been able to land squarely on his feet no matter what predicament his curiosity, pomposity, animosity, or thrill-a-minute urges got him into.

Miki was the charming stray: part insouciant Top Cat; part covetous Tom (usually of eating his "pal" Jerry); part mysterious, monosyllabic Midnight (from Andy Devine's *Buster Brown Show*); maybe even a little randy Fritz the Cat—not that he'd let on.

Less considered, less stylish and romantic, was another part of Miki's cat persona: the feral recluse, a virtual alley cat living under a Dumpster behind a restaurant, waiting to dart in and snatch the night's leftovers. Sometimes, the cat might slink out from under the bin and, if you held a tasty morsel in your fingers, approach—but remain ever ready to sink his claws or teeth into the outstretched hand, or run for cover at a suspicious glance or unexpected movement. However, if one had somehow earned this transient's trust, he might now and then let himself luxuriate in a scratch behind the ears and even purr a bit. Everyone needs a little love. But don't try to pick him up and hold him close. Don't ask for more than he can give. Take his gifts and be satisfied. Da Cat had been burned before.

"Maybe there's something to that," says Greg Noll. "'Da Cat' is the perfect label because a cat's independent. You can scratch his head but he might bite your ass or claw you. You can throw him up in the air or drop him off a ten-story building and he'll come out on his feet. I don't think there's a better description."

In the mid-'60s, Miki's growing popularity and mystique seemed the perfect opportunity for him to create a surfboard at a time when signature models had become the "in" thing. His only problem was how to go commercial without appearing to deny and deflate his anti-establishment, antisellout mythos. Once again, Dora needed to have it both ways: to sell his board and have it, too.

First he needed the board.

GREG NOLL: We were in the water, surfing at Manhattan Pier. Miki said, "You know, I've got this idea for a new board, blah, blah, blah." There was no "Will you make a board?" Miki was never that direct, always elusive. But I could see where he was going. That was the time of signature models and manufacturers having their riders. I didn't have anybody. I did stuff based on my trips to the Islands in the winter and I was kind of coasting off the exposure from riding big waves. Of course, I did it because I loved it, but if I could get any promotional value that would help my surfboards sell, all the better.

Over two or three conversations, Miki started making obvious overtures. He came into the shop and explained pretty much in detail what he wanted:

basically a Malibu-style board designed for his kind of California wave. A nice trim board for a long wall.

Miki had for years traveled up and down the California coast having boards made. There is hardly a major manufacturer that at one time or another hasn't made Miki a free board or two or three—or as many as he could squeeze out of them—before he moved on to pork the next guy. Velzy, Jacobs, Hobie, Weber, Sweet, Gordon & Smith, Yater. The list is pretty damn long. He'd get the board for free, sell it, and move on. That's one way he got by and managed to keep surfing. Anyway, he said he'd like to consider doing a Miki Dora model by Greg Noll board. We'd known each other since we were kids and had a mutual respect, I think.

The first thing I told him was, "You're not gonna fuck me out of a board, Dora. If you want to do this and you want to do it right, there's gonna be an agreement." Much to my surprise he said, "Fine, okay. Let's do it." But it was never quite that simple with Dora.

It was absolutely murder coming to the deal. He would go on and on. Paranoia would dribble out his ears about everything, particularly about how I was going to screw him by making more labels than I should and he wouldn't get his royalties. I was pretty hot-tempered when I was young and I didn't mind stepping up to the plate. I'd say, "I'm gonna take you outside and kick your goddamn ass, Miki." He'd just drive you nuts. Then he'd get paranoid and run away from me and not come back for a couple days.

Laura, who worked for me then and is now my wife, would follow Miki into the outer office. She'd pat him on the back, talk to him, and calm him down. I'd calm down and we'd get back together. It didn't happen every time, but it did on more than one occasion. Seems funny now.

After a week of screaming, yelling, and fist waving, we ended up with an agreement. It was one that we both looked at carefully, signed, and stuck to for over thirty years of what was at heart a very respectful relationship. I think Miki got $25 per board—maybe more. We started out selling them in 1966 for $175 each. Another thing: once Miki signed the deal, he fulfilled it. There was never any after-the-fact bullshit.

After the agreement, we started from scratch. I took some of my old board templates, and we shifted those around and came up with an outline template. After screwing so many different board makers, and riding virtually every kind of board on the coast, he'd taken the good ideas, fed them into the computer in his brain. We went through about five different designs in the process.

To Miki, a surfboard was like an extension of his body that allowed him to have his wonderful relationship with the wave. You can talk to most surfers and they can tell you every measurement of their first surfboard. It was so long, so thick; it was so wide and had a certain type of fin; it rode a certain way. Ask the same guy what his first chick was like, he can't tell you.

Our first board didn't have a scoop deck—which is where the board is thinner or scooped out near the nose to make it lighter. I remember clear as a bell Miki looking at me and saying, "This board is not different enough. I want a rocket ship. Something completely spacey looking. What can we do about getting a thinner nose?"

I told him that I didn't want to do it. I didn't want a bunch of boards breaking in half because they were too thin-nosed. Scoop noses were nothing new; Bob Simmons made scooped-nose boards in 1948. Joe Quigg made some I rode when I was twelve years old. I've seen ancient Hawaiian boards that had scooped-out decks in one form or another. Yater did a step deck. I think Morey did something, and there were two or three others out there. But that's what Miki wanted, so I came up with a completely new design, totally different from anything done before. We went about an inch and a half in the rail, scooped about 30 to 40 percent of the nose, came back to the deck and put a V in it. (If you're standing on the board, the point of the V is centered and faces toward the nose.) I tried to put as many compound curves into the fiberglass as I could, to strengthen it. We went through several boards, making adjustments here and there. Flatter. Rounder. Wider. It took about a week or so to get to the final version.

Once we had the board, we had to name it, and sell it. Dick Graham and Miki and I sat in my office and said, "What do we call this?" Dora criticized every idea. Finally we focused on a cat, because people referred to him as a sly cat and a cat burglar, and that he had more lives than a cat when it came to ripping off people and not getting put in jail. They didn't refer to him as "The Cat," just as catlike.

I said, "How about 'The Cat?'" The room stopped. Everybody else liked it. Miki folded his arms and said, "The Cat. I can see it now. You can take the label off a Puss 'n Boots cat food can and we can use that."

He had to grumble about everything, but he liked it. I could tell because he didn't yap all that violently about it.

From there, because of my Hawaiian connection, I thought about how we could make it better. "Da" is "The" in Hawaiian. I was known as Da Bull, so we called it "Da Cat" and it stuck. We also used a cat paw print on the label, under our signatures.

When we were done, you could not find another board on the coast that looked or surfed like ours. The Da Cat board continued to evolve for the next four years: a pintail, stabilizing channels, removable fin, and many other subtle changes in rocker, rail thickness, and so on. Like Miki, Da Cat was an ever-changing and evolving creature.

I never knew Dora's reasons for coming to me. Maybe it was that I was more able to commit to production. Maybe it was because we were kids at San Onofre. Maybe it was because I saved his ass when I shoved him through the impact zone on that big wave at Waimea during *Ride the Wild Surf*. Maybe it's because I'd never screwed him over; I mean, I'd steal his trunks, I'd put him down, and I'd argue with him, but I never porked him big-time. Maybe all these things came together. The guy was a purist. He was really serious about the connection between himself and our board. I told Pezman once that for Miki to do a signature model with me must have felt like he was cutting off a finger or a hand. But it was his call. I didn't come to him. He came to me and said, "You want to make a board?"

Ultimately, the board was successful for a number of reasons. One, it was unique. Two, Miki could ride the shit out of the board, and he endorsed it in print. Three, we did an advertising campaign that Miki was involved in 100 percent. Those ads are funny, man. The best Miki Dora ever did was when you gave him a paragraph or two to summarize the situation. Those ads said more about Miki and about his philosophy than anything he's ever done. It allowed him, in his own particular way, to express himself to the surf community about what he was all about. It was a peek into his brain, and people have never gotten tired of trying to get a glimpse of what was inside his head.

2

Da Cat model offered a belief in an escape from the ordinary.
            —Mark Fragale, "Out of the Bag: The Story of Miki Dora's
                    Da Cat Model," *Longboard Magazine*, April 2003

From 1966 through 1969, Miki and Noll rolled out a print advertising campaign considered to be the most clever and memorable in surfboard advertising history.

The first ad appeared in the April/May 1966 issue of *International Surfing* magazine, whose editor, Dick Graham, had worked with Dora and Noll and Duke Boyd in formulating the campaign. A second ran in *ISM* the following month, along with a Miki interview laid out with three pictures like the classic *Playboy* interview.

Noll says the ads cost "four grand a page." The first featured Noll, in jacket and tie, standing in half-shadow against a black background, at the tail end of a board draped in silk, much like a veiled new model car. Noll's pet ocelot, Sylvester, lay on the board. The headline: "The CAT is King."

The ad revealed nothing. The text was similarly ambiguous. "Noll overlooks what represents a first, a completely new evolution in the surfing world. Under gold silk cloth lies a surfboard designed, tested, and proven by a rider whom many big name and influential surfers refer to as the best all-around surfer in the world . . . the #1 Cat."

Hipster lingo anyone? Testimonials from an assortment of respected surfers followed, including this comment from Phil Edwards: "I surfed with him a whole summer, which changed my outlook on surfing; he was so progressive everyone thought he was nuts—except me."

The first ad in *Surfer* magazine was a double-page spread all in red. The left-hand page featured the words "The Cat" and two paw prints. The right-hand page continued with "is coming" and a trail of prints. The body copy mimicked the first ad, but without testimonials. Again, no mention of Miki.

The next *Surfer* ad spilled the beans. Laid out again on a red background, the headline blares: "Da Cat is here." There are five pictures, two of Miki surfing solo and going, uncharacteristically, left. Another shows him pushing Johnny Fain off a wave in the 1965 Malibu contest. A fourth has Miki in sports coat, slacks, and Wayfarers—with an unnamed friend—posing next to an upright board. The fifth shows Miki in a sweater, leaning over a board on the shaping stand, elbows on the deck, one hand pressed to his forehead in concentration, possibly wondering if he'd really get his royalty money, or figuring out how to RF Noll as soon as possible.

These ads were the first salvo in a singular campaign in which Miki fired at multiple targets, at will. His ad copy combined imaginatively abrasive put-downs, outlandish opinion, supreme hauteur about his own skills, antiestablishment agitprop, and pungent social observation—all of which played neatly into the mid-'60s times that were a-changing.

If Miki played the outspoken iconoclast in his magazine interviews—at that point he'd appeared in *Surf Guide, Surfer, ISM,* and so on—the ad copy, totally under his control, fleshed out further depths of his personality. Not only did he get to play dress-up and pose with iconic symbols—from angels and crucifixes in a graveyard, the German Blue Max flying medal, his trophy from the Duke Kahanamoku Invitational (photographed spilling out of a trash can on the beach)—his unabridged and unfiltered voice spoke directly to the audience on topics of his own choosing.

Miki's genius was in his ability to frame his edgy criticisms and radical behavior as that of a truth teller's. In one ad for the new 1967 model, he wrote, "Hoodwinking the public is generally against my principles, naturally. That goes double when my name appears on a product." Anyone savvy enough to read between the lines knew that while the second sentence was true, the first was not, and the whole was delightful.

Even those who didn't want to buy Dora's board eagerly awaited each new installment of his provocative marketing serial. Says Greg Noll: "(Board builder and friend) Bing Copeland once told me, "Before I'd even look at my own ad I'd go to your ad and see what Dora was up to, and hope to shit I wasn't on the chopping block."

In some ads he raged against the surf machine; in others he spat back at naysayers; in yet others he inflamed controversy or seemed to allow fan-dancer glimpses into his twisted psychology.

In all, he embellished the "Dora" persona without apology, and one never knew where the line between fact and fantasy lay.

GREG NOLL: To even get the ads published was a whole knock-down, drag-out deal with the magazines. They wanted him to lighten up, play the game. Dora was forever pissed off because they tried to censor him. I was in the middle, on Dora's side basically, but just trying to get the damn things to run. I had huge contention with *Surfer*—though it wasn't Severson as much as his guys. They'd complain that material was too graphic or not socially acceptable. I'd tell Miki, "We've got to do something about this to get it printed." At times we were damn near on the floor wrestling over words. Hot arguments. No magazine would run "fuck" and certain other language. I'd have to say, "Miki, it's a great ad, man, but we've got to get it published. If you don't get it published, you and I can sit here and agree it's a great ad, but magazines aren't going to take it."

"Oh, those assholes, they're trying to destroy me. They're ruining my

reputation by making me do this marshmallow bullshit. They're trying to censor me! They're trying to keep me in a box!"

I could do what I wanted to do with the ads, but I also realized that if I pissed off Miki bad enough, he'd walk away—and I couldn't do the ads like he
could. When I tried, it came out bland, like a GMC ad. Miki, on the other hand,
wrote: "I don't want some acne adolescent in Pratt Falls, Iowa, using Da Cat
as a car ornament or some show-biz creep in the Malibu Colony using Da Cat
as a coffee table. Da Cat is too pure and sensitive for the clumsy touch of the
occasional pseudo-surfer."

When an ad came out, I'd have surfers say, "Jesus Christ, man, can you
tone Dora down? He's on my ass something fierce." I think Fain said that. But
those of the era knew that the worst thing you could do if you were getting
razzed or put down was to make an issue of it. Your sensitivity would come
right back and bite you in the ass.

Appearing in the July 1967 issue of *Surfer*, "Da Cat's Theory of
Evolution" is acknowledged as perhaps the greatest surfboard ad of
all time—certainly the most memorable. Not only did it "blatantly
mock well known figures in surfing," according to surf historian and
collector Mark Fragale, but it drew on artwork already iconic in every
American high school science textbook: the ascent of man from earliest hominid to *Homo sapiens*.

Perhaps unknown to Noll, Dora often had help with his concepts
and prose before bringing them in. Darryl Stolper supplied some words
and ideas. A teenaged Pat Darrin, whose dad knew Miki's dad from the
Westside Tennis club in the '30s and '40s, took some photos.

Dora and Stolper brainstormed the evolution ad, and Stolper wrote
an early draft in longhand on a piece of notebook paper that was recently discovered in a Dora collector's possession.

DARRYL STOLPER: I came up with "Da Cat's Theory of Evolution." I was an
anthropology major. Time/Life's book on evolution had just come out. I suggested equating each development stage with a different well-known surfer.
I lifted the ape-to-man pictures directly out of the book. The surfers we used
changed a little. Originally, one was Mike Doyle. We substituted Bob Cooper
for Doyle. That was Homo Cooperi. The one he really wanted to nail of course
was Johnny Fain.

da CATS' Theory of Evolution

RETARDESS KOOKUS

The earliest stage, unworthy of discussion.

PIGMIO PHAINAS

Characterized by small structure and jerky, uncoordinated movements, little ability.

MALIBUIS MASOCHSCUS

Recognized by determined expression on face, but no ability. This short structured musclehead resorts to throwing of objects and threats abortive attempts to make waves.

VALLEI SAN FERNANDO

This small-brained inland migrant is only mentioned because of the peculiar habits they have of traveling in packs and futile attempts to look skilled on waves over one foot. It is hoped that they will soon become extinct.

HOMO COOPERI

The first stage with any skill. This form was unable to move in a limited way . . . however, this form was unable to compete with the earlier forms and became extinct.

EXCLUSIVE GREG NOLL SURFBOARDS DEALER FRANCHISES AVAILABLE. WRITE FOR INFORMATION.

I have been asked by several leading Universities to clarify the various stages of evolution in the history of surfing. Much time and research has gone into these studies and the final results. *Mickey Dora*

da CAT

MAFIAS DANA POINTIS

This form will survive only as long as its food supply lasts. This being the earlier stage of evolution with their dull wit and idle worship. This form is easily recognized by its pleasant smile and gaudy outfits. It is quick to sell out to any side.

DECENTUS INDIVIDUALIST

Easily recognized once it is spotted. Although this is a very rare form it is serious and intelligent in its action. He possesses skill and cunning, and his type probably led to the final stage.

HOMOSAPENS MICKEY DORA

The peak of perfection has all the qualities of the latter stage plus more advanced knowledge and ability. Uses only one model . . . da Cat . . . a very rare form, the only one known.

"Da Cat's Theory of Evolution" ad, *Surfer*, July 1967. Courtesy of the Noll Family Collection.

At one point Dora even had an artist draw apes that actually looked like the parodied surfers, but they were not used, cutting too close to the bone. This artwork, by Ivan Hosoi, was recently discovered in a stash of Miki's effects.

DARRYL STOLPER: Then I heard nothing else about the ad. I asked Miki what had happened. He said that either *Surfer* magazine or Greg wouldn't approve because they thought it was too insulting. I didn't think any more about it. Then one day Robbie Dick brought in the issue and showed me the ad. "Have you seen Dora's ad with the monkey people in it?" My ad. I don't have the temperament to get pissed off, but I was disappointed. When I confronted him, he told me they changed their mind at the last minute and accepted it. At that point I was like, I've been friends with this guy for seven or eight years and he lies to me? Of course, I continued to work with him on stuff. I enjoyed Miki's creative mind. I never got paid, but it was fun.

JOHNNY FAIN: Pygmio Phainas. The most outrageous thing. Character assassination. When that ad came out, I knew it was all-out warfare. He tried to get me off that beach and he thought he couldn't do it any other way except to humiliate me. Here I am, almost as good as he is, if not as good, and he decides to hurt my feelings. It was like he'd said, "Enough is enough. I gave you a certain amount of time, and now your time's up." He withdrew his affection from me entirely. It broke my heart and hurt me very badly. . . . Just give me a moment. I'm sorry; that hits a nerve.

He made me the laughingstock of the beach. No matter how good I was, Miki upped me. This was his way of saying, "I'm still better than you." He was ten years older, he was smarter, he'd been around longer. For Greg Noll to go along with this ad . . .

Besides defamation of character, he tried to demoralize me. He did a good job. I was young. My mother said, "Sue." I said, "Forget it." She was outraged. "The nerve of him doing this." If I'd sued, I could have taken Noll and Dora out badly; but I cared so much about surfing, I didn't want the politics or the money.

My friends tried to rally around me—but in truth they thought it was hilarious, and only Miki could have thought of it. I thought it was too smart even for him. I hope somebody else thought of that. I'd feel better. That would help me, if I knew that this idea didn't just come to Miki overnight.

When he came to the beach the next day, lots of people had the magazine and wanted to see what we would do. All I could think of to say was, "Is that your best idea?" He laughed and said, "It's good enough."

From then on, whenever we both went in the water at the same time, there were bets about who was going to come in alive.

Soon after, I entered the Hermosa Beach Surf Contest. I wanted Jacobs to do a Fain model but he put all his money on Mike Purpus. But I went there—a point break rider, into a beach break—and beat David Nuuhiwa, Corky Carroll, Mike Purpus, and the rest. I beat them all and won the whole contest.

The next day I went to Greg Noll's shop. I told him I was thinking of manufacturing a board in my name. He goes, "Well, I already got three with Da Cat. I don't know if I'm gonna do any more signature model boards." I said, "Yeah, you probably aren't, but I just won the Hermosa Open yesterday." "Okay, kid," he said. "You're on." We sold a lot of boards together.

That was my way of getting back at Miki for the Pygmio Phainas ad. That's the only reason I did it. I could have gone to another manufacturer, but I didn't, and it probably really made him mad.

GREG NOLL: Johnny was a great surfer, but Miki never had a nice thing to say about poor Johnny. When Miki's model was over, Johnny came in to me and said, "Can you make a Johnny Fain model board?" And I did. Then he'd always ask, "Are my numbers getting close to Dora's yet?"

All he could think of was coming close to Dora.

CHAPTER **EIGHT**

The Point of No Return

1

Meanwhile, all Miki could think about was getting away from it all.

[Letter to Greg Meisenholder]
*I finally stumbled on one of the last true South Pacific
paradises. This island is a tiny circle of life in a big ocean. I can only
tell you at this time it's about 2000 miles north of New Zealand, quite
near Micronesia, a true coral atoll about fifteen miles in diameter.
The water is incredibly clear and one can see 200 feet underwater in
any direction, compared with the average 15 feet in tropical waters.
The side of the atoll shelves steeply away and disappears into a deep
blue haze. . . .*

*It has abundant coconut trees and fish trapped in the shallow coral
reef. Yet it is the precious coconut which sustains life. Their entire
culture is based on coconuts. Strange, but on the island every coconut
tree is named by somebody. The trees are never cut down. They are far
too valuable and are highly respected. . . .*

*Half of the 500 people living on the island are young. The old
custom of infanticide was stopped by the missionaries at the turn of the
century. When the Christian religion was introduced the missionaries
also tried to persuade the young girls not to go topless. It didn't have
any effect on the girls who are still bare-chested. . . .*

GREG MEISENHOLDER: Miki believed Armageddon was at hand in the Western world. He wanted to find someplace safe—which to me was as much of an inner place, as well as a physical place—where he could get away from the demons about to descend. He never said where this dark view came from. Maybe he'd invented it because he loved the search or because it somehow justified his behavior. But to me, this quest for the Holy Grail, a place where he could seek inner salvation, was simply metaphoric.

Part of Miki's free-floating paranoia stemmed from his being a conspiracy theorist—or is it the other way around? A particular obsession was the assassination of President John F. Kennedy. When interviewed by *Surfer* magazine publisher John Severson, for his film *Pacific Vibrations*, Dora said, "I'm really modest, but I was one of the first persons to solve the JFK assassination in 1964."

What was the solution?
DORA: I solved the case, that's all I'm saying.
What was the solution, your solution?
DORA: Well, that's to be debated. We could spend all afternoon charting it out, certain international banking circles, the Federal Reserve system, the World Bank, and these things.

DARRYL STOLPER: I was with Miki the day that JFK was assassinated. We met at State Beach. There were no waves. Miki said he was going to the E. F. Hutton office on Fifth and Wilshire and "watch the market crash." Afterward, he was obsessed with the assassination. He was sure of a conspiracy. He later told *Surfer* that on November 22, 1963, a "curse" had fallen on the world.
JOHN MILIUS: I spent hours and hours talking to him about who killed President Kennedy. He was the most astute and learned conspiracy theorist I knew until I met Oliver Stone. And Miki was a better conspiracy theorist, because Stone just threw everything in. If you see *JFK,* that mirrors Miki's belief. He thought Jim Garrison knew the answers. Miki had every newspaper article about the investigation.
ROBBIE DICK: Miki actually brought clippings about Garrison, and some artwork, into the surf shop where I worked and said, "Hey, do you think you guys could put some of this stuff on my board? We glassed it on and he rode it pretty well.

DARRYL STOLPER: Miki was also a big Mort Sahl fan. We'd be late for parties sometimes so he could stay home and watch Sahl obsess about JFK.

BOB COOPER: Sahl used to go to the Daisy in Beverly Hills. George Samama told me how Miki got into his ear and convinced him he had to talk to Sahl. He begged and pleaded to be let into Daisy when Sahl was there. Samama, being the good buddy to Miki that he was, went to Mort and asked a favor. "Look, I have this friend who has this incredible need to speak to you about some things he feels are very important." Mort said, "Oh sure, George, no problem. Okay, yeah. A favor to you, George."

This was totally against the Daisy rules and George put his job on the line. He let Miki in through the back door and introduced him to Sahl who sat at a corner table. Miki began to babble about an impending world cataclysm. He said Mort could stop it and that Mort needed his help. But he was so bombed—I don't know what he was on—he was almost inarticulate. Meanwhile, George stood off to the side thinking, Oh no, I have totally blown this.

Finally, Mort got up, walked over to George, and said, "Get rid of this guy."

That was it. Miki had totally imploded. George immediately told him to get out and shot him through the back door. George knew that if Sahl ever complained, he'd lose his job. He was totally embarrassed.

PETER BARNETT: Miki saw conspiracies everywhere. He believed the World Court would morph into a One World government. He said the media was training us into accepting the One World paradigm through the United Nations. I could get more out of Miki on that kind of stuff than he ever would reveal about a scam. The former was cocktail conversation; the latter a lecture. I majored in history so I'd challenge him, but he'd have more answers than I had questions. He'd go, "Don't you see . . . ?" and try to reason with you. He'd never get worked up, never get mad. It was just: "Don't you see? That's what they've convinced you to believe. The books are all printed by them. They're controlling your thoughts. You're only getting the one side so of course that's all you think, man. That's the fallacy of the whole system. If you get beyond that, you'll see that this is what's happening."

My argument was always, "You're influenced by the same things I am. You went to the same schools I did and had the same kind of education I did. Why didn't it affect you?"

"Because I'm Miki," basically.

JOHNNY FAIN: He had a vision: Put all your money in gold; the economy will be in turmoil because the Mexicans and, sorry to use the word he did, niggers, are going to become so abundant they'll drain our economy. He goes: "They're gonna come over here; the borders will be overrun. I'm telling you right now, man, it's all for yourself. Protect yourself because nobody else will." He also said, "The world will become unsafe. It'll be a fascist regime. Everybody will be untrustworthy." Of course, he didn't trust anybody—maybe not even himself.

PEACHES: Yet when it came to doing something good politically in the world, he was a coward. He was a complainer who expected others to do what he wouldn't.

MARTIN SUGARMAN: His worldview was not coherent. It wasn't systematic or well thought out. It was kind of bits and pieces, a mixture of fascism and liberalism and communism and fundamentalism, all smashed together. But he had the gift of gab, a silver tongue. He was very witty and funny, so people listened and believed. But if you put him in an academic setting at Harvard or Yale or UCLA, I don't think he'd do very well. Remember, his following was high school kids on the beach, and this is during the '50s and '60s, before critical thinking was introduced.

GREG NOLL: I thought he was out to lunch. I said, "Dora, you're full of bullshit, man. You're seeing spiders where there's butterflies."

At the same time as Miki saw conspiracies everywhere, he occasionally took mind-bending psychotropic drugs. C. R. Stecyk III wrote that "Miki knew about acid from the good doctors at the UCLA Neuropsychiatric Institute who liked to dose surfers to test their hand-eye coordination and balance while in altered states." Although he never actually confirms that Miki took acid, Stecyk—like Miki, a master of innuendo and suggesting linkages where they may or may not exist—also reports that "Dr. Timothy Leary had Miki on stage as a performer during his Freak Out at the Santa Monica Civic Auditorium," where Leary appeared for four days in mid-January 1967, to raise money to keep his League for Spiritual Discovery headquartered in Millbrook, New York, afloat. Was Miki's drug experimentation real or only apparently real?

The idea of Miki taking any mind-altering or expanding drugs seems on the surface counterintuitive. He was relentlessly committed to his health, a lifelong gobbler of vitamins, supplements, and organic foods—not that he minded a great steak. He even had a touch of hypochondria. Moreover, it must seem odd that this charmingly remote character with a paranoid streak was willing to experience the loss of any control.

But one has to look no deeper than the intersection of man, board, and wave, to realize that control is at best temporary and mostly an illusion. Stiffness on the high wire almost guarantees a fall. Drugs demanded new reactive skills, and Miki was a relentless explorer who consistently lurked on the fringes of the zeitgeist. He realized that the rhythm and balance of life is unceasing and dwells in the uncertain quantum regions where the difference between mastery and helplessness is but a fine point on the razor's edge. Traveling through the doors of perception was part of the ride because to Miki, life was actually less about being in control than it was about being awake; he cherished the feeling of being supremely alive that full consciousness offered. If the whole point of life is the thrill of negotiating one's survival between inevitable uncertainty and mastery of the game, Miki wanted to feel it fully. Or something like that. Plus, it could be fun. Maybe.

DOUGLAS CAVANAUGH: John Peck told me he had given Miki some LSD and then gone off with two other people to sit on a hilltop looking at the moon. Miki had wanted to stay behind. When they came back, he was just little Miki Chapin scared in the corner, with the boogeyman coming after him.

MIKE HYNSON: Miki knew I took LSD, and he was really interested in it. He told me someone had given him some and he got into a real bad trip with devils and mayhem. I also think he said he had gone to a Hollywood party and someone had dosed him. That happened a lot. It was rude. Miki told me he understood what it was all about but he'd never gotten the true experience.

I told him, "I'll help you out anytime." It took him a while. When he finally said, "I want to go," that was really something. I wasn't secure enough to go by myself with him, so I had my team with me. The people I took LSD with considered it a sacrament. We planned for it and paired for it. That kept me straight. He got the best experience from the best I know. We were down in Mexico. We got in the ocean. We surfed a little bit. It wasn't big, but it was beautiful and clear. Dolphins came up to us. Miki was as godly as he could be. His whole presence glowed. He went off smiling.

RICK "SPIDER" JOSEPHSON: In those days people took a lot of psychedelics. I remember Miki saying that after he took something and caught a wave, a medicine man, sitting on the beach, would inhabit his body. He also said he could surf way better than he ever imagined. Most of us had surfed on acid. I surfed Pipeline that way. In fact, I believe the whole shortboard evolution happened to a large extent because of acid. Eventually, most of the smart ones quit the drugs and pursued yoga and meditation. Some didn't. Some are dead now from drug-related incidents. Others still walk the beach.

At the time, I was the spiritual guru, if you will, of the beach crowd. I was like the stoner on peyote half the time, but somehow I always kept it together in my head. Later I became a Buddhist monk, fully ordained, for ten years. Then I went to Nepal for an additional ten and studied Buddhism.

One morning I asked Miki if he wanted to drive up to Rincon. He said okay, and we spent the day together, and for the first time I talked to Miki when he wasn't around other people. To my surprise, he opened up. He had a lot of questions about life in general, and the mind, specifically: mind games and how real they are. He had questions about identity. He wanted to know how people are related to each other, what the hell we were doing on the planet in this drama we call life. Very fundamental questions. I was surprised by how deeply these questions concerned him.

Miki said his questions all arose out of an experience he'd recently had with a medicine man, some kind of yogi. The meeting had apparently shaken his reality.

I wasn't surprised that some mystic could get into his mind stream and manipulate it. But it had left him wondering how it could have happened; how was it possible that someone could get into *his* head like that? He was supposed to be the in-control guy.

I told him about meditation. "If you want to find out, you have to do the work." He asked how to meditate. "How do you practice? How do you find a teacher?" But I sensed that he wasn't willing to do the work. He just wanted to find a path that agreed with him. That's not how it works. The first thing a teacher tells you to do is something you don't want to do. Miki didn't want to hear any of that. He wanted a magic pill that would get him over all this insecurity. He was searching for some form of happiness.

Women didn't seem to provide the answer, either.

"At parties, he never bragged to women about being a surf star," says his lawyer friend Paul Fegen, who used to throw wild soirees in the Hollywood Hills and let girls in for free. "I'd say, 'You like that girl, talk to her.' He'd say no. Though he was physically agile, he was socially awkward. Ofttimes he grunted rather than communicated. I'd bring girls over and he'd say, 'Paul, don't say that. Stop that.' He'd pretend that he didn't want to meet them. He was embarrassed to be rejected—though I never saw him rejected. All I could say was, 'Carol, here's Miki,' and walk away. Or, 'This is my friend Miki. What are you girls doing tonight?' He liked that. He also liked blondes."

Miki's women tended to have a similar look: lithe, blond, winsome, eyes that held a promise of adventure, maybe danger. His darker-haired companions were more like he perhaps wished his mother had been: independent, stable, cultured.

While most of Miki's girlfriends say he could experience and enjoy emotional intimacy, they generally agree he couldn't sustain it. When emotions kicked in they were just too dangerous, unpredictable, and distracting. Though he could be romantic, most women were eventually too traditional for him, and wanted too much. Miki could easily juggle intellectual points of view, but he couldn't find an inner emotional consistency.

Still, with rare exception, like Peaches, whom he met when she was seventeen and dated for three years—she calls Miki "arrogant. He was unkind. Dismissive. He would put down people, tease them, fault-find them. Miki was far from being a considerate and evolved person. He wasn't the kind of guy to call you 'baby.' He was not into romance. His sexuality, on an intimate basis, I can tell you straight out . . . he was beyond having a little trouble; he was shut down. He didn't have any sexual energy. He had no sex vibe at all. None. Zero. None"—nearly every woman in Miki's life came away feeling that they knew him, as one paramour claimed, "Better than anyone else on Earth."

More than one claim to have been the love of his life, and themselves his. "At one point he gave me a gold wedding band and said, 'You will understand the significance of this ring someday,'" says Peggy Barr, who thought Miki "a prince" when she first laid eyes on him. "I realized then and there that Miki considered us married from that time on. So if what Peaches says is true, then I'm a stone. Sex is a very private matter, so I'll just say that Miki was the best lover a woman could have. Apparently Peaches, whom he mentioned to me once or twice, just didn't do it for him."

This much is clear: When Miki decided to open up, he did so intensely. And he could back off and shut down just as intensely. In between he often worked hard to create for himself and each lover their own private world—even when he saw more than one woman at a time. Many relationships, particularly those that endured after the physical part ended, were conducted from afar through letters and faxes that reinforced the original romance and passion. Distance also made it safer for Miki to stay both connected—and free.

2

. . . I can't help feeling there's something happening and things are not going to stay the same. New philosophies are taking hold. There is a great deal of change accruing in certain segments of the sport, and I hope you want the same things I want: freedom to live and ride nature's waves without the oppressive hang-up of the mad, insane complex that runs the world and this sick, sick war.

Things are going to change drastically in the next year or so, for all of us, whether we like it or not. Maybe a few will go forward and make it a better world. These are incredible times.

Thank God for a few free waves.

— **"Mickey on Malibu,"** *Surfer,* **January 1968**

Hopeful prose, atypical of Miki; a moment of repose, his personal shield down to beam out an acknowledgment of the changing times, both literally and spiritually, as well as his shifting place in the great design. As he had so often repeated, Malibu was over. Now Miki had acknowledged his heyday there had passed as well.

"The Malibu surfing lifestyle gives you a false set of values," says Johnny Fain. "I say that because life changes, and when you're at Malibu you think it never will. Miki never wanted it to change. But Miki knew his time was coming, and maybe that infuriated him. Maybe that's what made him bitter. Something ticked him off; I don't know what it was. It couldn't have just been me."

Tired of constructing self-interviews in "Dora character" (which, time has shown, was really how he felt, dressed in a baroque hipster patois) for surf publications, Miki next decided to try writing an article in which he more or less signaled his intent to depart the center stage. The result was "The Crackerjack Conspiracy," a return to the critical voice, which appeared in the May 1969 issue of *Surfer*.

During a multitude of years on the California coast I've watched the once dominant individuals of our art phased out by an uncomprehending bureaucracy. In an apparently useless endeavor, I devoted my energies and thoughts to warn the unenlightened of the plight of the times. . . . Now, the "hardened" lifeguards with the extension of power fantasies, the oldies but uglies, and the thousands of other plebeian fruit flies that compose the alleged surfing sub-sub-culture are forcing me to seek greener pastures. Bad omens are in the air.

As a parting shot or gift, Miki writes that he's going into exile on an island near Madagascar, and "Since I am leaving I have chosen to divulge the last area on the coast in which a person may exercise his wave-riding urge unhampered. I hope that this knowledge will act as payment for any misunderstandings we have had between us over the years." This last area? The right-in-front-of-your-faces-all-along breaks of Santa Monica and environs. No doubt readers had expected something entirely exotic; instead, Miki was having a laugh.

"He brought the story in unsolicited," recalled Drew Kampion, then-editor of *Surfer*. "At the same time, Miki made it very clear to his outlaw compadres that he only did this sort of thing because we paid him a lot of money. I have no idea how much, but I made $500 a month as editor, so it wasn't much."

The story also marks the official beginning of a ambiguous mentorlike symbiosis between then-eighteen-year-old C. R. Stecyk III, a young photographer, writer, surfer, skateboarder, and, lately, freelance curator, and Miki. Stecyk's two takes on Malibu culture—"Curse of the Chumash" in *Surfer*, and 1993's "Humaliwu," in *The Surfer's Journal*—are classics of bullet-point cultural anthropology.

Stecyk was certainly in the right place when he met Miki. As he told Ovidio Salazar and Peter Day, in an interview for their 1996 documentary on Miki, *In Search of Da Cat*, he was at the beach—his mother took him surfing—when he made a cutback that hit Miki in the knees. "(Later) this man comes out of the water and goes 'Jesus, you know you're a drowning rat. You're trying to take me out.' And we were friends ever since. (Before that), growing up on the beach, I don't remember him ever not being around. He was always there, a dark moving presence, always very polite. I never had any real conception of who he was or what he was supposed to be doing."

Miki took young Stecyk under his wing, going to concerts and cultural events. They traveled together to Mexico, the Islands, and Europe, where they visited "the Louvre and the Rembrandt Museum. We'd argue over paintings," Stecyk recalled. "He liked Vermeer and I liked the obvious pyrotechnics of Rembrandt. I could never get it that he was the maestro, but he was always very polite, always completely aboveboard, very honest, very quiet, and very concerned about his privacy and just being left alone. I've always gotten along with him because I gave him enough space to do whatever he had to do.

"The most amazing thing about him was . . . I wasn't completely naive to his influence . . . there was a point when he was considered the best surfer in the world and that was probably a portion of the time I was around him. But if you knew someone day to day, if they came over and were having tea with your mother, you didn't take it all that seriously. This was just some guy who was having tea in my living room, who people think is the best surfer in the world."

To the world at large, Miki was a charming, unpredictable, mysterious character, but Stecyk got a more intimate look. "I think there were times when he honestly couldn't understand (the hero worship) at all, he just wanted to be accepted as an individual, and as long as you allowed him to be his idiosyncratic best, he was fine with it. I know people he's done incredible acts of kindness for. He used to drive me to high school, I suspect in retrospect, so I wouldn't cut. I was provided with surfboards. He got me work from Greg Noll, he helped me out in a lot of different ways and in a certain sense it was like a brother or a paternalistic guidance influence. Dale Velzy . . . if you could carve, he'd give you a draw knife. People then took care of the kids that were coming up; there's always a group of kids that are being brought up and are kind of the extended family. And he was just someone that was there before me.

"Miki and I would argue in the way that friends argue, and he would tell me that surfing was a total illusion and I would argue that it was an absolute reality, a total reality, and he'd say no, it was fictitious," Stecyk told Salazar and Day. "A dream. The ultimate illusion. It was much the same as arguing over Vermeer or Rembrandt."

Stecyk would continue to help Miki, or "just be on hand" for various projects through the years. "I don't know if it's true, but this is what Miki told me about Craig Stecyk," says filmmaker Stacy Peralta, who directed the *Dogtown and Z-Boys* documentary, which he cowrote with Stecyk. "Miki said that he had the ideas, but that he didn't have the talent of the pen. That's what he found with Stecyk. He needed him to work the pen."

"Craig is like Miki," says Miki's dad. "There's a beautiful German expression about a person whom you can't make out; you talk to him and you never know where you are. You call him a 'drehkopf': a twisty head. I like Craig, but like Miki, I can't pin him down."

"Craig made Miki aware that if you just wrote stuff, you could create the universe you desired—which, again, goes back to control," says Skip Engblom. "Writing was a new area of control for Miki and he knew he could sell the stuff to the magazine guys at a premium price because they would take anything he'd give them, and he only gave them a little bit every few years. Miki's wanderings and writing let these guys who were too timid to go out into the world themselves be voyeurs. The editors and readers lived vicariously through Miki Dora. And once the Miki Dora persona was in place he just had to work at being Miki Dora."

<hr>

3

In 1967, longboards began to give way to shorter boards and, once again, newer materials and technologies. According to the *Encyclopedia of Surfing*, the redesign phase lasted until 1970, with "average board specifications dropping from 9'6" by 22" and 26 pounds, to 6'6" by 20" and ten pounds; accompanied by an equally radical shift in wave-riding styles and techniques . . . *Surfer* editor Drew Kampion called it 'the greatest conceptual shift in surfing history.'"

This transitional period took place within the context of larger social changes: the Summer of Love, anti–Vietnam War protests, the Chicago Seven, Richard Nixon's election. The Beach Boys blew the Beatles' minds with *Pet Sounds*, which led to *Sgt. Pepper* and mind blow-back. The Beatles quit performing. The Manson murders. Landing on the moon. Kent State. Mai Lai. Martin Luther King's and Robert Kennedy's assassinations. The Tet offensive. Chappaquidick. The draft lottery. Woodstock. Altamont.

Meanwhile, the crowds at Malibu, and elsewhere on the California coast, were there to stay, so the better surfers and the just plain adventurous spread out, searching for a few perfect waves on un-cluttered beaches around the world, often finding indigenous surf cultures already there. Exploring the undiscovered country became part of the game, to boldly surf where no man (or woman) had surfed before. In the spirit of *The Endless Summer*, many of these adventures were filmed, hence an explosion of professional movies from Grant Rohloff, MacGillivray/Freeman, Hal Jepsen, Bruce Brown, Bud Browne, Dale Davis, and John Severson, and many more.

Miki systematically expanded his globe-trotting, and in some respects led the way. He'd already been to Argentina to visit his father in 1949 and 1951, and to Haiti to visit his stepmom Lorraine, half-sister Pauline, and stepbrother Tony McBride (Lorraine's son by a previous marriage) in 1953. Trips to Baja and Hawaii were old hat. He'd seen France, Italy, and Spain. But times had changed; this was different. In the wake of stateside assassinations, Miki's deepening paranoia, political and financial shock waves—and crowded surf—he was increasingly uncomfortable in the United States. Home no longer felt like home.

And what a long, strange trip it turned out to be, as Miki later became fond of writing in letters from abroad, with a tip of the hat to the Grateful Dead and R. Crumb. Miki gained what he called "an international concept of the world. I knew how to function in it. I'm not like the average American, who, once they get out of America, can't survive."

In 1969, Miki let *Surfer* interview him for the September issue. After the more wistful sentiments of "Miki on Malibu" and the irony of "The Crackerjack Conspiracy," he reverted to his usual amalgam of bombast, denunciation, humor, uncanny prognostication, and elliptical revelation. For some, Miki's incantations had begun to sound tired. But he wouldn't be denied:

> *The only people to survive this fall will be the true independents, those who will have nothing to do with the upper echelon of this current illusionary prosperity. Any person who complies with the current ruling faction will only provoke his own downfall through corruption and association. People who play ball by reading publications such as this are dooming themselves to extinction.*

Nothing like chewing on the hand that feeds.

Accompanying the piece: a hand-drawn chart illustrating Miki's private time line of surfing's significant social and cultural developments, much as a paleontologist might chart evolutionary epochs from the

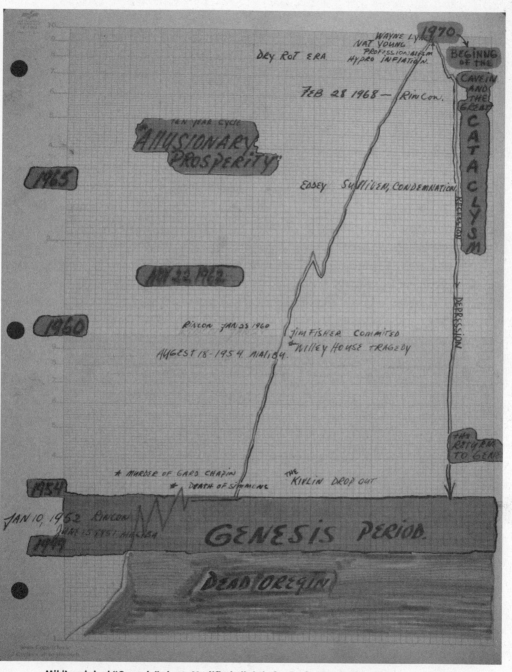

Miki's original "Genesis" chart. Modified slightly for *Surfer*, September 1969.
Courtesy Dora Estate/Refrigerator Collection.

Paleocene to the Pleistocene—and history didn't end well. His apocalyptic visual provided another access point into how Miki's mind worked. The chart published in *Surfer* was almost identical to the one Miki submitted (shown here). The editors corrected some spellings, but not all. In black marker on an orange oval, the date Nov 22, 1962, referring to JFK's assassination, was off by a year, but the editors left it, says Drew Kampion, for a WYSIWYG authenticity.

The entry labeled "Willie House Tragedy" was probably the most obscure of all—who was Willie House?—and Miki, of course, was not about to enlighten anyone.

WILLIE HOUSE: Miki had many notions of tragedy. Malibu: wonderful waves, glassy days, is overrun. Tourists park and never take their boards off their cars. Another was the guys at San Onofre. Miki said, "These guys: the surf's a little big, they're all white, they're all fat, they get out there and they can't handle it." Miki thought it lamentable.

But the tragedy involving me is one of a surfer's lost soul. Lost, forever, probably. I had a wife who didn't take care of our daughter. I had to take over in the early '60s. From the guy sleeping beside the road at Cotton's Point, all of a sudden I'm living in the Valley. The first tragedy. Then I sold my sandal shop because I had to take my daughter to a Waldorf School and get a job as a gardener. Another tragedy. Now I'm not surfing much anymore because I couldn't work it all out somehow. The third tragedy.

Miki saw a guy who really loved to surf, with whom he'd had good times, just lose it. To be from the Valley was a sin; to move there, worse. He thought it tragic to be forced to change by circumstance and responsibility, and lose interest in surfing. Of course, when you have a little child and you're all alone with her, you're not thinking about who gets the best waves. I imagine this scared the heck out of him because he believed the biggest tragedy would be if the same fate happened to him.

After the perfect swells of 1968, and before the 1970 Malibu fire, rainstorms pummeled Southern California in 1969. Creek runoff and shifting bottom contours washed away the waves. State Beach and Malibu were completely sanded in. First Point Malibu stopped breaking temporarily—and State Beach, forever—and Malibu got a whole new surf spot: Third Point.

The downpour and the unexpected downtime were an irrefutable harbinger of what, for Miki, was the end of an era. A perfect mood painting in ominous cloud gray. Miki's defiance had been unable to alter events, and all the king's horses and all the king's men couldn't put Malibu together again.

GLENN HENING: At one point in the summer of 1969 the surf was actually good for two days and Hal Jepsen was at Malibu to shoot film for his movie *Cosmic Children*—the segment using "Sympathy for the Devil" as the sound track. Dora happened to be in the water. He wore a short-john wet suit that said "Cat." He actually surfed Third Point well, ripping it as much as anybody, doing cutbacks, and off-the-lips, crossover steps and crouches, using a short board.

His last wave was little and Jepsen caught it. The wave slowed down, and Miki wound up in the shallow water. He fell back, his legs went up in the air, he got out and left. It seemed sad.

Miki continued to surf Malibu, but less and less frequently. The era was over. While a new generation still dug his entertaining antiheroics, Miki had tired of them. The We Decade had become the Me Decade. Making the scene meant escaping the scene.

Perhaps much like Greg Noll's helpful hand on that huge Waimea wave six years earlier, Miki now felt Poseidon's hand at his back, pushing to force him out of the collapsing cultural impact zone while the sea god's mermaids whispered in Miki's ear: "Time to leave. Remember, you have to ride the wave in the direction it's going. But be careful what you wish for."

OUTLAW

Man would yield his sovereignty to an immense power . . . one that does not destroy, or even tyrannize, but one that serves to stupefy a people, reducing them to nothing better than a flock of timid and industrious sheep.

—Alexis de Tocqueville

I was a little bit smarter and quicker than everyone else so I've been able to live the way I've wanted to live. But I wouldn't recommend it.

—Miki Dora

CHAPTER **NINE**

Horseman of the Apocalypse

1

No problem is so big or so complicated that it can't be run away from.
—Miki, fax to Steven Taussig

According to the *New York Times*, "Biarritz, on France's Basque coast about 15 miles north of the border with Spain, is especially alluring for surfers because of its rocky shore and its climate, which is not unlike that of Monterey and Carmel in Northern California. . . . The first French surf club formed in 1959, but the sport didn't really take hold until the 1970s, when adventurous surfers from as far away as Australia made the pilgrimage. Now Biarritz (and environs) is a regular stop for the Association of Surf Professionals, culminating in the European longboard championships at the annual festival that turns the beaches into a little Oahu every July."

Biarritz in 1854 became a destination for royalty when Emperor Napoleon III built the summer palace, La Villa Eugénie, by the ocean for his wife, the Empress Eugénie. When seen from above, the building and its wings are laid out in the shape of a giant "E." For sixteen years, the imperial couple never missed a season in Biarritz and the world's aristocracy followed. The palace is now the Hotel du Palais.

Nearby surf breaks include Anglet, Bidart, Guéthary, Hendaye, Lafiténia, Les Alcyons, and St.-Jean-de-Luz. American screenwriter

Peter Viertel (*African Queen*) came to town in 1956 with his wife, Deborah Kerr, while filming *The Sun Also Rises*. Noticing the waves, he sent for a surfboard and astonished the locals by gliding across the break on a plank.

According to Jim Kempton, once an expatriate resident, "Biarritz was a way station for Australians coming up across Asia, and Americans going the other way. It's the September stopping spot. The mountains begin to get cold and create offshore winds. You get the big swells, but still warm, hot sunny days. Indian summer."

In 1968, the Basque breaks were still the frontier, especially to someone like Miki, groomed in the urban nightmare that Malibu had become.

"The summers of 1968 and 1969 were unbelievable: beautiful weather, perfect wind, excellent drugs, happening chicks, good surf— and almost totally undiscovered," says local surf veteran François Lartigau. "You got high just walking around. Even the cops on the beach didn't know what was going on.

"I grew up in Biarritz and was one of the first to surf there in 1960 with my brother Jean-Marie. We were the two best surfers around. We spoke a little English, and my mother always wanted us to travel, so we were attracted to people from overseas.

"I saw Miki arrive in Côte des Basque in a convertible Mercedes, with another guy, two beautiful chicks, and two brand-new big boards in the back. He looked like he had stepped out of a Hollywood movie. Then he disappeared for a while and came back with nothing, like a hobo. But the next time I saw him he had a Porsche.

"Everyone gathered at a restaurant called the Steakhouse. It was an international rendezvous, the easy place to meet. Because the owner spoke good English, all the young travelers used to go there at night: GIs dropping out of the army, California surfers on their way to the army who never went any further than the Côte des Basque.

"In 1969, there was a big bust at the Steakhouse. It seems funny now; it wasn't at the time. Of course, everyone smoked. Also, no big companies sponsored surfing at the time, so if you wanted to travel and surf, you needed a lot of money, and dealing drugs was one way to get it. But someone used a hollowed-out balsa board and filled it full of hash in Lebanon. After he took out the hash, he threw the board on the rocks by the water. The cops found it and went, "Oh, the surfers are up to no good." So they waited and one day they busted about thirty people at the Steakhouse. The whole thing collapsed. From a nice summer, it went to a big bummer."

Miki didn't stick around long enough to get caught up. Besides, he had his own misadventures to pursue.

In the summer of 1969, two young California surfers, Richard Slade and Ron Smerling, drove from Paris to Biarritz in Smerling's Westphalia VW van, on a search for waves. In Biarritz, they ran into Miki and his friend Craig Stecyk, and by August, minus Stecyk, the remaining three headed down the Spanish and Portuguese coasts to Morocco.

"Every day Miki had a different personality," said Smerling, a self-described Dora protégé. "Sometimes he was serious like a professor. Or into classical music. He could also act really juvenile, or like a drunk. Some days happy, some days sad. We'd go into museums and he'd take spears right off the walls and pop wild animal heads into his coat. Then he'd go out and stick them in my car. I was scared shitless."

As they drove, Miki would also talk about his apocalyptic vision for America's crash and fall. "He said the world's economies were based on false pretenses, and that the gold standard of $35 an ounce would be dropped and he was going to make thousands of dollars an ounce. He also showed us some of his gold stash—he bought some while we were together—but we were afraid to touch it."

Before the trio were ready to return from the Moroccan side to Algeciras, in Spain, they wandered through a marketplace where Miki would take items and tell the vendors his friends would pay. "We got really scared," says Slade, "so we told Miki we'd see him at the ferry."

But when it came time to board, Miki wasn't around. "I said not to worry," remembers Smerling. "Miki always showed up when he had to."

He didn't, not even when the captain blew the horn, closed the gates, and the ferry left. "We had his passport, his sleeping bag, every-thing," says Slade. "Ron told me not to worry. I took Miki's passport and his duffel bag to the captain and said, 'We just left a friend of ours in Africa. Here's his stuff, maybe when you go back you could help him get to Europe.'"

"I left him because I knew he wanted to smuggle bars of hashish, which you could smell a block and a half away," says Smerling. "I told him, 'Are you crazy? I'm not taking that on my bus.' I wasn't going to end up in the middle of *Midnight Express.*

"During the ferry trip I told Rick we'd better go through the car, because Miki might have set us up. But we found nothing."

Smerling and Slade drove back to Biarritz, where the former kicked the latter out of his van.

"I took off on my own for a final shower," says Smerling. "I paid for one at a campsite way off the beaten path. As I came out, with a towel around my waist, I saw Miki in this classic silver, black-convertible-top Porsche. He pulled right up to my knees and stopped. He got out, shot the blade out of a stiletto, and said, 'I'm going to kill you for what you did to me.'

"I said, 'Miki, first you were trying to smuggle hashish in my car. Then I told you to show up at 12:30 and you didn't.' I was pretty scared. He put the blade right against my throat. Then, suddenly his eyes turned red and started to water. He closed the blade. We looked at each other. He turned around, got in the in the car, pulled away—and tried to run me over. I had to jump to the side of the road.

"The next morning I drove to the ELF station to gas up the van and the attendant began jumping up and down, going, 'Monsieur, Monsieur.' He showed me sugar around the gas tank opening. Fortunately I was on empty, so they took ten gallons of gas and washed it out. Then I realized my passport, my plane ticket, my health certificate, and all my traveler's checks were gone. Everything. I had nothing."

2

There are people who think that honesty is always the best policy. This is a superstition. There are times when the appearance of it is worth six of it.

—Mark Twain

The late Don Wilson, tall, blond, and thin, was a contractor/investor and, some might say, the ne'er-do-well son of a well-to-do developer from Pacific Palisades. Others saw him as the "White Knight" to Miki's "Black Knight," not that color denoted virtue. Allan Carter called Wilson the Pirate Captain, which was more accurate since he'd been in and out of jail on a variety of nonviolent charges. "Don once told me he needed some money and I told him the quickest way was to write *Don Wilson's Guide to the Cuisine of International Slammers*," says Carter. "He could rate all the jails in the world because Don had been in most of them. He told me the one in Marseilles served an acceptable rosé for lunch and a pretty good burgundy for dinner."

Carter was a young writer from a wealthy family. He also had a strong paterfamilias: His father, a highly placed and powerful aerospace pioneer involved with Boeing, Douglas, and Lockheed, had known and done business with Howard Hughes since 1924.

Carter and Miki were longtime associates who'd met at the beach in the mid-'50s. One had money and connections, the other had pretensions to both. Carter, who called Miki "Gypsy Darling," was easygoing, intelligent, engaging—and wanted nothing from Miki but the pleasure of his always entertaining company. Miki found in Carter a lively and perceptive compadre who liked to have a good time and enjoyed surfing with him. The pairing was mutually beneficial. Both knew Wilson, a surfer at Malibu and State Beach, who knew Greg Meisenholder—the Mad Mongoose. Meisenholder had no fortune, and grounded himself as a landscape architect and family man. Wilson and Meisenholder were high school friends.

Dora called the troupe the "Four Horsemen of the Apocalypse."

GREG MEISENHOLDER: Don always had get-rich-quick schemes. The trouble is, he had a propensity for writing bad checks. His somewhat wealthy father bailed him out for a while, but by 1969 the habit had gotten worse and he wrote a bad check to pay for our flight down to Acapulco.

We stayed at the El Mirador, where they had the cliff diving. On the flight down, Don said, "We're gonna check in and do a W.O." A "walk out"—on the bill.

I said, "Those people weren't born yesterday."

I saw the handwriting on the wall. I didn't want to be any part of it. Allan and I stayed one night and paid for our end of the bill, then checked in to an inexpensive place. Miki and Don stayed another three or four days.

We got together every day. We went to surf spots out by Puerto Marquez, below the airport. We went waterskiing one day in Acapulco Harbor.

Eventually, the El Mirador management smelled something going on with the high-flying American surfers, so they said, "We'd appreciate you settling up now. It's our policy." I think Miki got stuck using his Diners Club credit card, which maybe later was the infamous credit card that got him in trouble.

After the November 1969 trip to Acapulco, the Four Horsemen went to Rio de Janeiro for Carnivale in February 1970. Trouble followed them like a lost dog.

ALLAN CARTER: After we got back from Acapulco, Don said, "They're having Carnivale in Rio. We've gotta go." I got Miki to come along. I had friends in Brazil. When Dr. Carlos Lacerda, the governor of Rio de Janeiro state, would come to California, he'd get bored at all these Beverly Hills parties, so Raul de Smandek, the Brazilian cultural attaché, would bring them out to my (father's) house in Malibu and we'd have barbecues. Raul was a dear friend, and he had a cousin in Rio, named Selma. I made a call, and we stayed in the attaché's condo on Copacabana Beach. We flew together from Miami to Rio. Don got the airplane tickets. My friends gave us entrance to all the best clubs, introduced us to Sergio Mendez, and took us to a private performance by Brazil 66.

One night, Miki came up the elevator with a street prostitute and walked into a fancy party that the governor's cousin threw for us. Selma said, "Allan, we don't have these kinds of people in our house. You must speak to your friend." It was the equivalent of going to a debutante ball and dropping a camel turd in the middle of the punch bowl.

During the Carnivale festivities in the street, they had dancing carnival dolls with carnival hats. Miki ran around buying pulp magazines. One was about Nazis in South America, with a picture of the Führer the exact size as the carnival doll's head. He cut out the picture and glued it on the carnival doll. Now he had the Dancing Führer.

BOB BEADLE: I lived in Rio from the late 1960s until 1971 and met up with Miki there. He had the idea to go to the Governor's Ball. They held the ball at Teatro Municipale, on the main drag, an ornate, old colonial building that was home to one of the greatest opera companies in the world.

We saw a block-and-a-half-long line of really fine people. People don't like to stand in line, especially in Latin America, and these were all people of a

ABOVE LEFT: The Four Horsemen arrive in Rio, 1970. Left to right: Don Wilson, Miki, Allan Carter, Greg Meisenholder. Courtesy Greg Meisenholder.

ABOVE: Miki at the back entrance to the Gran Hotel Dora, Buenos Aires, 1970. Courtesy Dora Estate.

LEFT: Allan "The Eagle" Carter on the Grand Tour. Norway, 1970. Photo: Marcia McMartin.

certain social importance. I had no idea what Miki had in mind, but we passed by the line and walked toward the entrance.

I stood right at his elbow. He reached into his coat pocket, pulled out his wallet, and opened it with one hand, flashing his international driver's license. With the other hand he waved at someone inside who wasn't there, saying, "Hey, Saul! How's it going?" Then he replaced his wallet and walked right by the ticket taker. I walked in with him. When we got five paces in, we ducked behind a column and stood there while the burly guys ran right by us. Quintessential Miki.

DON WILSON: While in Rio, we wanted to see what jewelry was available that we could make some money by reselling it. Miki went into a store recommended by the family, wrote a check for thirty or forty thousand dollars. The check was no good and he absconded with a bagful of gems. He jumped on a flight south, and didn't say good-bye to anyone. Raul de Smandek's family had to come up with the money and pay off the store. It caused a tremendous grievance and loss of good friends that we all cherished.

ALLAN CARTER: Don did the same thing in Brazil, scammed jewels like crazy, only he went into Sterns and did it impersonally, without using a friend to get credibility. He told me about it afterward, so anything he might say about someone else, I'd take with a grain of salt.

Raul never said anything to me about Miki's escapade. My Brazilian socialite friends didn't, either. When I found out and inquired, they said it had nothing to do with me. I must have been horribly naïve then because I really didn't think Miki would do something like that.

All I know is, Miki ended up with this jewelry and I wasn't privy to how he got it. I've said it before and I'll say it again: Miki was a like a chimpanzee on a motorcycle with a loaded shotgun. Everything's flying and you don't want to get in the way.

Don returned to Los Angeles, and Miki and I kept going. We went everywhere in South America except Chile and Ecuador. Greg tagged along.

If you're a man between the ages of eighteen and ninety, when you travel in South America, you've got to arrive at the airport in a tan suit if you want to be well received at Customs. Miki and I also always traveled with medals because in South America, with all these dictatorships, they love anyone who looks like the military. I had a Good Conduct medal because I was once in the army, and I stuck it on this tan wash-and-wear suit from New Orleans. The minute they saw me they kicked old ladies out of the way to roll out the red carpet.

Everything was fine until the Customs people popped open Miki's luggage. There on top was the Dancing Führer. Miki had to spend about two hours explaining, while I had drinks in the lounge. Meanwhile, I met this really nice fellow. He said, "Isn't that Miki Dora, the surfer?" I said, "Yeah." He said, "My father's the top general in the Paraguayan army." I thought, This doesn't sound good. He said, "We'd love to have you guys come to our house. We have an estancia on the River Paraguay. We're going to have a wonderful dinner party tonight that my father is hosting for President of Paraguay [for life] Alfredo Ströessner, and I want you to come."

Miki and I discussed it and frankly we were afraid to go because we'd be forty miles from nowhere, at a place with a driveway thirty miles long, and we might be listening to the strains of *Lohengrin, Parsifal,* and *Die Meistersinger*—if our hosts were in a light mood. We decided we didn't want to end up on the wrong end of a guest list if this was a Wermacht SS unit having their reunion party. Maybe, because Miki didn't look Aryan, we'd end up as food for Burpee's hybrid corn somewhere in a field. I mean, what if Miki said something confrontational? They'd cut our throats out in the middle of nowhere. Though we considered ourselves to be courageous, we realized we weren't *that* courageous.

Nonetheless, the entire trip eventually served as fodder for Miki's classic magazine travelogue, "To Whom It May Underestimate," published in the October 1971 issue of *Surfer.* The story described balmy afternoons on the estancia of Martino Bormanito, a camera-shy European gentleman then residing in Paraguay. (A picture of "Bormanito" was actually a shot of an unsuspecting traveler on a boat near Stockholm.) Later, they traveled to Dora's ostensible final destination: the (actual) Gran Hotel Dora in Mar del Plata, Argentina, to meet his ailing uncle Kornel and, as his only living heir, to discuss his will and Dora's eventual interest in the hotel. A picture of Dora near the hotel sign accompanied the text.

DREW KAMPION: In May or June of 1970, about the time I was leaving *Surfer,* "To Whom It May Underestimate" came in. Miki dropped it off himself. He drove a Porsche Speedster, walked upstairs carrying an attaché case, and wanted to see Mr. Severson. When I saw him coming, I scooted up to the front to meet him and make sure I got involved. I didn't want to miss anything.

I told Severson he'd arrived. We went into the film room between John's office and my office. Miki said, "I have something to show you. I just returned from South America. Knowing that you're a person of some erudition and discernment, I thought you'd appreciate these artifacts." He opened up his little case, which was velvet lined on both sides, and extracted a little velvet bag. He poured out a dozen or so yellowish-green topazes onto the foldout table and, using tweezers, began to show them off to John.

STEVE PEZMAN: Drew later described Dora going through the stones with the tweezers, "like turning jumbo prawns in a fryer."

DREW KAMPION: All the while Miki talked about their clarity and quality. "Rare Brazilian topaz." He led John forward and forward. "This is something your wife would like." "Once in a lifetime." But he never actually said they were for sale. Finally John said, "How much are they? Maybe I'd like to buy one or two." At that, Miki scooped them all into the bag, snapped the case shut, and huffed: "I'm personally offended. These are family heirlooms. They're treasure. They'd never be for sale. It was actually very bold, rude, and venal of you to suggest that I might actually offer them."

He hustled out, down the stairs, into the car, and—*vroom!*—away.

This was classic Dora. He drove to Dana Point just to do a number on John, to set him up, switch him, and adios. He lived in the moment. Doing the thing was its own reward. He did it for the chuckle, for the grin.

In the summer of 1970, Allan Carter and his then-girlfriend Annabelle "Terry" Harkness McBride, Miki, and Marcia McMartin, an adventurous dark-haired beauty whom Dora had met through Carter, took an extended trip through Europe. They arrived in London on July 15 and didn't return to the States until the end of November. Their itinerary wound through the Continent and adjacent countries like an animated cartoon map, from the northernmost point in Europe to Marrakesh, Morocco.

ALLAN CARTER: Marcia met Miki on my doorstep. She was good-looking, thin, very attractive, and very rich. Her father and brother were heirs to Hollinger Consolidated, which is the biggest gold-mining enterprise in the history of the Western Hemisphere. They eventually had a big battle with Lord Black, who took over the company. Duncan McMartin's income in the '40s was something like $85,000 a week. He was also a world-famous big-game hunter. They had two houses in Bermuda: Elephant Walk I and Elephant Walk II. When Marcia's father died in '83, they sold Elephant Walk I for $19.5 million. They also owned a nine-acre estate on Tower Road in Beverly Hills. Her mother, "Tits," came from a very wealthy family that owned a lot of commercial property in San Diego. Money on both sides.

I figured Marcia might straighten up Miki a little bit.

At the time I was going out with Terry Harkness, whose family owned Villa Capricorn at Lyford Cay. Her money came from Standard Oil. John D. Rockefeller I and William Hill Harkness founded Standard Oil.

MARCIA MCMARTIN: Allan, Miki, and Terry needed a fourth person to go to Europe. Allan had had a car accident years before, and had a bad leg, so driving was difficult. Terry didn't want to drive all over Europe, and Miki didn't want to be the only one driving. I happened to be the most available candidate.

Between meeting and leaving, Miki began to call me. I'd been divorced only a year and the last thing I wanted to do was get tied down. I figured he just wanted to get to know me as the fourth person, but we quickly had a rapport, and that was that. We didn't tell Allan and Terry, but at the hotel in England, when Miki and I split off to go to our room, Allan was dumbfounded. I think he had imagined sharing a room with Miki while I roomed with Terry. I'll never forget the expression on his face.

As I was the last to join the group, I was unable to get a ticket for the boat in the Baltic. If I wanted to go, I'd have to stow away. It didn't take much encouragement; I didn't want to be left behind. Naturally, I was found out, but since we'd already left port, I just had to pay my fare. Unfortunately, they had no other cabin for me, and Miki had a single. But he graciously gave up his cabin for me and was put down in the bowels of the ship in one of the crew cabins.

Miki loved to pull pranks and live dangerously. In France, British Petroleum issued replicas of ancient French coins as part of an ad campaign. One side had a BP slogan, the other side looked authentic. In Biarritz, Miki pretended he'd dug up a treasure trove of coins. He tried to make us think they were ancient. In Switzerland, he had bought pills and monogrammed them with his initials MSD. Then he claimed they were LSD and passed it around. I liked LSD and took it about seven or eight times. He asked if I wanted one and I said sure. But it was fake. He kept asking, "Are you feeling anything," thinking I'd imagine something happening to me, or be too embarrassed to admit it was nothing.

After Norway we took a boat trip up the Rhine to Basel, Switzerland. Miki and Allan went to Munich to pick up a Mercedes Terry had ordered in Germany, and we went to Spain to see her mother's ballet, the Harkness Ballet, perform in Barcelona. We finally arrived in Biarritz on September 25. Miki was finally able to surf for the first time, a good thing, since he was a bit stir-crazy and we'd been lugging a bag of boards with us since Los Angeles. At that point Terry and Allan split up to go back home, and Miki and I continued. We stayed in the south of France for a few weeks, then went to Spain, Gibraltar, Tangiers, Casablanca, and Marrakesh, before driving back to Le Havre and Southhampton.

Miki had turned thirty-six while we were in Norway. I knew he liked gold coins, so I secretly bought him three or four. I gave him the jewelry box the morning we packed to leave. He thought it was some old watch or a ring, so he refused it without even opening the box. I was so hurt I left the damn box there; whoever cleaned got a nice surprise. I never told him. But I knew Allan would.

ALLAN CARTER: Miki was ready to shoot himself when he found out what he had refused.

MARCIA MCMARTIN: It may sound trite, but Miki was really the love of my life. He rarely said I love you—maybe once or twice; he was not a demonstrative man, in that sense—but on this trip, somewhere in France, he actually asked me to marry him. That really surprised me. But we'd had a lot of wine, so I said, "Ask me in the morning," and well, of course, he never did. If he had asked me in the morning, I probably would have said yes.

3

Linda Cuy, who passed muster as a surfer, and was nothing like Annette Funicello or Kathy Kohner, was Miki's lover for the next ten years, sharing his waves and his scams, getting close but never too close. . . . She had his attention, and they ran together. On the sly the pair pulled down the walls of jailhouses with a Land Rover, sequestered jewels in the hideaway heels of their boots of Spanish leather, and kited monetary exchange instruments into the stratosphere. . . . Linda was Miki's match, and his accomplice.

—Drew Kampion, *Dora Lives*

We traveled and got into trouble.

—Linda Cuy, *Dora Lives*

LINDA CUY: I met Miki when I was roughly seventeen. I already knew who Miki was. I read *Surfer* magazine; you *had* to get a subscription and study up to know what was going on. I saw him at Malibu. I could tell that he was interested, but I think he thought I was too young—and I was, just a silly girl, with girlfriends, surfing.

I was born in North Hollywood. I got to the beach the first time with a neighbor when I was fifteen. He used to drive a big Cadillac convertible every Saturday morning, and I'd see this big board sticking out of the back. I talked to him and found out he was about sixty-five years old and strong—a real waterman. He said, "I'm going down to Malibu, to surf." I said, "What's surf-ing?" He said, "Come on. I'll show you this weekend." My parents said it would be okay.

I watched Miki from a distance, and in the beginning we just made passing comments to each other. I thought Miki was different. I thought I was different. It felt like he was searching for something, and I knew I was searching, too. Then one day, at the lighthouse jetty in Santa Monica, when I was twenty-one, we were surfing, and he asked, "Would you like to go out to dinner?" I was blown away because he was fifteen years older than me. I think about it now and I realize that he spent the best years of his life with me.

JOHN MILIUS: Miki took Linda away from her previous boyfriend, but I could never understand the great fascination. She was a little surfer girl: sexy, but not that sexy. She didn't know how to sell herself that way yet. It was more like Miki was the prince riding through town, saying, "Over there. That one interests me. Bring her. She has a curious look in her eye, and nice form. I think I will let her warm my feet."

LINDA CUY: I was attracted to Miki because he was the best for everything. He looked fantastic, was excellent in what he did, had different feelings about the world. He's like art. I believe what he always told me about the ecology of stuff, how everything was commercializing and breaking down. He always talked about how clean the beaches were, how free everything was when he was young: no parking restrictions, no crowds. I was on a whole nature thing, too, and I related. In the '60s there were crowds, it was hard to park, but everything was still okay. But when you think about how things are now—oh my God. Miki was right.

ANONYMOUS: I also dated Linda Cuy back then. She walked like a cat, had no fat on her. It made some guys' tongues hang out. We played tennis, surfed, did everything together. But it was more like a friendship thing than a love thing—though it went to that, too, maybe one night here and there. The downside was that she wasn't very well educated and was embarrassed to talk about where she came from, what her mom and dad did.

I didn't care when she and Miki started hanging out because he was my idol. I remember Linda telling me Miki was great in bed. He could go a long time, she said. But he wanted no competition and put sugar in my gas tank. So I did something that probably got him busted.

By that time, Miki was into counterfeit credit cards. I also heard he was making explosives—pipe bombs—from someone who saw them. This is secondhand: Maybe it's not true, but I did hear it. So I sent a letter to the FBI in the Federal Building on Wilshire. I wrote it out by hand, with a ruler and a pen, wearing surgical gloves. Then I cut some old photos out of that classic *Surf Guide* story, "The Angry Young Man of Surfing"—there are side shots and forward shots of him—and put them on the letter and sent them off to the FBI.

I had to do it, because he was really trying to hurt me. He destroyed my car. He had the devil's eye, man. He could give you a look that put the fear of God in you, if he thought you were screwing around with him.

In that letter to the FBI I told them about the pipe bombs. I'd also heard he had a ton of Diners Club cards, and a bunch of weapons, those really nasty hunter's bow and arrows. And his house was booby-trapped, so if you tried to enter something really bad would happen to you. I don't know if the FBI thought my letter was a prank or not. There wasn't a fingerprint on it. I'm sure they checked for all that. But I wrote it very seriously. Anyway, after that I think the FBI was on to him and watched him, and that's how he landed in hot water. [Author's note: Not found in Miki's FBI file.]

LINDA CUY: Miki and I got really, really involved—in everything. We used to play tennis together at Barrington Courts. We'd take his camper up the coast, surf and camp. Took a couple trips to Baja. He had told me, "Every summer get out of here. Go to France. It's fantastic. You'll love it." I went to Biarritz by myself when I was twenty-one, looking for him. I saved up three hundred dollars and hitchhiked around with my surfboard. I saw Miki briefly at Guéthary. He was with Marcia.

I had the key to his apartment. I could come and go as I wanted. But sometimes he'd go away in the evenings. I knew about Marcia, of course, and I finally thought, What's all this about? So I did a little sneaking around and found out where Marcia lived. I used to pull up by her house in my van and wait outside for Miki to come to me. Or I was on the property next door, up in the tree, looking down through the window to figure out what Miki's fascination was all about. Marcia was my competition and you have to size up your competition.

JIM KEMPTON: Linda told me that she moved into Miki's flat by showing up on his doorstep, deciding to be his girl. She cooked for him, cleaned for him, was in bed at night, and wouldn't go away. And if he didn't come home because he was with another girl, that was okay, too. Years later, in the mid-'70s, Linda and I were lovers. She was a great love. She gave herself to you completely, unbelievably, beyond what you could imagine both physically and spiritually. Yet, it was only for a term. Marcia was the "Debutante," what Linda could never be. Linda had no title, no money, nothing that Miki could transport on to. But Marcia inherited half a billion dollars. I know Miki hoped to capitalize on that, and that would have been his best scam. But he missed out because Miki never had much capacity to have a real relationship or even fake one very well.

LINDA CUY: Eventually, I made a big to-do about Marcia with this girl on the beach, and somehow word got back. Then I let the cat out of the bag—my displeasure—and made a big stink with Miki, and said, "I'm your girlfriend during the day. It's fine and dandy to play sports with me and stuff, but at night you go over to Marcia's to eat, and have dinner parties." Miki loved dinner parties. She had the perfect place, nicely decorated, lots of friends. And I had nothing. I was just a beach person. I couldn't entertain like Marcia did. I felt like I was cut off.

When I made the big hoo-ha, Miki threw me out. I was all bummed and crying. So I went to State Beach one sunny day, at my wit's end about the whole thing: I really liked Miki, he had another girlfriend, he liked her cooking, she was a multimillionaire, and I was a nobody, a surf bum. While tearing my hair out I heard two guys talking. I lay on the sand, half-dozed, sun-stroked, in an emotional state, listening. One said, "Well, Shelly's driving her Mercedes now. That bum Mexican." And I thought, Shelly? What do they mean? They were talking about Shelly Riskin, who had been my boyfriend before Miki and was, at the time, going out with Terry McBride—she's how Marcia found out about me—and he was driving her Mercedes. So I popped up and said, "He's not a Mexican. He's a friend of mine." They both turned around like, Who's this upstart, this little thing, and what's she saying to us?

Don Wilson, the Pirate Captain, said, "Who are you? What do you have to do with any of this? It's not any of your business."

"Well," I said, "I'm Miki's girlfriend, the one no one knows about."

And then it started. Don said, "We're having a big barbecue up at my house." He lived in Santa Monica. "Why don't you come up. Don't be depressed. Have some fun." I did and had a great time. Met a lot of characters.

Allan. Mongoose. Don said, "If you don't want to go back to the Valley, park your van here, use the shower."

I thought, This is great. Don and I started going out, playing tennis. I found he liked to do lots of interesting things, too.

Don and Miki were so completely opposites. Don had blond hair, was fair-skinned, had blue eyes; Miki was tanned, had dark hair, was glamorous. And Miki hated Don and Don hated Miki. I don't know what started the conflict. I only know it preceded me.

DON WILSON: I met Linda about the same time Miki did, and we started seeing each other quite a bit. Miki came to me one day and said, "That's my woman. I saw her first." Then it finally came down to the statement, "May the better man win." All of a sudden the police would knock on my door and say "We understand you have stolen surfboards," etc. Totally untrue. Miki tried to set me up to get busted. He was pissed and vindictive and would do anything and everything to get Linda away from me.

LINDA CUY: With Miki everything was a game and a challenge. With Don it was win or nothing. The big difference between Don and Miki was that in his soul Miki liked to surf. He was a low-key guy who thought he would win, but by secret methods. He would do it more in the shadows than in someone's face. Yet both were so interesting. I don't know how I got strapped into the middle, but I put up with them battling over me because it was fun.

JIM KEMPTON: Linda was the quintessential cosmic girl, an archetype, as much as Miki and Don. The books she used to send me to read are so amazing, like *The World's Desire*. Which is what Linda was. She personified this gypsy queen, and whoever had the queen is the king.

Why? I'm sure she had her reasons. To Linda, Malibu and Miki meant escape. He was nobility. It was like the milkmaid meeting the handsome prince. He was in magazines and was adored by millions. He and his surfing buddies could seemingly go anywhere and do anything. She wanted to get the fuck out of the Valley. Fortunately, she had a great body and, as Bob Seger once sang, she was "blessed with a face that would let her get her way."

DON WILSON: In 1971, I started traveling but made the mistake of coming back to the U.S. after six months. I got arrested on a nonsufficient funds charge. Meanwhile, my attorney had fallen in love with my wife and wanted me out of the picture. When I got out, I got divorced and got a job in Costa Rica building a tennis club. I sent money home to support my family. At the same time, Linda came down to live with me. At some point I had to fly to Panama.

Miki found out that I had flown into Panama. He called the authorities and they arrested me in the hotel room and put me in jail. I was in there for three weeks until I finally paid off the doctor and jumped out the prison's second-floor window, escaped into the American zone, and worked my way back to Costa Rica.

When I got back, Miki was with Linda. How did Miki know I was there? Good question. It seems there was a little communication going on between Miki and Linda. She would write letters and postcards: "Hi, how are you? We're headed here and etc.," without knowing how it undermined us. I didn't know about it until later when Linda told me.

LINDA CUY: These adventures with Miki and myself and Don feel to me now like *Breathless,* with Richard Gere. I felt like the woman in that film, and Miki was kind of like this nut. He was eccentric and had energy, the craving and the craziness—the "arrghh" I want to do something—but not the police part of the film where he gets killed in the end. There was also a taste of *The Endless Summer,* which was like the total opposite energy. We were on this adventure trip, it was light, everyone was friends, and let's look for the perfect surf spot. And then you throw in *Catch Me If You Can* and it's like a carousel of different feelings from intensity and spirit and craziness to this mellow let's go surfing, relaxed vibe. I'm not the normal, settle-down-get-a-house person. I wanted to go surfing. I would be with one guy and then get physically sick from roughing it and moving, moving, moving—and go home. Or one would get in trouble and I'd have to bail out. It's confusing. It's spaghetti. But in the end I went around the world roughly three times. What Miki and I did together was way over that, over the top. I'd like to get that out and have the whole world read that story.

Thinking about it now, though, is difficult because I have to relive every minute of it, and it makes me ill mentally to go through all the emotions again. The stress. It's so hard: remembering being interrogated and running and forging things. It's hard to settle down after going through this and then go out into the real world. What we did was not the real world.

(Our adventures) turned into this exodus out of California. Along the way, Don got into trouble and went to prison. Miki got into trouble, too. And all because of what we did between the three of us. It was all for fun. It was a wild time. Sometimes we were in big trouble. Sometimes we lived the high life. I'd be with one guy and the other would show up and the first would try to get the other arrested. And vice versa. All over the world, this little chase and craziness went on. It was fun *and* stressful, and everybody got sick, especially me.

Don and I ended up with malaria, and I had tapeworm. You can get all kinds of nasty stuff when you're running around Africa. There were lots of times when we were being questioned and I'd spend the night on the floor in some interrogation room. It was a time of giant highs and giant lows.

4

9.16.1971 [Postcard to Ramona from Africa]
   Johannesburg: I find somehow that I've bumbled my way to the ends of the earth, once again absolutely mystified with my surroundings. Planning to spend a few months in the interland Zulu countries, Rhodesia and the Congo. Life is going well, but a strange feeling of isolation always prevails. Always on the run makes for interesting times, but highly exhausting without any time to relax.

After Miki and Marcia's first trip, they took at least one grand tour a year, sometimes lasting three months. In 1971, they returned to London and drove around England and France, stopping to surf at Guéthary and Biarritz. Next they went to Andorra and Zürich, then Rome, Pompeii, and Capri. A flight to Johannesburg, South Africa, with a side trip to Durban, Pietermarizburg, and Port Elizabeth, followed. They rented a car and drove to Capetown, staying in Jeffreys Bay on the way. There Miki was awed by the challenging and perfect surf. Rhodesia (Zimbabwe) and Victoria Falls ended the journey.

   "These trips were all Miki's idea," Marcia recalls. "We'd go at the spur of the moment, stay as long as we wanted. When it was boring, we'd move on to the next place. Miki seemed to only want to live for the moment."

   The following July, Miki and Marcia went to New York, Australia, New Zealand, Bali, Jakarta, Java, Thailand, Singapore, Hong Kong, and Tokyo. In Australia and New Zealand he tried to hit as many surf spots as possible. Says Marcia, "Miki couldn't be away from the water for too long."

   Miki may have acted the casual traveler, but surfers who ran into him often found him unusually wary and circumspect. Mike Tabeling, who found Miki sitting on a bench in Guéthary in 1971, remembers him as "paranoid that people were after him."

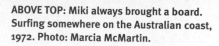

ABOVE TOP: Miki always brought a board. Surfing somewhere on the Australian coast, 1972. Photo: Marcia McMartin.

RIGHT: Jeffreys Bay, 1971. Empty and beautiful, like Malibu before the deluge. Photo: Marcia McMartin.

ABOVE: Marcia McMartin, Thailand, 1972. Courtesy Marcia McMartin.

ABOVE: Miki entranced by the empty waves at Guéthary, 1970. Photo: Marcia McMartin.

RIGHT: The only surfer boy in NYC, 1970s. Courtesy Gard Chapin Jr. Photographer unknown.

BELOW: Miki at Victoria Falls, 1971. Photo: Marcia McMartin.

BELOW RIGHT: International man of mystery, Biarritz, 1971. Photo: Marcia McMartin.

Miki was correct. He'd been footing much of his travel on an altered credit card, or just not paying the bills on his own card. At the time, the consequences took much longer to catch up with you, but they always did.

According to Los Angeles attorney Jan Handzlik, who represented Dora almost ten years later, "The card was originally obtained in 1958. I'm pretty sure it was his own card. I can see from my records that he signed the slips Miklos S. Dora Jr. I see a date of August 6, 1972, in Auckland. Also receipts from Australia, Nairobi, Germany, Beirut, Munich, Ceylon, and so on and so forth. It's nothing unusual: hotels, car rentals, airline tickets. It's possible, I guess, that Miki could have gotten cash advances from Diners Club. I don't know if he did it or not."

According to Miki's FBI file, obtained through the Freedom of Information Act, he used a card that originally expired in 1966 and altered the expiration date to 1976. However, he may have used an assortment of cards either in his own name or lifted from others. One Diners Club estimate of fraudulent charges as of September 1975, just on his own card, was $19,785. By 1976, the amount had reached $22,000.

Miki ran other scams as well. His friend Peter Barnett, a surfer and real estate salesman who lived for a time in Marcia McMartin's basement guest quarters—and to whom Miki gave power of attorney to handle his mail and bank account so Barnett could deposit Miki's tiny movie residual checks—says, "He used to get food stamps under the name Michael Chapin. I still have his Food Stamp Identification Card and some of the coupons for Mayfair Markets and Vons."

It's likely that Dora didn't need the food stamps, but he got them for the same reason a dog licks his private parts: because he could. Besides his own Social Security card, he also had one numbered 558-27-3816, in the name of Michael Chapin.

"We opened an account at a bank on the corner of Fifth and Santa Monica, California Federal," says Barnett. "The biggest check was probably less than $25. I used the money to pay any bills, or sent it to him when he asked for it.

"He also had a post office box in the Palisades and gave me the combination. The three-digit combination spelled D-I-E. That was classic Miki Dora. He wrote it out for me in boldface and underlined it. If he wanted to mail something secretly, he'd send it there."

~

In early 1973, trouble finally snared Miki in California, and this time he couldn't wriggle free. On a ski trip to Mammoth, he had written a check to pay for equipment rental, then stopped the check. In a handwritten statement found in his FBI file, Miki called the incident a "misunderstanding" and asked for consideration so that he could return to "work" as soon as possible, since he was "running low on funds." Not that he worked.

One source interviewed by the FBI—name redacted—described Miki as "emotionally unstable," and as someone who "had a large ego and was idolized by (Malibu) kids for the capers he had pulled off."

A complaint was filed in the Mammoth incident on March 23, 1973, in the Justice Court of Mono Judicial District, County of Mono, State of California, against Michael Chapin aka Miklos Dora, thirty-nine, for allegedly violating section 484 (larceny or theft) of the California Penal Code. A warrant was issued and Miki located via an anonymous tip.

MARCIA MCMARTIN: The police came to my home and banged on the door. I had worked as a meter maid six or seven years prior, so of course I answered. I told the detective that Miki wasn't there. He said, "His car's here," and I said, "Well, he has more than one car." I could tell this guy was really psyched up and that he wanted to push me out of the way and get into the house, but I closed the door.

Miki *was* there and we talked about what to do. We thought we might put him up in the attic, but I didn't have a ladder. The police knocked again. I kept saying "Miki's not here." Then Miki decided to come out.

Later, I heard from my next-door neighbor that the police were everywhere. The entrance to my house was on the side, not the front, so I only saw the one policeman and I don't believe he said he had a warrant.

After they took Miki away my neighbor said, "What was it? A parking ticket?" And of course I said, "Yes." I don't know how they knew he was at my house. Maybe they'd been following him for a while.

The judge set bail of $2,500 on June 11, 1973, and scheduled an arraignment for June 26. Miki didn't appear until July 19. He pled not guilty and demanded a jury trial, but his attorney, Don Chapman, advised the court that he would be making a motion to dismiss the charges. Eventually trial was scheduled for November 12, 1973.

GARDNER CHAPIN JR.: I was really amazed when Miki got arrested. He told me he was totally innocent, that he had bought this merchandise and it was defective, so he had returned it and stopped payment. That sounded strange to me, but I wasn't going to argue.

MIKLOS DORA SR.: He didn't do it maliciously, but stupidly. It was a good check and then he stopped it. If he would have come to me and said he needed $100 or $200. . . . It was chickenshit. He thought he could get away with it. This unfortunately was instilled in him when he was a young man by Gard Chapin, who always tried to finagle. He also had my example—not that I am innocent of everything—but I am a correct citizen. I didn't cheat anybody, and anywhere I go they respect my integrity. Listen, for $100 to wind up in jail is asinine. Of course I told him that. But then his mother was on his side: "Oh my poor child. This judge is a crook." I had to make good for the bad check, plus expenses.

DENNY AABERG: Miki called and wanted me to testify on his behalf at the trial. I'd been in Mammoth with him, Nat Young, Joey Cabell, Mike Doyle, and Alema Kalama, in a condo. All I remember is saying that it would be perjury and that I couldn't do it.

Despite his legal woes, Miki didn't sit around waiting for the justice system to decide his fate. Instead he continued his travels, visiting New Zealand with Linda. When he returned, he went to see Marcia McMartin.

MARCIA MCMARTIN: We were outside, standing near my rose garden around noon. I knew Miki had something on his mind, but he had trouble telling me. Finally, he said, "I think I'm in love with someone else." I knew who. He'd been bouncing back and forth between me and this other woman, Linda, for about a year. I only saw her once. She was tan, petite, long hair. Not a real beauty, but attractive. I never asked how they'd met; I assumed through surfing. What surprised me was that he also said that for some reason he thought I didn't really love *him*. I *would* get frustrated with him; I guess the lack of warmth got to me. He said he thought I was just smitten by the fact that he was *Miki Dora*. He later told me that when he said that and saw my face, he immediately realized he'd been wrong. But the words had been said. I was dumbfounded. I had no inkling.

I don't know what I did the rest of that day, but a few days later, I told him, "You'd better spend some time with this girl, just see her, decide what you're going to do." And we stopped seeing each other. This was *hell* for me. Two or three weeks went by, and I didn't hear from him. So I called and asked what was going on. We saw each other, and he began bouncing back and forth again. He'd see me; he'd see her. Then I found out that Linda was seeing someone named Don Wilson because Miki told me Wilson had taken Linda to Costa Rica and he was going there to pick her up.

CHRISTINE DORA: Marcia was crazy about Miki. But Miklos once told her, "You should be so happy he's gone off with somebody else. One day you'll be very thankful about this."

MARCIA MCMARTIN: When he returned from Costa Rica I found out that Linda had decided to stay with Don. So he came back to me. He knew I'd take him back. I thought, "Now he's gotten it out of his system." Stupid me.

I went with Miki to the trial. My late stepfather, Richard Ney—an actor who later wrote a well-known financial newsletter—had written him a letter of recommendation. Miki didn't seem nervous. He assumed he wouldn't be locked up. In fact, he got probation, but the judge said if he got caught doing anything again he'd go right to jail.

Miki had been out of the country for his November 12, 1973, trial date, so the proceedings were postponed until early April 1974. When he showed up, the police took him into custody for having failed to appear. He was released on bond the next day and ordered to undergo a medical exam. Miki missed his next trial date, too, and the court issued a bench warrant. This pattern of promised appearances, no-shows, and warrants continued until September 26, when Miki came to court and was again taken into custody. At the time of his arrest, he wore a tie and sports coat. He had two Chapsticks in his pocket. Papers described him as six feet tall, 185 pounds, single. His occupation: self-employed salesman.

The next day, Miki appeared. The judge said he'd read the probation report and considered its suggestions. Then he pronounced sentence:

1. $1,500 fine, $100/month to Mono County probation officer, due 11/1/74
2. Restitution to: Mammoth Ski Lift, $401.89; Eddie Crespell, $18.81; T. C. Lu, Hong Kong, $1,028.00—paid in monthly installments of $50 until #1 paid off, then at $150/mo
3. Maintain only one bank account
4. Report to probation officer
5. No credit cards

The court also directed Miki to consent to examination of his banking records at any time, by his probation officer (PO). Other conditions were that he couldn't stop payment on any checks during probation without authorization of his PO. He also was required to maintain residence and employment as approved by the PO; obey all laws—state, federal, and local—orders, rules, and regulations of the court and PO; and report to the PO not less than once per month, in writing, and as directed in person by the PO.

On September 27, 1974, the judge told Miki that if he fulfilled all the probation requirements that the matter would be dismissed after three years.

According to the FBI, on October 3, 1974, Miki (allegedly) applied for a passport in the name of Richard Austin Roche Jr.

5

ROBBIE DICK: Richard Roche was a buddy of Dora's, a really good surfer and brilliant guy into higher mathematics. But he died crashing into the back of a trash truck.

JOHNNY FAIN: Miki immediately went to the house after the funeral to console Roche's wife. He said, "I'm sorry about this" and "I know how it is," and got her to trust him. He got all the information he possibly could about Richard, who had been establishing a company that built tennis courts. Miki got her at the right time and sucked all the information out of her.

He became Richard Roche and charged $58,000 to the estate in forged credit cards.

It took a few months, but on March 6, 1975, in Los Angeles, Miki was charged with making a false statement on a passport application.

JAN HANDZLIK: It was actually a John Doe warrant; that's what they use when they don't know your true name. He was John Doe, aka Richard Austin Roche Jr. Allegedly, using Roche's birth certificate, Miki had applied for a passport as Richard Austin Roche Jr., who had been born in Fullerton, California, in July 1944 and died on March 22, 1973.

Whoever had applied for a passport in Roche's name had submitted Miki's picture. Was it Miki? Still operating in the dark, the FBI decided to nail the culprit. First they set a trap, planting a dummy registered letter that required a signature when "Roche" picked up the documents. No one showed. Then the FBI began to interview Roche's family and friends and ask if anyone recognized the man in the application photo.

In June 1975, someone finally did.

Pulling Miki's files, police reports, driver's license records, and past passport applications, the FBI slowly pieced together the puzzle. They discovered some of Miki's many aliases, which included: Miklos Dora Jr., Michael S. Chapin, Mickey Dora, Alexander Dora, Kornel Dora, Michael Spring Chapin, and Mickel Spring Chapin. They discovered his numerous addresses around Los Angeles, as well as his various "occupations" such as salesman for "Greg Knoll [*sic*] surfboards," for his friend Joel Laykin's National Estate Preservation company, for Laykin Jewelers, and as an actor supposedly under contract to Warner Brothers. They put together a file that by 1976 ran almost 250 pages; it would later grow to almost 800 pages. Included were interviews with Miki's father, as well as "friends" who would only talk in strict confidence. Also in the file were Miki's passport applications dating back to 1949, including the latest (at the time), issued on July 13, 1971. A note in the file reported that this passport had been "lost" and replaced on October 25, 1971. Miki's official explanation

was that a "dog had ripped it to shreds." (Goes well with homework?)
The new passport expiration date was extended until July 13, 1976.

When the FBI finally connected Miki with the Mammoth incident
and his California criminal record, they unearthed a rap sheet of petty
incidents, ranging from driving an unregistered car from out of state,
to old arrests and dropped charges. The circle around Miki began to
close. But he already knew it.

MARCIA MCMARTIN: By then Miki had already decided to leave the country.
He was just fed up. Maybe he realized his other shenanigans might catch
up with him, I don't know. Miki wanted to live in New Zealand. He'd already
made several trips there, one with me. I thought it was a good idea. We were
going together. I knew Miki was on probation, but it didn't seem to bother me
at the time. I just knew if I didn't go with him, I'd be left behind. And that was
that. But honestly I was delighted to leave Los Angeles myself. We'd always
had these wonderful adventures. We had round-the-world airplane tickets in
case it didn't work out. It was a Miki ticket. I don't know how he got them, but
I know he didn't pay full price.

DON WILSON: Someone—I don't know who—had burglarized the Cardillo
Travel Agency in Los Angeles, and Miki wound up with some of the tickets. He
also had the embossing plate and machine that validated and authenticated
the tickets.

DIANE SWANSON OOSTERVEEN: Miki wanted my husband and me to take off
with him to New Zealand, to meet him there and help create a sanctuary. He
offered us tickets. I said, "Miki, I don't want hot tickets. I'm cool now. I'm a
vegetarian. Make love not war. I don't want to lead the bad life anymore."

LINDA CUY: Miki had really wanted to go to South Africa, and he had taken a
first trip there with Marcia. Evidently, and it's written in a note I made, he said
she gave him too much trouble in South Africa; she didn't trust the country,
she thought it was a little backward. Miki told me this. He also said, "God, they
had the best surf break. Jeffreys Bay was a perfect right. But she wanted to go
touring to Capetown. We went during a twelve-foot swell." He missed the swell
of the year and was furious.

When he told me, I threw my hands in the air and said, "See. You go with
Marcia and you're going to end up missing surf all over the place. If you'd
been with me that wouldn't have happened." He knew I didn't have the class
or artistry of Marcia, but I'd go surfing. He knew I'd look out for his interests.
I'd always opt for surfing over shopping.

I finally met Marcia the day Miki and I packed his Volkswagen van in 1974, getting everything ready to go to New Zealand. I was just dying. I said, "If you take Marcia you'll regret it because she doesn't surf. You'll be this little houseboy running around, doing stuff for her because that's what she's used to. If you want someone who is a companion, who'll do sports with you, play tennis, go surfing, rough it, ride horses, hunt wild pigs in New Zealand, then you want to go with me. So you decide." He went with her. He made a big mistake. I would have gone to South Africa in a second.

MARCIA MCMARTIN: We'd planned to start our way around the world in the fall of 1974 and end up in New Zealand. But Miki and I didn't leave together. He was a health fanatic and months earlier we had booked a couple weeks with a doctor and spa clinic in San Francisco, and planned to leave the country afterward. Then he decided he couldn't wait and didn't want to go to San Francisco. I did, and he went on ahead.

CYNTHIA APPLEWHITE: I had been in Tahiti for six weeks and when I got back I called Miki to tell him about my trip. His phone was disconnected. I went by his apartment and it so happened that the guy who had rented it was someone I knew; he'd waited on me in an antique store. He said Miki had taken off. I called his probation officer in Bishop, and he said, "He had our permission to leave. All he has to do is write to us and keep in touch."

As was common in DoraWorld, maybe yes, maybe no. Nonetheless, on April 11, 1975, the Superior Court of California for the County of Mono issued a bench warrant for Miklos Dora Jr. aka Michael Chapin. The charge: violating probation. If sighted, Miki was to be arrested. There would be no bail. On April 24, 1975, LAPD Chief Ed Davis's office sent a letter to Mono County Sheriff William B. Evans, stating that Dora was known to the LAPD, and that "all efforts to locate him have met with negative results." They reported that they had checked his address at 824 Gretna Green Way, Apt. 4, and discovered that he had "left that location in February of this year."

He hadn't. By February, Miki had already been long gone.

The FBI posted a memorandum to its field offices and representatives worldwide, as well as a "Look Out" card on Miki. A note said that he was "armed and dangerous, known to carry a large knife, and may be emotionally unstable."

Again, maybe yes, maybe no.

The LAPD letter also indicated that "Special Agent John Leake,

Diners Club Corporation, had informed investigators that Miklos Dora was in Switzerland."

The FBI's file suggested he was in Australia.

He had been in both locations, but not for long. As always, Miki kept two or three steps ahead of his pursuers. They should have known: Da Cat wouldn't be caged.

CHAPTER **TEN**

Whereabouts Unknown

1

A: I always have an escape route in my life. Everything I do I try to think on a 360-degree level. In this situation I was in a hole, which I couldn't get out of. I was painted into a corner. They were ready to put me away for three or four years, and they had a kangaroo court all set up—and I can prove this, it's all documented—and I thought, I'm going to leave this country anyway. I was planning for years to go to New Zealand, to set up a survival home. . . . So I decided I'm not going to fight these bastards. I don't pay taxes and I get nothing in return. If I wanted to live under socialism I could go to Europe or elsewhere. So I said to hell with it.

Q: And all of a sudden you become an international fugitive?
A: Right.
Q: And you're how old at this point?
A: It was 1974. I was born in 1934.
Q: Wow. That's fairly late in your career, to go on the run like that.
A: Not to go on the run. I was leaving, anyhow. That was my escape route from corruption. My days in Southern California were finished, because they had taken over everything—lifeguard control, the police were on my back everywhere. Before that, I lived like a king. It was all crumbling. It was the end. But my life continued, like it did before.

—Miki, from a conversation with film producer Michael McDonnell, 1999

JAN MAYER: I was a young hippie leather worker living out of my VW van in Bidart, just north on the Côte Basque from Guéthary. My friend Gregg Blue (formerly Marsh), and his girlfriend, Lynne, lived "next door" in their VW van. Both vans were parked just outside the Hotel du Fronton, a charming, Basque-style building located right above the surf in Bidart, just south of Biarritz.

Miki showed up in the late fall of 1974, with friends, and checked into the hotel. Despite the nineteenth-century royal pretensions, Biarritz is in many ways a small town, and he became part of the family.

Miki and I bonded, although we had differences. He didn't comprehend why I wanted to work so hard. He did propose to me, on at least one occasion, "Why don't I just crash into your car and sue you, and we'll split the money." I said, "Well, I don't work that way."

I also introduced him to a very close friend of mine, Philippe Lauga, who worked for the Bank Nacional de Paris, now BNP Paribas. Philippe became one of Miki's most faithful and loyal French/Basque friends. He was there for Miki in every way imaginable, for decades, and yet they were from totally different worlds. Philippe played by the rules, and Miki had no respect for anyone's rules except his own. Yet Miki knew when the going got tough, he could always count on Philippe, like you count on parents and family.

MARCIA MCMARTIN: I showed up in France about two weeks after Miki. We took a trip to Spain with Nat Young and an American girl—with whom Miki might have had an affair before I got there—but we had to leave her behind on the way back because she'd forgotten her passport. Eventually, Miki and I went to Val d'Isère to ski, which he'd booked through Club Med. For the holidays we went to stay with our friend Peter Bruhoffer in Switzerland and planned to go to London next to get our visas for the rest of the trip.

Then, suddenly, at Peter's, Miki broke up with me. He said he'd decided to be with Linda after all. Maybe he'd heard that she didn't want to be with Don Wilson; maybe she'd contacted him. All I know is that he said he'd sent her a plane ticket so she could come meet him.

It was Christmas. I was terribly upset. I walked around the little town by myself and cried.

LINDA CUY: Miki decided to be with me. We'd been writing letters and calling and talking the whole time. I kept making my case. We were the same type. I thought we were right for each other.

I don't want to sound cold about Marcia. There's nothing wrong with Marcia. Miki even said, "She's a sweet girl and I love her very much, but . . . I don't think I could settle down and be the kind of person she wants me to be." He realized that wherever he and Marcia went, she'd have nothing to do. So he left her in Switzerland, and I joined up.

Miki wanted a mad adventurous spirit, which was me. I couldn't sit in one place too long, making a home. I'd do it for a while and then the roller-coaster ride would start again. Let's go surfing. Let's go wild. That's what his spirit gravitated toward and that's what hooked us together for so long.

Miki told me that it made him nuts to be torn between two people and that it hurt to tell Marcia that he'd had to make a choice. The thing between Miki and Marcia was a very strong connection, but I was on Miki's level. We were soul mates. It's the struggle, the yin and yang battle between passion and security.

MARCIA MCMARTIN: Of course, Miki didn't totally break it off with me. He kept me on the string. He told me to go to Christine's—Miklos's wife's—father's farm, outside Manchester. He said he'd call. I waited almost two weeks. When he finally called, it was some Miki conversation where nothing was cut and dried, never committing, and I realized nothing would happen. At the end of the week I knew: This is really it. Quite a turn of events, considering that we had once planned to marry in Biarritz. Quite frankly, I'm glad he never did marry me, with all his legal problems and credit card stuff that came up afterward.

I had my plane ticket and could have gone home, but I thought, Hell no, I'm going to take advantage of this. I went to London, as we'd originally planned, to get visas to go to Iran, Burma, and places like that. I had to drop off my passport each morning at a different embassy, and then pick it up in the afternoon and take it to the next. I had just come from one when I heard, "Marcia, Marcia turn around! It's Miki!" He had also been collecting visas. We talked for a few minutes. My birthday was the next day, January 29. He asked about my hotel and I told him. I also told him, "Just leave me alone, Miki. Stop torturing me." And I walked off. But he had said he would call for my birthday, and there I was, sitting in my hotel the next day waiting. He never did call. That was the last time I saw him.

After traveling with Linda from Switzerland through Austria, Greece, Egypt, Turkey, Lebanon, India, Ceylon, and Australia on his "Miki tickets," the couple landed in New Zealand with plans to settle on the Mahia Peninsula located in the Wairoa District of northern Hawkes Bay, on the east side of New Zealand's North Island. It is also a surfing paradise, and for Miki's purposes, a hideaway far from the Western civilization he despised.

"I can't live in the Northern Hemisphere," Miki explained some years later to filmmaker Bill Delaney. "I must live back, back into time, where all these animals, all this sea life, shellfish, crustaceans, is part of the smell. Everything has to come into the focus of the whole experience. If you don't understand that, then you're only a pretender. The whole magnificence of riding waves is that living being, that communication between you and the whole existence of reality on this planet."

"Miki was still looking for that Garden of Eden with the perfect break," said Greg Meisenholder. "Perhaps this time he'd found it."

CLIVE NEESON: In the early '70s, New Zealand was little known by the rest of the world. Even the hippie trail seemed to have overlooked it. The economy was tightly controlled and the government right-wing. We had hardly any concept of how our own country rated in all aspects, including surf. But a small network of early global surfers did, and it seemed they left each country as soon as they got the notion that the *rest* of the surfing world had got wind of it. Rumors suggested that at times their moves were also influenced when certain of their unorthodox lifestyle-sustaining enterprises caught up with them. Some of the American surfers who came were escapees from the Vietnam draft. But not all. A small contingent of regular Californians lived in Raglan, a tiny harbor town on the west side of the north island, populated mainly by old war veterans and local Maoris. They enjoyed the perfection of the legendary Indicators break for themselves. In the winter they disappeared to Bali, then back to Raglan for the New Zealand summer, which is the American winter.

DON WILSON: Miki had gone to New Zealand a couple times in the early 1970s and applied for a visa to live there. They granted it. So he bought everything he possibly could on his credit cards, used all of his charge accounts right to the max, and put it all in a huge shipping container. He also bought a Volkswagen camper, and an insurance contract guaranteeing that if he was injured or out of work that the loan would be paid off. Not long after he got the car, he put in a disability claim with the insurance company. They paid off the VW and gave him the pink slip. He drove it into the shipping container and sent it to New Zealand, where it sat at the port for a couple years.

CLIVE NEESON: The first time I saw Miki was in 1973. He arrived in Raglan, in a taxi. It pulled up on the other side of a muddy puddle next to our clapped-out Austin mini. A taxi was a rare sight at a remote surf break. He sat in the backseat in formal attire. He seemed older and was definitely transfixed by the waves, as he surveyed every set. Meanwhile, we contemplated the taxi meter still running and speculated on the small fortune clocking up during the lulls.

Dora stayed initially in the Hotel, which was unthinkable then for a surfer. On our level, a Ford station wagon was a surfer's home and secondarily a mode of transport.

During his first visit, Dora scored two back-to-back five-day swells. It was an unforgettable stretch. I guess that had made up his mind he was in the right place, which is why he came back a couple years later.

At the time, Miki was almost forty years old. Few people in New Zealand knew of his background, or were even interested. As such, he was very approachable and mellow. He had a way of embracing your company by asking questions and your opinions. This was unusual for an older guy.

Miki's maturity and politeness made him a good mentor for young surfers, though I think this was lost on many of the undirected renegades of the era. My brother and I were greenhorn grommets whose father owned the Raglan Pub (Harbour View Hotel). Because we didn't harass or threaten Miki, he invited us round one night to his place and showed us through his picture albums. He lived in what we called a granny cottage on Harbourside Drive, at the end of Bow Street, a typical waterside weatherboard house usually occupied by old and retired people.

He didn't seem to miss his California days. He just seemed quietly proud.

At the time, I wondered how he could bear to exist in a sea of people, surfers, who were basically school dropouts. New Zealand could be a paradise in terms of anonymity, but it was no place for someone with an active mind.

Nonetheless, Miki had returned.

YVES BESSAS: I had met Miki in 1968 in France and we became friends. In Chinese astrology, Miki and I were both dogs looking for freedom. When dogs don't get their freedom, they become rebels. When I saw him in Los Angeles in 1974, I told Miki that I would meet him in New Zealand. I was sitting on a bench when he and Linda showed up. We decided to rent a house together for a month. Miki told me, "I go to Auckland tomorrow to pick up my gear," and he asked me to come along in his VW bus. He wore a red corduroy jacket with a round pin with a stripe. It was very flashy.

We arrived at Customs at nine in the morning. I waited in the bus with Linda while he tried to clear up his gear. At three o'clock we saw Miki. His jacket was torn in pieces and falling apart. I don't know what he did, but I think he was fooling around. He said, "They gave me such a hard time, I'm naked now. I'm ruined."

We were on the sidewalk, talking about what had happened, when an Indian guy, an immigrant like Miki, fell down in front of us and died. I tried to make respiration efforts so he would breathe. Miki said, "Don't do that, he may be sick!" He also said, "Look: The Customs people killed this guy! He's got five kids and they gave him such a hard time he died. By luck I didn't die."

Then Miki put out all his gear, and it was incredible. Motorcycle, surfboard, all the tools from America you can imagine. Juicer. Clothes. The bus was packed full.

I was in New Zealand with a friend, and when we stayed with Miki he was on an Adele Davis diet trip and ate a lot of cow liver. My friend Jacques and I were vegetarians full-on. After a month we couldn't live there anymore. Miki got upset. We said, "Miki, we're both looking for the perfect food, but I think Adele Davis is wrong. Besides, we can't stand the smell. You eat like shit." We remained friends after that, but I moved out.

JACKIE SMITH: He'd even blend up liver for breakfast. In fact, his and Linda's two Cavalier King Charles spaniels were named Epinard and Rognon: spinach and kidney, in French.

CLIVE NEESON: We never knew if was true, but the French guys—Jacques and Yves were their names—told me that while they were away Miki sold their furniture. They said they would write to *Surfer* magazine to complain. They were funny. I don't know if they were gay, but Miki used to call them "a couple of faggots." I went round their place once or twice for dinner. They had all these dreams about forming a commune. They were a bit in la-la land.

Then Miki decided it was time to move on from Raglan. We assumed he'd gone back to the U.S.A. But that winter, during a surf trip, we ran into him on Mahia Peninsula.

SHANE GRIMES: Mahia, on the other side of the island from Raglan, is rural farming and fishing country south of Gisborne, on a railway that's now unused. It's pretty hard-core living. Many places then didn't have power or hot water. The winters are cold; it's not the South Pacific. Miki could be anonymous, but this was not a suburban reality.

Miki and Linda looked for a little clapboard country house. They had the dogs. They wanted to settle in. A few years later Miki would show friends in France a slide show of his time in New Zealand. "He had pictures of the house, of him digging the garden," says one. "He was very domestic, making vegetables grow. There was a shot of Linda on the side of the house, in a bathing suit; and the mountains and the ocean." For fun, Miki and some Mormon missionaries he met would occasionally hunt goats and make stew.

MIKE HISCHIER: He rented his place from Joe and Bette Olsen, who also wanted to sell it. Miki told them he had a bunch of money coming from an inheritance. "There's no need to charge me rent, because I'm just going to buy it from you when the money comes in."

CLIVE NEESON: Miki invited us round one evening to a comfortable two-story house with panoramic views of the bay. We asked him how much he paid for this flash joint. "Nothing," he said. "The guy just asked me to look after it." Classic. That was Dora. Styling it again.

2

Pleased to meet you, hope you guess my name. But what's puzzling you is the nature of my game.
        —Mick Jagger/Keith Richards, "Sympathy for the Devil"

8.13.75 [Letter to Ramona and Gardner]
    I spent my XLI birthday like every other day in New Zealand, trying to keep warm and gather sufficient food to keep the old bones from becoming too brittle. Where I am residing it's about 25 miles to the nearest town. It looks like the dump in The Last Picture Show . . . *Nothing works, everything seems to collapse. I have no phone, no electricity, just my two fateful companions Epinard and Rognon; they're eight months of age and keep a consistent vigilance on our sanctuary . . . My ambiguous intentions to come to New Zealand were my anticipated fears of a predicted depression in the United Snakes of America. It seems I was a bit premature in my departure . . . Yet I'm still here. Why you ask? Because where I am there is no outside*

world . . . In California I had my home burgled three different occasions and most everything of value taken. After months of my own investigating I discovered who the house-breaking marauder was. I notified the authorities to my find but as usual they're not keen to do anything to help the citizen. Way down here I do not have any of these problems. I have nothing anymore, so what's to take? In the U.S. I'm known by name only to some 100,000 crazed spoiled surf bum brats who use my name for every conceivable caper under the sun to make me look like an idiot. I have had good humor for the most part but some of it has had financial repercussions that have cost me dearly.

Considering all factors, I'm very fortunate I have none of these long gone pressures anymore. I fish and hunt, plant my garden, wash, sew, clean, work for myself only and am relatively content in my life. Most people in all probability would be bored stiff, yet every day brings something new in nature's treachery, which plays on one's survival instincts.

STEVE CONNERS: In early 1975, I was a Mormon missionary in New Zealand. I was nineteen or twenty at the time and posted to Nuhaka and Mahia Beach. My mission partner, Rod Hughes, and I met some of the surf guys. "Surf bums" is what we called them. Some were Americans, and being Americans, we immediately tried to make friends. We'd bring them to the church on Monday, our day off. The church was probably the biggest building for sixty miles. They'd play basketball. The Cramer brothers, twins in their thirties, knew Miki well. One day they brought him along. I could tell he'd never played basketball, but he had incredible athletic ability. I was also amazed, because I later found out he was forty years old, and he sure didn't look it.

That day Miki heard organ music coming from the chapel, and he wandered off. He seemed awestruck. The organist was twelve years old. He said, "I can't believe this little kid playing the organ." Of course, being a missionary, I jumped all over the slightest indication of interest.

Miki invited us to his house, a little beach place up on stilts. He drove a VW van. We met Linda Cuy. Miki told us they were married. She was kind of hedgy about that, but wouldn't say one way or the other. I thought that was strange. I guess us being religious folk, maybe they didn't want us to think badly of them. Linda told me they'd come through Bali, and that she'd gotten malaria there.

The house was a stone's throw from the beach. They had more stuff crammed inside than seemed possible: coins from Alexander the Great, Chinese gold carvings, Persian rugs, steamer trunks, a leopard skin jacket. I remember wondering, Where in the world did you get this stuff, and where'd you get your money? He told me he'd had it shipped from America in a crate, along with the van.

Rod and I wanted to teach them about our church. They seemed very, very interested. But one thing was strange: Every time we'd have a standard prayer with Miki, like, "Our father in heaven, we're thankful to be here meeting with Miki and Linda. We hope the spirit will be here," he'd start laughing. He'd get hysterical, bust up and walk around the room with a big grin. We'd go, "What's so funny?" He'd say, "I don't know, I guess it's just the spirit." Linda seemed a little embarrassed by his behavior.

Miki always talked a lot about his mother. She was heavy into this radio preacher named Herbert Armstrong, and his show "The World Tomorrow." She sent a lot of money to him. I couldn't tell if he was okay with it or not, even though he insisted she could do what she wanted.

We had many religious discussions. One time he brought a friend by, a white-blond-haired surfer named David Caldwell, who seemed to know Miki really well. A handsome kid. If he was over thirty he sure didn't look it. Miki wanted us to teach him, too. We ended up getting in an argument with the guy. Miki got mad at us. He said, "What're you doing getting into an argument for? Just sit him down and explain it to him like you explained it to me." Eventually we went, "You know, this guy's too strange. We don't want to hang out here too much."

DAVID CALDWELL: I'm sure I was very anti-anybody who was into one-way religious thinking. I thought Miki was completely putting them on. But maybe secretly Miki believed and wanted to belong. Maybe he thought that was his ticket to heaven. But I don't think Miki believed in anything.

STEVE CONNERS: About a week later, Miki and Linda waltzed into our place one evening. He went, "Hey, I've been reading this book you gave me. I had a dream last night that these two men dressed in white came to visit me and told me I needed to listen to what you have to say." He seemed hard-core serious. Rod and I looked at each other and went, "Well . . . Okay." We kept teaching him. His interest seemed to grow and grow, and Linda also seemed very interested. I had my reservations, but I kept them to myself.

Miki's questions were stereotypical: Why is there death and badness in the world if God is good? I asked him if he lived the Commandments. He said, "Yeah, I'm living all of them. There's not one I'm breaking. I'm living a perfect life, what else do I have to do?" In retrospect, I totally think he was pulling our

ABOVE TOP: Linda Cuy and Miki in New Zealand, 1975. Photo courtesy Rod Hughes.

ABOVE: Baptism day, July 19, 1975. Miki and Rod Hughes in the pool. Linda Cuy and David Caldwell in upper left corner. Photo courtesy Rod Hughes.

legs. You got to realize the mentality: I was barely twenty, eager for success, for converts. You have a tendency to overlook a lot of things.

We'd been talking to Miki and Linda for about a month when the Cramers told us Miki was famous and rich. I see that I wrote in my journal that I asked Miki about it and he just blew it off. He also tried to get us to go surfing, but being missionaries, we aren't even allowed to go swimming.

At a certain point, it's laid out in the discussions that you are to flat-out ask, "Do you want to be baptized?" When we asked, he said yes. Linda said no. I was shocked. She was more quiet than Miki, but from the questions she asked, she seemed to be more into it. So we set a time, then finished up our discussions—there were seven or eight steps that we went through to prepare for baptism. He was interviewed by a local bishop, Andrew Brown. Brown seemed to think everything was okay.

CONNERS JOURNAL: 7/4/75
Linda is unhappy and wants to go to Tahiti. She said she was too cold here. Well, apparently they *are* married and were married in the States—so he says. I still wonder if they really are married. Linda said the closing prayer and they were both in a strange mood. He wants to know if the church could find him a good wife. He asked us a lot about it, and it was kind of funny really. It was an unusual day, and we left.

HUGHES DIARY: 7/8/75
Linda was in good spirits tonight. They were especially impressed with the power of the priesthood. Boy, Miki could sure do a lot of missionary work for us.

CONNERS JOURNAL: 7/14/75
I got Miki in the corner after ping-pong and had a good talk with him about Linda. He told me a few things that have to do with her being sick. Sometimes she was real happy and other times she wasn't. Then at the close of things we gave the prayer—and Miki started to laugh again.

HUGHES DIARY: 7/19/75
I baptized Miklos S. Dora today. It was one of the greatest experiences of my life. It started at about 8:45 in the Mahia chapel. A lot of people were there. The baptism was at Morere (local hot springs). It was great. President Ormond confirmed him and gave him the

Holy Ghost. Mickey was real humble all the way through. He didn't even laugh during the confirmation. That's the part I was worried the most about.

ROD HUGHES: I remember him coming up out of the water after the baptism with a smile on his face, saying something like, "This feels right." It was an exciting experience for me. He was the first person I converted. I thought Miki was sincere.

STEVE CONNERS: Afterward, Miki was shaking, almost in tears. He said, "This is just wonderful. I've never felt this way in my whole life. I could just float," or words to that effect. At the time I thought, Okay, now he's really interested. But in retrospect, I think that might have been an act, too. I came to that conclusion when I learned years later that when he had been in New Zealand, he was hiding out. He was a wanted man! We had no clue. If we had, there's no way they'd ever let him be baptized.

DAVID CALDWELL: During the baptism Linda and I sat by the pool, very sacrilegiously doing the silent laugh while looking at Miki. It was complete immersion. He kept a straight face, but it was the funniest thing I ever saw. Afterwards, we asked Miki, "Why'd you do it?" He smiled and gave a one-line answer: "Because nobody ever asked me to go to heaven with them before!"

3

11.25.75 [Letter to Miklos]

New Zealand: Dear Father, I had to take a tranquilizer after your last letter. I can only tell you this: There is in this creature by the name Don Wilson, the poor man's Dillinger of our times. This person is an escaped convict. A record of forgery, credit card theft and many other offenses, I'm quite sure. He's been dashing around the US and elsewhere using my checks and credit cards and identifications. His father, a Pacific Palisades financier financing his son's swashbuckling adventures. It's too strange to comprehend. Only by contacting the LA police will anyone be able to find out some of this assailant's past history. I lived in the US 40 years with not a blemish on my record, as a citizen in good standing . . . (There is) only the Bridgeport problem in which I was blackmailed by a corrupted judge and made to plead guilty. My consternation and apprehensiveness towards the US, its turbulent and violent life patterns, were some of the contributing factors for finding a peaceful land to settle and raise a family. I was sure New Zealand was this land, a self-sufficient home with garden-grown foods, with some of the comforts and pleasures to make a life a happy one. I sure hope things are going to work out. Please advise me what you think I should do in this matter. I'm so sorry for the trouble this has caused you and Max [Author note: Christine's nickname]. *Love, Miki.*

Two days later, Miki wrote literally the same letter to his brother, Gardner, adding only this sentence: "I now understand the FBI is looking for me on a number of charges."

LINDA CUY: New Zealand was a bad deal. We got in a lot of trouble there. It started out with good intentions but it sure ended up in a mess. The whole thing just had a bad mix. First of all, New Zealand was Marcia's choice, but Miki and I had to go and live there. The whole reason for leaving the U.S. was to go to another spot that had nice surf. Well, it didn't have great surf. We went, "What's this all about? This place isn't the greatest. It had left-hand points. Miki rode them fine, but he hated lefts. Also, at a lot of the little spots in Mahia, you had to wait weeks for surf to come; then it was usually very, very windy. An onshore wind. Maybe we didn't give it enough time, but I think what Miki really wanted was the lifestyle of France—the abundance of food and that European charm—and a little surf spot like Malibu, with just a few friends to watch him surf.

And then out of the blue, Don Wilson shows up and there's this whole scene. It was doomed.

JIM KEMPTON: I won't get it exactly right, but in terms of a Shakespearean cross, double-cross, triple-cross, there's nothing I've ever heard that tops their trip to New Zealand.

Linda is with Miki, and Don comes. It's 1975. Don spirits her away to some exotic corner of New Zealand, and then she asks Miki to come and save her. Miki comes and spirits her away. Don, knowing that Miki took her, calls the New Zealand authorities and has Miki stopped at the airport. Linda, who was with Miki, then goes back with Don. It's full of romantic plot details that I've heard, but only the participants *really* know. Let's just say that everyone betrays someone else in order to get revenge, satisfaction, or escape.

DON WILSON: Linda finally dropped me a line in France and said, "Please come rescue me." I flew to New Zealand and walked up to their door. Miki answered with a shotgun in his hands. His comment was, "How did you find me here? Who told you I'm living here? Do the police know I'm here?" Always the questions trying to put you on the defensive. Never, "Hi, how are you?" Anyhow . . . I grabbed Linda and we took off. Miki called the police immediately and said there's a world-famous bandit in town and he has just kidnapped my wife and they're in such and such a car going south. Miki, of course, had stolen Linda's passport and identification, so she had to go to the embassy and apply for a new one. I hung off to the side and they arrested me in a hotel under false charges that Miki had made up.

WAYNE SPEEDS: Don told me that after Miki came to the door with a shotgun, they had a screaming match, and Don went to the police. Of course, Linda was the instigator. How else would Don have found out where Miki was in New Zealand? She would write letters saying "Rescue me." That's what got Don going. He was encouraged. He went down there like Mighty Mouse, with an attitude of "Kill Mickey!" I can almost see it in my mind's eye, him pounding on the door and Dora telling him to go away. Maybe Dora also called the police on Don.

LINDA CUY: Miki got him arrested and that left me in the lurch.

DON WILSON: I spent three months in jail in New Zealand. They let Linda go immediately. Miki realized right away that he was in trouble and fled the country. Of course, the New Zealand police confiscated everything Miki had obtained under false pretenses in the U.S.—all his little toys, coin collection, Persian rugs, etc. He wasn't penniless, because he always had a money belt. They also wanted him because he'd been doing scams there with credit cards and bad checks.

According to Miki's FBI file, the bureau had heard from Interpol that Miki was in Wellington, New Zealand, on December 10, 1975. He'd been noticed because of bad debts. The FBI was advised that he might attempt to leave the country soon. Interpol alerted the New Zealand authorities about Miki's situation with the U.S. federal authorities, but the Extradition Section of the U.S. Department of Justice also noted that according to the new treaty between the United States and New Zealand, the charges were not an extraditable offense. By January 20, 1976, New Zealand police authorities in

Auckland knew of Miki's whereabouts, and the Diners Club company thought it would be no problem to get a complaint and arrest warrant on counterfeit credit card charges. Miki had allegedly changed his own card from #5130 0836 7 to #5180 0836 7.

As usual, in addition to Don Wilson's rendition, a multiplicity of stories sought to explain Miki's troubles and escape.

PETER DAY: He'd been writing bad checks and the feds found him in New Zealand. He had to leave immediately, basically with the steam still rising from his soup. They came in the front door while he went out the back.

MIKE HISCHIER: His landlords said that he just left in the middle of the night. He drove petty much from Mahia to Auckland and split.

DAVID CALDWELL: We left New Zealand and went to Australia together. He said he was just traveling. If he left on the run, there were no sirens after him. I didn't sense that at all.

CHRIS MALLOY: Miki once told me that New Zealand was the best part of his life. He'd finally gotten away from America, then the FBI came and took it all. I asked him what he did and he said, "Nothing." I said, "Come on, what'd you do?" He said, "Lookit, if you were twenty-five years old and they gave you all these checkbooks and credit cards and told you to spend money, what would you do?" He said they took everything. I said, "Everything?" He said, "Yeah. I don't care about any of it but I wish I could get my Duke trophy back. Can you help me get my Duke trophy back?"

Miki probably had time enough to pack a bag, but this much is apparently true: After more or less a year in New Zealand, he left virtually empty-handed. His many possessions—surfboards, diaries, family heirlooms, clothes, childhood memorabilia, tourist trinkets, Duke contest trophies, Third Reich leather trench coat, personal surfing films, magazines, books, and a Volkswagen bus—were left behind.

Perhaps his dearest possessions were the photo and memorabilia albums he had to abandon. He'd filled one, the cover of which read in faded handwriting, "Today Malibu Tomorrow Whole World," with copies of magazine stories about him, copies of various "Da Cat" board ads, wine labels, classic surf photos of his heroes (Bob Simmons at "Point Doom" in 1951. Matt Kivlin at Rincon on November 18, 1951, Phil Edwards at Makaha in 1958, a shot of himself as a teenager captioned "Boy Squinting," Simmons at Malibu in September 1949, a photo captioned "Makaha Jim Fisher Winter 1954/The Beginning of the End" with Fisher on a very large wave), letters from surf magazines inviting him to functions or congratulating him on his making the *Surfer* poll, personal notes from the likes of Tom Morey, and stories he'd written. Also part of the booty: guns.

Meanwhile, Miki headed for Australia, where he broke his arm while riding a horse. He spent a month recovering at Nat Young's ranch. David Caldwell dropped by and took gag photos of himself and Miki arm-wrestling. "He didn't look too happy, but I thought it was pretty funny," says Caldwell.

Inevitably, the journey continued. In Bali, Miki saw François Lartigau, whom he'd befriended years before in Biarritz. "I was watching the sunset, I see this guy walking in the shore break with a tennis racket," says Lartigau. "He looked really clean and different from all the hippies who hung around that place. The next day I was at Uluwatu, surfing. I was in the shade, resting and cooling off and when I opened my eyes, Miki was sitting next to me. I said, 'Hey, what are you doing? Where's Linda?' He said, 'I didn't take her, she didn't come over here. She hates going left.' He didn't surf much in Bali because he'd broken his arm. He played tennis instead."

Miki traveled next to Mauritius and Kenya, where, on March 26, 1976, he used his expired Diners Club card in Nairobi.

Eventually, Miki returned to the Pays Basque, alone.

On August 12, 1976, a Colorado federal grand jury charged that from January 1, 1975, to March 31, 1975, "Dora did use and attempt to use a counterfeit, fictitious, altered and forged" Diners Club card, to obtain goods in excess of $1,000 in value. A warrant for his arrest was issued under federal jurisdiction in Denver to return Miki there to "answer to an indictment charging him with fraudulent use of a credit card." Bail: $5,000.

The same year, Mattel debuted its Malibu Barbie.

4

DON WILSON: After Miki broke his arm at Noosa Heads, things seemed to go downhill because everywhere he went it always seemed that Interpol was trying to get him. The only safe and civilized place where there was no extradition agreement with American law was France. I had told Miki about this many years ago, so he set up base in France in 1976. When it was warm, he lived in and around Biarritz. He'd spend winters skiing in Val d'Isère, which is about six hundred miles north. Periodically, he would jump out of France and go into, say, Germany or Italy to do a scam and then go back to France. I think he spent some time in the Canary Islands and traveled around Europe and maybe went to Morocco with Linda. Baron Philippe de Rothschild, for whom Miki's father worked, gave Miki a letter on Rothschild letterhead saying that the family extended its financial arm and respect to Miki Dora. In other words it was a carte blanche letter saying Miki could do anything he wanted to. And whenever he was arrested he would show the letter to the police and they would say "bye-bye."

GREGG BLUE: All I know is that he had Baron de Rothschild's phone number and said that the baron gave it to him. He had a case of Château Mouton Rothschild in his van. Using the number, we could call anywhere in the world. He'd go into the phone booth, turn his back, and block my view of the dial. He'd say, "Hello? I'm a friend of Baron Philippe." The operator would say, "Yes. What number would you like to dial?" He'd read off the number and the operator would dial it.

MIKLOS DORA SR.: I had introduced Miki to Baron Philippe de Rothschild in Mouton. Baron Philippe always, even though he was ancient, liked good-looking women. He got very friendly with Miki and Linda—she was a hot potato—and they played Ping-Pong, walked, had lunch and dinner together. But I don't think that Baron Philippe would give him that kind of letter. Miki indulged in too much fantasy. All the baron would give Miki is a recommendation for another château to welcome him.

JIM KEMPTON: I'm sure Miki could have fabricated something after the baron had written the first part. Or he could easily have gotten letterhead from the baron's desk. I know that he worked the baron for everything he could get. Linda told me they often had dinner at the baron's house. But he was an old man . . . needed a son. He was known to spend millions on endowments. Miki had this scam he tried to work on the baron. It was about finding this incredible wave in New Guinea. He wanted to take a team of National Geographic people, or Jacques Cousteau, to study it. The baron was going to fund that, but it fell through. In those days anything was possible. We'd sit around spouting our get-rich scams. We were always full of dreams and plans.

However, Miki's plan to find the wave of all waves was authentic.

PHILIPPE LAUGA: I found a typed pamphlet Miki wrote sometime in early 1977 in order to raise funds and sponsorship for this quest for the "episonic wave," the rogue wave. People involved in this expedition were supposed to be: Ian Faulkner, a Welsh fellow who now is foreman for BMW in Bayonne; Yves Bessas; Gregg Blue—then known as Gregg Marsh; Philippe Dacsma, who lived in Brazil; and Ronny Bell from New Zealand.

The four-page prospectus is a masterwork of hyperbole with utopian spin appeal. By selectively doling out facts, the language manages to suggest more substance than actually exists, not to the wave—that's the legitimate mystery—but to Miki. All of it was true as long as you didn't look too closely.

The "episonic wave" itself was, according to Miki, "a Bermuda Triangle–like phenomenon supposedly accountable for the mysterious disappearance of many ships. It is a wave of enormous proportions not caused by any of the usual means, e.g.: storms, earth tremors, or quakes." He planned to begin looking near New Guinea, where, in the same place, even when there are no other waves on the coastline for hundreds of miles, "a remarkable wave breaks with monotonous regularity and without apparent cause—a wave "of a size capable of swallowing and taking to the bottom even a supertanker."

He'd also get to do some exotic surfing in remote locations.

LOUIS ZAMPERINI: Miki sent my wife, Cynthia, and me a letter about the episonic wave in which he included an algebraic formula for the wave itself, and how to find it. We always thought he was a nice guy—he'd store his surfboards in our attic when he wasn't in the country, and he always called us to pick him up at the airport in Los Angeles, and he stayed with us until he made other arrangements—but with this wave thing we thought he'd gone slightly off his rocker.

Actually, Miki hadn't. A story by William J. Broad in the July 11, 2006, *New York Times* should finally put an end to any speculation about his sanity and, possibly, his motivation. Episonic/rogue waves are indeed real. According to the *Times*, "Enormous waves that sweep the ocean are traditionally called rogue waves, implying that they have a kind of freakish rarity. Over the decades, skeptical oceanographers have doubted their existence and tended to lump them together with sightings of mermaids and sea monsters. But scientists are now finding that these giants of the sea are far more common and destructive than once imagined, prompting a rush of new studies and research projects."

5

Grenoble, 01.10.77
Dear Father & Max . . .

Please forgive me for not writing before this . . . I've tried many times to phone you to no avail. I must walk 2 kilometer in the snow to find a phone system. You see I'm tucked away in a small village in the Swiss Alps completely snowed in for the season. I work 7 days a week & up by 6:00 A.M. I haven't had a free day in over 4 months . . . look forward to seeing you all in May. I sure hope you make it this year. Thanks so much for the Christmas gift, just got it the other day. Things take a long time in this part of the world. Thanks again. Love, Miki Jr.

Grenoble, 02.28.77
Dear Father,

. . . My life still has a bit of adventure, every day bring's forth new unexpected delights, its interesting living with new-found friends I would never have imagined in the U.S. Still I have glorious memories of my life growing up in California and find myself day-dreaming often of those amazingly uncluttered and uncomplicated times, wandering alone, riding isolated waves on deserted beaches for years of great pleasure that will never ever happen again to anyone. I thank you for this gift. —Miki

GREGG BLUE: I didn't know Miki was on the run when he came up to Val d'Isère. He drove and lived in a green Mercedes camper van. I had a funky house up in the old village; it was like a monastery: 350 years old, made of stone and trees. Miki parked outside my house and I passed him an extension cord. That's where he spent a winter so cold that in the morning the toilet water was frozen. Our neighbor was a dairy farmer with fifty cows who lived underneath his house in the winter. One of us would walk through the cow shit in the morning with a jug and bring back a bucket of hot, fresh milk right from the udders. We'd use pure Van Houten's cocoa powder and honey, and that would be our breakfast with some French bread. Then we'd go ski our brains out.

LINDA CUY: When we lived in the camper, there were always dishes to wash. I used to do my part but it would get to the point where Miki wanted to play backgammon to break up the evening. Everything was like a bet to Miki. He loved games, the sport of it, but he never played for fun. And if he lost he'd get very upset. I'd say, "If you win, you don't have to wash the dishes, I'll wash them." Then we bet on back massages and I won all the time. He ended up in debt to me for a ten-minute massage, then a thirty-minute massage, then, eventually, an hour-and-forty-five-minute massage. I said, "When are you gonna pay this debt?" Miki, in his chivalrous way, would say, "Let's go out for a nice meal and cancel that whole debt." He couldn't stand it anymore. The idea of massaging someone for that long made him squirm. He was a good massager, but not good at paying a debt.

GREGG BLUE: I opened my house and myself to Miki. Unfortunately, he stole my passport, and one belonging to a guy named Peter who rented out a thirty-passenger bus I had in front of my house for the winter. They were found together in a trash can in a train station. I had heard that Miki stole passports so I asked him point-blank, "Miki, my passport is gone. Do you know anything about it?" He looked me straight in the face and said, "No." I wanted to believe him, but it was just too much of a coincidence. I had to go get a new passport and it was a big hassle.

JIM KEMPTON: I'm pretty positive that Miki also stole my passport. I know Miki had a gig selling passports. I met a South African guy who was trying to get out of the country. We were having a pipe of hash. He told me he knew where he could get a fake passport. A few days later, I find out he's talking about Miki Dora. The cost was $300 U.S. Miki's mind was criminal but his gain was minimal, just like with the credit cards: so small-time as to make you wonder if he was really as crafty as everyone thought. Also, stealing passports is a slimy thing since it puts the person you do it to in heavy jeopardy.

Meanwhile, rumors about him being on the lam had begun to spread. Back in California, I saw "Dora Lives" bumper stickers. Speculation was hot. What was Miki Dora doing? Why was he hiding? Had he ripped somebody off? I had taken it all with a grain of salt until my passport disappeared.

Miki needed passports and was on a tear. In 1976, when attempting to renew his own soon-to-expire document at the American consulate in Genoa, Italy, the clerk noticed the FBI's "Look Out" card, and pulled it. Miki spotted the move, grabbed his application photos, and disappeared on the run.

JAN MAYER: One day, in early 1977, on a ski trip, Linda Cuy came to me, Yves, and his wife, Maritxu. She wanted to leave Miki and return to the States. She was comfortable living in the van, but sometimes their relationship could be pretty tough. Now she was homesick and wanted to see her parents. Miki did not want her to go, she said, because she knew more about him than he wanted her to know. Linda had begun to feel like she was in prison. None of us really knew the magnitude of Miki's other life, and I guess Miki felt she'd go back to the States and spill the beans on him if the FBI ever interviewed her—and then he'd get nailed.

Linda said she had no money, and that she didn't know how to go about getting away. I said, "Call your parents, they'll send you an airline ticket." We then masterminded a plan where we basically "kidnapped" her and put her on a plane without Miki knowing it. We kept Miki occupied skiing and rushed her to the airport in Geneva.

JIM KEMPTON: Linda had, in her interpretation, escaped Miki. I could buy into that because I knew the power that Miki had psychologically. I had seen Linda's unhappiness at living in a van for eight months.

At some point later she and I also had a relationship.

I went back to France in September 1977. I took American products, which always bothered Miki, and helped commercialize the Biarritz area. The kids loved T-shirts and Hawaiian silkies and slaps, last year's models that I'd pick up for half price and make enough money from to travel and have a good time. In Biarritz I ran into Miki. Eventually, the subject of Linda came up and I said, "What's the deal with you two?" And he said, "She's gone." I didn't want to say anything about my relationship with her or that I knew where she'd gone. He continued, "Yeah, she was a great fuck, but other than that, what is she?" He had no respect.

Miki could never stand Don Wilson being involved with her, and when he finally found out about me and Linda, he couldn't stand that, either. He called Linda once about 6:00 A.M. Los Angeles time and I answered the phone. Of course, he knew my voice; no sense trying to conceal the situation. He figured it out in about ten seconds and he and Linda had an intensely heated conversation, and—presto!—that was it.

In the end Linda had to make a choice. I was a total gypsy, living in beach shacks, traveling the world and scamming. Miki was Miki. So she chose Don. She imagined him as her savior. He was certainly the one with family money. I like to think of myself as the one with the love. Miki was out on both counts.

Linda and Don married on November 27, 1977. They divorced eighteen months later.

6

As the '70s faded, Miki was stuck in France. After Linda divorced Don, she eventually returned to Miki's side. Jim Kempton took a job in California. Miki stayed in touch with his mother and father. The Mongoose practiced architecture. The Eagle dabbled in screenwriting. John Milius made his surf epic, *Big Wednesday*, but the Dora-esque character played only a minor role because Milius thought a whole movie about Miki would be too complicated.

In the surfing world, new performers and hot waves graced the magazine covers, film output rose, contests multiplied, and new winners took home the trophies and cash. Skateboarding got popular and the Z-Boys ruled the Santa Monica and Venice, California area known as Dogtown. Surf apparel company profits grew. Commercialization, Miki's bête noire, rushed relentlessly ahead, balanced by a renewed ecological mind-set and an umbilical connection to the sport's soulful origins. Fortunately, the Apocalypse remained on hold, but with Miki not around to proclaim it—and not writing his polemic travelogues—he became a cherished icon to some and an object of curiosity to others.

Beyond surfing, some of Miki's predictions did come true as world tensions increased and financial markets reeled—and, to his benefit, gold had not only earlier been deregulated by Richard Nixon, but shot up in price. Gasoline rationing began in the United States, and interest rates skyrocketed. The first test-tube baby was born, the first commercial cell phone became available, and President Jimmy Carter presided over the Israel/Egypt talks at Camp David. Soon, Ayatollah Khomeini would oust the Iranian shah, and militants would seize the American embassy in Tehran. Three Mile Island's nuclear plant failed, and the Soviets invaded Afghanistan.

Miki's priorities were simply to avoid capture, and worry about his health. He regularly wrote to his mother, asking her to send him assorted vitamin packets and concoctions, saying, "This is the magic mastication that keeps your old boy on his toes and fancy free, dancing miles away from the maddening crowds. Asking Miklos to do anything for me is like pulling giant nails from an oak tree with my two front teeth, painful and impossible. He has as much interest in me as a tea leaf has in the workings of the East India Company."

Sometimes he signed his letters to Ramona, "Your paranoid son." It was no offhand joke. While he lay low in France, the FBI had been busy visiting his friends and relatives.

ANNABELLE MCBRIDE: The FBI came by the Miramar Hotel in Montecito when I was there, looking for Miki. Someone at the beach had told them I was his girlfriend! The FBI said they wanted to talk about him selling jewelry. This very silly FBI man showed me pictures of Miki and asked if I'd seen him, and where he was living. It had been such a long time that I figured if the FBI came to see me, they were getting desperate.

JIM KEMPTON: The FBI came to my house twice. I told them nothing. If anything, I misled them. I didn't give them any other names, either, though people have heard things secondhand and made assumptions. But I was pissed off; I was living with my parents and the FBI had come at dinnertime.

Somehow, this got back to Miki. He figured that I had spilled the beans on him. He wrote me a very nasty threatening letter and I sent one back that probably burned up on the way, it was so scathing. I received a couple nice letters after that.

MIKLOS DORA SR.: Two big FBI agents sat in in my living room and accused Miki of many things, including holding up banks. I told them, "This is absolute bullshit. Even though I don't know my son too well, I know him well enough to know that he wouldn't ever use force. So don't give me this nonsense." They made it up. [Author note: Miki's FBI files reveals no mention of bank robbery.]

I knew where he was but I wouldn't tell. They left and never came back. Anyway, they indicated they knew *exactly* where he was anyway, and that he would very soon be picked up. Afterward, I talked to Miki. I said, "You better come back on your own because they will catch you."

JAN MAYER: One morning, the FBI came to my house in the French Alps. I told them I had no idea where Miki was. Miki showed up that afternoon. I told him the FBI had come; man, he took off. Later, the FBI visited me in Berkeley. They showed me pictures of his van. They showed me—and this kind of freaked me out—pictures of Uzis and a whole artillery cache that he apparently carried in his van. Miki never talked to me about guns, never talked to me about blowing somebody away. I was pretty shocked when I saw all these weapons. But I had nothing to tell them. I swear, man, they had helicopters flying over my house with mercury lights. They told me that he was the second-most-wanted criminal in the world for credit card violations.

The FBI even offered a $50,000 reward to a friend of mine, to whom I had introduced Miki years earlier, to turn him in. She declined.

The FBI also stopped by to ask Johnny Fain if he knew Miki Dora. Said Fain: "Do I know Miki Dora? I know things about Dora you guys never dreamed of."

GERRY KANTOR: One night in France Miki walked into this restaurant holding a copy of his FBI dossier. I don't know how he got it, but he seemed pretty proud of it. The front cover looked real super official. I read through it and it was scary: Every credit card transaction he'd made was listed. Somehow, Miki had also obtained a tape of Johnny Fain talking to some girl. She said, "Hey, did the FBI come and talk to you? They came and talked to me. What did you tell them?" He said, "I said, 'Go to the square in Biarritz. Put the gaudiest piece of costume jewelry you can find out in the middle of the square. After a while he'll slither in like a snake through black sand.'"

Miki said, "That rat, telling them where I am," but he was half laughing.

How did Miki get ahold of his file? Don Wilson suggested that Miki worked as a snitch for the FBI. C. R. Stecyk has added fuel to that fire by obliquely intimating that Miki's travels were not spontaneous and had something to do with being at world hot spots at propitious times.

Did Miki move about in some unofficial capacity for some unofficial agency whose unofficials would disavow any knowledge of his unofficial existence? One Dora associate says, "It came up that Miki had made deals with people to get out of trouble—this was all in the early '70s—and that he was questioned by government agencies far more than anyone was aware of. Miki also said he was 'interrogated' by people, and so maybe he did make compromises and deals to get out of difficult situations. I'd always heard that Miki worked for the FBI, and I always thought it was nonsense, a complete fabrication. Then I asked one of Miki's [girlfriends] about some things in that vein and [her answer] wasn't, 'Oh, that's so far out.'"

Miklos Sr. is unequivocal in his opinion: "Bullshit. I don't believe it."

Based on informal discussions with someone intimately familiar with bureau procedures, here is a possible answer: "If he was overseas or had contact with foreign officials or their family and friends, he might have been used as an 'asset'—which is like an informant but it's the counterintelligence way of looking at it."

But why then pursue Miki on various charges if he was an "asset"?

"A lot of times there's a investigation file open at the same time as an asset file. So while it seems like agents are following this guy around, they're actually probably meeting him a lot so he can provide information for them—so they know what's going on in his life criminally, as well. Bad boys often continue to be bad boys while, at the same time, they're an asset or informant; and when they screw up, depending on what they give the bureau, the bureau can often help them out of their 'issues.' Or not."

7

Another fall in Biarritz, another winter in the Alps, another spring and summer wandering and looking over his shoulder. "Miki didn't seem particularly stressed," says his friend Alan Tiegen. "He just killed time hanging out in public places and going about his personal business."

Chris Clements and his wife, Muriel, ran into Miki at Cavalier Beach, near Biarritz. "Most mornings he would sit outside our camper and have coffee with us. His green camper was very tidy. Inside he kept a huge gas pressure cooker. I always wondered what would happen if that cooker ever exploded. He told me he took the camper to Austria during the winter for the skiing season and would still live in it despite the subzero temperatures.

"He'd surf in the morning and play tennis in the afternoon. Sometimes he'd walk along the beach with a backgammon board under his arm asking anyone if they'd like to play, and perhaps make the game a little more exciting by putting a little cash at stake.

"At the time, *Big Wednesday* had just been released. He said he hadn't seen it but for some reason or another he didn't speak of the director, John Milius, in glowing terms.

"However, every few days he'd call California to speak with Johnny Fain. He said Fain was auditioning for minor movie roles and he was very interested in his progress.

"I remember, he was absolutely paranoid about having his photo taken. I couldn't resist, though. I got one of Miki standing in front of his camper with his wetsuit hanging out to dry over the open passenger door. He was in a good mood at the time and actually smiled for the camera. Other times he'd give me a bloody awful glare, which meant 'Don't point that thing at me.'"

Miki also passed the time trading books with Philippe Lauga, who gave him Maugham, Huxley, du Maurier, Hemingway, Poe, Jack London, Emerson, Galbraith, Paul Erdman. "He also asked me to buy him the bestseller *Shogun*," says Lauga. Miki gave Lauga *How to Prosper During the Coming Bad Years* by Howard Ruff, *How to Win through Intimidation*, and the book that embodied his mantra: *How to Live Free in an Unfree World*.

"We used to bet a grand meal for whomever had loaned the best book that year. In 1977 I won by giving him *The Crash of '79*. In 1978, I won with *On the Brink*. The dinner took place on New Year's Eve, at our favorite restaurant then, a former sheep barn, called La Bergerie in Urrugne."

GERRY KANTOR: I first saw Miki sitting on a bench overlooking the beach break at Anglet. It was early fall. He was dressed in tennis whites and held a wineglass filled with Perrier water. The bottle was on the bench. He wore Sony headphones and a pair of Vuarnets. Everything just reeked of wealth. He looked like he lived up on the hill, a retired aristocrat or trust-fund guy who had come down to enjoy the sunshine and ocean view.

I suspected that it might be Dora and I said, "Hey. Speak English?" In an accent, he said, "No." Then I made some small talk about the waves: "Those don't look too bad." He continued, speaking in broken English: "Yeah. Looks okay."

Eventually I paddled out. Got some good small waves. When I came in, Miki said, "Oh, very nice. Yes, I saw your waves. Very nice." He didn't talk like a standard surfer: "Dude, you got some barrels. Hey, that was cool." But the accent had disappeared.

French lunchtime. I went back to my car, a Citroen Braque that I had borrowed from Lulu and Zuzu, the women at whose house I was staying. My wallet, which I'd put underneath the front mat, was gone.

I went back to Dora and said, "Dude, come on. My wallet's missing and you're the only guy here." He had a cagey reaction and weird hand mannerisms, but no answer. "Look, you can have whatever francs," I said. "I just need my driver's license and stuff out of it." I wanted to be tactful, but the guy went into a tirade about how wherever he goes a black cloud follows him around. "I don't need your wallet," he said, more frustrated than pissed. "I don't need your ID."

Then he opened the back of his deluxe Mercedes van, reached under a mattress, and pulled out five different European passports. German, Swiss, I forget what else. He flipped each one open and each had his picture and his name. They looked like real bad paste-up jobs. He said, "Are these going to work? Do they look any good?" I said no. He said, "I need to get out of here." He'd been in Biarritz for years and he wanted to go to South Africa.

When I got back to Lulu and Zuzu's, my wallet was on the foyer table.

The next time I saw Miki I apologized. "Hey, sorry. I left my wallet in the foyer." Then it was, "Okay. From California?" Yes. "Are the orange groves still there?" Some. "Yeah. I used to run away from home and survive on oranges."

Then he said, "Do you play tennis?" I didn't.

Anglet that year was pretty much Mik's camp. He really wasn't wealthy, of course; I'd see him cooking a pot of potatoes in the van. I once bought him a sack of them as a gift and he ate those for weeks. Or he'd eat road-catch stew, which was basically a vegetable stew. Then he'd have some Chivas Regal and offer you a glass. Later I saw him filling the Chivas bottle from a Johnny Walker bottle.

Around the corner from where he parked was the Sable d'Or, a big hangout for traveling surfers. You got a big plate of frites for dinner, a big bowl of coffee in the morning. And you could use their bathroom.

One day we compared our pictures and realized that although he had a wider jaw, we had the same skin tone and same hair, and looked almost alike. That's when Miki said he wanted my passport and he'd trade it for letting me write a story about him. Him being Miki Dora, the King of California Surf, and me being a native Californian whose dad and uncle had surfed, I could respect that. I figured since I looked like Miki Dora, if I could get him out of Biarritz with my passport, I'd look into it.

I went to Paris to get another passport. At the passport office I read posters and discovered that getting another passport wasn't like getting another driver's license when you've lost it. So I completely chickened out because of the penalties.

Miki continued to defy the odds despite being on the run—or perhaps because of it. In any case, he grew increasingly boxed in and desperate.

RHONDA CHAGOURIE: In 1979, I went to Biarritz for twelve months, traveling with a friend named Bruce. We arrived at the end of winter and met Miki in the car park the first week. Bruce made surfboards and I sold jewelry I'd bought in Sri Lanka. We stayed in an apartment unit up from the Grand Plage. Sometimes Miki would have dinner and watch television with us.

Miki and Linda were together. I liked her, and he was incredibly friendly. Of course we'd heard about the famous Miki Dora. His age was a shock: He was in his midforties and we were in our twenties. But he hung out with a whole crew of kids half his age and seemed to have a ball with everyone.

A nunnery or monastery stood on the outskirts of Biarritz. Miki used to steal from their veggie garden, take eggs from their hens and fruit from their trees. One night he wanted me to go with him but I wouldn't. He always stole. Or got you to. Outside the supermarket was a huge barrel of peaches with a sign over it. I didn't read much French. He said, "The sign says it's seconds fruit and you can take as much as you want." So I filled a bag and walked away and everyone ran after me. He thought this was hilarious.

Miki would eat codeine tablets when there was no surf and just sleep for days. He'd park in the woods somewhere and just check out. "The big sleep," he called it. He seemed very depressed at times, with all sorts of demons.

One night a little something happened between Miki and me. It was basically a drunken evening. It was quick and over and done with.

Miki was also seeing a Frenchwoman. We never met her, but he would

ABOVE TOP: Left to right: Epinard, Linda Cuy, and Rognon, in New Zealand. Courtesy Dora Estate.

ABOVE: Miki, 1978, in Cavalier Beach parking lot, France. Photo: Chris Clements.

boast that she had a lot of money. He also told me he'd take me to Brazil and showed me amazing jewelry. God knows where he had gotten it. It seemed quite expensive.

Bruce and I were about to leave for London and then South Africa. We had made and saved a lot of money. One afternoon, while reading on the beach, I looked up at our apartment and saw Miki on our veranda. When I went home that afternoon, our money was gone. Afterward, Miki avoided us like the plague. We had to search for him. When we tried to speak to him, he wouldn't come out of his van. We had our plane tickets and just enough money left to get out of town.

When I got back to Australia, I got a strange phone call from him at my parents' house. He'd left a couple of little Cavalier King Charles spaniels in Melbourne. He wanted me to pick them up and send them to him. But first he wanted me to look after them. I said, "No, that's impossible." Then he said, "Can you send them to me? I don't have any money right now but I'll pay you back." I told him to go to hell.

LINDA CUY: One day we had a fight and Miki blew up as a result of him being really anxious and stressed out. It was all bottled up. We still lived in a camper van. We were both on edge. He was in a lot of trouble. We'd go to the Alps during the winter and find a safe spot. We had an electric heater inside, but the camper was like an igloo, covered with snow and ice. Eggs were frozen. Wine bottles popped. Sometimes we'd have a better accommodation. Miki usually hired out to do an early morning waiter service and deliver breakfasts to lodge rooms in exchange for half-a-day's ski pass and a permit. But I had nothing. If I got into trouble, there was no one to bail me out.

When Miki blew up, I moved out of the camper and stayed with a girlfriend. I had been talking to this Irish guy and I asked him about the beaches there and he said they were beautiful, all reefs and points. I asked if one got beatings (from the surf) when they paddled out and he said it was easy. France is not like that. We always surfed rough spots and got pounded in the shore break.

I asked the Irish guy when he was going back. He said a couple weeks and I said, "I'm going." I had some money and I asked if I paid for some of the gas could I get a ride and he said sure.

When I told Miki, he said, "Linda, don't leave." He sat on a step at the bottom of the winding stairs, in this little hallway. Tears streamed down his face. So much emotion; I'd never ever seen him like that. He said, "Don't go. I don't want you to go. Don't leave. Don't leave me." But I'd had it. He'd blown up and, to tell you the truth, I guess I was just tired of surfing in France. I hated France.

One of his common expressions was, "You're gonna leave me one day." It was almost like this purveyor-of-doom thing. If you think about it, women do leave one day. I guess he was bringing on his own fortune, somehow.

RHONDA CHAGOURIE: I received a letter from Linda later saying all was well, and she was really happy she had finally gotten away from Miki.

In August 1980, Peter Barnett got a postcard from Linda Cuy, from Dublin, Ireland. She raved about a fun summer surfing, sailing, and three months of skiing with Miki. She suggested she might return to California by September—and made no mention of the breakup. But it was over and Miki did what he always did: he moved on.

Not one to suffer for companionship, Miki took up with another young woman, Carole, twenty years his junior. Slim and beautiful, with long blond hair and an international pedigree, Carole had been featured in *Elle*, enjoyed outdoor activities, and "was attracted to adventure"—a perfect match for Miki. They met while Miki was with Linda, and Carole was with the man who would later become her husband. But when both significant others left town, Miki and Carole began spending time together. "My boyfriend asked Miki to take care of me, and Miki took him at his word," Carole recalls with a laugh. "He was charming and such a nice guy. And we were all free spirits in those days."

Although Carole had her own apartment in Biarritz, "Most of the time we lived in his van, at Chambre d'Amour, Lafiténia, Guéthary. The van *was* Miki. It had his heart, soul, story, travels, his secrets—which were in a black briefcase. Also, his scent, which was quite like . . . a lion."

The relationship lasted until Carole left for Australia in April of 1981, but Miki didn't have much of a chance to miss her. Too soon, the lion had to confront the cage.

CHAPTER **ELEVEN**

Honorable Gentleman, Guest of the State

1

2.7.81 [Letter to Ramona, from France]
  Dear mother. Thank you again for your kindness in sending all this information to my friend Philippe. He will always forward my mail to me. I'm working very hard seven days a week. Maybe I will get a few days free later in the season. My best thoughts go out to you all for 1981. As for myself, I'm stuck deep in the Swiss Alps, frozen in for the winter . . . We are beset by uncertainty and insecurity. When everything else is uncertain, what lasts? The good feelings between members of the family lasts. They last whether certain members of the family have become wealthy or gone broke. They last as long as people last and even after they have left us. Le bon grace. —Miki

ALAIN GARDINIER: In 1981, I wanted to go to California by myself and spend a few months. Miki said, "Hey, Genius, you don't go like that. I will take care of you." He gave me his dad's information and said, "I have a good friend called Frenchie. Go to see him in Malibu." He also promised to call ahead for me. This was a Friday. I went to Paris for the weekend, and Miki called America from a phone booth that was broken and let him make the call for free.
PHILIPPE LAUGA: In those days the phone was a long yellow box, not too

wide, with a slot to allow the coin to slide in. Miki would insert in a long, flat, metal rod instead of the coin. Then he pushed to squeeze down some piece inside. Then he'd burrow through his big address book and make as many calls as he fancied. Once, while calling, he pounded on the booth doors at the same time, pretending—and telling his correspondent—that he had to fend off some fiend attack, since he was calling from an uncivilized country!

BILL FREY-MCLEAN: Miki's favorite booth was out of the way, in St.-Jean-de-Luz, near some apartments. He'd call Linda, and the States. I'd sit in the van and wait and then it was my turn. He said the booth could be seen from the apartment of some ex-girlfriend—one of them—and he always told me we shouldn't be too conspicuous because she was angry with him. However, he usually parked his van quite close to the booth, so it's not like we hid.

One day he asked if I wanted to make some calls, but I went surfing instead.

ALAIN GARDINIER: The police were watching the phone booth, but not just for the phone company. Terrorists from ETA, the Basque separatist movement, used the same booth. The police wanted to catch guys from ETA, and while they watched, they saw Miki.

MIKE MCNEILL: They busted Miki, searched his van, and found six or seven passports under the mattress, in various states of being forged. They didn't know who he really was. They tried to get him to explain the passports, but Miki had never bothered to learn French. At the police station, they checked his papers and found out that they were all screwed up, and that he was wanted by the FBI and Interpol. Credit card fraud, airline tickets, bounced checks. All the charges came from the States except for the telephone calls.

Miki was arrested on May 9, 1981. The FBI couldn't extradite, but that didn't mean they hadn't known of Miki's whereabouts and activities all along. In fact, they'd been quietly setting up grounds for at least an "informal extradition," meaning "kicked out of France" with a choice of which country to enter next. But should extradition become possible, Diners Club was eager to prosecute.

According to Miki's FBI file, the bureau had monitored his general location and movements through interviews with informants, traveling surfers, and the friends and family he contacted in the States either by phone or mail. They knew he moved between surf and ski areas. They knew about the green Mercedes van, about a woman he traveled with who in one 1977 interview told the special agents about how the "constant arguments" over his travel plans caused her to plot a "midnight escape" and leave Miki in Chamonix. She also told the FBI that Miki had no gun or knife (his FBI jacket always warned of them), and that she didn't know how he made a living. The FBI also tracked down a hodgepodge of phony leads and cataloged unconfirmable sightings of Miki from India to Hawaii—mostly due to Miki having friends misdirect the authorities by mailing his letters during their world travels.

The FBI had also compiled a list of alleged misdeeds that ranged from the original credit card fraud and passport violations to alleged drug running and possession of firearms, a batch of blank airline tickets, and a ticket imprinter stolen from a Los Angeles travel bureau in 1972 or 1973. Agents even speculated he'd arranged for counterfeit U.S. currency to be shipped to Singapore and had been told that Miki stole jewelry and fenced it to a jeweler connection in Los Angeles. Two sources claimed Miki had "swindled" them out of $50,000 and $40,000, respectively. Another said Miki wanted to finance a film to be shot in New Guinea, but in reality intended to "abscond with the funds."

As usual, what's true or possible is anybody's guess.

Although some declined, most of the sources periodically interviewed by the FBI promised to contact the bureau if and when they heard from Miki or discovered his location, especially after special agents explained the statutes regarding harboring fugitives. One "friend" even offered to find Miki for the FBI if they would pay for his trip to Europe. They declined.

At one point in late 1979, Miki had briefly negotiated with New Zealand authorities to turn himself in, but it fell through. One reason was that he had for years tried to find a way to reclaim the possessions he'd left behind. The FBI knew because Miki had written to the storage company—Direct Transport Limited, in Gisborne—about his goods, and the company had turned over the letter (postmarked August 25, 1976, from Seignosse, France) to Diners Club.

It was too late to make any deals. On August 11, 1976, Miki's forty-second birthday, a search warrant had been executed at Direct Transport Limited in New Zealand, and the storage compartment was opened. According to the FBI, among the eclectic treasures, they found: a 30-caliber USM rifle, folding stock, fully loaded, unlawful in New Zealand; a .22 automatic Walther pistol, fully loaded; a Winchester 1897 pump 12-gauge shotgun; twenty-four used airline tickets; sixty credit cards, may of which were altered or defaced, all in the name of Dora; documents indicating large-scale fraudulent purchasing of goods throughout the world, and other belongings in excess of $100,000 including antiques, coins, rare books and paintings; identification in the name of Eric Dean Welton and Michael Chapin, both containing Dora's photograph.

The FBI's pursuit and monitoring had continued until the spring of 1980. The French authorities declined to "informally" deport Miki, though if they ever caught him, they said they might still ask him to leave because his real passport had expired, leaving him without valid travel documents. The FBI put Miki's case on a "pending inactive" status.

Late in 1980, the FBI caught a little break. A bag of Miki's possessions was found on a bus in Grenoble. The contents included "numerous photos and identifying documents in the names of Mick Dora, Mickel Dora, and Mickey Doro. Also in the bag were two altered passports, not Miki's. But the discovery led nowhere.

Then the FBI got another break. Miki was arrested in the phone booth at St.-Jean-de-Luz for "tampering with the phone" and for "having phony French identification documents." No collection of passports was mentioned in the file.

Da Cat was caught and held in the Bayonne jail, called by the locals the Villa Chagrin. "Chagrin," explains Quiksilver's Maritxu Darrigrand, "is when you feel bad."

PHILIPPE LAUGA: The police came almost immediately to my family home because they found some mail in the van addressed to Miki in care of my parents. My father was an ex-cop and it didn't please him to have the police asking questions about his son, and affecting his reputation. The Bayonne police asked to interview me about my connection to Miki. I said we were friends and he was a journalist and we played tennis and shared time together. All true. They told me the reason they couldn't stop him earlier, by finding out his name was on the FBI list, was that he lived in his van and didn't use hotels. So there was no way to trace him. No address. That's why he asked if he could have his mail sent to my address.

MIKLOS DORA SR.: Philippe Cotin, the managing director of Mouton Rothschild, called me at two in the morning my time. "Your son is in jail in Bayonne." It had been in the local paper, *Sud Ouest*. My friend got him a lawyer and I went over to see Miki. In France, to see somebody in a jail you have to be photographed and fingerprinted and carry a certificate, just like you were a felon yourself. Inside, I asked him, "What goes on?" "Nothing," he said.

PHILIPPE LAUGA: Miki requested to the police that his van be kept in my custody. So I went to the station in St.-Jean-de-Luz to drive it back to our yard. It sat there a couple months until my parents began to get fed up by the inconvenience and the inquiries—especially from fellow cops—about why we had to put up with the "convict's" car in our yard. Miklos Sr. came to retrieve it with Philippe Coutin. They drove it to St. Vincent de Tyrosse, where Philippe Coutin's in-laws had a family home.

MIKE MCNEILL: Miki was in jail for three months or so, and it was pretty horrible. Stone cells. Wet. Moldy. You could hear the water drip off the ceiling. He went crazy. "Get me outta here. Get. Me. Out. Of. Here." Because he was an older guy it was probably much tougher on him.

WILLIE DIX: It's pretty grim. An old prison that hasn't changed much since the nineteenth century. Very few people would go see him. Inside the walls was a little cabin with booths and a grill separating the sides. He was miserable. We took him the basics: toothbrush and paste. He wanted books, but I didn't think we could get books through. They were in English and the guards couldn't read them and tell if they were subversive and contained the instructions for how to get out of prison.

Although Miki's FBI file indicates that on July 23, 1981, Miki was actually sentenced to time served in Villa Chagrin, his father says that "Miki got out on an amnesty because of the election of Francois Mitterand. The attorney arranged everything. Also, they found out that the telephone calls weren't illegal. He didn't change the setup, just figured out how to punch in certain numbers to get all the overseas telephone calls free. So he got off. They put him in jail absolutely under false arrest and had nothing against him."

ALAN TIEGEN: When Miki was released, I stood at the prison entrance with the Rothschild attorney, an elegant lawyer right out of a novel. Miki came charging out and we headed off. The attorney told me that although Miki had walked out as a free man, he still had a big cloud hanging over his head, and a big decision to make: whether or not to go back to America and face the music.

Within a few weeks he came to stay with me on my farm.

We'd have breakfast together, then we'd reconvene in the afternoons and surf, or talk, or listen to music. In the evening he'd crack a bit of red wine, as long as it was good red wine, and shoot the shit.

Miki had a major case of the blues. He'd say, "You know, Alan, that jail, I hated it. I hate jail. I don't want to go back to the States." Then, "So what do you think?" meaning: should he go back? This would go on day after day after day. I knew he must be talking to other people about the same thing. I didn't ask, "What did you do that they want to get you for in America?" Instead, I said, "Do you want to go? Obviously it's serious." He told me he didn't want to go, but that his father had said maybe he could keep him from doing more than a month or two in jail—but it could be longer. "They might put me in jail for a year or two." I said, "Well, that's a long time."

MIKLOS DORA SR.: The FBI was still after him, of course. I told him to come back and face the music—the credit card thing, the passport, and the probation charges in Mammoth. I said, "Eventually you will be caught and it will be much tougher." You know how it is: even if you get a lousy ticket on the highway and you don't respond, eventually that will catch up with you.

ALAN TIEGEN: I said, "Well, Miki, I've been watching you live over the years, and I don't know what to tell you—except that I have a gut feeling that someday you're going to get old, that one day you're going to want to travel again, that you're going to want to live where you want to live and get on with life. Freely. I think you really have to consider your options on this. I know your dad wants you to come home and face the music."

He said, "Nobody else is telling me that."

I pushed him on it pretty heavily. One day he said, "Okay, I'm gonna go back." I didn't say, "Bravo." I said, "I think that'll be a good decision."

MIKLOS DORA SR.: I sent him a plane ticket.

SUSAN MCNEILL: Miki insisted on first class. But I still don't understand it. He was free. He didn't have to do a damn thing. So why did he end up on a plane to come back to America?

MIKE MCNEILL: He couldn't stay in France after he was let out of jail because he didn't have a valid passport. He had to do something.

PHILIPPE LAUGA: He told me he was extradited.

MIKE MCNEILL: He left voluntarily.

MIKLOS DORA SR.: I said, "You can't have the sword of Damocles hanging over your head constantly. You have to finish it. You got into this shit, you have to get out of it."

In July, Miki was issued a temporary certificate of identity, good for one month, and was expected to return directly to Los Angeles on July 24, 1981, to be met by special agents. He never got on the plane. His attorney later advised the FBI that Miki's no-show was the result of him needing medical attention "due to having been beaten during incarceration" in France. His lawyer also wanted Miki to avoid a protracted stay in a U.S. jail while he awaited arraignment on the passport, credit card, and probation violation charges.

Miki was next scheduled to fly to Los Angeles on August 15, 1981. Again, he missed his flight.

Miki made another reservation for September 1, 1981, on Air France Flight 003, nonstop Paris to Los Angeles. Knowing that he'd missed his July and August departures, the FBI made this entry in his file: "Paris: aware of Dora's hedonic pilgrimage, magniloquently described heretofore, realize he may alter his plans." The note goes on to describe him as, "A quintessential albeit aging boy of summer on a perennial quest for the legendary ninth wave," and suggested he "may have returned to Biarritz instead of Los Angeles, as originally planned given his surf compulsion and legendary lack of responsibility."

But this time Miki came through. He later told a friend that he laughed and joked with the passengers on the flight, sharing wine and stories. One traveler even offered him a lift home from the airport. But Miki already had a ride. FBI agents met him at LAX with handcuffs and whisked him to a holding cell at Terminal Island.

The next day, Miki's dad arrived, ready to help.

Miki's half brother, Gard Jr., also visited.

At least one phase of the long ordeal was over for the enigmatic outlaw surfer. And another had just begun.

2

In 1949, Frank McNamara schedules a business meal at a New York restaurant called Major's Cabin Grill. Prior to dinner, he changes suits.

After dinner, the waiter presents the bill. Frank reaches for his wallet . . .
and realizes that he has left it in his other suit. McNamara finesses
the situation, but that night he has a thought: Why should people be
limited to spending what they are carrying in cash, instead of being able
to spend what they can afford? In February 1950, McNamara and
his partner, Ralph Schneider, return to Major's Cabin Grill and order
dinner. When the bill comes, McNamara presents a small, cardboard
card—a Diners Club Card—and signs for the purchase. In the credit
card industry, this event is still known as the First Supper.

People soon grasped the "charge it" concept and began using the
Diners Club Card. . . .

The Diners Club Card soon became a cultural icon. Hollywood
cashed in on the charge craze with the 1962 release of The Man from
the Diners Club, *starring Danny Kaye and Telly Savalas. The Ideal*
Toy Corporation followed suit with a board game—the Diners Club
game. The idea quickly expanded outside the United States. Diners
Club became the first international charge card in 1952 with franchises
in Canada, France, and Cuba. . . .

In 1955, Western Airlines became the first airline to accept the Diners
Club. Ten years later, every major domestic airline accepted the Card.
—A brief history of the Diners Club Card, from Diners Club International

When Miki arrived in Los Angeles, he was arrested on federal charges
of passport fraud and credit card fraud—as well as on the California
charge of violating probation—and taken to Terminal Island, at the
time a medium-security federal prison. He went before a magistrate
on September 2, 1981.

MIKLOS DORA SR.: The morning after the FBI took Miki, I saw him downtown
at the hearing. I told Miki I would help him every way I could. I posted bail. I
also spoke to his mother. We hadn't spoken for maybe twenty years. She was
very upset. But Ramona wasn't a smart lady. She condemned the Mammoth
judge as unfair to Miki and said Miki was innocent. I said, "Ramona, Miki
didn't follow the ruling and he's in the shithouse right now." She said, "Are
you taking care of Miki?" I said, "Yes. I have an attorney and it will cost me lots
of money." She said, "I have a thousand dollars I will send you." I said, "Don't
send me money." But she sent it anyway, and I told Miki. He said, "Send back

the check. She needs the money." I did. I thought that was unusual for Miki, and I was proud of him. It was the first time I saw that Miki loved Ramona.

On the other hand, once, while Miki was out on bail, I got really pissed off at him. We were coming back from the attorney. Somehow I had money that belonged to Miki—a few hundred dollars. The legal expenses were already quite high and I thought Miki should say something like, "Take this money to cover the expenses." Instead, he said, "Give me the money. I want to buy myself a new tennis racket."

"Goddammit," I said. "Here we are spending money like crazy, you have prison hanging over you, and you want to buy a new tennis racket?" Those big steel rackets had just come out. I said, "Here's your money." It wasn't the money; it was the attitude.

To represent Miki, his father had retained Los Angeles attorney Jan Handzlik in July 1981.

MIKLOS DORA SR.: Miki's attorney asked him, "Did you do it?" Miki wouldn't answer him. I said, "Miki, tell him: Is it true what they are charging you with, or not?" He wouldn't commit himself. We sat there for four hours. I had a luncheon date with somebody and I was an hour and a half late. I said, "Miki, it costs me every minute you are hesitating here!" He came up with cock-and-bull stories. I said, "Miki, give him something to work with." He denied the credit cards also. I said, "Miki, your signature is on it." I saw the signatures on the credit card receipts. They were his signatures. He said, "They're not mine. A friend took advantage and forged my name to it."

JAN HANDZLIK: Obviously, the idea was to get the charges reduced or dropped. Diners Club alleged that Miki had altered his credit card expiration dates and run up a $14,000 bill. But for some reason, I seem to recall it being a great deal higher than that: $400,000 or $500,000. Miki originally got the card in 1958. It was canceled in 1967. It was reactivated in 1969 and canceled in 1971. He ran up $14,000 in charges between October 1971 and September 1972. In September 1972, $1,400. From January 1975 through March 1975, $5,062 in charges in a hunting lodge in London, somewhere in Munich, a duty-free men's shop, Hotel Ceylon in Ceylon. In March 1976, $2,000 in Nairobi. In April 1976, $300 at the Old Hickory Restaurant somewhere in Germany. He was an opportunist and lived well using someone else's money.

If Miki said he was chased around the globe, I think he just wanted to glamorize his existence. I don't know if he suffered from a persecution complex or not, but he certainly had the desire—according to the records, that is—to portray himself as something other than what he was. He was a big guy, garrulous and talkative. But you could tell from a number of public sources that he was basically a whiner.

At the hearing, I requested a new handwriting examination be done to ascertain whether Miki had actually signed the disputed passport application in the name of Richard Roche. It turns out that on November 20, 1973, Miki had been arrested on a forgery charge. It wasn't the Mammoth or the passport thing, but something else. [Author's note: He was quickly released, the charges dropped.] He gave handwriting exemplars to the Los Angeles Police Department then. The handwriting examiner working on the passport violation used those exemplars as samples of his known handwriting. But the authorities were unable to match the handwriting and prove that Miki had passed himself off as Roche, and the charges were dismissed.

TIMELINE: 1981

September 10: Miki ordered to appear 9/21/81 in Mono County.

September 11: Miki released from Terminal Island on bond.

September 21: Miki (aka Michael Chapin), appeared in Mono County Superior Court. Edward Denton represented the People. Clark Vaughn represented Miki. Vaughn asked for a couple weeks' continuance since he'd just met his client thirty minutes earlier and was not familiar with the case. He also suggested that since Miki returned voluntarily to the United States to face the charges, he would not be a flight risk. The judge, Harry Roberts—the same judge who presided over Miki's trial in 1973—said, "Are you aware that he's been in flight for about seven years?"

Mr. Vaughn: "Yes, Your Honor."

Judge Roberts: "If that isn't proof of the pudding I don't know what is."

A discussion ensued about the continuance as well as Miki's trustworthiness. "All this talk of the defendant's voluntary return does not impress me," said Roberts. "Nor does a mere $10,000 bail. I can tell you this: he didn't himself post the $10,000 bail."

Denton said he could live with a continuance. Judge Roberts wanted Miki to admit or deny the probation violation charges with all due speed. "This file is not that complicated," he said. "This man [already] pled guilty to grand theft. I remember him quite well." Nonetheless, Roberts granted a continuance.

October 6: Vaughn, Miki, and David Cross (for the People), appeared before Judge Roberts. Miki responded to each charge:

1. Failure to report to PO: Admits.
2. Absconded to whereabouts unknown: Admits.
3. Failure to make restitution. Admits.
4. Failure to pay fine. Admits.

November 24: Miki appeared for sentencing. Attorney Vaughn argued for county jail time. Cross wanted state prison. Roberts sent Miki to the California Department of Corrections medical facility in Vacaville for diagnostic study, but stayed the date until January 2, 1982. When the psychological examinations were complete, he'd pass sentence.

Out on bail, Miki had six weeks of relative freedom. He stayed with his dad, played tennis, saw friends, but mostly kept a low profile. Not all of his time was his own, however. He still had another appointment with the law, in Denver, on the alleged worldwide Diners Club credit card spending spree.

December 10: The Feds took Miki from California to Denver. He spent the night at a New Horizons Community Center in the Mile High City. In Denver, public defender John Richilano[2] represented Miki.

Richilano's motion to let Miki return to California was denied. His financial affidavit showed that he was not employed, had no checking or savings accounts, owned no property, stocks, or bonds—not quite true, given his Swiss account, if it was still active—and had "no debts other than doctor bills." He also had $6.00 cash.

By December 18, Richilano had secured permission for Miki to travel to California and stay with his mother in Newport Beach until he entered the California Superior Court–ordered diagnostic study in January 1982.

---

[2] Richilano has since been involved in a variety of fascinating cases, among them, international extraditions involving counterfeit Russian rubles spread around by Russian émigrés in the United States illegally from Canada, and as a lawyer for Oklahoma City bomber Terry Nichols.

JOHN RICHILANO: I was an assistant federal defender and I simply got assigned the case. I recall the charges had to do with phony credit cards, and also he had multiple identities. He even had a claim to some peerage or royalty, and some woman believing he was a prince.

Miki was one of the most interesting, deep men I've ever met. He seemed to have his own reality. He had movie-star looks despite his age. He complained about his health but he was in shape.

Miki's father is a very, very distinguished, kindly gentleman. He came to Denver a couple times. We went to lunch. Very concerned about his wayward son. He sent me a case of Mouton-Cadet after it was all over.

Miki was reluctant to talk to me about his past and stayed matter-of-fact. However, he was surprised that I'd never heard of him. Being raised in Ohio, surfing was far from my reality, though I'd read about it. I did vaguely recall a character in the vanguard of surfing in the '50s and early '60s, and I think it was him.

It's difficult to get a feel for a guy when you're representing him, you've heard a lot about him, and you don't know much of him beyond the immediate circumstances. I never felt Miki was dishonest with me; everyone is entitled to their view of the world. He certainly had his own, which seemed basically to be: I am Miki Dora, the individual, unique person, and why doesn't everybody realize that?

3

On January 2, 1982, after celebrating the holidays, Miki walked into the Bridgeport sheriff's station, surrendered as ordered, and entered the penal system. He was forty-seven years old. The booking sheet notes that he carried $47.93 in cash, a brown wallet, a watch, two keys in a black box, a yellow metal pen, a soft brown suitcase, a red sweater, yellow shirt, light brown pants, tennis shoes, and "various meds." Occupation: Salesman. Marital Status: Single. Religious Preference: Christian.

01.05.82 [Letter to Cynthia Applewhite from Mono County Jail in Bridgeport, CA]
> *Happy New Year from Bridgeport-bastille*
> *This is my fifth imprisonment since returning to this great country.*
> *This incarceration is domestic hospitality at its very best, polished and*

refined as subjection rarely is. Next week my keepers say I'll be transferred to the lunatic prison hospital somewhere. Will write you when I arrive at my new headquarters. Until then love & God's grace go with you in 1982.

On January 8, Miki arrived at the California Medical Facility in Vacaville. Set on six hundred sprawling acres off Highway 80, due east of Napa, halfway between Vallejo, at the northeast end of San Francisco Bay, and Sacramento, the CMF opened in 1955 to (according to their website) ". . . provide a centrally-located medical and psychiatric institution for the health care needs of the male felon population in California's prisons. CMF includes a general acute care hospital, in-patient and out-patient psychiatric facilities, a hospice unit for terminally ill inmates, housing and treatment for inmates identified with AIDS/HIV, general population, and other specialized inmate housing. Additionally, the Department of Mental Health operates a licensed, acute care psychiatric hospital within CMF."

Miki didn't care for any of it, but he approached the experience with his characteristic mixture of complaint, apocalypse, conspiracy, and humor.

01.15.82 [Letter to Cynthia Applewhite, from Vacaville]
   La Mer, La mer. La Vagues, La vagues.
   In the wonderful luxuriousness of Chateau du Vacaville, entre les tombs, bon surroundings. I am presently going through psychological deprogramming process, unintellectuality of a cockroach's gray matter, results guaranteed. Shock therapy is the only form of organic therapy, as defined by law, which may be used in the treatment of persons committed to the custody of Chateau du Vacaville. Psychosurgery, including lobotomy stereotactic surgery, chemic or other destruction of brain tissue, or implantation of electrodes into brain tissue, is not performed at this time at the Chateau. However, if by chance one survives with soundness of mind, it's a different matter during residency. If you care to write, I shall be here for some time, unfortunately.

On April 15, 1982, Vacaville discharged Miki. Later, when asked about the psychological testing, he said, "I was never tested. I sat there for four months. It was hell. I don't know if you've ever been in jail or prison, but they're insane asylums. People get killed in there every day, easily."

Miki returned to Mono County and appeared before Judge Roberts on April 20, 1982. The court considered the diagnostic report and Judge Roberts imposed sentence: three years in state prison, suspended; three years of probation upon the following terms and conditions.

1. Two hundred seventy days in county jail, minus 109 time served (160 to serve)
2. Additional fine of $2,500
3. Restitution to art dealer in Hong Kong + inflation and interest, total $2,056
4. No credit cards
5. Stay in California

Miki told Roberts he had a blood disorder. Judge Roberts sent Miki directly to the hospital for an exam. On his release he entered Mono County Jail to serve his sentence.

04.25.82 [Letter to Steven Taussig from Mono County Jail]
D'autrefois Amitie,

I am now decomposing. So sorry I've lost all count in time of my State sabbatical. I have been found guilty beyond any hope by the people of California, who have a negative sense of humor. They seem unimpressed by my International status for all my bewildering indiscretions, one of which is of being disinclined to do anything which requires effort, and the other great sin of riding more waves than any other of the species in the history of mankind.

Upon entry to Le Grand Chateau, I proclaimed my service as an Honorable Gentleman, to do my duty as prescribed by law. The management was so impressed by my presence that they instantly confiscated my luggage, including all my interesting reading matter, and threw it all in the trash dump—vitamins and all. There's one thing I can tell you for certain, I'm not tipping on this trip.

It is not easy to reconstruct any moment of pure emotion, and for one reason or another it seems hardest of all to recapture my feelings, being cast into the heart of America's psychotic Mexican v. Black street gang ambitions. If there's one lasting lesson which I've been taught during this period of time it is that no institution can ever hope to become great unless culture is at the core of its progress.

In Le Chateau, a type of confined warfare, a doctrine of the survival of the fittest persists, as in the ruthless struggle for survival beast contends against beast and insect against insect. So prison is the means by which the man best fitted to survive, be they purest Aryan brotherhood or strugglers for Black gorilla power, will inevitably crush the puny ones who stand against them. My limited reason tells me that I don't have a chance in this crazy system and I'd rather take the better odds with the unleashed forces of nature on this purely physical planet, where I neither have a God destroyer to save me, nor a God protector to save me . . .

Realizing my chief aim is of wasting time as gracefully as possible. However, when one is locked away 22 hours per day, there is not that absorption for business which spoils a man and dulls his brain. Please accept my apologies and excuse these ramblings of such an uninteresting letter, but when you take an amphiba from its waters, one undergoes a total metamorphosis . . .

Twenty-two hours locked away, each and every day, makes a man hardly know what to say. Ding dong bell, Pussy's in the well. Who put her in? (you see I've cracked up). A while back, I heard that there might be a Ping-Pong tournament. I'll do anything with reason to get the hell out of this cell. Well, I bribed one of the overlords to sign me up for the coming amusement. The other day I was given a pass to go to the arena to intervene and launch forth my performance. When I arrived I discovered to my horror it was an all out Boxing tournament. I immediately tried to escape my fate, but was forced to fight a 22-year-old six-four Black giant with a reach and hands like a Goliath. I didn't last one round and was carried back to my cell whimpering and twitching. My body now feels like someone has used a ball pen hammer over every inch of my frame. I'm very happy now to be back in my cell.

Some time ago, I don't quite remember, due to this blood clot to the brain, while looking at nothing, I decided to construct a backgammon set. I used discarded trash to construct the game board, and molded wet toilet paper into cubes and let dry for the dice. Sometimes if I'm a good old boy, I'm let out for one hour at night to watch Wonder

America *through T.V. Thus I was able to find a few diehards who would play for cigarettes. By the way, it's amazing if you have enough of the damn things, what can be accomplished. Well, to get to the point of all this, I was playing this character and had him strategized to the best of my ability. Under these rules, a player may offer to double the stakes at any junction. This confronts the opponent with the choice of accepting higher risk or resigning immediately. Halfway through the game he asked me if I knew who he was. I said no and asked him if he knew who I was. He said no. I said good. He then, in no uncertain terms, informed me he was the renowned Backgammon Murderer of San Francisco; that he plays for lines of coke, and if the opponent doesn't pay off . . . Well, ??? I conceded the match at once, thereupon taking the set back to my cell and flushing it into eternity. Well, so much for enjoyment . . .*

. . . However I want to thank you again for you Comradeship and generous reception last October . . . I'm very grateful for the friendship and hospitality received, after ten years abroad. Consequently, whether we become stinking rich or wind up dead broke, it's the good feelings among friends that last.

P.S. No need to write. I'll be off to Denver, Colorado to face Federal charges. With this now-pending case against me, I could face up to ten years in Federal prison and a substantial fine, for non payment of taxes for 35 years."

To Cynthia Applewhite, he wrote:

Completely dumbfounded, I was given a copy of the Bible, which I use everyday to put myself in a coma from around eight   Ñ Ñto six ı Ñ Ñı It's the trigger mechanism that sets me off after the first few lines. Then I'm off riding perfect waves somewhere in the Indian Ocean for the next ten hours.

The sun is my only God, its light reaches me in a little less than nine minutes, other sun God's take billions of years at 186,000 miles per second. My sun creates all the things I love but how many sun Gods are there? There are estimated over 30,000,000,000 suns for every human on earth if divided into the inhabitants of this globe. It's stupefying. But who really understands or worships this God. Only me. I have been betrayed, and left stranded on the darkest side of the moon.

This disabilitating chest infection that has keep me in rather low spirits for the last six weeks, flared up last week into asthma. Its under control at the present time. With approximately 4,000 inmates incarcerated in this pit of germs its hell to keep healthy. . . . After three months I finally confronted my psychologist. They cannot understand why I was put in state prison—that the case seems ridiculous. By the way I had to agree with their analyzation. They have recommended no probation restrictions whatsoever, with the freedom to return to France at once. Two dilemmas down; now if this crazed judge has won satisfaction for his pound of flesh there's only one more big hurdle to vault and then freedom. If there's anything left by then. I truthfully don't know anything of my release date. It could be as late as April 8, 82. The bureaucracy and paper work in transporting back to Bridgeport takes time. Then off to Denver for my Federal Case. It's endless. Thank you very much for all your kindness again. Your most obedient humble servant.

SKIP ENGBLOM: Miki was in the worst possible situation for a person like him whose whole life was based on controlling his personal freedom. Instead, he's being controlled by the government, the thing that he's always warned about. The hand finally reached out and got him. At the same time, there's this insane gallows humor. He created whole universes inside the prison through these letters, and what's amazing is that he got them out of prison.

Despite the attempt to put a black comic mask on his incarceration in order to come to grips with his fate, Miki was quite concerned about some of the facility's other inhabitants.

In one letter he shared his fear and disdain and recalled having encountered a familiar face at Vacaville: "With a personality like mine it could prove extremely unwise to converse with anyone. When I try, I find it ludicrous that my embittered neighbors, which included Charlie Manson and friends, just respond with an icicle stare. I'm quite certain that I'm the only person in this snake pit who doesn't have a mosaic tattooed torso or multiple gunshot wounds."

Manson? Was it true?

PETER DAY: Miki said that one day, while sitting in his cell, "I heard this voice from a cell down the hall. I knew that it was Charlie Manson, so I yelled out to him, 'Hey Charlie! Is that you?' And Charlie went, 'Miki. Surfer Boy. Is that you?'"

ALAIN GARDINIER: Miki said Charles Manson knew him through partying with Dennis Wilson, from the Beach Boys. Manson was like a king in jail and suddenly Miki was a star, and it was really inconvenient for him.

PHIL GRACE: In the version he told me, while being taken across the exercise yard by some guards, Miki said he saw this wild-eyed guy who looked at him and straightaway said, "Hey, Mick the Prick! Great party!" Miki went into great detail, so even if he made it up, I thought, Great story!

Few later believed Miki and Manson knew each other, even if only casually. In April 2005, TheReporter.com, a Vacaville online newspaper, did a series of articles that, according to its website, "explored the impact of California Medical Facility on Vacaville, to coincide with the 50th anniversary of the prison which houses some of California's most dangerous, troubled, sick or frail inmates."

One installment, by senior writer Brian Hamlin, settles any argument of proximity, though not of what actually transpired. "(CMF is) Perhaps best known as the prison where convicted cult leader–mass murderer Charlie Manson was housed between 1976 and 1986."

Miki was there in 1982.

Hey, Mick the Prick. Great party!

4

In June 1982, Miki returned to Denver to face federal charges. The road to the Mile High City involved many stops, with Miki spending each night in a different jail: San Luis Obispo; Sacramento; Laramie, Wyoming; Denver City Jail. Finally, on July 1, 1982, in Denver federal court, Miki pleaded not to felony fraud, but to a misdemeanor: "Desertion of mail."

As part of the proceedings, Gary R. Crooks, a probation officer, tendered a pre-sentencing report that read, in part: "Defendant is serving the custody portion of his sentence at the Mono County Jail, Bridgeport, California. He is scheduled to be released sometime in September, 1982 and will be under California State Probation supervision until April 19, 1985. Defendant advised that he is afraid to return to the Mono County jail because several people have it in for him there, and he has been treated unfairly, even cruelly, including treatment that has jeopardized his physical health and emotional well-being. United States Probation Officer Michael Robinson made inquiry with the Mono County Jail regarding defendant's alleged problems there. Deputy Padillas described defendant as 'the biggest crybaby and hypochondriac we have ever seen. He refuses to do anything and won't even clean his own cell. He always claims he is too ill to do anything, but is always the first to go out for exercise.'"

On July 22, 1982, Miki was found guilty in Colorado of having "knowingly quit and deserted a letter addressed to himself . . ." from Diners Club. He was sentenced to six months, to start when his current sentence in California was finished.

JOHN RICHILANO: The charge was reduced to a misdemeanor mainly because it was old and the prosecutors in Denver didn't think it was a big deal. But Diners Club sued Miki and got judgments against him all over the world. They moved to attach his property in New Zealand.

On October 8, 1982, Miki arrived at FCI Lompoc (Federal Correctional Institution), a low-security area housing males. On the Security Designation form he was rated a "one" out of "six"—very low risk. He listed his last employer and address as Hotel du Golf.

Medical intake approved Miki for general population housing, for temporary work assignment, for continued transport. Remarks: "Claims he is an asthmatic. Arrived with meds."

HEALTH:

Physical: Defendant is 5 feet 11 inches and weights 180 pounds, he has black hair, brown eyes, and no tattoos or other marks of identification. He denies any history of drug or alcohol problems but states that he has an asthma condition, is a borderline diabetic, and describes his health as only fair at best. He feels in need of a complete medical examination but has not been able to receive same at the Mono County Jail.

Mental and emotional: Early this year, defendant underwent a diagnostic study ordered by the Superior Court at Bridgeport. That report concluded, in part: "The subject seems to be an elusive, nomadic and unreliable person. His claim of various physical illnesses or disabilities is not supported by our medical examinations and evaluations. On the contrary, he is a healthy person. Psychologically he is immature, unstable and irresponsible. Probation is indicated in order to maintain legal control and jurisdiction; and probation could be considered only if the subject is willing to abide with the Court orders. If granted probation, any further violation of probation or the law will be adequate reason for prompt commitment to the Department of Corrections." [Sic] March 29, 1982—Gary R. Crooks, Probation Officer

4.25.82 [Letter to Steven Taussig, from the Mono County Jail]
   I see no end to my dilemma. Since returning to America I've been incarcerated into six suppressive institutions & yet I have never been convicted or sentenced in a court of law for any crime in my entire life.
   Like the Inquisition, the state has accused me of being a Sociopath even though I haven't been part of this society for over ten years. I've been given a clean bill of mental health by the psychiatric overlords here, who think this case is completely ridiculous and recommend my immediate release and return to France. Its obvious to me, nevertheless, that I'm being made an example of by certain individuals who disapprove of the way I live my life. So I still sit here.
   It's sometimes hard to believe that this country could so completely have lost sight of the principles it preached a mere ten years ago: tolerance, charity, humility, and brotherly love (a monstrous clerical error).

Miki also insisted that he had been made an example of by a biased judge in Mono County—Harry Roberts—who had it in for him. In a later letter to Ramona he wrote: "Have you heard anything new on that sadistic judge, Harry Roberts? I hope they hang that SOB. I still have nightmares of that stinking place, buried alive for six months.

   "I had a crazy judge up in Bridgeport, Judge Roberts," he later told film producer Michael McDonnell, while discussing a possible movie of his life. "They wanted blood and they wanted a payback. So they were very revengeful. This judge is totally insane, and an alcoholic.

Seventy years old. He's been disbarred for corruption, had a long history of violence. He foams at the mouth, throws a Bible at me. My lawyer ran out of the court, terrified of this man. I'm not dramatizing. This is all documented. I can tell you about this character and his personal vendetta to put me away for, I don't know, four years, for nothing, for stopped payment on a check.

"And the reason this all came about: in the early '60s I had a . . . Well, it's very difficult to explain my life in California with these beaches and with the lifeguard system and the takeover of Malibu by the state, and how a few of us fought against this takeover. We sabotaged and held them back for many years.

"These same lifeguards made money out of the system and retired and moved to Mammoth, and were in the skiing business. And when I stopped payment on those checks, which is absolutely legal, and which is a civil matter, and must be settled in civil court under the seventh amendment of the Constitution, I did everything in my power to go to Mammoth and pay off the provo. In Los Angeles, they would have written it off in two seconds. But no, they made it Grand Theft, a felony. Due to the lifeguard contingent and my prior reputation. The controlling of the small community, of the judicial system up there. Totally corrupted. And I can go in detail and prove to you this whole conspiracy against me. It was a bunch of the good old boys who set this thing up. It's a big story, and I'd discuss it with you in a lot of detail."

JOHN RICHILANO: After putting Miki on probation the first time around, trusting him, Miki just left. This time the judge gave him the whole ride and treated him like public enemy number one. From what I understand, the judge was pretty much out of line and had been cited by the bar for abuses and indiscretions.

True. On April 25, 1983, the California Commission on Judicial Performance recommended that Judge Roberts should be publicly censured. "The commission found several instances of misconduct warranting censure," the report stated, "including impermissible personal involvement in litigation; rude, hostile, and intimidating treatment of litigants, witnesses, and counsel; and a misdemeanor conviction for resisting, delaying, or obstructing public officers (Pen. Code 148) in the course of their investigation of a possible intoxicated driving offense of the judge's son, all of which constituted either willful misconduct or conduct prejudicial to the administration of justice that brings the judicial office into disrepute."

~

Miki became a short-term citizen of FCI Lompoc. Nearby, he could see Lompoc's high-security United States Penitentiary, part of a complex located in California, 175 miles northwest of Los Angeles, adjacent to Vandenberg Air Force Base. Perhaps, with a strong onshore breeze, he could even smell the ocean just a few miles west. So near, yet so far.

CHRISTINE DORA: We used to take a picnic lunch to him on some weekends. Miki would request certain foods. He was obsessed because the food there was all starch and he gained weight. He'd always want fruit and a big salad, and Miklos would make chicken paprikash. He also liked cold cuts and good French bread, and nuts and dried fruit. We brought him yogurt. One day he put some nuts in his pocket and they stopped him going back in and said, "You leave it outside."

MIKLOS DORA SR.: To visit was not difficult. We were not searched. We ate at picnic tables, outside. No fence, no barbed wire. If Miki wanted to walk away, he could have. He had a gymnasium and could exercise. Miki didn't even wear a uniform, just jeans and a shirt. Lompoc was a country club. I told Miki, "Lompoc is nicer than the Jesuit boarding school I went to."

Everyone at Lompoc had a job, and Miki was sent to the warden's home, to take care of the garden.

[Nov. 1982 letter to Cynthia Applewhite from Lompoc]
Once again I find myself back in the Federal prison system. Only one notch up from the State nightmare. Spending one hour in such a place would turn Cheech & Chong into Trapist monks. Niggers & Mexicans screaming threats 24 hours and sleeping with only one eye closed. My head has become a Cabbage. Well over 18 state jails, six months in Bridgeport solitary confinement. Now I'm a P.O.W. of this new socialistic paradise. Fresh air and sun has improved my appearance considerably. When first arrived I was gray-green in color, a cross between General Westmorland and the tin man. It took me a week to

walk a few hundred feet at one time. The lack of any exercise over a ten
month period destroys all the body's fundamentals. I am told over and
over again that everyone must do an honest days work in this place, or
be put in the main prison hole for 15 days punishment. The one thing I
can't stand in life is to do a honest day work—especially at 8¢ per hour.

My first assignment, possibly due to my mature age, was to be the
personal gardener to the warden's private residence. The first hour on
the job I discovered a huge fig tree. I hadn't seen anything like this in
over 10 months. Bee's buzzing, green grass, and plump purple figs. I ate
some, and O.D.'d in the hot sun. I was rudely awakened by the Warden's
wife screaming that I was a no good thief. I was fired on the spot.

The next day I was put on a work gang pouring 100 lb sacks of
white lye powder around the prison fences, a deterrent toward escape.
One look-see was enough. I didn't have to fake an asthma attack. I was
put on sick call at once. Then I was threatened once again to be put in
the hole for not working. I was given more chances. I was sent by bus
to work at Vandenberg Air Base with about 20 other slaves. My duties
were to make the M.X. missile headquarters more attractive by doing
landscaping type work. By the way, this is the type of guidance system
that goes into orbit around the Earth with multiple warheads that
plunge back to earth on command and destroy everything no matter
where. I refused to do anything to glorify World War III. At once I
qualified for the prison psych. Its no different in or out of prison. I'm
hated by all who work for the end. At least now I'm not working for
the pigs anymore. A few days ago the G-bosses took me to the operating
room and chopped out one of my bumps on my arm. Its one big package
deal; maybe I'll be out by Christmas. Who knows? They're working me
over and over. I would love to see you but it's a big expensive trip up this
way. And I'm not looking so well since my head has been shaven. Happy
Thanksgiving.

11.19.82 [Letter to Linda Cuy from Lompoc]
    48 Years old. Sheet.
    With a loaf of bread beneath thine oak; a flask of wine, a book
of verse, and thou besides me singing and running naked with
[unintelligible] and [unreadable] in the wilderness, always together
doing research in episonic theory to form part of a team to investigate
the tidal wave factor with a view to world domination. Salary will

> Dear Phillip,
>
> I hope everything with my Father went smoothly, and the hrs is out of your place with not to much inconvence to you, and your house hold.
>
> It looks like I'll be returning to the U.S. some time in the near future, I hope its not true, its not a pleasnt thing to think about. Maybe I'll see the sun there some time, here I don't have such a pleasure.
>
> Please give my best thoughts to your Mother and Father, & thank them Again for me.
>
> I hope your playing lots of Golf & Pelota by now,
>
> Very Truly,
>
> Miki

ABOVE: Letter from Miki, in "Villa Chagrin," to Philippe Lauga, Spring 1981. Courtesy Philippe Lauga and the Dora Estate.

RIGHT: *California* magazine cover, August 1983.

BELOW: Miki booking photo, January 8, 1982. Courtesy Dora Estate.

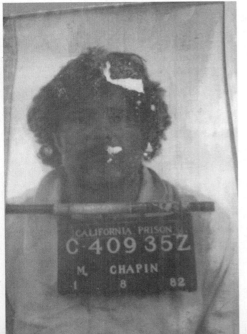

California

$1.75 AUGUST 1983

Deukmejian's Nomi...
Worse Than James

In Defense of Infid...
By Michael Fessie...

Underwater Adven...
A Splashy Vacation...

The Endless Summer

From surfing legend to
international fugitive—
the wild ride of Mickey Dora,
by David Rensin

be on a profit sharing basis. It is expected to be low at first, but rising within a year or two, depending on satisfactory results, to ten million pounds P.A., with annual increments thereafter as nation after nation capitulates to our demands. Are you with me for the next earth trembling trip? My life here is hell on earth. You could never believe what kind of scum exists. You're the only sane one left on earth. Your letters keep me alive. I haven't seen the sun in six months. 270 days for being anti-society. From now on I love American Nazis. I am sorry I haven't written. I have been locked down 24 hours a day for the last two months. Nothing to write with. Sadists. —Miki

Sentenced to six months, Miki's full ride would expire on March 6, 1983; however, with estimated time off for good behavior, the government predicted his statutory release date as February 4, 1983.

5

When nobody bothers you, you're anybody's friend / But draw a circle in the sand, and everybody wants in.

—Rickie Lee Jones, "Circle in the Sand"

SAM GEORGE: I worked for *Surfing* magazine as a contributing editor. We'd heard that Miki Dora had been extradited from Europe. Dave, the editor, said, "Hey, Sam, why don't you try to find out where Miki Dora is?" I thought it'd be pretty easy.

I lived in Santa Barbara at the time. Eventually, a surfer who heard I was looking for Miki called and said, "Miki's at Terminal Island. I've got letters from prison."

When I called Terminal Island, they told me he'd been sent to Lompoc.

I wrote a funny little story about the search and how this guy showed me the letters. I didn't take it any further. It seemed a little invasive to me to actually try and track him down. My search for Miki was the interesting story. That some sad little criminal career came to an end and he had to do some time in Lompoc isn't very romantic.

DAVID RENSIN: In late 1982, when I approached Janet Duckworth, an editor at *California* magazine, and proposed a story on discovering Miki's whereabouts, I had no idea that Miki was in jail. I was just a former surfer, looking for something to write about and curious about what had become of my favorite antihero. I gave Janet an overview of what I knew then of Miki's life and times and impact, told her about his disappearance from the scene in the early '70s, and described the endless speculation and some of the rumors circulating among surfing pals about his fate. Duckworth and editor-in-chief Scott Kaufer assigned the story.

It wasn't Miki's style to leave many clues, so I sought out a cross section of those who'd known him. Almost immediately, and despite what I assumed was my familiarity with the surfing world, I realized that I'd crossed over into an intense and fraternal land populated with obsessive, committed characters who lived, at least in their hearts, and sometimes in reality, on society's edge. They were territorial, loyal, fiercely protective. Some talked, some didn't, but to all Miki was a cherished anomaly. Good or bad, he was one of their own.

Soon I discovered two articles in the *Rocky Mountain News* under the headlines "Ex-Surfer King Surfaces in Cheyenne Jail" and "Surfer to Serve Six Months." The stories told of Miki's arrest in France, return to the States, indictment by a Denver grand jury, and the allegations that went with it.

I made some calls and tracked his progress through various penal institutions until I discovered his last residence was the Lompoc Correctional Facility. I learned of his whereabouts on December 19, 1982. I called Lompoc. He'd been released two days earlier. His exit photo showed him with very short hair and a ZZ Top beard. He looked like Rip van Winkle after the Apocalypse, or a wandering mad monk.

CYNTHIA APPLEWHITE: I saw Miki a few days after he got out. He had a long beard and he told me that he'd just cut his fingernails; that he had let them grow real long to serve as weapons. But every time I saw him afterward, he looked better. He said he had to make himself look as ugly as possible because of the homosexuals who'd want to rape him. One thing really touched me: he spent so much time inside—and he's such an outside person. That's why, before jail, he got as much sun and surf as he could. But he didn't think he would have to stay in jail as long as he did.

DAVID RENSIN: With Miki free and required to reside somewhere in California, I called Miki's father in Montecito on the off chance that his son might be living there. He wasn't. Still, I asked Dora Sr. if we could meet and talk. He courteously declined. "It would complicate things," he said. "My son and I are on speaking terms but we have a completely different outlook on life." Did he not approve of his son's behavior? "Those are your words. To comment would be unfair. Of course . . . I have a certain great feeling for Miki . . . but I can say nothing." He offered, however, to give my number to Miki when they next spoke and tell him about my interest. Miki never called. But his friend Cynthia Applewhite did.

We met at a Studio City coffee shop and sat at a table near the kitchen, talking about Miki while lunchtime dishes and silverware clattered around us. "Miki's tired and sick and wants to be left alone," Cynthia said. But she also felt a story might help him, that he needed to be remembered well.

I asked where he lived. She said he was with his mother, Ramona, in Newport Beach.

NAT YOUNG: Miki worked at a soup kitchen somewhere around Huntington Beach in the mornings and afternoons, to pay his fines. Apparently he had told the court that he hated old people, so part of his entry back into society was to live in his mother's house and serve soup to old people. He had two days off, and I took him to Malibu. We stayed at a friend's house and played some tennis.

GERRY KANTOR: He also worked for this guy a couple nights a week, folding shirts. He'd play tennis every day. We'd drive along the coast and check out the surf. I trusted him enough to give him a key to my place and tell him he could stay there, but also, "Don't go through my stuff." He always had this thing of, wherever we'd go, opening up drawers to look through little bric-a-brac stuff, like a garbologist. He'd never take anything, just look.

DAVID RENSIN: I asked Cynthia if she could arrange a meeting between Miki and me. A couple days later, I got the answer. "Miki thinks this piece is just another example of his being exploited. He doesn't care about the negative things he knows will be in there, or about defending himself. He knows people hate him. Miki says you ought to write about the Pirate Captain and the Eagle; that their exploits are a gourmet meal and he's only a wet teabag.

"In fact, Miki wondered if you'd heard the Eagle's jackdaw theory for catching Miki Dora?" I hadn't. "It's simple: You put some cheap jewelry on a park bench in Biarritz and Miki Dora, like an eel, will slither out and take it. Drop a net and you've got him. Miki thinks that is pretty funny." Cynthia paused, deciding something, then said, "Actually, Miki is afraid. He thinks this story will blow his cover. He thinks the authorities are going to try and jail him again. He thinks the Pirate Captain wants to bump him off. Miki feels . . . trapped."

The Pirate Captain, whom I'd already interviewed, could find Miki anytime without me, I said. I paid the check and asked Cynthia to keep trying. She agreed.

I heard from her a few days later. "Miki wants to leave the country. He's trying to get written permission. He'll talk to you in exchange for a one-way ticket to Europe. First class. He's searching for this mysterious rogue wave. Miki has been talking a lot about the ocean lately," she said with a sigh. "Just the ocean, not even surfing. It's as if he wants to become part of it. He thinks he'll find his salvation there." Of course, I couldn't give him a ticket, nor would the magazine allow it.

As the weeks passed I continued to get messages from Miki. Each time, he would suggest a new price for his cooperation. I also got some mysterious phone calls. One man identifying himself only as "Art" claimed that Miki had burned him on a business deal in Europe. He wanted to tell me about it. Another caller refused to identify himself at all, but said he was a friend of Miki's who wanted to anonymously "shade my piece with positive input." Miki couldn't know he helped. He also sounded an ominous warning: "The story of Miki Dora is the story of getting the story. The real story is not publishable. It's more than a simple journalistic undertaking. There's more to it than words on a page."

I declined both anonymous offers. Besides, Miki had my phone number and since neither caller would reveal where they'd gotten mine, perhaps Miki had put them up to it—or he had called himself, disguising his voice.

GERRY KANTOR: Miki told me, "Here's Rensin's phone number. Call him and feed him some lies." The only actual lie that got through, and which actually made it into the story, is that in his wallet he has a picture of a wave and a picture of his dad. They were not in his wallet, but in a photo album. But from that one quote he said his dad felt great and got him a ticket back to Europe, and "Thanks a lot."

What's funny is that the whole time he kept going at me to write a book about him, but I wouldn't. I knew that once you start doing business with Miki that's when he ceases to be your friend. I thought it was better to hang out with Mick. Still, he always said, "Hey, we're going to do the big story."

LINDA CUY: When we lived together in his van in France, he would complain about any magazine that wrote a story about him and say he'd sue. Then the next minute he'd say, "Where's my spotlight?" Miki was of two minds about the *California* magazine article—or any article. He would rather not have anyone write about him, but he wanted to be known. He just didn't want problems.

DAVID RENSIN: I felt as if any hope of my meeting Miki had evaporated. Being written about represented for Miki a loss of control over the image he'd crafted in the surf magazines, the image that sustained his global welcome and survival. He didn't want any unapproved information about himself out in the world. And what celebrity does? The situation was disquieting. To Miki, the gratification of getting the piece killed, or getting a payoff like a plane ticket, was like a dose of anti-anxiety medication. Until the next time someone wanted to write about him.

Weeks passed. Then Cynthia called.

"Miki wants to meet you on Sunday, May 29, at the Good Earth restaurant in Newport Beach. He feels he may have handled this situation wrong. You can bring your tape recorder. Miki is bringing his. I'm excited. Good luck."

I agreed and set about revising my questions. A few hours later she called again. "He wants to meet you tomorrow at 7:00 P.M. in the fourth-floor taping room of the Orange Coast College Library."

Cynthia suggested he would want to talk about politics and—to my surprise—turning the story into a movie property. "If you get along," she said, "you should be prepared to send some articles that you're proud of to Miki's attorney." "He doesn't really care about the negative implications of the story," she added. "He doesn't care a bit. It even amuses him."

I arrived at the college library thirty minutes early and waited in a reading area on the second floor. I kept one eye on the entrance and the other on the elevator. I wanted to see Miki before he saw me, to gauge the man, if only by his carriage, before what I was sure would be our uneasy meeting. I knew I would recognize him, but by 6:55 P.M. I was still waiting. Perhaps Miki wouldn't show. I quickly walked downstairs to check the first-floor entrance. Nothing. It was time. I punched the button for the fourth floor and rode up.

Miki was slumped on a Naugahyde ottoman, waiting. He was darkly tanned and wore loose, rust-colored, wide-wale corduroys; a black and khaki shirt, untucked; a down vest; and tennis shoes. His curly hair was black and silver and matted. Cynthia had mentioned a beard, but now only a thin wisp of mustache lined his upper lip. More wisps formed the outlines of a translucent goatee.

Miki stood up warily; we shook hands.

"I'm, uh, I apologize that it's taken so long for us to meet," he said, in a small, carefully modulated voice. "But I'm certain that you understand that when I discovered some of the people you'd spoken to about me, I had to be cautious. I don't want to go back to jail. These people have no love for me."

"I have no desire to see you harmed," I said. "I would have spoken to more of your friends if you'd encouraged it." I kept my tone light. I was absolutely sincere, but I didn't want to sell hard.

We settled into a glassed-in taping room with yellow walls, beanbag chairs, and a long vinyl couch divided by a boxy Formica trash bin that doubled as a tabletop. It was the kind of room you see used in movies for group encounter sessions. Miki and I sat on opposite sides of the divider and turned on our tape recorders. Miki's dark eyes watched me carefully.

DORA: I've been an expatriate for over twelve years. I've been away from California and surfing and the media. Why have you taken an interest in me?

I've wondered where you've been.

DORA: Well, so has everyone else; so have the authorities.

They found you.

DORA: They didn't find me. I came back voluntarily, to settle this up, as an honorable gentleman. I thought they would reciprocate in the same way. But things like that don't occur anymore. Now I have to make a living in this country. I have to pay fines. I have to live up to the obligations of my probation, with the bureaucrats, the state, the people who are controlling me and you. I must be very circumspect in my behavior. If I do one thing wrong, I can go back to jail. I don't see where this article is going to help me. Do you see it giving me more employment or making me a happier person? The probation officer or judge reads this article, people who seem to think that I'm a sociopath . . . I went to jail in Vacaville, not for any crime, but because I smiled at the judge . . . I had a wonderful life in Europe. There was no reason to come back here.

But you did.

DORA: I felt I was innocent and that it could be taken care of in a court of law by fair play. But that didn't occur. I thought I'd be here one or two months. My lawyer said this is nothing; the charges against me are ridiculous, and that we'll settle them quickly and you'll be on your way. And 99 percent were gossip, just like your magazine is going to talk about. Hearsay. Unsubstantiated rumor.

Are you saying that the Diners Club problem, the Mammoth incident, jumping probation—that is all gossip?

DORA: I'm saying that I did not do any crime in this country. But a judge can say "You plead guilty to these charges, and if not, if you are found guilty, we'll put you away for ten years."

I'd say you lucked out, then. The federal charges were reduced to a misdemeanor. That was six months instead of ten years in jail.

DORA: Ten for what?

According to you, ten years for nothing—or six months for nothing. Take your pick. I'm not saying you were fairly treated. . . .

DORA: Well, are we in the Dark Ages or the enlightened twentieth century? I didn't have to come back to all this.

But you did.

DORA: I said I made a mistake, that's all. . . . I would leave tomorrow if I could.

Where would you go?

DORA: [smiles] There are islands in the Pacific I could live on and never be found. . . .

I'm a healthy human being and I want to find happiness in this world and live a good life. I'm known all over the world. I'm respected in Australia, Europe . . . it's only in this country that I have problems with these people. [pauses] Will I be able to see what you've written about me or is that going to be a big secret until the last moment until it blazes and blows up in the *California* magazine, in my face?

Why assume the worst? Anyway, that's not how it's done.

DORA: So everyone else can see it.

Only Cynthia and my editors have seen what I've written. Ask her what's in the story.

DORA: Cynthia is a friend of mine from a long distance, and I keep her at a distance. And I hope I can trust her and I hope that she doesn't get overexcited about this project. I can only tell you that she relays some information to me and that's all. [pauses] She told me she was upset about reading about Linda in the article. Sometimes I think she's just an aging debutante who can be neurotic. [Author's note: Linda was not mentioned by name in the final article; she may have been in an earlier draft read by Cynthia.]

What's your relationship with Linda now?

DORA: Linda is someone I liked—I like a lot of women—but she betrayed me, my confidence, my intimacy. I give a lot to a relationship. [pauses] After this article comes out, everyone will look at me like I'm some sort of freak of nature? Some untrustworthy individual?

Why? Is that what you think of yourself?

DORA: I'm quite sure that you put in print my, uh [smiles] . . . escapades of the last thirty to forty years.

Yeah. Some of them.

DORA: Well, people interpret that as nefarious sometimes. [laughs] I don't want to suffer. I'm an old man. The sport is for young people, not people like me.

This is not just a surfing story. It's about a unique individual. It's about mystique created by absence. Look at Garbo.

DORA: But she was a talented person. I have no talent. None.

What do you call it, then?

DORA: I don't know what you're talking about.

Your surfing ability is not a talent?

DORA: There are thousands of these kids, millions of them all over the world like polliwogs. What's that got to do with me? They can do ten times what I can do.

You're avoiding the question.

DORA: The only talent I have is to try and live a free life. And that's been taken from me. It was a different sport in those days. It was a small community and everyone respected each other. Now that world and that life are gone forever.

And that's exactly what you predicted.

DORA: But what's to discuss? It's an illusion, off the face of the earth. The point is that I don't go back and dwell upon what I used to do, that I was popular or unpopular when I lived in California twelve years ago. My life is completely changed. I'm not happy in America. Simple. And I'm sure that many people here don't want to make me happy, they want to make me miserable and, if they can, put me back in prison.

Why do they want to make you miserable?

DORA: Why is there violence in this country? Why is everyone . . . why is there this upheaval, this tremendous crime?

Good questions. Why?

DORA: You should look deep into the society. Why are the prisons filled? Why are . . . the psychiatric clinics filled? Why is the whole country neurotic?

I'd be interested in you telling me.

DORA: This system isn't working, that's what's happening. People here think only of money. That's not in my psyche and it's hard for me to adjust to people that I don't know and to be candid unless . . . it takes time to get to know somebody. And since I don't know you, I just can't tell you what I really think or fulfill my presentation to you.

So let's take the time.

DORA: Let me digest all of this.

Many consider you a legend in your own time. Is that difficult or does it please you?

DORA: [quickly] I never considered myself a legend. I never considered myself anything as a way of surviving, of living in a very competitive sport.

Many consider you an enigma.

DORA: I don't think of myself as an enigma. California is all screwed up. The movie stars have simpering fans, but I don't want that. People on the beach never worshipped me—that's just your viewpoint. There are four billion people on this planet and they're all fucked up except for a few. But I don't see why I have to tell that to the world. What does my philosophy matter? I just want to live my life as I see fit. But I guess I'm paying the price now for my charades with the surf magazines in the past. All those stories were just satires putting down surf culture. The judge had them stacked up and used them as evidence against me, as proof of my "antisocial attitudes." This is what I get for having lived here in the '50s and '60s. I feel ripped off. Like I have a gun to my head. Like I'm being held hostage."

DAVID RENSIN: The college campus was empty. Night school was in session. Miki declined my offer of dinner and a ride home. He said he couldn't eat because of a dietary problem. Then he showed me some bumps on his arms. Also, he said he had borrowed and had to return a friend's car. For a while we walked in silence. Then he began to talk, unbidden. "I don't have the same kind of profile as the normal American," he said. "I don't have a house or a car payment, or kids who hate me, or three or four marriages."

Perhaps he was referring to his father, who'd been married a few times. I asked if I could call him, if he'd okay it.

"Don't talk to my father. We're not close. He doesn't know me. My parents threw me away when I was four years old and I've been on my own since then. I've had to survive." It would be years before I found out that this wasn't exactly true.

Miki continued to insist he didn't "do stuff with credit cards. I reported my Diners Club card stolen years ago." He suggested his signature had been forged.

"Would you be willing to take a handwriting analysis test?" I asked.

Miki smiled. "I did certain things in Europe; I had ways of avoiding the

FBI, which chased me around the globe for years and spent millions of dollars doing it. But, I'm not going to reveal those ways because I'm afraid of going back to the pen."

By this time I could tell by the widening of his eyes and a little smirk, when he knew I knew something that he wouldn't admit to—or wanted to give me that impression.

As we neared my car I couldn't help thinking, as ironic as it might sound, how it seemed as if Miki and California had grown up together. Miki's life was a microcosm of the California experience, breathtaking, explosive, and confused. California had been a more natural place before the 1960s. Rapid growth and the media selling the California Dream had had an enormous effect on the social, physical, and economic environment. It became a state defined by paradox: mysterious, trendy, superficial, dangerous, welcoming, innovative, entertaining, unstable, original, traditional, and eternal in its natural beauty—all qualities that inspire awe and love, and invite cynicism. California has always had to deal with relentless criticism by anyone who lived a more "normal" American lifestyle, where the skies were not cloudy all day. California's dilemma was now embodied by the struggle between trying to define itself and coexist with its multitude of media images, and with resisting definition at the same time. It made for a fragile, gorgeous, and at times stigmatized, existence. Much like Miki's life.

We lingered in the parking lot still making small talk. I wanted to meet again. Miki promised to think it over. I searched for some ammunition to convince him, but we'd reached an impasse. We shook hands. I took a quarter from my pocket and flipped it in the air. Mickey read it as his signal to leave, spun slowly, and sauntered gracefully away. He was an individualist in a world that both loved and hated exceptions to the rules. As I watched I remembered something Cynthia Applewhite had said of Miki: "His attitude is that 'They'll never beat me.'" She'd also told me, "Mickey's always had this disappearing fantasy. He once told me that he just wanted to paddle out past some second point and just disappear in the fog, leaving his surfboard to wash up on the shore."

I caught the coin and cupped it on the back of my left hand. Heads, he would call me. Tails he wouldn't. It came up tails.

After Miki's story came out in the August 1983 issue of *California*, the David Geffen Company called about buying an option to develop a movie. I called Cynthia and asked her to tell Miki and said he should be involved. Soon, Cynthia called back. Miki wanted to meet me at her house on September 4, 1983.

~

I walked in, we shook hands, and Miki immediately berated me about my "shoddy journalistic practices" for having talked to sources "who knew little or nothing about him." "You've spoken to a bunch of liars," he said. It didn't seem that way to me, and I told Miki again that had he encouraged some of his closer friends to speak, then maybe the story would have felt more balanced to him. In any case, his legal hassles and jail time were hardly the focus of the piece.

He told me that my story had caused problems with his father. "My dad was embarrassed by the reaction of some of his friends, like the Rothschild family." But Miki also said the story had pushed his father to do what he'd been asking him to do all along: pay his fines. Dora Sr. had also bought his son a ticket on a charter flight to Germany.

Miki said that the story had even caused some personal confrontations. "I've been in a few fights," he complained, "and I injured my arm."

I don't know what kind of reaction he expected. I just listened.

Then, suddenly, he dropped the attitude completely, flashed his trademark grin, and said, "Let's make a movie."

Almost in the same breath Miki added that he really didn't trust "the Hollywood system. I'm afraid that any information I give you would be stolen and a movie made and I'll get cut out of any financial compensation." He asked questions about his legal rights. I referred him to his agent or lawyer for factual information and tried to soothe his paranoia. Or was it just pragmatic caution?

As for the film story, he wanted to address the early days, but dwell more on the '60s and early '70s. He talked about the changes that had taken place at Malibu and in surfing itself, with the commercialization and competition and crowds. He said his buddies were a tight-knit group of territorial surfers with their own conventions and codes of honor, all caught in a tide of social change. "They're also like sheep that one by one were caught and dragged off by the wolf, leaving only me to survive."

"I wasn't liked on the beach," he said, but didn't explain why. "I never—or rarely—went to their parties. I was in the water crowd. Maybe that had something to do with my popularity.

"People constantly wondered about what I did when I wasn't surfing and I think that's why all these rumors about me began." People were insatiably curious, he said, about this character who dedicated his life to the art and challenge of riding a "temporary bit of water. So they made up myths." Miki was compelling and convincing, even as I tried to remember that not everything said about him was a myth.

At the outset, Miki seemed animated and light, sometimes cynical. As our conversation progressed, he grew more serious. "Is life meaningless? Are we just ants? Is the world going to blow itself up, anyway?

"Look," he said, "I've lived my life in the tube, with the law, and my disappearance, and my disappearing friends, and the various hassles I've confronted, just crashing over my head until I decided to kick out and leave the country. I wouldn't have come back except that my father suckered me. Since then I was in more than twenty prisons, including one in Sacramento where inmates are hung up and beaten for just laughing at the authorities."

"So you've said," I reminded him.

When we got back to talking about the movie, Miki said he envisioned his life story told in two parts. The story of his escape and travels around the world would be part two.

I asked Miki what he had lost in the '60s and whether he regained it.

"Honor and respect and the ability to stay true to my feelings about the environment and how one should live. I can't stop the system changing everything, but I didn't fail. I just got out."

Miki had someplace to be, and as we said good-bye he said he would not be "averse to working together," and that we should meet again. We did. At the same time, he busily worked at ending his probation, paying off his debts, seeing and avoiding "old friends," and planning his escape.

GARTH BULLOCK: In 1965, I surfed a lot at Hollywood by the Sea/Silver Strand, which is by Oxnard. We'd see Miki there occasionally. He'd surf either at Twin Poles or he'd be up where very few of us rode, a place called the Rivermouth. He would never drop in on your wave, but he expected that if he was farthest out, you'd get the hell off his wave.

I'd talk about him a lot, so much so that after he got out of Lompoc, my wife encouraged me to get in touch with him.

I'd heard he was in Orange County. Knowing he liked to play tennis, I tried calling Orange Coast College. I got through to this lady who knew him. She was very protective. I told her who I was. She said, "Well, yes, he occasionally works down here." She said she belonged to a group that held gourmet dinners—and he sold the wine by the case. She told me to try calling his father.

On my third call, I got Miki. He decided he had to test me. "Well, the name 'Garth' is really familiar. I don't remember your last name. Give me something to key into." I said, "March 1965, Twin Poles, Hollywood by the Sea, eight-foot-plus."

"You mean Rivermouth?"

"No. Twin Poles. Eight-feet-plus. You were taking off behind us. Sometimes you'd put your arms straight up and couldn't make the section, the wave would just take you off and you'd have to swim to the beach."

"Ah yeah, I remember you," he said. "I'd love to meet with you and talk things over." He said he had to go to Newport Beach. I said I'd be taking my family to Disneyland for two nights at the same time. "One of those days, if you can arrange it, I could leave them at Disneyland and meet with you."

"Okay," he said, and picked a place.

"Let's have brunch," I said. "My treat."

A couple weeks later, Miki waited for me in the restaurant foyer. He was thinner than when I'd last seen him. He had a full beard. He had longer hair, curled a little bit. He wore a loose T-shirt and slacks, both black, and a sports coat with the sleeves rolled up. A tennis racket handle stuck out of his gym bag.

The hostess asked if we wanted to be seated. I wanted to sit in a corner booth but Miki picked a table in the middle of the room. The waitress brought water, then brought another waitress with her when she came back to take our order. They never looked at me, only him. "Can we help you, sir? Is there anything extra you would like?" He made that funny little smirk because he knew what was happening. It's like Marilyn Monroe. She could walk downtown and not be recognized, but she could also turn on that "thing."

The champagne brunch cost $7 or $8 a plate. I wanted to be gracious. I said, "Anything you want, Miki. Let's order up." He didn't feel like eating, but ordered a bran muffin and an iced coffee in a tall glass.

I wasn't sure how to start the conversation, so I said, "So, what've you been doing?" He looked at me with a silly grin and we both started laughing. I was so stupid. It was a great icebreaker.

Occasionally he did his little cry thing: "God, I wish I had my van right now."

"Where is it?" I asked.

"It's parked next to a rock wall in a friend's villa in France. It's got two surfboards in it."

He explained his arrest in France. "I made a call from a phone booth in the south of France, near Basque country. You know I'm Basque, right? I speak three languages."

Yes, of course you do, I thought. Who doesn't? I could hear the embell-ishment.

"Were you extradited?" I asked.

"No. I could have stayed. But I took the wrong advice."

Then he told me about his problems in Mono County.

"There's a judge in northern California, in some ski village. I went up there with friends six or seven years ago. I rented some ski poles and bind-ings. They were those new step-in boots that the back closes in on you. The damn things were no good. I wrote a check and they broke after two hours' skiing. I brought them back to the guy and said, 'This equipment is broken. Here, take it back. Give me my money back.'

"The guy said, 'Bullshit, I'm not giving you your check back.' I said, 'Well, I'll stop payment on the check. I'm not going to pay for something that's broken.' The guy kept the check after I stopped payment and the judge threw the book at me. If anything it should have been a civil case, not a criminal case."

He said the judge went off on him about why didn't he have a driver's license, why didn't he have a Social Security card, what did he do for a living? "I explained that I was in one of the oldest professions: barter. I do some-thing for people and they do something for me." He said that didn't go over well. "Part of the deal was, they made me get a Social Security number and a license, and all this crap.

"Coming back cost me over a year of my life in prison. I could still be in France with my van and free."

"What was prison like?" I asked.

"It was terrible." The upshot was that he, Miki Dora, had been locked up with *criminals*.

"They had me talk to a psychiatrist in the prison. Then the warden said, 'You are a sociopath.' They locked me in solitary for a couple months. I could never have imagined what it would be like losing my freedom, let alone being locked up by myself except for the meals." He said it reminded him of military school.

We talked for three hours. He kept saying, "You've got to get back to your family," and I said, "No, I don't. My family's always there. They see me all the time. This is important for us now." He was gracious, but, at the same time, I could tell he enjoyed talking this out with someone who wouldn't judge him.

Miki said they finally got him on the credit card charge. He claimed the bills were sent to a friend's post office box. "When they came in, they were dumped in a trash can, unopened. Now I have to pay back a portion of the money. It's going to take about a year. I also can't leave the country until the debt is settled."

I asked how he planned to pay it off. He wouldn't go into it.

"So what are you going to do after that?" I asked.

He paused, and shook his head up and down, intent, determined. "I'm going back to France, Garth. I'm going back."

WANDERER

To what avail the plough or sail, or love, or life—if freedom fail?
Freedom. Freedom to what? Escape, run, wander turning your
back on a cowed society that stutters, staggers, and stagnates
every man for himself and fuck you Jack I've got mine?

To be truly challenging, a voyage, like life, must rest on a
firm foundation of financial unrest. Otherwise you are doomed
to a routine traverse, the kind known to yachtsmen, who play
with their boats at sea—"cruising" it is called. Voyaging belongs
to sea men, and to the wanderers of the world who cannot or will
not fit in.

Little has been said or written about the ways a man may
blast himself free. Why? I don't know, unless the answer lies
in our diseased values. . . . Men are enmeshed in the cancerous
discipline of "security," and in the worship of security we fling
our lives beneath the wheels of routine—and before we know it
our lives are gone.

What does a man really need—really need? A few pounds
of food each day, heat and shelter, six feet to lie down in—and
some form of working activity that will yield a sense of
accomplishment. That's all—in the material sense. But we are
brainwashed by our economic system until we end up in a tomb
beneath a pyramid of time payments, mortgages, preposterous
gadgetry, playthings that divert our attention from the sheer
idiocy of the charade.

The years thunder by. The dreams of youth grow dim where
they lie caked in dust on the shelves of patience. Before we know
it, the tomb is sealed.

Dedication to the sea is the symbol of migration and movement
and wandering. It is the barbaric place and it stands opposed to
society and it is a constant symbol in all of literature, too.

As Thomas Wolfe said, "It is the state of barbaric disorder
out of which civilization has emerged and into which it is liable
to return."

—Sterling Hayden, *Wanderer*, 1964

CHAPTER **TWELVE**

Sink or Swim

1

ADVERTISEMENT BARWICKS AUCTIONS
AUCTION SALE - SPECIAL SALE
THIS FRIDAY NIGHT MARCH 16

STARTING 7PM SHARP

Synchronex 8mm movie camera - Wooden snuff box - Double brass bedstead - Cabin slide projector - Asst linen and sheets - Burmese wood gilt figurine - German SS leather coat - Small writing compendium - Stoneware china - Danish milk jug - Ski clothing - Projection screen - Ski boots and poles - Electric dog prod - Student's microscope - Camera tripod - Sony cassette recorder - Trinket box and asst stones - Brass scales - Nepalese shield - Jade figurine - Leather briefcase - Many interesting books - 4 big cabin trunks - Carved horn - Whale's tooth - Haiti wooden writing box - Leather satchel - Globe map - Snakes skin - Kitset furniture - 4 sets snow skis - Chinese trinket box - Electric engraver - Brand new Sony 4-channel stereo - Plated ewer - Ruby 7X30 binoculars - Bottle cognac - Sleeping bag - new clothing galore

AUCTIONEERS NOTE:

This sale consists of many interesting items collected from all over the world. Everything must be sold. TERMS strictly cash, all must be settled the night of the sale. On view now.

"The stage looked like a set from a Valentino epic." Dora auction, Gisborne, New Zealand, 1984. Photos: Rick Hodgson.

BRIAN EDDY: I was the auctioneer in Gisborne who sold Miki's goods. We were contacted by the local police in 1983 and asked to inspect a consignment of half a dozen cabin trunks housed at a local storage firm. When opened in the presence of the police, Barwicks's role was to advise if the chattels had any commercial value.

The trunks revealed a treasure trove of interesting items, including an automatic assault rifle, hand grenade, and other weapons. Also, a fine array of beautiful handwoven materials, travel memorabilia, expensive clothing from Beverly Hills, hand-tooled Eastern carvings, a long black Nazi leather jacket and armband, a selection of surf magazines and photo albums, skiing equipment, antiques.

The police took the guns. Shortly after, we were contacted by Diners Club, regarding the best manner of disposing of the goods. My business partner, Michael, and I—who had taken over Barwicks in Gisborne—suggested an auction. We were asked by Diners Club to take the goods to our place of business, lay them out for a week, then advertise them as an "unknown owner auction." They stressed that we weren't allowed to use Miki's name. Usually there's a rule where we provide a name, address, some detail that helps promote an auction. For Dora they wanted a simple ad and a sale. "No matter what you get, just get rid of it." We were of the opinion that had we been allowed to use Dora's name, especially in a surfing location like Gisborne, that the attendance and prices would have been greatly enhanced. I suppose that was their little bit of a comeback at Dora.

The auction took place Friday March 16, 1984. It started at 7:00 P.M. and finished at 9:30 P.M. About ninety people attended. Some movie reels were sold to a gentleman from Malibu who, we understand, returned the reels to Dora.

RICK HODGSON: The night of the auction I walked into my house, the phone rang, and a friend said, "Get down here, they're auctioning off all Miki's stuff." I went to this funky old mart where they only sell off the left-behinds of poor dead New Zealanders, like used Tupperware. But now the stage was full of the most amazing stuff that anyone had ever seen. The humble audience of old Maoris, who just go to hear the banter of the auctioneer and hopefully pick up an old knife or fork, were confronted with a vision that looked like the set of a silent movie, with treasure chests and all kinds of strange African jewelry and suits from J. Carroll of Beverly Hills, and tuxedos, and a pink paisley silk sleeping bag, cashmere everything, dinner jackets never worn, ritualistic carvings, Rolls-Royce hood ornaments, the street corner sign from Hollywood and Vine, a Nazi SS leather coat. It was so amazing. I could only stare. All of

Miki's treasures in this humble building in the most remote city in the most remote country in the world.

The auctioneer was usually completely comatose about the crap he had to get rid of, but this night he rose to the occasion, selling ostrich eggs, bibles with the centers cut out of them—one Maori called it a "heroin Bible." Another Maori about Miki's size, named Mickey, bought all his clothing.

When three reels of 16 mm film came up, I bid every cent I had on me, which was $36. People knew that I was going to return them to Dora, and nobody bid against me. There were 8 mm and 16 mm films taken by Hal Jepsen, and an original Kodacolor film Grant Rohloff took in Hawaii. Miki must have obtained the print from Grant somehow.

Before I returned the film, I rented a projector and set it up in my garage. All of a sudden there was Miki at Sunset Beach, and Malibu, then Topanga, and there *I was* at eleven years old taking off in front of Miki, on the first surfboard I ever had, an old Jacobs with baby blue rails. Jim Fitzpatrick and Bruce Bernstein are in front of me, and Miki is behind me. Miki comes up and tries to push me off, but he ends up going over the falls. I go up on one foot but catch my balance and make it.

I started screaming in the garage. To feel the karma of this stuff released and given to Maoris for pennies was so inspiring that the energy in that room was biblical. The closets, both literally and metaphorically, had been opened and the secrets finally laid bare. And in a way it also freed Miki and his soul, released him from his past. As I later wrote: "It's been forgiven. It all got laid out in the sand, the tide came and took it away, and now it's gone."

Just before the sale started, Brian Eddy had called me over. He had a couple boxes. He said, "Look, this is really personal stuff of Miki's. We want to give this back to him and his family." They knew I was originally from Malibu because Miki's lawyers—Dan Winters, Doug Rishworth, and Peter Wahl—were my friends, and they'd told him.

The boxes contained some diaries and family photo albums, also drawings he did when he was young: guys surfing and stuff.

I decided to mail everything to his mom because I didn't want the responsibility of carrying it—or Miki even knowing it had been me. I addressed the boxes to "Da Cat, Miki Dora" and sent it to his mom, and put my address down as "The Phantom of Topanga Beach."

When Ramona informed Miki what the Phantom had sent, he wrote Hodgson:

*It's not easy to reconstruct any moment of pure emotion and for one
reason or another it seems hardest of all to recapture my feelings of
hearing from California that two very large and heavy packages
arrived: photos. I got the hell out of the US as soon as I could
and am now living in France . . . Please understand how much I
APPRECIATE your kindness. I had given up ever seeing anything
again. If there's anything I could do for you from this side of the globe
please write as soon as possible. Please send a bill for all expenses. You
give me new hope for human nature. Thanks forever. Miki.*

DOUGLAS RISHWORTH: Meanwhile, we got the leftovers from the auction,
which included some personal items that we held on to for years and finally
managed to return to him shortly before his death. I know he was particularly
anxious to locate that Duke trophy. There's a chap who runs a surf museum
up in Manganui, and I suspect it might have ended up there.

It did. According to the Mount Maunganui, New Zealand–based,
Mount Surf Museum's website, "Among the collection are valuable
private possessions of the legendary Malibu surfer Mickey 'Da Cat'
Dora . . . The possessions of the charismatic one-time stuntman and
movie star, which had been locked away since 1972[3] were put up for
auction in Gisborne in the early 1980s. They went to a surfing-mad
local collector, who stored them in a bank vault until recently, when
museum proprietor Dusty Waddell acquired them. Items on show
include personal photographs, a childhood silver ID bracelet, specta-
cles, nail kit, snuffbox, a wetsuit, and a Duke Kahanamoku Big Wave
Invitation Trophy."[4]

---

[3] Dora's possessions were not confiscated earlier than 1976.
[4] Additionally, other Dora memorabilia still floats in the shadows, much of it in the
Refrigerator Collection, a stack of papers, boxes, photos, drawings, documents, and more,
discovered by Wayne Speeds in a refrigerator in Marcia McMartin's garage in 1979.
Speeds eventually sold the collection and it's since been kept in a very secure location.
The cache fills two large storage containers and includes Miki's skateboard; surf trunks;
Hawaiian driver's license; his original certificate of Holy Communion at St. Victoria's
Church, dated May 17, 1942, under the name Miki; a draft of the text for Da Cat
"Evolution" ad, and sketchbooks that include drawings of surfers, waves, cowboys, a
sabertooth cat in a tux with red eyes and red bow tie, Oriental surfers, Tommy Zahn, and
more; his Los Angeles City High School diploma from Hollywood High School, dated
June 18, 1954; a copy of the check Miki wrote to enter the Tom Morey Invitational

Miki would spend the rest of his life trying to recover his posses-sions only to find bits and pieces put up for sale on the Internet for thousands upon thousands of dollars by anonymous sellers acting for other anonymous sellers in a collectibles shell game. And depending on who wanted to do the buying, the price could go up or down until even Miki or those acting on his behalf were no longer interested. As he once wrote to Bob Simpson and Steven Taussig, after running into yet another brick wall, "Memorabilia meltdown! Another pie in the face. My personal property was seized illegally. This is theft in the first degree. This is a personal affront, a travesty of justice and an insult to the History of Surfing. It's greed for money only!! And the total disre-gard for private property that can only bring more disgrace to surfing, which it will never recover from. Who breeds these morons?"

2

PHILIPPE LAUGA: When Miki returned to France and recovered his van, he didn't park as before, away from the scene. He parked right on the spot where every-body hangs about. He didn't avoid the crowd; he stayed in the limelight!

His behavior, which was quite smooth before he went to prison, got rot-ten when he resurfaced on the Basque scene. Before, there was some sort of balance between his frolics and his naughty behavior, a kind of childish game in which everybody played, no winner or loser, just friends sharing a common experience of life. On his return, the curtain rose on a totally different second act. The Pied Piper had given way to Humbug. The screenplay was cheap and nasty and the actor all deceit.

Humbug meant using his friends to abuse. We would use my car to go to the gym, the golf courses, the restaurants, to Spain, and he never offered to share the expenses. He gave me a hard time in front of a friend because I didn't supply him fast enough with a medical prescription I was supposed to obtain for free from another friend. That's neither kind nor honest.

He had been a perfect gentleman who had found refuge in the Pays Basque, a lion in winter. Now, perhaps having brushed against other criminals in prison

---

Contest, which bounced because of nonsufficient funds; an invite to the first Duke contest; a certificate of "Registry of Marriage" dated April 10, 1967, for the state of California—but never exercised—in the names of Miki and Mary Jacqueline Booke; a Social Security card for Michael Chapin, as well as one for Miklos Dora—and much, much more. Others have boards Miki rode, as well as scrapbooks, tapes, and other items.

had affected his nature and revealed his darker side. I was ready to jump to that conclusion at the time.

His physical appearance also began to reflect his inner self. He was a slouch, a sloven, untidy in dressing, in his behavior. He was on a guest list at a sport center but was sent off for having cleaned his clothes in the Jacuzzi and storing them in the sauna to dry.

His van also showed the deterioration from exposure to salty winds and severe weather. And inside, where he had once kept it in good condition, decay set it.

MIKE MCNEILL: After he got out of jail, Miki had his own passport, his own driver's license, his own Social Security card. He used to get movie residual checks from America, then go to restaurants in Biarritz and try to pay for his meals, knowing in advance there was no way they were going to accept third-party checks. He'd also use the same check over and over. If you were aware of what was going on, you'd pay your portion and get out before they got to him to pay. But he always did stuff like that. Before he went to prison he was once stopped at the Carefour supermarket where you return a bottle into a device and get a refund. He'd put in the bottle over and over and over, just for 20 centimes each time. Everyone used to do it. But Miki got caught.

Mike McNeill's then-wife, Susan, had met Miki at Lafiténia in the late '70s. Like Miki, she lived in her van. Unlike Miki, she was married, but her husband had gone to England with friends. One cold winter day Miki burst into her van without knocking, looking for someone. She asked him to leave—he did—but began to see him around town. One night she attended a party at which Miki showed slides of himself and Linda in New Zealand. Shortly afterward, Miki knocked on Susan's van door again and asked her out for coffee.

"Soon Miki and I spent every day together," Susan recalls. "I never asked about Linda; it was none of my business. Miki made me think about life. He had the BBC on the radio all the time. He taught me about the world situation, about stocks and gold. Every morning we'd have tea and read the *Wall Street Journal* and of course the *International Herald Tribune*."

"It took several weeks together—doing laundry, trying to find showers, going to the bathhouses—to become lovers. I think I initiated it. One evening in his van I said, 'Why don't you kiss me?' He said, 'Because if I do, you'll have to get a crowbar to get me off of you.'

I said, 'Well, I don't have a crowbar . . . and I don't think we'll need to use one.' He was wonderful with me. Wonderful."

The relationship was short-lived. Susan's husband returned from an extended trip—broke—and eventually the couple moved back to California.

SUSAN MCNEILL: Miki said, "Don't go. I'll never see you again." I told him not to worry. In America I was miserable. Miki called every night, in the middle of the night. He sent me an airline ticket. But I chose not to come back because I realized that Miki didn't live in the real world and I didn't know if I could live that way.

Miki and I saw each other again when I went back to France in 1984. I wasn't married anymore. We picked up from where we'd left off. He was in a pretty tight spot. He had no money, nowhere to live, nowhere to go. He didn't do the stuff he'd done before—credit cards, telephone. I didn't know what he was going to do. It was really sink or swim.

Then, one day, while we were lying in Miki's van in back of the youth hostel at Anglet, the door opened and there stood Harry Hodge. In a way, Harry opened the door to the rest of Miki's life.

HARRY HODGE: When I was making the surf film *Band on the Run,* in 1976–77, I had met Miki in the campground at Lafiténia, two miles south of Guéthary. We saw his van, and my friends and I thought that to meet him would be huge. One day he strolled over and said, "Where you guys from?" We had a few beers, he went surfing with the guys. I didn't film him because we knew that was a no-no.

We were there during an off month. Miki hung out with us from time to time. He played a lot of tennis with Rabbit Bartholomew. We put no demands on him. Before we left he said to keep in touch, and we wrote letters for a while.

I came back to France from Australia to visit. Miki had agreed to do an interview with me and have dinner. He said, "If we tape this, I want to keep the tapes until we finish the whole process because I want to do it really well and I'm really into it." We talked for quite a while.

I'd written Paul Holmes at *Surfer* a note saying he owed me lunch if I could pull off the interview. When I saw Miki the next time, I asked him about the interview tapes, and he said, "Oh no. I don't remember the tapes. I thought you kept the tapes? Why would I take the tapes?" I said, "Why would I lose the tapes?"

You have to hand it to him. He says yes, but in fact he's saying no. In my mind I had the interview, but in my hand . . . no tapes, no story.

In 1984, I moved to France to start the European Quiksilver operation with Jeff Hakman. Miki would come to the offices every day and hang out. He faxed letters from our machine. He was a fatalist, but funny. "Everything's rigged," he'd say. "The system. The drug companies." He asked if I knew the Charlton Heston movie *Soylent Green*. I did. "That's what's going on," he said.

"I have to back the system, Miki," I said, "because I have to go to work. I have no other choice. I'll be just like all those other lemmings who jump off the cliff. But I don't think we're eating people—at least not yet."

One night during a philosophical discourse over six bottles of red wine— we were really geniuses by then—someone at the table said, "What's the most valuable thing to you in life, Harry?" I said "time." Miki concurred.

Miki didn't talk easily about surfing. Current events, golf, Quiksilver: He was always interested. And he'd talk about his projects: a surfing contest at Jeffreys Bay that used only organic and environmentally friendly materials, from surfboards to wet suits. He had ideas on surfboard design. His friends. The episonic wave. But surfing: "What's there to talk about? I had a great surf today?"

SUSAN MCNEILL: Like everyone else, Harry was enamored of Miki. Miki kind of made fun of him in the beginning, like he did with everybody, but Harry is one of the few people I know who Miki genuinely respected.

HARRY HODGE: Miki and I slowly concocted a relationship. I say concocted because we both worked at making it happen. Of all the people he had relationships with, I was probably the most commercially entrepreneurial in the surf industry. Contrary to conventional wisdom—actually, myth—Miki was fascinated with how to make money from surfing, as he'd tried to do with the Hollywood movies, with his Da Cat board, and I told him I didn't buy into the argument that you shouldn't make money off surfing, or that *real* surfers don't want to. In fact, they'd been doing it for years. Even Duke Kahanamoku. He did world tours, TV, movies—and his hook was surfing and swimming. He was a Hawaiian legend. Then in the late 1940s, early 1950s, Jack O'Neill invented the wet suit. You can't call Jack O'Neill not a true, hard-core surfer, one of the originals. And why do you do it? So you can spend more time going surfing. Who wants to get a job in a bank?

Miki watched me and Jeff Hakman, two guys in their thirties, try to make a career by selling surf lifestyle clothing when everyone thought the money was in surfboards. Wrong. Today, Quiksilver and other clothing companies are a multibillion-dollar industry competing on a global scale with the mainstream companies like Ralph Lauren and Levis. And surfing is better for it. I think Miki really liked that.

If Miki was the complete iconoclast that some of his devotees think he was, he never would have tolerated or spoken to me. He could have taken a stance. But Miki didn't have a problem with that as long it was done by the surfers instead of the Wall Street suits. This is a myth that some of Miki's disciples want to perpetuate for their own agendas, to satisfy their self-need and self-importance. Even though Quiksilver is now on Wall Street, we're still run largely by surfers.

As Miki had said, exposure and growth did bring the crowds. But they would have come anyway. In time, the situation evolved. Surfers are pioneers and explorers; we figured out ways to find new waves. Instead of surfing one break our whole lives, we had the means to expand the resources. Now surfers go to Indonesia and Tahiti and everywhere else, to ride waves that would never have been found if the surf and apparel industry didn't provide the wherewithal for surfers to travel. That's what Miki realized—no matter what he said out loud. After all, Miki was one of the original surf travelers.

Miki also knew he'd been part of bringing jerk-offs to the beach. Compare Miki to Kelly Slater. Both did movies, stunt work, book deals, ads, sponsorship, surfboard models, surfing contests. And yet, people go, "Kelly's a commercial surfer; Miki was a soul surfer." It's a bunch of crap. Both represent that spirit of travel and that purity of concept. I don't buy these people who have fabricated this myth that Miki hated *anything* to do with commercialization of surfing.

Miki and I became good friends because he liked being around people who were their own people. He didn't tolerate fools or followers, or imitators. I'm not saying I was an original, but when Jeff and I went to Europe, people said there's no way you'll be successful. "You're in France and Germany and Spain. They don't even know about surfing."

Miki would question me often about business. He wanted to understand. And I talked freely about it. I felt I had an opportunity to make sure that this legendary, mythic guy understood the ethic behind our process and our goals.

Miki's goal after prison was to create and maintain the lifestyle that he desired. He made it up as he went along. He'd already paid a tremendous price: he had to live outside the box and scam a bit. Loneliness. Lack of a consistent group of friends and advisers. That makes one introverted. He never talked to me about being lonely, though, or even acknowledged it. But I know what it's like when I'm on the road by myself. When you saw his possessions, and the way he lived, well, it was obvious: He spent a lot of time by himself.

3

Miki ferried his van to Ireland in the summer of 1985 and drove to see Linda Cuy. He'd visited her there the previous summer, considered buying land, but didn't like the cold or the surf.

LINDA CUY: (This time) he tried to pry me out of there to go to South Africa with him. "Look, we'll go to Jeffreys Bay," he said. "It's perfect." He showed me photos. "It's a perfect right." But with Miki I'd always been one step behind his shoulder. He was in the spotlight and he loved that. He couldn't figure out why I wanted to be in a cold country where there weren't a lot of people to watch you surf. Miki wanted an audience. He didn't want to ride a secret spot. I mean he'd do it for the novelty, but he wouldn't want to live that way. Even Jeffreys Bay, where he went, eventually had major competitions. It was on the map. It was an important spot for surfers.

Miki wanted me because of his ego and whole manly thing, "You come here!" I said no. I'd established my own little fun group to surf with. I didn't want to get into the whole mess again.

> *7.1.85 [Letter to Ramona, from Ireland]*
> *. . . I wish I could tell you something about south Ireland. Why in God's name I come here is beyond me. It must be a repressed death wish . . . This part of Ireland hasn't moved an inch since the 1929 crash. The conquering of the darkness of night, the weather, pain, disease, space, and time will never happen here. The inhabitants if not dead drunk on Guinness, toil desperately from dawn to dark, unwashed, unshaven, uncombed, with lousy hair, mangy skin, and rotting teeth to eke out their meager existence in the bog-waters of never-ending rains. Sometimes there's good waves breaking on distant deserted beaches which have gone unridden since the beginning of time. (For damn good reasons, obviously) . . . Every night I dream of a sunshine cruise to Africa. In the morning I awake gasping for breath. I try to remember what transpired, but the shock of the day's reality devours all memories.*

ANDY HILL: While visiting, Miki saw our wee dog Stubby, a King Charles Cavalier spaniel, and decided he wanted one like it. Dad gave him the address of the breeder. Linda and her friend Johnny Vance, a legendary surfer here, took Miki to see the pups.

LINDA CUY: Miki was nuts for King Charles spaniels. We'd had two females in New Zealand and had to leave them with a very nice woman in Australia because we couldn't quarantine them everywhere we traveled. Miki wanted to get them back, but he never did. We got so far afield that it became the Impossible Task.

In Northern Ireland he pestered everybody: "I've got to find these dogs. They're the perfect dog." He liked their shape and size. They weren't big sloppy and drooly dogs. Nice disposition.

Finally, we found some puppies just outside of Belfast. One, a little tricolor mix, was Scooter Boy. He was from County Antrim.

Scooter Boy lived in Miki's van as a puppy. He built a ramp for the dog so he could go in and out of the open door and do his business. Miki always pictured Scooter Boy on a little satin pillow, eating chocolates. Miki always pictured himself on a satin pillow, eating chocolates, too. Everything became geared around Scooter Boy; he was Miki's little partner—or child. In fact, in letters Miki referred to Scooter Boy as "our son."

BOB SIMPSON: Miki would travel everywhere with Scooter Boy. He could get him on the planes, with him in his seat, not in the hold with other animals. He'd do all sorts of tricks like wear dark glasses and say he was functionally blind, and Scooter Boy was his guide dog. The flight attendants always took pity. Once, on a trip, he saw a surfer who knew him. He whispered, "Act like you don't know me." Miki said that when the plane landed, the flight attendant felt so bad for him that she drove him all the way to his house.

PHIL GRACE: Eventually he had a letter from a mate in Geneva, an optometrist, saying, "Mr. Dora is partially blind, he can only see so far in front of him, please take all care"—and he'd get Scooter Boy on free as a Seeing Eye dog.

Not only was Scooter Boy an ersatz Seeing Eye dog, apparently he was also an accomplished wordsmith. After Miki had a fiery four-day romance in Biarritz with Kris Kruseski, a friend of Susan McNeill's, Kris returned to Southern California and corresponded with Miki, waiting for him to arrive in the States and—as he'd promised—to sweep her off her feet. They exchanged many letters, including a postcard on which Miki had placed four tiny diamonds under some green tape. Although Miki's letters were emotionally revealing, sometimes torturously so, a note Kruseski got from Scooter Boy was easy enough to read between the lines.

Dear Kris,

I would like to introduce myself. My name is Scooter Boy! My master always talks of you and shows me your pictures. You are very nice looking and have a very kind face. I think I'm in love with you. How can I get rid of Miki??? He wants to take me to America, so I need him to pick up all the bills.

I probably have a higher IQ than my master—but he doesn't know that. He spends all day chauffeuring me around, feeding me, and generally entertaining me. And you know, Kris, I do absolutely nothing for him. You tell me: who do you think is the bigger fool, him or me? You'll never catch me washing dishes, putting petrol in the van, cooking my own meals. I might as well let these suckers do it all for us. Just act stupid all day and you won't have to do anything except sleep and eat.

You should see him play golf. (Hopeless.) He's got a new club. It's shaped like a boomerang. When he throws his club it's the only one that returns. He's got this one club he calls OO in his bag. It looks like a shotgun. He swears that the next time I laugh at him he's going to blow my yapping head off. Ha ha. Must go now. It's time to get fed again. See you soon. Love, Scooter Boy

ALLAN CARTER: Miki had never assumed responsibility for anything, but when he got Scooter Boy, the dog profoundly changed Miki's whole outlook on life.

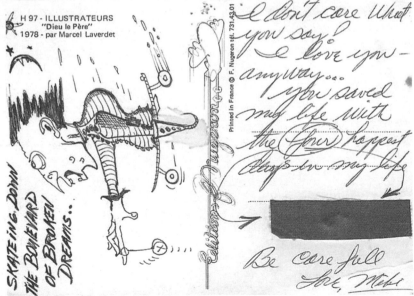

ABOVE TOP: Scooter Boy at the table enjoying a petit dejeuner. "Attend upon his squire," Miki wrote on the back. "I'm just a yah-suh, yah-suh everlasting deathless bondslave. Groom me, feed me, chauffeur me to the beach . . . "
Photo: Miki. Courtesy Dora Estate.

ABOVE: Postcard from Miki to Kris Kruseski. Four tiny diamonds were hidden under the tape. Courtesy K. Kruseski and Dora Estate.

CHAPTER THIRTEEN

Deep Cover

1

Anyhow, free again, I wasn't about to sit around waiting amid all the trappings of modern urban materialism and let TV rigor mortis infest my mind. I stand or fall, live or die, by my own decisions . . . What better place to end one's life than in Primordial Africa?

By adopting my particular type of self-imposed exile I can outdistance these scourgers of mankind: those who believe in consciousness without existence and those who believe in existence without consciousness—these caricatures who go to ludicrous lengths to assert their own importance, their own grotesque, overblown ambition.

The preconceived, hypocritical values of these scourges are their calling cards to the temples of mediocrity and cultural impoverishment. These schizos are forever in motion, spinning out of control, unable to slow down for fear someone might get a glimpse of their hollowness, their vulnerability and lack of moral courage. . . .

Africa represents a last chance for the Human Spirit; one of its few remaining opportunities to return to the place from whence it came.

—Miki, "Million Days to Darkness," *Surfer, July 1989*

In the spring of 1986, Miki parked his green Mercedes van next to the Quiksilver office/factory in St.-Jean-de-Luz, gave Harry Hodge the keys, and left for South Africa. Miki had asked Linda to come.

He'd asked Kris Kruseski. He'd asked C.C., a girlfriend from Orange County whom he'd met in 1985 during a trip back to Southern California. They all declined. Bad idea? Bad timing? "Miki sought sanctuary," C.C. explained. In the end, no longer on the run from the law, and free to again discover himself in the world, Miki arrived in South Africa with his board, a few suitcases full of stuff, his trusty companion Scooter Boy, and his eternal hope for a safe and idyllic life.

STEVE PEZMAN: Miki had spent so much of his life looking for uncrowded surf that he was starting to seem like an old vaudeville act on the road: France. Spain. Morocco. Fiji. New Zealand. Australia. France again. Ireland. But it was always temporary. Wherever he'd go, the place became overrun—not because he was there, but because he was there *early*—and it ended up being like the end of a marriage: You were alone again and you had to go out and seek another new reality. Miki went through a series of those transitions, finding a place that for a moment seemed like it could be the place that would be home. It would solve his needs for a while and then slowly begin to disqualify itself according to his values. Eventually, he ended up in Jeffreys Bay, South Africa, which was symbolically another Malibu circa 1947.

DEREK HYND: Africa of the '80s and '90s was far closer to America of the '30s than the America of today. You wake up in the morning in that Steinbeck-like era and you wonder what you're going to do to make it work today, to make it productive. I think Dora found that spirit wonderful. He loved the challenge of the frontier day.   •

MIKE TABELING: In the early days, the area had sheep farms right down to the beach and a population of two white people to every black person, which is the opposite of the rest of the country, which is five blacks to one white. The reason is because there were no townships close by—and the area just so happens to have the best waves ever discovered: Jeffreys Bay and Cape St. Francis.

SCOTT HULET: He raved endlessly about that wave. He wrote letters to everyone saying, "You've got to come here and ride this wave."

Located where the Benguela and the Mozambique currents meet, just a few miles east along the coast from Cape St. Francis, and an hour's drive west of Port Elizabeth, Jeffreys Bay is on the Baio de San Francisco, or, in the local Xhosa language "Ndawu Yama Phupo"—

which means "Place of Dreams." The name is apt: Jeffreys Bay boasts a collection of in-your-wildest-dreams breaks, from Albatross at the east end, through the Point, Tubes, Salad Bowls, Supertubes, Boneyards, Magnatubes, and Kitchen Window. These waves were, by any modern measure, still largely empty when Dora arrived in May 1986.

Though not nearly as barren as when Miki had visited in 1971, the community was still sparse and undeveloped, with homes set back in the low hills on the other side of the main road that itself spurred off the highway and ran through the town and countryside. The bluffs were mostly open and green, the beaches blanketed with shells and, at low tide, rocky bottoms cut with perfect paddle-out channels. And when he gazed into the star-saturated night sky, the Southern Cross hovered high, and the constellations familiar to Northern Hemisphere dwellers were all upside down.

Dora, himself the spawn of mingling currents, had seen the clean beaches and unsullied waves of the southern tip of southernmost Africa and never forgotten them. Bruce Brown and the *Endless Summer* crew had preceded him in 1963, of course, and had been astounded by the perfectly peeling rights off Cape St. Francis. But during the intervening years only the most adventurous travelers made the journey to this still remote region of the globe. Call it cost, distance, political turmoil and, of course, apartheid—the long-existing segregation policies written into law in 1948 by the National Party government.

DEREK HYND: There is a wild smell in Jeffreys Bay, from the west wind rushing through, and it blows that sense of something's coming: another storm, and with the storm, the swell. Sometimes you'd know three or four days in advance and get set. You could almost hear the drums as the surf just lifted. All of a sudden it didn't matter how many houses were stuck on the beach, it was just a surfer on the windswept sand with his board, standing on the rocks, trying to get set for a go-out, hoping he wouldn't get smashed.

MIKEY MEYER: The wave at Jeffreys Bay is very fast. With a short board, you can get in when the lip throws, you can go underneath it, and you can change direction. If you're young and fit, you can ride with quick, jerky little movements. With a longboard, you're looking into the future of the wave. You've got to read the wave yet to come to make it through the sections at the right time. For a longboarder it's all happening twenty or thirty yards down the line. You can't just whip it around and get acceleration. You've got to keep that constant speed, so that when you do run into a section that you need to make, you can. It's very difficult, but even at his age, Miki could do it.

Out of the water, Miki found the pace slow, the land wide open, the few cars driving on the left-hand side of the road, and the locals unin-terested, unaware, and unencumbered by his past. For the first time, Miki Dora was virtually alone, with the perfect wave, in the remote location he said he'd dreamed of: no crowds, no law, no friends, no fuss, no fans, no fame.

In Jeffreys Bay, Miki had a choice. Far removed from the assaultive society and values he said he abhorred, he was able, if he desired, to be more open, more giving for its own sake to people who wanted noth-ing from him. He could be kind, shaking off the fear that kindness left him unacceptably vulnerable. He could let go of the insecurity and the fading cover story of narcissistic recklessness. He could transform his lifelong instinct that offense is the best defense into a less cynical and more pastoral existence.

That was the hope, anyway—and he made some progress. All he had to do was follow the advice that Mariel Hemingway gave Woody Allen at the end of *Manhattan*: "Have a little faith in people."

DEREK HYND: Miki came to Jeffreys Bay in his midfifties. I think his ability to feel and conquer the sway of nature at such an old age is akin to someone like Edmund Hillary or Jacques Cousteau. The most interesting thing in this act of Dora's life is that without even knowing who Dora was, the people in the surf-ing community had always expected someone like him to one day rock into Jeffreys Bay, and they knew that once this person found the place, he would find a new gear entirely.

Mick had a great respect for the waves of Jeffreys Bay. He felt them as his end. He would not casually paddle out. He'd stand first up at Cheron Kraak's house and then he'd stand down on the rocks, just waiting and watching, sometimes for hours. If he didn't jump in, something inside would switch off and he'd wait until the next swell, then he'd disappear from view and hang out in his one-bedroom cave. People mistook him walking away some days for dogging it, backing out. But I'm pretty sure that he could feel that it wasn't his time and that he would be a fool to challenge Mother Nature and get creamed. Besides, on many days he'd be out in far bigger conditions than the days he walked away from. It comes back to what I figured out about the lore of the tramp or the hobo who rides the rail: A lot of hobo royals did not catch every train they looked at. They had a sixth sense that pulled them back. They'd wait for the right train at the right time, another time.

It was as if every day of his life Miki woke up wherever he was and trod the same steps. It didn't matter if he was in France, California, New Zealand, Australia, South Africa, anywhere. . . . Much like Peter Sellers's character, Chauncy Gardner, he just loved being there.

Yet he was perhaps not such a quixotic figure as a lot of people paint him. I'm pretty sure Mick wandered through his head in Jeffreys Bay as much as he physically wandered the world. Who knows what he actually thought when he waited on those rocks? He might have just been in a bit of a trance, in reflection. It could also have been quite vicious; he might have been seeing "kooks," as he liked to just say, riding waves the way they should not be, and things like that triggering massive flashbacks to '58, '59, '60, as the crowds arrived at Malibu and elsewhere without a clue. What's to say that he didn't have some sort of post-traumatic syndrome that lasted forty, fifty, sixty years. Perhaps with every new arrival at a new location, he just flashed back to the unworkability of the surfing experience if people weren't wholly with the wave, wherever that wave was.

2

6.10.86 [Letter to Ramona from Jeffreys Bay]

Just now have got settled in after a very long and exhausting trip. Now I'm in the little town of Jeffreys Bay, a wonderful beach with good waves, golf club, tennis, and everything I need for a happy life. I'm living in a home facing the Indian Ocean; two bedrooms with everything for $50 a month and the world's greatest views. Hard to believe. Everyone is friendly to me. The Blacks are all nice people. All the trouble is hundreds of miles away from me in the townships of Black workers. I see and hear nothing. Will keep you posted as things develop. Thanks again for helping me in my time of need. I still don't know how that happened to me.

BRUCE GOLD: After finding a place to live, Miki went first to the surfboard factory. If I was a board maker and Miki came to town, geez! I'd just *give* him several boards. But no one gave him anything. Africans are hard: They made him pay for everything, including places to stay. I saw Miki through the window at the factory and ducked off. We hadn't met and I was avoiding him, the charisma to confront him being suddenly unavailable. Later that day he accosted me on the corner of Vasco Da Gama Road and St. Francis Road. I was minding everyone's business as usual when he strolled up with a too-cute long-eared, runty spaniel. I was a bit in awe, but he was perfectly friendly and charming. Now this is in the days before "Ahoy" so we shake hands. He said, "Hey, how are you? I'm Miki." He said he'd heard a bit about me. I said, "Well, maybe you *are* Miki Dora." Teased him a bit. He didn't mind. We became friends.

MIKE TABELING: Miki and Bruce were an odd couple. I've known Bruce a long time. He's strange and cool and really stands out. He's never worked. He used to pick up oysters on the beach and sell them for a quarter apiece, but otherwise, where did he get his money? How did he live? He had to pay rent and buy food, but he never, ever had a job. Like Miki.

BRUCE GOLD: I did work. I was a policeman for three years. In South Africa it's compulsory service. We had to go to the army or the police force. I should have just ducked to Hawaii or something, but what did we know? We were all pretty brainwashed. I was a flag worshipper until I was twenty-one. Then my baby sister came home one day with a hollowed-out whale's tooth filled with marijuana. Doors of perception were opened! Can you Adam-and-Eve it? Yes. Then I drove taxis in Durban for a couple years, night beat, surfing in the day. Bought a couple new surfboards and came to Jeffreys Bay in the winter. Every time I came to Jeffreys Bay I'd stay a bit longer.

GARY YOSH: Bruce has got a good heart. Most people only do things for money; anything for a dollar. Bruce helps people for free. The only people Miki wouldn't take advantage of, even in the mildest way, were Bruce, because Bruce used to massage him, and Tony "Doc" Van Den Huevel, a great surfer who literally lived on the beach—and died there as well. He told me they were the only people he'd ever *give* money to. They were genuine comrades.

BRUCE GOLD: At first, Miki had to be a bit wary in the water. Some of the young Afrikaans guys, they're not that friendly. They all went to the same school and had their own little private surf club. They're quite protective of this place and there's always been the odd barb in the water at Supertubes. Sometimes there's been quite a bit of violence, too. These guys all used to wear white vests. They were called Jeffreys Bay Underground. But they mellowed out. They take their vests off now.

They eventually got to know Miki, but they still weren't going to give much respect to someone they'd never really heard of. He wasn't king here. I heard a rumor that one guy punched Miki over Scooter Boy doing something to his dog. They also didn't appreciate that Miki would sit out the back and take all the good waves. I lost my temper at these guys—who could have easily put me in my place—when I stood up for Miki and told them not to pick on him: "You have no idea who that is." It helped that he befriended Cheron Kraak. She even employed some of these territorial kids at Billabong.

Cheron Kraak had turned hand-sewing a pair of board shorts into her own highly successful Jeffreys Bay apparel brand and shop, Country Feeling. In 1984, Gordon Merchant, cofounder of Australian surfwear giant Billabong, awarded Kraak that company's license for South Africa, and she turned that piece of paper into an empire. Today, Kraak is regarded as the unofficial mayoress of Jeffreys Bay. Although she recently left Billabong to return to her own Country Feeling retail empire, she still employs many in Jeffreys Bay. Kraak also started the Jeffreys Bay surfing tournament in the early 1980s, which has since grown into the most prestigious and longest-running event on the South African coastline, helping to turn Jeffreys Bay from a small fishing village into a booming surf center.

CHERON KRAAK: I'd heard Miki was an old surfer from America who ran away with contest money once, but that's all. Then I went to a conference and said something to a friend about "that American guy, Miki Dora." He went: "Miki Dora!"

At first, he was simply a tennis partner. He's a really good tennis player, very calculated. Absolutely hates losing. He hugged the baseline. I'm a net player, so we used to have the most amazing rallies. We used to play every Sunday for two, two and a half hours until we were dripping sweat. Then we started chatting, and he'd come around and have a cup of coffee. I found him hilarious. My friendship with Miki grew from our tennis relationship. It's not like I needed to meet someone famous. Besides, Miki always gave the impression he didn't want a legacy or to be remembered. He didn't want anyone writing about him. He didn't let anyone take photos of him. How dare they invade his privacy? And yet, I discovered later, he sometimes needed to be famous.

Every morning he used to walk along the beach with Scooter Boy as I went to work. Sometimes even if I wasn't around, he'd come into the kitchen, pour himself coffee, read the newspaper, take the rusks out, feed Scooter Boy, feed himself, feed Scooter Boy, feed himself—check please! He loved smoothies and anything healthy that the girls who worked for me made. He was always very effusive, "Thank you very much, that was very nice."

I always gave him a Christmas present, and one on his birthday. We never had a Christmas lunch without Miki. We don't have the traditional roast meat thing, because it's usually boiling hot here in December. We have a big seafood dinner and whatever we can find that's exotic enough. The first year that Miki wasn't here, we all looked at the bowl of crayfish and went, "My God, why are there so many crayfish left?" Simple: Miki wasn't there!

3

9.19.86 [Letter to Linda Cuy]

Time is running out and Africa is a good place to die. A mixture of California in the '50s and Ireland. Come spend some time. With waves like this all year around I won't have to put up with the French Frogs and the U.S.A. Young Republicans in love with themselves. They're rich. They're happy. They're white. They're over the world. They have no shame. They take no blame. They worship fame. And they're smug about it. There are many reasons why you can't go home again. One of the reasons is yourself. You are part of all that you have met; and because you have learned that never, never, never can you go home again to that land of fools—Los Angeles. For myself, I shall never return until after the nuclear holocaust has destroyed the pestilence that over-ran my kingdom. I am the one and only rightful king of Malibu, and you are my queen. Until that day I must take second best and live in banishment and exile in this land of lovely beauty.

Love, his majestic, magnificent M.

PS: Don't listen to a word he's saying. My master's been smoking the loco weed; besides he's a terminal nutcase. He thinks he's Bob Geldof. To be continued . . . Signed: Scooter Boy Mandela

With his whereabouts generally unknown and mostly inaccessible, Miki led a quiet, often happy life, hanging out with locals and legends like Tony "Doc" Van Den Heuvel, who, according to *Surfer*, "was the youngest member of the adventurous crew who discovered Jeffreys Bay six months after the *Endless Summer* crew unknowingly passed it

on their way to Durban" in 1963. "Doc" lived outdoors in a homemade scrub shelter at Supertubes and died there of an apparent heart
attack when he was sixty.

A year after arriving in Jeffreys Bay, Miki received an audiotape
from Tubesteak, who, acting as master of ceremonies, had recorded
a score of hellos and remember-mes, and we've-not-forgotten-yous,
from a diverse group of well-wishers, including David Nuuhiwa, Sean
Tompson, Skip Frye, Herbie Fletcher, Paul and MJ Luten, and more.
"Well, Meatball and Scooter Boy," Tubesteak said in closing, "that was
quite an emotional few minutes; there wasn't a dry eye in the van."

The surf press still wondered about Miki as well and made occasional
interview requests, always turned down, or agreed to for a price—an
airline ticket, a favor—but never carried through. And if a surf journalist showed up for any reason, Miki was, as always, on guard and
critical.

In 1986, after Sam George paddled in from a surf session at Jeffreys
Bay, "an older guy sitting in the dunes with Bruce Gold, wearing a hat
and dark glasses, said 'I really like your style.'"

Later, at a party, George met Miki—and realized he was the older
guy in the dunes. But when Miki found out George worked for *Surfing*,
a debate ensued.

SAM GEORGE: Miki said, "So, you work for the magazines. The great commercial conglomerate."

"I'm a surfer," I said. "I just have to figure out a way to keep surfing."
He said, "You seem like such an intelligent young man. I don't understand
how you can put up with the incredible hypocrisy of living in California and in
America the way it is today." He went off on how I condoned everything by living there. "Why don't you stand up and make a difference or move away?" He
kept ranting in that quiet, insistent monotone voice. It bugged me a little. "I
don't know how you can endure the political situation there," he added. "The
enlightened wanderer would have to leave, or die trying to change it."

Finally he said, "I don't understand why you're willing to suffer the sins
of your fathers."

"Well, that's funny coming from you, Miki," I said. "I've suffered your sins
my whole life. My whole life."

He stopped. "I don't know what you're talking about."

"Who taught you to kick your board at another surfer? You invented localism.

ABOVE TOP: Miki, Bruce Gold, Clive Barber, and Edward Godfrey at the Breakers restaurant in Jeffreys Bay. Photo: Juliette Godfrey, family friend.

ABOVE: Christmas in Jeffreys Bay. Miki and Christine Liepner, best of friends. Photo: Jessica Naude.

You ruined surfing for the next generation. You did it. So don't talk to me about suffering the sins of my father. I've grown up suffering from your sin, Miki."

I don't know what got into me. He stood there for a second with everyone looking and then he said, "I'm sorry, but this is starting to sound like a magazine interview. Thank you very much." And he walked off. I thought, Oh my God, I've just insulted Miki Dora. What have I done?! But people came up and said, "That was great! Finally, someone who talked back to him!" I said, "I didn't mean to! That's the first time I even met him." I felt so bad.

The next day, while waiting to paddle out, Miki walked up and said, "It's looking pretty good out there." I said, "Yeah, looks good." He said, "Well, let's go." Off we went. Never said another word about the night before.

4

7.25.86 [Letter to Gardner Jr.]

Happy birthday and greetings from deepest darkest Africa, the last outpost. Try looking up a Mau Mau's mau mau. Flat on your back with a 100 power field glasses. Pee-U. Things are very cheap here, including human life. They're not like the blacks in the US who just kick your ass and take your wallet. These MF's are flesh-eaters. Give these guys the rights and you'll get white-man jerky for export. This continent is going up in smoke. It just might be one of the bloody and gruesome insurrections to hit Africa in the history of this planet. Nonetheless, I'm calm and at peace with this bloodthirsty world. Momentarily.

Just down the road a piece in Port Elizabeth, the blacks are roasting blacks. Just like a huge weenie roast on the 4th. The red-hot necklace parties are going on every day. The victim is forced to drink gasoline and then a used tire is forced over the poor screaming and flailing wretch, dowsed with petrol, and set a light. It doesn't matter who you are or what age male or female, your incineration papers are certain. A terrible way to die. Down here, the Goodyear "torture test" doesn't mean road wear. Yet in the back of my mind I know it's only a matter of time. What I must always go through to try and enjoy some waves alone. Such a wonderful and beautiful geographical region. There's no tourists. Every one has been frightened off by the terrorist warfare.

NAT YOUNG: Miki got very upset about the whole Afrikaans thing. Sometimes he also sounded like a fucking full-on bigot. I don't know where he got it from.

People say Gard Chapin. I suppose it's more accurate to say that he was an equal-opportunity insulter. Sometimes he could be pretty outrageous.

DALE VELZY: He came to see me once, on a trip to California, and he asked me if I had ever been to South Africa, and I said yeah, during the war. He said, "Where I live, you should see what I have. I have a black man who wakes me up in the morning, gives me my orange juice, gives me my robe, carries my board to the beach. Everybody ought to live in Africa. I have a coolie for everything for I do. Everyone should own a coolie." And of course it was bullshit.

JESSICA NAUDE: Miki wasn't for apartheid, he just wasn't for what he thought would happen to the country with the ANC coming in. He didn't believe that they could actually run things.

Whatever final shape Miki's amalgam of political and social theories finally took, he explored a variety of philosophies. For example, he subscribed to a newsletter from Americans for Sane Policies,[5] but as *Mrs.* M. Dora. "He didn't want to be traced," says Bruce Gold. Miki would ask Jessica Naude and her sister, Christine Liepner, to read them, and then they'd discuss the various points of view. "We'd talk about the issue on the drives to Port Elizabeth, or if he came to the restaurant for lunch," says Christine.

DEREK HYND: Miki liked to walk with the black women along the beach in the early morning. They'd look for shells to sell. He'd immerse himself in their world. It is simple and unaffected. Sometimes the pink flamingos would cruise along that stretch of Supertubes, just before sunup. If you were lucky enough to see them, it'd really set up the day. I'm sure Miki was very clandestine in what he did with the blacks. There were rumors of liaisons with, shall we say, girls of a color that the white authorities didn't particularly respect.

BRUCE GOLD: Miki liked certain shells. One, you could make into a big funky ring. He took a lot of these to Thailand or Vietnam and he sold them. The hole is D-shaped. He also liked a shell that looks like a lion's claw, a cat's paw. It's brown and very beautiful and you can make holes in it for a necklace.

---

[5] A virulent right-wing, America-first newsletter edited by Major Alyn Denham, a former mercenary, anti-Communist, and onetime chairman of the Committee to Impeach Bill Clinton (CIBC), out of Cullman, Alabama.

RUPERT CHADWICK: At night, in the locations,[6] you don't get mugged; but you can lose your life. The Africans would be open to you being there to drink beers, but if you flashed your gold watch around, they'd take advantage of you. Miki never had to deal with any of that shit. He'd just cruise in. It's hard to describe and appreciate his ability to do it. Miki was somehow accepted, even as a foreigner. I'm not saying he made friends or would be remembered, but somehow, almost mystically, he was allowed to wander through.

He went in his beat-up car that he couldn't even lock. Maybe you'd think, nah, there can't be anything there. But the local population don't think like that. Doesn't matter how your car looks; they'll break in just to see if they're wrong.

I saw him plenty of times with people from the township in the car, driving without any hassle when it really hadn't been done yet. Here, when white people drive, the African guy sits in the back. You could be forgiven for thinking you'd never seen so many blacks with chauffeurs. Miki could drive around in full public view, down the main street, with two or three black people in the car. Miki could rub shoulders with the town fathers, two hours later be down in a squatter camp, and two hours later play tennis with the owner of Billabong.

DEREK HYND: What Miki did was not without severe risk. Cheron's maids and nannies, whom Miki knew very well, would have given Dora an easier entry by dint of their own respected position amongst township society. But a wild card, and dangerous despite any cachet Miki had, were the teenage kids who returned from weeks alone in the bush after their tribal circumcision rituals. They were never the same after that. Dora's younger years in California were not unlike the normal Xhosa kid—literally including the circumcision, and metaphorically the weeks in the beach wilderness to see if he could hack it and survive. That thread and commonality bred respect from Dora toward the Xhosa tribe, and perhaps, if they could sense it, given what he'd been through, from them to him.

---

[6]Townships for nonwhites were also called locations or lokasie (Afrikaans translation) and are often still referred to by that name in smaller towns. The term "kasie," a popular short version of "lokasie," is also used sometimes to refer to townships.

5

EXPLOIT
Pronunciation: ik-'sploit, 'ek-'
Function: transitive verb
1 : to make productive use of : UTILIZE <exploiting your talents>
<exploit your opponent's weakness>
2 : to make use of meanly or unjustly for one's own advantage
<exploiting migrant farm workers>
—Merriam Webster Online

If *exploited* was not one of Miki's favorite words, he certainly used it often enough in conversation and letters to make one think so, and, as in his earlier days, it dominated the tone of his wary relationship with all forms of media. Only this time, with surf culture having undergone many revolutions since his reign at Malibu, Miki in Africa was more a ghost in the machine than someone actually on the scene. This was not a negative to Miki. He cared most about the waves and little about the circus that surrounded them. As he had recently written to his mother, "Somewhere there's good waves breaking on distant deserted beaches which have gone unridden since the beginning of time."

Yet Miki had hardly been forgotten, and his celebrated surfing style and outsized personality—however much an artifact of an earlier generation—became all the more attractive to the media because it was a unique story of a rogue life that had somehow endured, that still generated whispers down the waves. So every once in a while, a filmmaker or a surf magazine got the idea that they should look into Miki. Some wished to focus on his crimes and punishment, others on the mythic—and all wanted to understand him.

Miki just wanted to be left alone, except, of course, when he saw some advantage to playing along.

Miki's mantra required that only Miki be allowed to exploit Miki, and that wasn't really exploitation, but Miki legitimately controlling his public image, access, use of his name and likeness, the terms under which his story could be told, and the price for which it would be sold. Miki exploiting Miki was framed as Miki getting his due, his just reward for . . . well, for being Miki and all that implied.

Yet Miki was also a public figure, a situation he refused to accept—he claimed the media had come after him, not the other way around—that eventually had to be decided in court. But had the media forced him to enter surf contests, attend legends events, sit for interviews, or write magazine articles, not to mention do whatever had landed him in jail, embarrassed him, and become part of the public record?

Like other larger-than-life figures, willing or unwilling, Miki didn't want to pay the personal tax of simpering cretins being inconveniently interested in the character he'd created (that bored him), or the real Miki (why should he have to explain himself to anyone?). Which is not to say he kept everyone at arm's length. Although he enjoyed the pursuit and the game, in a deeper part of himself, he relished an authentic meeting of the minds, and someone who could get him right.

Whenever confronted with a potential article that he'd declined to cooperate with—and often even when he had cooperated—Miki would fire off an angry letter and famously quote Ayn Rand's *The Fountainhead*. "I do not recognize anyone's right to pilfer one minute of my life, nor to any achievement of mine, no matter who makes the claim, how large their number, or how great their need." He did not credit Rand.

To guard his reputation, Miki's need included threatening lawsuits to prevent being written about, pictured, or somehow "used" in a manner he disagreed with. He based his estimated monetary compensation not on any quantifiable real damage, but on "having been there at the beginning." He felt he was owed not what one might reasonably expect from an individual or company, based on the severity of the slight, but rather a percentage of the multibillion-dollar surf industry overall gross. The money symbolized a payoff for having had to leave Malibu, for being "chased" around the world, for being incarcerated, for having fewer empty waves to ride. The money was long-overdue salve for mental and spiritual wounds that wouldn't heal, afflictions that, however much rooted in the detritus of an unstable childhood and the beaches full of kooks—and there was always an element of truth to his remonstrations—were also based on a sense of entitlement and perceived opportunity.

The society was screwed up; he'd had to reject it. It wasn't his fault. He'd suffered. We owed him. "He created this entitled victim position," says Ken Price, a well-known Los Angeles artist who surfed with Miki in the '50s. "I think he was comfortable as the underdog. I couldn't figure that out."

Miki also felt that no one, least of all the press and the "idiots" who ran it, would ever truly understand him. After all, his experience in the world was virtually unique. So how could they accurately tell his story? Especially since he wouldn't share it. In other words, if we had some ham, we could have some ham and eggs, if we had some eggs.

KIM FOWLEY: Miki didn't learn how to take the surfing torch and run through the future with it. He sat on the beach and based everything on a culture of a post–James Dean rebellion, pre-Beatles alternate lifestyle. He didn't take the audacity of the party crasher and learn how to package that rebellion into something that somebody would pay for.

James T. Farrell writes about it in his Danny O'Neil trilogy, which, to me, were really significant Irish-Catholic 1930s books. There were all these great guys in the eighth grade and ninth grade at the Catholic school, who fucked the girls with big tits on the fire escape. Then they could go into the street and be gods. Later in the book they become their uncles and their dads who died young as butchers or plumbers; but for that brief moment they're heroic and geniuses and could lead armies just by walking to the store and stealing a tomato.

Probably Johnny Fain and Miki Dora had great moments in a small window of time, and when that window of time passed, they didn't break the pattern and reinvent. They stayed there, and that's the tragedy. In life there's hardly anyone who's both charismatic and good at something. When there is, even for a brief moment, they're one of the privileged. Like Miki. I had no idea what happened to him. All I ever heard was, "Oh, bad boy. Buccaneer Bandito stuff." I said, "Oh, good. Well, tragedy poster boy." When you're given gifts of male beauty or athletic prowess, then the world is your wastebasket. Even if you make mistakes, you look good doing it. It's like waiting to see Johnny Thunder die onstage. People would go to see these guys fall apart. The rapid ascent is a turn-on, and the descent is equally fascinating.

Miki didn't so much reinvent as relocate. Yet here we are, all these years later, still talking about him.

STEVE PEZMAN: Guys like Mike Doyle and Joey Cabell in particular, and Mickey Muñoz to a lesser extent, bent life to their purpose, versus being bent to life's purpose. They've lived in optimum locations, doing more or less what they wanted, occasionally working at things that are unpleasant and distasteful, like selling condos as Doyle did. Cabell built a restaurant business, backed away when it got big, corporate, and ugly, and then took his slice of the

Charthouse to Hawaii and played it up, becoming Mr. Lucky, sitting at the end of the bar with the coffee and the chick. Doyle worshipped the buck, but never quite got it until he discovered how much people were willing to pay for his paintings. Now, he lives in Mexico where the dollar goes a long way. They all acquired wealth and a kind of stability and operated within the confines of society to the point where they didn't become fugitives. It was a more comfortable and established version of the surf nomad.

Dora worshipped the buck, but he was willing to give up less of himself to get it.

Even if Miki wanted to follow Fowley's advice, he still had a problem: He had hamstrung himself in a paradox of his own devise. Miki had to hold back the goods or risk destroying the mythos that was his most marketable commodity. It wasn't his critics who would attack him, but his staunch adherents, if, after discovering a chink in the façade, they became disaffected and spread the word that he'd sold out. Miki could usually spin his way out of any situation and justify his behavior. Plus, no one could ever take away the surfing skill, or having lived at the crossroads of surfing history upon which his bona fides were built. But for the rebel to enthusiastically endorse a project—even genuinely felt, and no matter how cannily rationalized for himself and his fans—might eventually betray, disprove, and devalue the commodity.

Miki understood the relationship between scarcity and desire. He'd occasionally tiptoed across the line: beach movies, articles, Da Cat boards. But the next step might always be the step too far, the ultimate giveaway. Miki realized that his treasured calling card depended not only on his past exploits in and out of the water, but on his unavailability.

He was like Moses, given a view of the Promised Land that he could nonetheless never enter. Not that he wanted to, of course.

That left the "hated" exploiters to get the story out. All he had to do was wait. Miki was correct when he insisted that various media and profiteers wanted to hunt, capture, and mount his acquiescence to analysis and caricature on their office walls. This included not only those who saw his life as a cheap crime caper, but those who genuinely admired his artistry and wanted only to laud him.

"At my house he'd always check to see if there were any new surfing magazines," Cheron Kraak recalls. "If he found an article on himself, or a picture, or whatever, he'd say, 'Tell Cheron I'm borrowing it,' then he'd make a photocopy—usually at my office—and bring the magazine back to the house. He had to save a buck. Then he'd take the photocopy back to my office and fax a copy to his lawyers. I don't know how many times he sued people, but he seemed to do that all the time."

"His favorite thing was to sue," Cristal Yosh recalls, with a wry laugh. "Once he offered to sue my parents for me. He said, 'Believe me, I can make it a court case.' He told me all the things that you can sue for."

In Jeffreys Bay, Miki's legend took a new twist: In his absence from the U.S., he'd morphed into an even bigger icon, a symbol of surfing's original rebellion that fit nicely into apparel and equipment companies' marketing plans. The exploitation might now include his name or likeness on a product—without his approval. But he'd cut himself off from the world so why should he mind?

The offenders didn't realize that Miki watched—always. And he went batshit. How dare they. He hadn't reinvented himself or his core philosophy, he hadn't changed, only moved to get away from the exploiters.

And still the bastards pursued him. He'd make them pay.

In 1986, Miki wrote to his lawyers Cooney & Fineman, in Los Angeles, to complain that a picture of him surfing at Jeffreys Bay had appeared in *Surfer* magazine. As evidence of major damage to his reputation (and, potentially, his pocketbook), he noted *Surfer*'s "projected readership of over one million." He characterized publisher Steve Pezman as "always eager for a fast buck, presumably in the interests of freedom of the press." He claimed that *Surfer* magazine "has been trying to acquire an interview from me for fifteen years. I've told them numerous times that I was not interested. (So) they get great pleasure in putting me in a bad light because I will not cooperate with their stinking magazine. Recently, they put my photograph in a contest to help promote subscriptions. Adding insult to injury they placed (alongside) a phony letter to the editor to make me look even more ridiculous. What can be done? Nothing."

There were many other instances, from suing Gotcha Sportswear for using a silhouette of what looked like his image on a T-shirt (he asked for $7,500 and took $3,000), to threatening *Surf Session*, a French surfing magazine, for running an interview with him that "has exposed my private life," when he thought the story was a photo spread only. "I don't know how Miki got this magazine in South Africa," says editor

Gibus de Soultrait. "I don't know if it was translated badly or what, but as soon as he got it, I received a fax at the office. The guy was really angry and upset."

Bob Simpson thought the article flattering and that Miki should back off. Miki's response: "This cheap outfit would not even send me a copy of the magazine. That says it all. I guess I'm just public property. Dead meat for the New World Order. I thought the French had a little more class than the United Snakes of America. Wrong again! It's my fault. I should have smelled a rat. . . . But you're absolutely right: It's not worth getting frustrated about."

Of all the lawsuits, two were the most intense.

In 1994, Miki found a Billabong catalog featuring a "Dora" board short. The company explained that the name was only used internally, for reference. They even apologized. Miki wrote to Bob Simpson: "Besides the dolphins, I'm probably the only one left that hasn't sold out my soul to the commercial piranha. I lived a frugal lifestyle with old-fashioned principles which went out to the Dumpster years ago. . . . I still have an underground following around the world. My integrity comes into question when I'm seen in catalogs with insipid boy models and my name is used to endorse products. (I'm entitled to punitive damages.) It makes me look like a complete idiot. If I went into a Billabong surf shop in Jeffreys Bay and stole a pair of Dora board shorts I'd get a month in jail and fined. Yet this company can rip off my name with impunity and privilege? It's a hell of a thing."

"When he wanted to sue Billabong, the company asked, 'Hey, isn't he your mate?'" says Cheron Kraak. "I think he'd seen the catalogue at my house, then contacted Australia. We definitely made the shorts and sold them, but his name wasn't on the shorts. It was just for the catalog so each garment can be identified. His problem didn't strain my relationship with Miki or with the company. They were all surfers; they understood Miki and what he was about."

Miki, however, could not let it go. He not only felt ripped off but he smelled big money. During a five-year period, he contacted attorneys on three continents to take the case. He called Billabong's tactics a "gross breach of what is known as intellectual property rights." He quoted Ayn Rand again and again. He attacked the "co-opting" of the "once noble" surf scene. He said these companies had "indoctrinated the imbecilic masses . . . I saw it all coming in the 1960s and have been trying to keep out of the way of the marching morons ever since. I've been ambulating throughout Africa now for over 30 years. If you don't die of disease, crocs, snake bites, cannibals, plus a few specialties on a long list of more exotic ends, consider yourself lucky in blood-soaked black Africa. I spend five months a year in Jeffreys Bay during the Winter Wave season. The Clothing Co. are even starting to make inroads here. This is my last year; it's time to move on. Webster's Dictionary defines 'FRAUD' as 'Intentional perversion of truth in order to induce another to part with something of value.'"

Miki's Australian solicitor, Andrew Cohen, was eager to handle the case, if only Miki would relocate to the country for the trial.

The most significant lawsuit involved the use of his likeness in a video called *The Legends of Malibu*. Five-time Emmy-winning producer/director Ira Opper's company, Frontline Video, secured the rights to film the first Malibu Legends event in the summer of 1986. "When we looked at the film we thought it would be very cool to make it into a documentary," Opper remembers. "Nobody had really told the Malibu story."

Opper eventually made a home video deal with Music+Plus and a TV syndication deal with the ABC network. Then, he said, "In July 1988, I got a letter from Miki Dora's lawyer. He had heard about the video and insisted we'd invaded his right to privacy."

Although Opper didn't interview Miki for the film, he did use some surfing footage and a bit of a taped conversation with Miki to which he'd secured the rights.

"I built a factual story line. End of story. When I told people what happened, they laughed. 'Dora wants money out of you, that's all. He does this to everybody!' Steve Pezman put his hand on my shoulder, looked me in the eyes, and said, 'You're a real surfer now.'"

Miki's case against Music+Plus and ABC was eventually dismissed. He rejected a modest settlement offer of $1,500 from Frontline—he wanted $15,000—and the lawsuit continued.

Miki told his lawyers that he wanted to "set a precedent," that he'd "been ripped off, not seeing a red cent out of a *$3–$4 billion industry*. It's not fair. I have to live in a Third World country. . . . The country in which I grew up as a free spirit is now ransacking my name and tearing my reputation to shreds by making films, videocassettes, clothing, books, advertisements, magazine articles, sports equipment, and all sorts of paraphernalia without my knowledge or permission. If there's any justice left in America, I must be compensated for my ability, style, skills, and individuality."

In April 1990, a judge declared Miki a public figure and dismissed the suit in a summary judgment. Miki's lawyers amended their complaint, appealed, the decision was reversed, and the case continued. Smelling vindication (and money), Miki wrote to his lawyers in November 1992, saying, "I'm astounded to know there's still some credibility in the justice treatment of the individual." In February 1993, he wrote, "How much time do you think will pass before we are able to make a settlement?" In October, his letter opened with, "What's going on? What about a settlement? What about the money?"

On October 27, 1993, lawyer Lee Fineman finally wrote to tell Miki he'd lost. He had been judged a public figure. Moreover, Miki had to pay Frontline's $25,000 attorney fees.

"The case went on to change the laws," Opper remembered, "and not in the way Miki would have liked."

Miki was outraged, and a series of desperate letters followed, containing his usual invective and accusations of payoffs and conspiracy. He invoked the Fourth Amendment and suggested suing the judge. It was left to Fineman to tell Miki that "All judges are immune from suit arising out of their judicial activities."

6

Even though Miki resented the "exploiters," he could just as easily embrace them—or at least make it look that way. From February 15 to February 19, 1989, he met in Fiji with representatives from Matte Box Films, of New Zealand. It was a get-to-know-you convocation to discuss the idea of developing a Dora-themed film called *Da Search for Da Cat*. Miki arrived via Los Angeles. His notes suggest an amiable time and that everyone agreed on Dora's need to be involved in writing the screenplay and general production. The story would be based on a yet-to-be-published article Miki had written for *Surfer*. Miki agreed to proceed once Matte Box paid him $7,500. They also agreed to a sportswear licensing deal and annual reimbursement for use of the Da Cat trademark.

The group met again a couple months later at a hotel on the Sunset Strip. Miki got a check and left immediately to cash it. "Later," said

Gerry Kantor, "he came back with a big bulge in his pants and said, 'Did I miss anything?'

"Miki cooperated to a certain extent, but as on any project he would never hand out any good information. He just scammed their money."

"There were other film projects," Rick Hodgson recalls. "Two young guys from Fox tried to get him together with Craig Stecyk to do a full Miki thing. Miki saw it as a sweeping epic, like *Lawrence of Arabia*, all his adventures, but making him look smarter than everyone else, which is what his thing was: that he got away with it. He had lots of opportunities but he never took them. Instead he milked everybody. I think he was scared that the reality would show that he was just a cheap grifter, a bunco guy. If anyone ever found out, he would lose the perceived genius of the conman image he'd cultivated."

"Miki always talked to me about *the movie deal*," says Steven Taussig, a close friend also of Hungarian extraction. "I knew it would never happen. Miki lived the lifestyle of someone with millions, and some Hollywood types would have given him a million dollars for his life story. But it wouldn't have made his lifestyle better; it would have made it worse. People would have gone, 'Hey, you have a million dollars now; *you* pay for dinner.'"

~

Despite the earlier lawsuit, in April 1989, Gotcha Sportswear sent Miki a letter asking if he'd like to get involved with a film they'd sponsored: Bill Delaney's *Surfers: The Movie*. An accompanying release agreement was quite comprehensive, and a check for $5,000 was included. Miki would eventually receive another $5,000 for expenses and $2,000 for wardrobe.

BILL DELANEY: I did a film in the '70s called *Free Ride,* with Shaun Tomson as the featured surfer. I also used some footage of Miki. He called; I explained I was a fan. He never sued.

Shaun's brother, Michael, created Gotcha Sportswear and, in the late '80s we talked about doing *Surfers: The Movie.* I said, "This needs to be not just about what's going on in surfing, but about where surfing came from. We need guys like Miki Dora in it." Michael agreed. We contacted Miki, who'd been visiting in Newport Beach, and set up a meeting.

He was pretty cool. He said, "I just want to be sure this is a pure film and not some Hollywood hack job." He wanted to be compensated, which we expected.

My father-in-law had a motor home. We parked it in front of my house above Ventura, California, so Miki and Scooter Boy could live there. He stayed three weeks, maybe a month. We went surfing at California Street and around the Overhead. Miki just liked to be in the water. Friends from the Ventura surfing community would come by and take him to play tennis and golf. He'd brought books and music. We had a barbecue.

Our plan was to fly to Cabo, coach, and rent a VW van. Miki came to LAX with Scooter Boy. He wore dark glasses and told the airline he was blind so he could keep Scooter Boy with him. They didn't believe him. It turned into a confrontation. We finally figured Miki wouldn't make it. We left Miki at the check-in. Somehow he got on the plane—with Scooter Boy.

We spent a week in Cabo and the filming was easy. At night we went to cantinas. Miki would drink beer and watch everything. When people approached, he stayed pleasant. Miki and [surfing champion Martin] Potter hung out a little bit, but Miki didn't want it to be like he and Potter were surfing *together* in Mexico. If I had to push for anything, it was to make that connection in the film.

Back in Ventura it was just him and me. He'd realized I would let him say what he wanted to say on camera. I set up the equipment in my front room. I gave him a list of topics I wanted to discuss: what was it like at Malibu in the '50s, how did he feel about the competitiveness of modern surfing—things I could play off of in the film. We had a couple beers and his stuff just started coming out.

After every take he'd say, "Is this good? Am I doing it right? Whaddaya think?" I'd say, "Sounds great to me. Talk about anything." I felt like he was digging down, trying to get his message out a little bit. Miki gave me great material to work with and it was easy to put together.

GREG NOLL: Dora and I had both done interviews for Delaney. We were in Southern California together and supposed to meet. Miki hadn't seen the film yet and asked me to bring a copy. When we watched it, he almost brought tears to my eyes. Miki hated almost everything he ever did—as far as the public is concerned; that's what he told people—but he was so immersed in this film, seeing it for the first time, that he reminded me of some of these old Hollywood stars who have their own projection rooms and will watch their old movies over and over. Like Gloria Swanson in *Sunset Boulevard*.

His bit about life and all the bullshit going over his head while he was shooting the tube is the best I've ever heard. It's an absolute classic. Anyone who's seen the film will always remember him for that. I looked over at him—he didn't smile a whole lot—and he had this shit-eating grin on his face. I could see his mouth moving as he spoke on the screen.

> *My whole life is this escape; my whole life is this wave I drop into, set the whole thing up, pull off a bottom turn, pull up into it, and shoot for my life, going for broke man. And behind me all this shit goes over my back: the screaming parents, teachers, the police [laughs], priests, politicians, kneeboarders, windsurfers—they're all going over the falls into the reef; headfirst into the motherfucking reef, and BWAH! And I'm shooting for my life. And when it starts to close out I pull out and go down the back, and catch another wave, and do the same goddamned thing again.*

CHAPTER FOURTEEN

You've Got to Ride the Wave in the Direction It's Going

1

If Miki's rant in *Surfers: The Movie* is his embryonic credo, then "Million Days to Darkness," a story he wrote for the July 1989 issue of *Surfer*, is its fully formed twin, Miki's ultimate manifesto, and belated confirmation of the rumors circulating about him. Parts biography, travelogue, adventure story, wave tale, environmental lecture, and sociological treatise, the piece is *Indiana Jones* meets Sartre meets Tom Robbins meets *Heart of Darkness*. In other words, it's all over the place, but curiously cohesive. It had been fifteen years since Miki's last *Surfer* story and this time, for all intents and purposes, between Jeffreys Bay and a trailer belonging to Linda Cuy's sister, in Bullhead City, Arizona, he wrote it himself. Full of vivid imagery and stylized language bordering on poetics, Miki reached for the most baroque metaphors and similes, that when parsed, and the words reduced to their root meanings, revealed the closest he would come to exposing his elemental self.

Miki being Miki, he wanted $10,000 for the piece at a time when the biggest fees at *Surfer* were $2,500 to $3,000. "We had to pay it because he'd endured all these hardships," recalls then-editor Paul Holmes. "It was as if the magazine owed him something. He also asked for total control over the piece. We couldn't fix anything but bits of grammar and punctuation.

"I wanted an update on his philosophies of life and what had been happening to him; and maybe a reflection on the state of surfing in the late '80s. The rumors were outrageous. I didn't ask specifically about prison, but I asked him to set the record straight.

"When the piece came in a couple months later, it was not at all what I expected. He'd written a travel adventure story about surfing in Namibia, with allusions to various international treaties and the machinations of global finance, gem smuggling, and God knows what-all. But that was cool."

According to former *Surfer* editor Drew Kampion, then working at *Windsurf* magazine, he got a call from someone at *Surfer* to edit the piece. "The story had no title and I ended up grabbing a phrase from inside the piece and calling it 'Million Days to Darkness.'"

Miki received a $1,000 advance, and after turning in the piece, he wrote to Holmes and publisher Steve Pezman saying if they liked his work they should send the balance due, $9,000, to his father, with a note saying that "this is from his son for his assistance he offered me in 1981 and all the hell I caused him from the *California* magazine article."

"I am glad to hear he felt this, but he never said it to me," says Miklos Sr. today. "To tell you the truth, if he'd apologized to me in person, I would have given him back the money. But I never got the money; I never saw a penny from Miki in my life."

After an intro that mimicked a bare-knuckles interrogation, Miki freely boasted about all the trouble it had taken to catch him:

> From 1974 to 1981 I covered well over 200,000 miles over four continents 90% of the time reconnoitering the coastal areas of India, Africa, the Far East, Indonesia, Australia, New Zealand, South America and hundreds of islands.
>
> Only in Europe did Interpol or the Feds ever get close. Only after five passports and millions of taxpayer dollars wasted on the hunt did I, with a gun pointed at my head, volunteer to return to the U.S.A. (just visiting, thanks), thus ending the most extraordinary surfing odyssey in the history of mankind.
>
> Better to be judged by 12 than carried by six.

Miki then introduced himself and tried out his concepts on a new generation of polliwogs and potential fans:

Since most of you are not yet intimate with my idiopathic mind, let me explain that I've been commissioned by SURFER *Magazine to formulate my general principles of self-aggrandizement. My hypothesis is 180° opposite to present-day logic (The Fool Plus One Theory); Quantum Wave riding being the prime factor in the equation.*

As child prodigies sometimes do, I continue to discover my aptitude, which has endured to this present moment. If you are willing to accept the assertion that surfing is a colossal waste of time, then I'll concede I've wasted my life. But in a better and more graceful manner than any of my two-legged counterparts, no matter what the cost or consequences.

As manifested in today's environment, it is extremely more hazardous to compete with the five billion out-of-control human beings endlessly copulating and howling to the gods of growth and planned waste, rewarded with IOU paper promises to their nonexistent Promised Land.

I've been globe-trotting since the age of three months. Getaway is the name of the game, and I've been burning up the road ever since. The flames are in my blood permanently.

Those who read the story never forgot it—though perhaps less for Dora's aptitude at eluding the law, and more for the way he wove his own real-life African treks into an intrepid adventure during which he supposedly found a black diamond in the beach sands of Namibia . . .

In short, tucked away in a safe deposit box in Paris are all the photographs, sketches, charts, and maps of the expedition, including a 10-carat black diamond encased in a fossilized oyster shell. . . .

Had he or hadn't he?

CLIVE BARBER: One day, Bruce Gold, myself, Miki, and Eddie Godfrey—who made buchu oil on his farm near Paarl, where Miki often stayed—and these two blondes, Karen and Jenny, took two vehicles up the west coast to Elands and had a couple good days' surf there. Finally, we ended up at Port Nolloth, the last seacoast before you get to the diamond area. All the surfers around dove for diamonds. You could find holes of diamonds down about three to five meters quite far out on the reefs. Two guys would go out with a massive suction pump; one would blow and one would suction. They'd get a swirl going and get the diamonds lying inside the mud and the clay.

It's illegal to take diamonds out of the area and sell them on your own. Of course, there is always a market in something illicit.

At one point, Miki disappeared with one of our cars, a big Cressida. He and one of the blondes said they were taking a tour. He said they drove right to the gates of the diamond area on the Orange River, said they wanted to check out the waves at the river mouth—and got in. I'm guessing Miki bribed his way in there somehow, although they did have surfboards on the car. He had Scooter Boy with him, and an American accent.

They were gone a whole night and when they came back he was totally stoked. But Miki didn't say anything. Obviously he'd found waves; I believe he found other items as well.

> *11.5.90 [Letter to Steve Taussig]*
>
> *I've come across some very intriguing objects of matter (retrieved from the restricted area). Perhaps you might know of persons, artisan or collectors who may have interest. I know of a Diamond Diver who has recovered a number of pieces. Weight from 1 kil to 25 kilos. These pieces are from an ancient prehistoric forest washed down by the Orange River millions of years ago, encased in the Diamond rocks hundred of feet under the sea petrified, fossilized into a mineral wonder. High density glowing golden grained substance. Its rarity and compressibility found once in a blue moon, is almost incomprehensible to modern man.*

Miki wrapped up the *Surfer* piece with a riveting replay of his encounter with an incredible wave:

> *Imagine a devastating, 100-yard, coiling stand-up cylinder breaking in 4' of water over a razor-sharp, crustacean-covered bottom. A split-second, vertical, semi-blind take-off must be executed with brute force for serious follow-through drive. Compulsory is maximum acceleration . . . and a full-out super trim.*
>
> *One miscalculation and you're a dead man, being carried out of this world. Injured-only is impossible.*

In the story's aftermath, Miki continued, as he'd always told Johnny Fain, to "go for broke." Even though he'd had complete control of his work, he still wrote a letter to his attorney claiming that "Hitting below the belt as always, I was double-crossed, with Breach of Contract and broken promises. My work was published, ripped to shreds."

2

In addition to his usual easygoing, last-frontier routine, Miki passed the time in Jeffreys Bay by corresponding with a far-flung phalanx of friends. His letters were usually on an onionskin aerogram decorated with flowers labeled with their Latin names. The faxes always bore a bold-faced header, in heavy black marker, that drew the eye: DEEP COVER, S.O.S., or CONFIDENTIAL. Often he'd use paper on which he'd earlier xeroxed an image from a scenic postcard or cigar box label; he'd write his message in ornate script around the graphic. Sometimes he'd include cartoons with sexual or drug themes copied from "underground" comix.

Miki's letters and faxes showed his peculiar habit of adopting language from his earlier letters and rants, as if he had a notebook full of prewritten text—lines, jokes, paragraphs, observations—to be swapped in and out as need and instinct dictated. His communications seemed casual but were actually carefully constructed to be entertaining and memorable. His introduction was often a funny story or outrageous provocation. The body contained the message. The sign-off was often surprisingly warm. (Did he realize most of his correspondents collected his letters?) No letter seemed written merely to say hello; he most always needed a favor. Perhaps, as one recipient of many missives speculated, "Miki's only way of communicating was to communicate his needs."

"Miki faxed obsessively," recalls Christine Liepner. "He'd give letters to me in a hard FedEx envelope. Twenty or thirty pages. Then he'd tell me, 'I'm expecting important faxes. Look for them and I'll phone you.' He never phoned. But when I got one I'd just put it in an envelope with his name and have it at my house for him to collect."

Miki also received regular letters from his father, especially on the holidays, steadfastly wishing him a Merry Christmas, Happy New Year, continued health, and love. Often, Miklos Sr. also enclosed a little monetary cheer.

Meanwhile, Miki continued to move from flat to flat in Jeffreys

Bay, often in a beat-up clunker on its last tires, eventually renting the guest quarters under Gary and Cristal Yosh's home, just walking distance from the beach, for 300 rand a month.

GARY YOSH: Miki had a daily routine. He'd walk down the hill from my house to Cheron's house at Supers and have the maids make him breakfast. Then he'd walk the dog along the beach and come back up to my house. By that time he would have loosened up his legs, warmed up. Then he'd go for a surf between eleven and noon. He'd paddle out, sit in a position, and just wait for the perfect wave, even if it took forever. If there wasn't any surf, he'd spend his day walking on the beach, picking up shells that looked like rings.

Miki lived with us for seven years and became part of our lives. My wife, Cristal, and I never thought of Miki as some superstar or legend. She could just as easily fix him a great dinner as be pissed off at him. Neither Cristal's or my parents lived anywhere close. If we wanted to go out, we'd ask Miki to babysit our kids. He was like a kid himself. When they got bigger they used to fight like mad. I'd step away to the restroom and I'd come back to see the kids and Miki throwing eggs at each other, fighting over what TV channel they could watch.

At the market, Miki always got the same things: health bread and a nice cut of meat. But he never, ever cleaned his place, or washed his plates, so he always got food poisoning. I used to tell him that's what did it, but it didn't seem to bother him.

Miki's routine also included a sports club membership. He played golf but was soon denied course privileges for letting the black caddies play with him. He played tennis as well, with the club president, a woman, as his doubles partner. Her husband, however, hated Miki's habit of discarding peanut shells on the club floor. One year, Miki won the senior championships in Port Elizabeth. Then he was kicked out for bathing Scooter Boy in the facilities and writing a note that read: "My son Scooter Boy has a grievance to make. He's just taken a shower in the men's locker room and there was no flea or tick shampoo. What are you going to do about that?"

Among Miki's closest friends in Jeffreys Bay were sisters Jessica Naude and Christine Liepner. Jessica owned the upscale Breakers restaurant, with an ocean view. Christine worked for Cheron Kraak. Around the ladies, as well as the Yoshes and Bruce Gold, Miki dropped most if not all pretense, artifice, and barrier; relaxed; and let himself be. It was as close to the natural, noncelebrity, unhassled state of his personality as one might get.

JESSICA NAUDE: I ran the restaurant business for five years. Miki often came for lunch. He loved filet steak, very rare, with pepper sauce and salad. He always shared with Scooter, who sat on the chair next to him. We closed on Mondays and I used to drive into Port Elizabeth to buy my stocks. Starting in 1989, Miki often came with me. We'd go shopping, then to Green Acres and have lunch. Often a movie in the afternoon. I found Miki intellectually stimulating, which I didn't get much from people around here. He was very clever and very wise. He could give you good tips on traveling: how to get your ticket quick and little things like that.

GARY YOSH: Miki had a self-made book, about two inches thick, of every traveling scam he could think of. He'd had it typed out like a dossier. He gave it to me once before I had to travel somewhere. He said, "Read this and you'll see what tricks you can pull." My wife also read it and said, "This is terrible."

JESSICA NAUDE: When Wimbledon tennis was on, he'd be at my house every night and eat everything. He had good manners, but somehow he always had to give Scooter Boy food on my white carpet. And take cookies from the glass jars and stuff them in his pockets.

When he cooked it was always in one pot. Oh my God, holy heaven, I remember that pot: a wok. Curries. Oats. Everything. Then he'd do a stew. He'd throw the oil in the pan—having not washed it. Afterward, he'd scrape it out into the sink. The drain grease would get thicker and thicker.

For a time he stayed in a little room here. It had been the servant's quarters but had been renovated into a beautiful little flatlet. I took him to the airport once and brought him home a month later, opened the door, and whoooo! He'd turned the fridge off but had left a whole fish inside. We'd also have to ask him to clean the toilet. It's amazing because he was so obsessive about cleanliness. He'd always inspect a glass before he drank out of it.

CRISTAL YOSH: Miki used to go through my makeup, find the face cream and the mask, put it on, and watch TV in my room, getting all prettied up. He was a looker, all right, and he liked to preserve himself as best as he could. He was a vain little boy. He drove me crazy at times, I must admit. Sometimes we had big fights about him not touching my stuff. They cost a fortune. I'd scream from upstairs, "You've been at my face cream again, I can see it! Don't touch my bloody stuff!" I did a French manicure for him once. It looked good.

JESSICA NAUDE: Once a week, in the evening, we'd go to a local hall and do ballroom dancing. Waltzes, the cha-cha, the two-step. We paid six months in advance. When the six months were up, he decided he didn't want to pay a further six months. He said he'd seen a book that had steps you could cut out, put on the floor, and practice on them with the music. Maybe in America you can get it, but you certainly can't here. So the dancing just dissolved.

CHRISTINE LIEPNER: Miki was so eccentric, he could always cheer me up. I never knew what to expect next. When my Siamese died, he was so apologetic for weeks. Like a different person: "I'm so sorry." Humble. He had such a good heart. If I came home exhausted, he'd say, "You're a slave. A slave!" That was his favorite. "A slave for what?" I'd say, "Well, are *you* going to pay my rent?"

I felt very comfortable with Miki. I'd tell him anything. I never felt I had to put up airs or graces or such. I used to fall asleep watching TV with him. He was a gentleman: "Would you like me to stay? Are you sure you'd like me to stay?" And: "Is there anything I can do for you?" Always.

JESSICA NAUDE: But sometimes he wouldn't leave. One night Christine had enough of him sitting in her house 'til late, so she said, "Oh, there's a fly!"— and she sprayed Doom, for cockroaches. He literally ran out the door.

GARY YOSH: Every nine months Miki would have to leave South Africa and get another visa to come in again. He'd try and time it to when Harry Hodge would pay his airfare to be a celebrity guest at some Quiksilver event in France. Or he'd go to America. Sometimes Derek Hynd would take him to Australia. A solicitor told Miki he must give 100,000 rand to get permanent residency, and he didn't want to do that. I thought he never had 100,000 rand. (Author's note: about $11,000 U.S. at the time.) He traveled, but always on someone else's bowl.

BRUCE GOLD: Every time he left to renew his visa he'd lug these big suitcases. He'd also stash stuff around for people to look after.

CHRISTINE LIEPNER: He always showed me pictures of his mother, black-and-white pictures of her in a black dress, very elegant hair. Like that French actress, Catherine Deneuve. His mother was totally the apple of his eye, yet he told me she was an alcoholic and in a home. He'd often excuse himself to go phone her. He despised his father. He'd show me movie residual checks for a few dollars and say, "Why does my father send me these checks? Why does he bother with this amount when he's so wealthy?" Miki believed his father was disappointed in him because he was just a surfer and never amounted to anything else. So Miki felt rejected. Maybe his father's opinion is indirectly why he didn't really like surfers. He said his father thought surfing was just a bum's life.

DEREK HYND: Christine was Miki's soul mate. She and Miki, if anyone, perhaps should have gotten married. They had a deep respect for each other. They seemed warm and natural together. Miki was impressed by people who could confess where they'd stuffed up. Christine had a lot of goodness in her, and a lot of pathos. Christine could have lived the most glamorous, successful life of many a beautiful woman had she not made a few decisions along the way. And yet, her mannerisms and self-deprecating manner were impressive. Dora was riddled with pathos, too, except he didn't really let it emerge too much.

CHRISTINE LIEPNER: He'd always say, "One day we'll get married." That way he could get his residency. And I could get a ticket to America. Marriage was my one-way ticket and his one-way ticket. A figure of speech. A convenience. We also said, if we were in pain and we were old, I would help him out or he would help me out. We'd find something that we could give to alleviate the pain so that we could slowly go off.

3

In March 1991, while relaxing on Eddie Godfrey's buchu farm, Miki read a long letter from Greg Noll in which Da Bull said that everywhere he went he got asked one question: when are you going to bring back some of your old-style board models, and "in particular the Miki board"? Noll had heard the question often enough to tell Miki, "This could really be a class thing." He said he understood that Miki had a certain lifestyle and image that he put ahead of any financial gains, but, "The way I see it both could be accomplished." Noll proposed a limited run. He would shape the boards himself, and another party would glass them, giving Miki a "second way" to verify his royalty per board. Noll offered Miki $50 per board, which, he said, was more than most shapers make. He suggested a run of four hundred boards, which would put $20,000 "in your pocket." Noll asked only for Dora's written approval and a commitment to do some ads, just like the old days. "Just think, Miki. You would get a chance to insult all those people one more time."

If Miki was interested, Noll said he didn't want any deal to get too complicated legally. He no longer had the energy for that, and he remembered that Miki was always worried about someone taking advantage of him. "All I want to do at this stage of my life is make a few boards, do it in a classy way, and have a little fun with the whole thing."

Noll also enclosed a copy of his autobiography, *Da Bull: Life Over the Edge*, saying he hoped some of the old stories would give Miki "a chuckle."

GREG NOLL: He was very proud his old boards were selling for up to ten grand, so it wasn't very hard for him to say yes. But I said, "Listen, man: Are you mellow enough to go through this thing without all this bullshit that we went through the first time around?"

"Oh yeah," he said, "I've completely changed. That's behind me. I'm a different person."

I should've known better.

Miki and I had preliminary talks about how we'd do the board, that it'd be a first-class deal, and that the details would be worked out at a meeting when he came to California. We also decided how the label would look: I would sign one side, he would sign the other side.

It went easily at first, but when we got down to the final deal, he had all this goddamn baggage. Again. His requirements just goddamn went on and on. At one point I got so pissed off I told him we ought to forget this goddamn thing and let's go out in the street and work it out between us. I'd said it years ago, but now I added, "Look, I'm just a fat old guy. You're in a lot better shape than I am, but I bet I can still whip your ass," or something to that effect. I was steamin' mad. Miki stomped out of the room and Laura went after Miki—just like she had the first time around. She got him settled down. She had to talk to both of us like we were little kids. If it hadn't been for Laura, we wouldn't have continued. By this time everybody in the room was sweating.

Miki also brought some guy he was staying with to the meeting. Miki let this guy talk for him and he was adversarial. "What's going on here with this deal? Why are you doing this to Miki? Why are you taking advantage?" I explained the facts and he'd say, "Oh. That's not the way I understood it." Half an hour later, he's going, "Miki, what's the matter? There's no problem here. Miki said, "So you're turning on me, too, you sonofabitch!" And he kicked his friend out.

GREG PERSON: We went six hours the first day, until Greg Noll and Laura and everybody else were beside themselves because Miki wouldn't sign. I think he just wanted to put Noll through hell. He'd took me aside once and said, "Look at how fat he is. Maybe he's gonna have a heart attack." That night at my house, Miki said, "I don't know if I want to sign." I said, "Who do you think you are, and where have you been? What do you have to lose?" He said, "Well, I'm not gettin' enough. He's selling me out." He'd just make a big deal out of everything. He had to have drama. He loved the attention, but he would fake it like something bothered him.

GREG NOLL: We finally got down to the wire. Everybody in the room's worn out. It's three days later. We've got six pieces of paper that need signatures. Miki wanted his money first. I counted out the cash. He watched, then counted the money. Then he counted it again. And again. He made a stack. Then he pulled a money pouch out of his shirt, the kind travelers use, and put the cash in. By this time I'm so nervous I'm pacing. Miki's in the middle of a long conference table. The door is at one end of the room. I'm opposite Miki. He looks at me and sneaks a look at the door, and I ran for the goddamn door. And I said, "You sonofabitch, I know what you're thinking. Don't even think about it."

He picked up the pen and looked over the agreements. By this time I'm panting. He looked at me, probably searching for something else to squawk about.

I'm not embellishing this a bit.

In big surf, when you take off on a wave, guys hyperventilate in order to get more oxygen into their system. It helps you live through the wipeouts. Dora started hyperventilating. The funniest thing I've ever seen. He's got the pen and he's going *ah-whooo, ah-whooo, ah-whooo,* hyperventilating.

Then he signed. Done deal. Never heard a word after that about anything, except how tickled he was. He could have done a hundred deals over the years. I was the only guy who would put up with his crap to the extent where he didn't kill his own deal.

We made 275 or 300 boards. The original boards sold for $700 or $800, then $1,000, then $1,500, then $2,000. The few we have left sell for $5,000 or $6,000. I put a bunch of them away for my kids, for their college. When I could finally afford it, I just bought all the decals and paid him off.

As part of the deal I asked him for two things. One was a new logo; and I needed the magazine ads. He sent me stuff, but I never used either. Still, his idea of how to promote the board was incredible genius. Honestly, I didn't use the new logo because it was too radical—though maybe not now.

Miki requested a "reliable artist" to do the fine, minute detail artwork the ad required. He never mentioned that he'd lifted the original art from an Americans for Sane Policies newsletter, whited out their text, and substituted his own.

GREG PERSON: After Miki signed, we drove home. On the way, I stopped at Hollywood Magic on Seventeenth Street. Miki bought a mask of clear plastic. You could see your face through it, but you really couldn't tell who it is. He also bought an invisible ink pen. He said, "Ah. Perfect. Now I can get money, sign, and when they get home they won't have my signature!"

A few days later was this guy Mike Marshall's fiftieth birthday. I tried to talk Miki into going to the party. He said, "I'm not going up there with all those fools. I'm gonna stay here with Scooter Boy."

A friend of mine, Pete Nickertz, went to the party. Pete saw this LeRoy Grannis photo of Miki—the classic one of him relaxed on the nose at Malibu, on the wall at Marshall's house. He took it without Marshall knowing and drove to my house and pounded on the door. Miki answered and saw this character with his picture. Miki said, "No. Uh, I don't sign. I don't sign."

"Man, if you could just do this for Marshall it would make his day."

"No, I don't sign."

But Nickertz hung in, and Miki remembered he had the pen. So he wrote, "To Mike. Happy birthday. Miki Dora." Nickertz said, "Oh man. How great. We love you. Thank you so much."

Nickertz drove back to the party. He got Marshall to show him the picture . . . and there's nothing but a wet spot where the signature is supposed to be.

But not everyone was willing to put up with Miki's idea of himself.

MIKE HISCHIER: I bought a board from Miki when he came to town, his personal board shaped on the North Shore by Chris Greene in 1967. It's a double-ender, in lavender. Steve Taussig told me Miki wanted to sell. I said, "I don't want to get into the middle of a scam, but I'll buy the board if he genuinely wants to sell it. Give me Miki's number and I'll call him." Taussig said, "Well, nobody calls Miki. I'll have Miki call you."

Half an hour later Miki called. I asked how much he wanted and he said,

ABOVE: Greg and Miki (in a favorite guise) checking out a garage full of latter-day Da Cats, 1992. Photo: Tom Servais.

RIGHT: Greg and Miki with a balsa Da Cat, 1998. Courtesy Noll Family Collection.

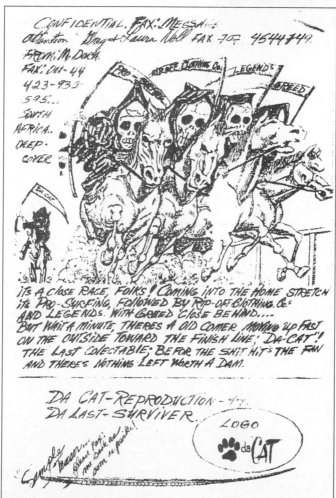

LEFT: Unpublished Da Cat ad, 1992. Unknown to anyone, Miki lifted the art from an ASP newsletter and added his own provocative text. Courtesy Noll Family Collection.

$1,000. I said okay. Then he said, "But it's already sold. I'm delivering it to Newport Beach tomorrow."

"Then why are you calling me?" I asked. But I knew he wanted me to make a move. He was in Santa Barbara. I said, "What if I come down tomorrow morning before you leave? I'll look at the board. If I buy it, it saves you the drive to Newport Beach."

My wife and I went together because she wanted to shop. On the way I told her Miki's story. In the typical non–surfer girl way, she didn't care.

I wanted to make sure that the board was legit, and that I didn't get talked into something else. I'd heard stories about dealing with Miki.

We met at his father's home in Montecito. The board turned out to be epic. Back then, having a lavender board was a pretty big move. You better be somebody out on the water to have that color. To verify it as an original, I looked closely at the sticker on the board . . . where it said, "Da Cat." In fact, it wasn't really a sticker. Miki had cut it out of a magazine, so you could see the type on the other side of the page. When he realized what I was doing he came over and said, "That was cut out of a magazine."

I said, "Why didn't you use a laminate?"

He explained the board was made on the North Shore by Chris Greene. Since it didn't come out of Greg Noll's factory, Greg wouldn't send him a laminate. It wasn't a step-deck Da Cat model, but Miki wanted his sticker on it because it was his personal board. I thought that was pretty cool, having it not be an actual laminate, but having it be where he just cut it out of a magazine. So I said, "Okay, let's do the deal."

He reminded me that "the price is fixed."

"Yeah, we talked about that yesterday. A thousand dollars."

"That's right."

I pulled the money out, handed him ten $100 bills, said, "Go ahead and count it."

"Nah, I don't need to."

"Oh, just go ahead and count it real quick."

While he did, I picked up the board. He said, "So what's the board worth?"

"A thousand dollars."

"No, I mean, what's the board really worth?"

He couldn't imagine anybody paying a fair price without planning to spin it for a profit.

I said, "Miki, I told you how I was going to use it. I own a surf shop. I collect surfboards. I'm going to put it in the shop. A thousand dollars is what it's worth."

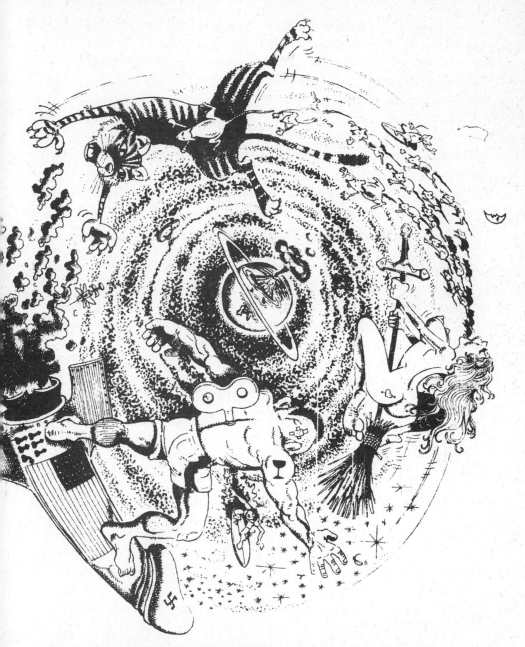

Never-seen Da Cat reissue series logo. "I thought it was too out there," says Noll. "But maybe now. . . ." Courtesy Noll Family Collection.

He looked at me skeptically. We started walking to the car, my wife third in line. Suddenly she said, "Oh, Mike, you wanted to get him to sign that . . ."

Miki whipped around, classic early 1960s stance, flipped his hand in the air, and said, "I'm sorry, I don't do autographs."

My wife snapped: "Why would we want your autograph? We want a bill of sale."

This absolutely devastated him. Miki had read her and the situation completely wrong. My wife didn't care about him; to her, he was just an older guy who surfed.

Miki said, "I'm sorry. I just don't know what people want sometimes. I can sign a bill of sale, that's not a problem." I drafted something real quick, and he signed it. I still have it, in a little frame that I keep in my office in the shop.

Later, I told my wife, "You have no idea what you just did to him."

"What are you talking about? He seemed like a nice enough guy."

"I don't think he's on solid ground," I said. "He's this master manipulator, chameleon-type guy. When you asked him that, he immediately thought you meant an autograph. In certain circles, he's a legend. But outside of those circles, he's just a guy who's gotten older and hasn't really done much, and nobody really cares."

I think that was Miki's worst nightmare, being just another guy.

CHAPTER FIFTEEN

In Search of Da Cat

1

While in Biarritz to attend an Oxbow Longboard Championship at the invitation of Nat Young, who'd been hired to coordinate everything, Miki shared with his attorney/tennis partner/friend Bob Simpson an idea he'd been long nurturing.

BOB SIMPSON: Miki needed to figure out a way to make money that didn't involve suing people—at which he was not successful, anyway. One day he said, "I've got this incredible idea. Very confidential." He gave me a sheet of paper—his Environmental Project—and asked me to read it. I said, "Yeah, that's very interesting, Miki. What do you want to do with it?" He said, "Bob, don't you realize? This is a major event. This is a unique surfing contest where the surfboard has to be made of all-natural, biodegradable materials, none of this polluting stuff—and you can't use a leash." He thought he'd organize and win the event at Jeffreys Bay, and he wanted a major sportswear company to sponsor it. I said, "Well, let's go to Harry. Maybe he'll be interested."

HARRY HODGE: We drew up a confidentiality agreement, I rang Quiksilver U.S.A. and ran the idea past a few people. The original philosophical concept wasn't bad—everything's natural. But it was just too deep in the too-hard basket and, as a company, we'd look foolish trying to pull it off. It would be like if Quiksilver said, "We are going to clean up the oceans of the world." No, we're not. That's impossible. We're going to contribute the best we can to the organizations that promote cleaner oceans. Miki never actually presented the idea to us in person, but I ran it by our international marketing committee anyway.

> [Letter from Harry Hodge to Bob Simpson]
> Whilst everyone was most impressed by the concept that companies such as Quiksilver should and will focus more on the environment and the subsequent issues, the meeting felt the concept of riding biodegradable surfboards could possibly develop into a very real political football or hot potato—ie, the surfboard industry is very defensive and aware of its problem. We felt that for a clothing company to point the finger of focus at them could create friction within the industry, whereas we are in fact colleagues. I will communicate the meeting's decision directly to Miki. . . .

BOB SIMPSON: I tried to get other companies interested over the next few years—Oxbow, Rip Curl, Billabong. Yvon Chouinard of Patagonia wrote to Miki saying he'd gotten his "curiosity up about the scheme"—but nobody expressed much actual interest in moving forward.

In 1994, Nat Young directed another Oxbow Longboard Championship, this time in Malibu. Again, he sent Miki a ticket. Perhaps he expected Miki to make a triumphant return, but as they say, you can never go home again—even if you're home. Unlike at Oxbow two years earlier, when Miki would only appear in public wearing the transparent plastic mask he'd bought at a magic supplies shop in Costa Mesa, this time Miki stayed close to the Malibu Inn. According to C. R. Stecyk III, "Miki was there for two and a half weeks and asked all his friends *not* to reveal he was there. It was the world's worst-kept secret . . . He'd go to a party and there'd be 150 people, and everyone pretending that Miki wasn't there . . . They expected he would need his privacy, and they allowed him to have it . . . under penalty of death. All the problems with him happen when people violate his privacy and they get confused."

SCOTT HULET: He phoned me at *Longboard* magazine and had me visit at the hotel. Miki had, in his words, "taken ill from the flight" and had kind of a phlegmy cough. His suite was dark and couldn't have been more gothic and mildly Transylvanian. I noticed a vaguely pneumonic smell. Bowls of fruit. Bottles of wine. Just a strange deal. He was really Bela Lugosi-ing it up, with dramatic facial gestures. He had dyed hair, grayish-dark, almost black, kinky-curly. Maybe it was a wig. He asked me, "Why do you continue printing things about me?" He asked that we never print anything about him again, without talking to him about it first. I said, "Sure."

We talked a bit more, and he went on about his love for the entire James Mason oeuvre. He talked about his hatred for Johnny Fain, which seemed strange and anachronistic.

JOHN MILIUS: Miki came to Paramount while he was in town and spent the day with me while I was filming *Clear and Present Danger.* I'd gone to observe the Gulf War, and he thought that was absolutely insane, unless maybe I was looking for Kuwaiti gold.

He told some great stories about South Africa. Very exotic stuff. Diamond smuggling fascinated him. He wanted to go back because of wild coastline where nobody went except to smuggle. He didn't say how he did it, except that he took the diamonds to Europe, then to New York, where he sold them.

What's interesting about Miki is that he was actually never an active opponent of society—but he never joined it, either. He was free of either side, which meant he was truly free. I owe a lot of my sense of social irresponsibility to Miki Dora. I thank him immensely.

People always ask if I considered doing a movie about Miki. Nah. I wanted to do a nostalgic movie about the bond of friendship. With *Big Wednesday* I took surfing into this John Ford-ian idea of years passing and people being ripped apart and a whole era of innocence disappearing. That's what I saw that was so dramatic.

When he came by, I tried to talk him into having a Miki Dora Day in Malibu. I'd arrange it, and we'd have a wonderful time. He said no, "There's a lot of guys there with scores to settle."

"Those guys are all gone," I said. "If they did have scores, they've given up. They're either old or dead." He wouldn't have it. I would have written it off to his narcissism in the old days, but this was different. He was really afraid someone would come after him.

2

I had some trouble sending (faxing) you this. I don't know why I am sending you this one. I hope you like it. I didn't. Rensin had a deadline for California *magazine. It could have been a good story, he had the raw material, but not the facts. He was bottom fishing and very confused. After all he's a carpet-bagger, an eastern low lifer third-rate writer for* Playboy *magazine, trying to make a name for himself. What the hell does he care about the rich history of California and the desecration of a lifestyle unique only to this part of the world? Millions like him came and destroyed, like Bolsheviks, all beauty and memory of a great land. I'm the last that knows the truth and I must be discredited at all costs.*

—Fax to unknown, potential collaborator

While Miki thought those with longtime grudges were out to discredit him—or worse—most, in fact, admired him and simply wanted to pierce the mystery and get the answers to the questions that Miki thought were no one's business. Or didn't believe mattered. Journalists just wanted *the story.* If Miki's friends and foes agreed on anything, it was the long-shared belief that his life was a great adventure, worth reading about. Naturally, Miki agreed with them—as long as he could tell it his way—and, according to Harry Hodge and Bob Simpson, Miki would send them Rensin's *California* magazine story as a primer.

As the surf-nostalgia trend took shape and a new generation of riders took to the waves, the timing for a book or movie about this seminal surfer began to seem ever more perfect. ("I'm just starting my book," he once wrote to pal Nat Young. "It's titled: *Mickey's a Prickey Dickey Mickey.*") Of course, what the story would be no one could know unless Miki spilled the beans and let his "friends" talk without restriction—and he never did that, no matter how much it seemed he might. "He always insinuated he had lots of inside information about the '50s," Gerry Kantor, once a candidate to coauthor the book, recalls: "Over the years, I came to think that his talk about all the secret information was probably BS to a great extent."

Still, like fairy-tale princes they came, suitors eager to perform the feat that would win the princess's hand and heart—or suffer the king's consequences.

BOB SIMPSON: Miki would say to me, "Wait 'til my book comes out. I'm gonna get even. There's a story that only I know. When I tell this story, and I have the names—surfers that you know from that time . . ." One story was about a Chinese homosexual at one of the piers in Southern California back in the '50s, and how these guys would get drunk and get blow jobs from this homosexual. Miki said, "I'm the only one who didn't get a blow job." He told me this story more than once.

I've always speculated on why Miki didn't just write his own story. I think he was just too lazy. I once talked with a very famous editor in Paris about Miki. She said, "Yeah, I'd be very interested. Have him write, in maybe ten pages, an outline of his book, and let him start on chapter one so I see what his writing looks like." I told Miki, and he actually sent me a four-page document.

> *Miki's PROPOSAL*
> *. . . Anyway, back to the book. Some revealing reminiscences of Malibu during the 1960s in a first chapter entitled "Throwing a Monkey Wrench into the Works." Here I will talk about the making of the film* Gidget. *Relating previously untold facts about my entanglement with the book and its characters and leading up to the making of the film and the ruination of surfing. As I was there, and in fact, being the only living person who knows the whole idiotic truth of events ranging from Columbia Studios to the off-beat and unconventional, this chapter will be powerfully convincing.*
>
> *Chapter 2: My link-in and link-out with Marilyn Monroe and Peter Lawford. John Kennedy and how three years before the Dallas shoot-out I almost lanced him in a surfing mishap.*
>
> *Chapter 3: Hollywood parties—the ghost of Marion Davies and the legacy of Conrad Hilton.*
>
> *Chapter 4: The last of the Kahanamokus and their sidekicks.*
>
> *Chapter 5: Relating to the Frank Sinatra Jr kidnapping and the sum of the ransom money that never showed up. Marlon Brando and the last of Mama Cass. Blast-off party. Lyezine: the real magic drug of the '60s.*
>
> *Chapter 6: On my back and off, and onto the Beach Boys home demolishment thrashing. My connection with Charlie Manson and family—Sharon Tate—George Hamilton and Polanski . . .*
>
> *What I have mentioned here is only a small sample teaser of what I am planning to write about, interspersed with wayfaring to Peru, Mexico, and the Islands.*

The remainder of his proposal laid out Miki's "requirements" for a writer—"An inborn talent and a professional facility with the English language"—and a series of instructions: "No meandering beginnings or clumsy expressions and redundancies. No preaching. I want the story just to get down to business right away." It was all fairly prosaic. Miki also described the necessary writer's mind-set. "The true writer will make time for the book if he has to give up time for all manner of other purposes. He is propelled. Whereas the man who says, 'If only I had the time,' is not propelled. People who say that if they had the time they would write a book never write one. I'm motivated to the highest degree possible."

Perhaps most surprising was Miki's promise that "the reader will gain insight into the protagonist's genetic makeup . . . as well as his assurance not to fill the readers' heads with unrealistic romantic dreams."

Given Miki's oft-stated desire to do a book, did he intend the irony? Did he not see the implicit self-criticism? If there was any insight or romantic dream, it was, perhaps, Miki's belief that he would ever actually do the book himself.

BOB SIMPSON: I never gave the proposal to the editor because I was too embarrassed. The problem was that with Miki every circumstance had to be right, at the outset: the person, the feeling that he was treated the right way, that the story would be handled the way he thought it should be handled. All very nice, but that's not a collaboration, it's dictation. And he couldn't focus enough to dictate, so he wouldn't agree to anything and all discussions ended up leading nowhere. Still, he would always egg them on, wanting them to do something, but I knew he'd never "spill the beans"—as he always put it.

Potential coauthors continued to surface. Bob Beadle, a longtime surfer and friend from the Topanga days, who'd become an expatriate himself, was thoughtful and literate and, in a more positive and self-preservational way than Miki, described himself as like-minded. He thought Miki should write the book in part to protect himself, in part to have his unfiltered say. Beadle was cautious, but willing. He wrote directly to Miki: "I think you might consider it because it might be your pleasure to do so, to make sure the truth as you know it is on record, to make some money to counter the illusions and fabrications, to snooker writers who can't get a life, for the psychotherapeutic experience, for all the reasons you won't realize until you do it."

A collaboration with Beadle never happened. Then, in June 1997,

Bob Simpson and Derek Hynd corresponded about a book. "I've been strongly encouraging Miki to get a book for years and we have discussed different arrangements with various people," Simpson wrote, adding, "Congratulations if you have worked out an agreement with Mickey Dora." After reviewing a history of missed or abandoned opportunities, Simpson assured Hynd that the book, if done right, would be "incredible, and attract publishers in various countries."

DEREK HYND: Dora was dead set about doing it. For about fifteen months he hassled me because he said he felt he wasn't getting any younger. Correspondence went back to Simpson. But whenever it came down to, "Okay, let's strike the deal," then it just wouldn't happen. In the meantime, there was a lot of conversation about what the book was about and how the structure should go, and what really happened in his life to make things worthwhile.

He never disputed anything. We never had arguments about it. When he'd come around it was always in the spirit of camaraderie. Pure stoke. But it never happened. The time had passed.

3

The story of Miki Dora is the story of getting the story.
                                        —Anonymous, to the author, 1983

OVIDIO SALAZAR: I'd grown up surfing in Southern California and I wanted to make a film about Miki. To me he'd always been much more charismatic than any of the movie stars. Also, the hungry ghosts of Malibu still haunted me. I approached two producers, Grant Keir and Peter Day. Peter was a partner in Faction Films, came from New Zealand, had surfed, and knew some of Miki's exploits. I'd been making films since leaving California in 1970. I went to work for NBC in Cairo, on the news desk, and then worked on films having to do with the Middle East, as a production assistant/coordinator/location manager/assistant director. *In Search of Da Cat* was my first documentary film as a director.

PETER DAY: We set the film up as a search, as if we didn't know where Miki was. But we did know because it was an open secret amongst surfing professionals and industry types on a high level. Still, when we shot our interview with Dale Velzy, for instance, we told him we were looking for Miki. He said, "Don't worry; he'll find you." I said, "How's that?" He said, "He'll smell the money."

OVIDIO SALAZAR: We had to know where we were going or we couldn't have gotten our funding. But it wouldn't have worked if I had said so. The point was that we are Miki's children, the disciples who manage to play the system like he would. Basically, I took *Apocalypse Now* and *The Heart of Darkness* as models. It was me going up the California Mekong, only instead of finding Kurtz I found Miklos, and he was a tabula rasa.

The filmmakers contacted Bob Simmons, and in April 1996 he advised Miki. Simpson said he'd suggested they make an offer that would include Miki's airfare to France, a few weeks' accommodation, and some fees. The usual stuff. "They seem serious. I spoke to the producer, Peter Day, told him it was a good idea, but that you should be paid," Simpson wrote.

PETER DAY: We knew Miki hung out at a particular board shop in Jeffreys Bay owned by Cheron Kraak. We faxed Cheron. Derek Hynd responded to that fax, and we quote his response in the film: "If you're looking for Malibu 1950, this place is maxed out worse than anything ever. Miki's a prophet." It was as if Derek was Dennis Hopper in *Apocalypse Now.* Derek brokered the deal. He said we could come down. There was no guarantee Miki would talk, but he left it open. We took the risk and figured if he didn't talk, we could still make it work in the film.

Ovidio and I went in first, to determine if there was any point in bringing the crew down, meaning, what would we film if he didn't talk? The night we arrived, we met with Derek. Then Miki agreed to meet Ovidio at a small restaurant.

When Ovidio came back from dinner he said, "Oh man, he's amazing. Wow, he's such a cool guy!" It was a Stanley moment: "Dr. Livingston, I presume." Ovidio was optimistic that Miki would be in the film.

My job was to get him to actually agree to be in the film. I'd seen that brilliant interview in *Surfers: The Movie.* As far as I was concerned, all he had to do was say that again. He could be obscure like Marlon Brando, mumble the old shit, and it would be great. Read the phone book, man, we don't care. A little Los Angeles cool would be good.

The next day we hung out with Miki while he, I suppose, contemplated how much money he could get out of us. I thought he was fabulous. He was in good shape. He had a very wicked sense of humor. He'd developed quite reactionary attitudes toward things politically speaking, but at the same time he was very live and let live.

We hung out for three or four days. Once he wore a blue sports jacket and slacks—unlike a surfer—and cool jewelry: little shells and a bracelet. He didn't wear a cravat but it would have fit.

One day, driving somewhere with Miki, he told us that he knew Elvis and was his stunt double for *Blue Hawaii.* He said he'd—let's not calling it pimping, let's call it procuring—helped facilitate movement of women to those Hollywood types.

I don't want to patronize, but he was very bright, lacking in stimulus, and starved of intellectual company. He was probably bored with the surfing community. Not a lot of people passed through. All they talked about was whether it was offshore or onshore, about the tides. Few talked about books. Miki got on very well with Ovidio because he could see there was a lot more going on with him than Ovidio immediately revealed. He also looked something like Miki then, but if Miki noticed, he didn't say anything. They were just two exiled Californians and they recognized each other.

A swell hit, so we went surfing. Once, two American boys went paddling past and one said to the other, "Hey, man, that's Miki Dora." The other said, "Nah nah, man. He's been dead a long time." I guess he had to put up with that a lot.

OVIDIO SALAZAR: Finally, I said, "Can we do an interview?"

PETER DAY: To convince Miki, we emphasized that the documentary would be on a prestigious channel that did films about artists and poets and painters and musicians; we'd help elevate him to that kind of pantheon. No doubt he believed he belonged there anyway.

Miki was very concerned about other people we'd spoken with. We stayed circumspect. But he gave us every indication he was prepared to talk, so we sent for the crew. Now we were under pressure.

DEREK HYND: I think they knew that it was a hopeless task from the outset because Miki would never go on the record. But he loved being a puppeteer again, and having these guys on a string. It was a little blast from the past. He enjoyed the game.

OVIDIO SALAZAR: And then, suddenly, the drawbridge went up—but only because he needed money. I think he wanted ten thousand dollars. Fair enough, but we didn't have it. So we asked if he'd give us the clearance to use his interview from *Surfers: The Movie.* I was desperate. We could only use so many shots of bushes, clouds, creeks, waves, and windswept beaches. I started to plead. I didn't know how to end the film.

PETER DAY: Ovidio and I went to see Dora and said, "C'mon. Have you thought about it? We thought the *Surfers* movie was really good. Saying something along those lines would be great, and we'll finish the film with you doing that. Wear your dark glasses, whatever. Just say something enigmatic."

We were at Derek's place. Beautiful view of the beach. We all sat on the terrace. Finally, we settled on paying him $5,000 US. I went inside to ring my commissioning editor in France to see if he'd agree. He did. I went out to tell Miki—and he'd gone. He'd said to Ovidio, "I don't want to do it. I can't do it." I said, Oh, fuck.

We were crestfallen. How would we finish the film? But as bad as I felt, Ovidio felt worse. Derek said, "Ah, it doesn't surprise me. I think he really wants to do it, but it doesn't surprise me."

DEREK HYND: I thought Dora played that situation perfectly. He knew these kooky guys were going to turn up and try to interview him. That was probably the only time I got to see Dora work his magic, or lack of magic. It was great.

OVIDIO SALAZAR: Then, amazingly, Dora came to our rescue. While he played the cat-and-mouse game, by the grace of God the waves picked up. If it had been flat, this would never have happened. We filmed him in the water, surfing. Classic shots. He knew we were shooting.

As he came out of the water, Peter said, "There he is. You've got to go talk to him! He's waiting for you." Was he? I was nervous and reluctant.

I went down to the beach and approached Miki, but he sensed the camera and set his surfboard on end and hid behind it. I leaned around it and talked to him. In the film I refused to say what Miki said to me because maintaining the myth was the whole point.

But this is what he said: "So, is this how the film ends?"

Brilliant. He knew.

He also said, "Why don't you come back and help me write my autobiography?"

After Salazar and Day left, Miki wrote to Bob Simpson: "Regarding the documentary team: I just could not work with them. We all got along quite well and I agreed on their subject matter. However, I felt the degeneracy of the surfing lifestyle was something I did not want my name to be 'accommodated' to and I could not sign their contract. Without my knowledge they filmed me nonetheless on the fourth of June when I got some good waves. It looks like they got what they came to South Africa for."

PETER DAY: The weird thing is that Miki called us often while we edited. We had a personal dialogue all through the process, because he was trying to control it, but he couldn't.

OVIDIO SALAZAR: He'd call the editing room and say, "What's going on?" He'd leave messages and send faxes. Although we emphasized lack of cooperation as a narrative thread in the film, without a doubt Miki was more cooperative than anyone thinks.

Tonally, I left out all of the worst allegations about him, and I never said exactly what he was in jail for. A lot of people I interviewed disparaged him, and I just didn't want to include that. Others said he was "damaged goods." That sounded more like envy. I liked his anarchic nature, the subversion, the most. His whole life, he threw our conformity with the system back on us. That's what a master does. He doesn't tell you everything; he creates the situation that you can learn from. But a master is like fire: If you're too close, you get burnt. If you're at just the right distance, you get warm. You have to know the safe distance. What one always had to keep in mind when approaching Miki was the need for some formality.

When Bob Simpson finally saw the film, he expressed palpable disappointment in a letter to Ovidio Salazar.

> . . . *As to the non-film on Mickey Dora, aside from the comments by John Milius and Steve Pezman and Mickey at the very end of the hour, it was of no interest. Worse, it shows that you have no insight into the man or the legend and nothing appropriate to say about him. Repeating the image of Mickey giving the finger is not only in very poor taste, but totally misses the point of what Mickey stands for—rebel or otherwise. I would suggest that his gesture is more appropriate as a comment on your film. . . . You owe the surfing world an apology. And please do not do any sequels.*

In Search of Da Cat aired in France and Germany on ARTE, in December of 1996. PBS in the United States featured it in 1997. Miki began to hear from friends and relatives who'd seen *In Search of Da*

Cat (not to be confused with Matte Box Films's *Da Search for Da Cat*). Miklos Sr. wrote that he thought it "quite good." In fact, the response from Miki's extended circle was largely positive. However, Miki continued whenever possible to inquire about the possibility of suing for defamation or invasion of privacy and hurt feelings. He engaged lawyers, drew up a list of "potentially defamatory allegations." The film also led to a falling out with Philippe Lauga, who he thought shouldn't have let himself be interviewed.

PHILIPPE LAUGA: I told Miki it was my choice to talk and you can be my friend or not. Take it or leave it.

JEAN-CHARLES CAZES: I mentioned to him seeing the documentary on French television. He said he was really disappointed in that movie. He said, "Don't believe a single word."

One day, Miki faxed Ovidio Salazar out of the blue.

CONFIDENTIAL. I'm taking for granted that this brief fax finds you in good spirits, health, and robustness. [A drawing of two almost feline eyes staring followed, then] WAS IT A HIT OR A MISS? I'm sure it missed the mark. Just another capsized, tawdry abortion. Fax me sometime for old times sake, if you ever get a chance. Aloha, M.

CHAPTER **SIXTEEN**

Da Cat in Search of Himself

1

Life is passing time as gracefully as possible.

—Miki

Too soon, Jeffreys Bay began to lose its once wild-at-heart innocence and palliative benefits. Boredom closed in on Miki, and his chronic restlessness flared. "Everything is going to hell in S.A. The good times are over," he wrote to Steven Taussig. "I'm trying to make a move to South America somewhere before the Blacks take everything. It was great while it lasted."

"I'm ready for the big tax shelter in the sky," he wrote to his brother Gardner in April 1996. "I thought you were going to move to Mexico? I was counting on you to have that ranch near the beach so I could move in with your wife and all your kids. Just me and Scooter Boy, my halfwit son. What happened? It sounds like you're just like me, up shit creek without a paddle. Don't give up yet and sell out to some evangelist. Mother gave all her money to them. What are they doing for her now? Just another hoax. Let's go live in Mexico."

Once again at emotional loose ends, Miki's friends could tell he was looking for something.

When Ian McCormack, "an itinerant evangelist for 24 years" who spends "most of my time traveling the world sharing the gospel," with an incredible story of having died from box jellyfish stings, spoken to God, and revived, came through Jeffreys Bay, Miki was especially intrigued.[7] "I shared my testimony," McCormack recalled. "Then I said, 'Everybody keep your head down and pray. If you've responded, just lift your hand up.' I remember seeing hands go up, including Miki's. Afterward, he wanted to talk. He was fascinated that I'd been dead and had come back to life, and I don't think he'd ever met anyone who'd had that happen. I could tell he'd had a real response in his heart . . . Miki's hunger fascinated me. People had always judged him, but he showed me another side. I realized that the guy was more than just a selfish person who didn't really relate to anybody except himself."

Yet, Jeffreys Bay resident Jackie Clemmons, who with her husband, Mike, was part of a Charismatic church, remembers that "Miki would always start these religious discussions, and be very provocative, just to check our reaction. He'd sound serious, but if you knew him, you knew he just liked to stir the pot. He wasn't afraid to say things to see how the group responded. He was very cynical about organized religion. He didn't want to join any sort of church, and he would be quite sarcastic to people who did have some belief. Maybe underneath he envied them in some way, because he wished he could have that faith. I'm sure Miki did believe in something, but nothing having to do with organized religion."

A serious religious commitment for Miki had always seemed unlikely. According to Gardner Jr., who had in 1990 become a Christian, he'd never told Miki because his brother "disliked Christians. He believed a television church had taken advantage of his mother through 10 percent tithes."

Cynthia Applewhite's husband, Louis Zamperini, had also tried, years earlier, to bring Miki to the Lord—or more to the point, respond to Miki's interest. "Miki seemed really serious, and then fanatic. 'All I want to do is learn more and more about Christ,' he'd said. For three months, Miki was the most dynamic Christian you ever met. Then he just fell apart. I said, 'Mick, I thought you made a decision for Christ. This doesn't make sense.'

"'Well,' he said, 'I now find God on a wave.'"

While casting about for his next move, Miki began to fax friends with increasing frequency. He also continued to hawk his environmentally correct contest concept where possible and concocted plans to

---

[7] www.aglimpseofeternity.org.

find the planet's best balsa wood to build boards to his specifications. In fact, Miki carried and often showed off a little box filled with tiny wood cylinders. All but one sample were labeled. "One was charcoal color and it was very hard, but much lighter than balsa wood," Jeff Hakman remembered. "I'd never seen wood like that."

"It was his secret wood from the Ivory Coast," says Mike McNeill.

"His idea was to do the Miki Dora signature-model balsa board," Phil Jarratt explains, "and sell them for squillions."

Miki entered into various arrangements on the balsa project, but nothing came of it.

~

In the summer of 1996, Miki traveled to France and stayed in Madame Jardine's Hotel Marienia, near the Bar Basque in the center of Guéthary.

MADAME JARDINE: He played tennis and golf—and surfed. Very, very sportif. And very handsome. He didn't like smoking, so he was always taking his breakfast here alone. And he always would go to Petit Casino, the little market across the street, to buy one or two fruits before his breakfast. He thought about his health. I gave him bread, butter, and jam. He wanted orange juice and tea. The room was paid for by Quiksilver. He had the smallest: number 4. He never complained.

He gave me some pictures and signed my guest book. [reads] "July 1996: Another edifying experience in Guéthary. Between Satan (a local dog) keeping me awake all night and breaking my right arm in the slime-pit of hell I still managed to have a good time. Now back to the salt mines in Jeffreys Bay, South Africa. It's a rough life. A.K.S. Mike Dorado."

According to a friend, Miki also delighted in buying cheap magic tricks, which he'd pull out at unexpected moments, often in third world countries, to play the shaman or mystic. "He had all these magic books, pamphlets like you'd see advertised in the back of *Boy's Life*."

MIKE CLEMMONS: He had a disappearing tissue trick. Or he'd pull a coin out of your ear. The kids loved that one. He would do the same tricks over and over and keep them entertained for ages.

FRANÇOIS LARTIGAU: At lunch in Guéthary with Mike McNeill, suddenly Miki said, "Hey, you know I light water on fire?" I don't know how he did it, but he poured water onto a plate, passed his hand above it, and all of a sudden the water was in flames.

SUSAN MCNEILL: He'd also do stupid jokes. Sometimes he'd laugh so hard he'd be crying. He had a copy of a photograph he'd taken of guys on the beach. But one guy was turned around with his ass showing. Miki had cut some bare ass out and put it in there, then photocopied it and made it look real. Miki thought that was hysterical.

Miki also liked tricks of another variety.

A FRIEND: I drove him to Spain a couple times. We'd go down to the brothels. They're totally legal. There's a big bar with chicks hanging around. You have drinks, you talk, you do whatever you want. They have rooms upstairs. There are all kinds of girls—Brazilians, Russians, Spanish. One time I gave him 1,000 francs. "Here Miki, I'll treat." Later, as we came out of the place Miki said, "I didn't spend all the money," and he gave me back 600. I couldn't believe it, but I was touched to see a side of Miki I hadn't seen.

JEAN-YVES ROBERT: We went also to the bordellos in Irun, just across the border, in Spain, maybe two or three times. He always asked for a cheaper price. [laughs] I don't remember what he got, but he asked the price many, many times. He bargained with all the girls. When he got a good price he'd go.

In 1997, Miki traveled through northern Thailand, Burma, and Vietnam and returned, sharing with Scooter Boy "some awful skin disorder." To Cynthia Applewhite he wrote: "Things haven't changed for me, still getting into pleasurable trouble and annoying everybody! Once again, I'm public enemy No. 1 in the Surfing World, this time in Australia. I think I've almost been forgiven in the U.$.A. Maybe its time to come back and start over. Only Joking! (I'll never come back there.) I'll tell you about it some day."

Other travel fantasies included a return to the beach at Phuket, Thailand—which he did a year later, always in search of better health—and, he told Applewhite, "Scooter-Boy wants me to take him to Chile and start a new life, this one is getting too dangerous. Do you know anyone there??? Neither do I. It doesn't matter, I've started over so many times. . . ."

DEREK HYND: As he got on in years, Miki became quite measured in his thinking and his search for the last great frontier staging post. He could live frugally and well among very basic people. He'd been through his great esoteric phase of getting his philosophical point across. And, just judging by the way he could still surf in his sixties, nothing was haphazard and chancy about the way he treated waves from the moment of paddle-out to taking the biggest. What did stand out is that his courage rose in the year before he rode, at Jeffreys Bay, what I think was his best wave.

MIKEY MEYER: He'd take off on the bombs. I was probably half his age, and I had to compete with him for these bombs. It was incredible. On a nine-foot surfboard, not a gun—big wide-nosed things, maybe shaped by me, maybe by someone else—it's not fun to paddle out at Supertubes with a board that doesn't easily go under the wave. It's twentyfold more difficult to paddle out, too. If you get caught it can drag you all across the rocks. But then he would take off on these pristine waves and have the rides of his life.

JEFF HAKMAN: Because he was older, he wanted something he could paddle into the wave, like on a longboard, but once he was on a wave he wanted to have a pointier nose—but not be a needly gun. He liked parallel wide tails. That really helped him get into waves because there was so much area. Once he got on a wave, the boards with a parallel shape would run through the water really well. And he could stand further on the tail and have more sensitivity.

DEREK HYND: As good as Jeffreys Bay can be, to really understand it you'd have to see it with dark, stormy clouds out the back and the wind howling at forty or fifty knots straight across, and viciously cold. Dora, in his deep black wet suit and dark blue board, would just sit way out the far back, waiting, waiting, on a mission. The crowd knew Dora was waiting to make the drop into the biggest, most critical wave, and take it all the way down the line. There's nothing quixotic about that. He wasn't just a glorified joke lost in clouds of depression. Some seasons he'd be bummed because nothing came together—but then it all came together.

I'll never forget Dora's great wave. I just got a shiver picturing it again.

There were just a few of us at the beach that day; I think Mikey Meyer was still out the back when Miki rode this wave. The wind was a light southerly onshore, making the swell most powerful. I'd caught the first wave of the set. Then I saw Dora ride past me as I was swimming into the rocks, having lost my brand-new Tom Parrish board. It looked like the Daytona 500, with Dora on his machine, way on top of the speed bank, almost going off the roof. He flew. "That's it," I thought as he went past. "That's his great wave. He's gone. We won't see him again for a long, long time." I reckon he knew it.

I'd seen him try it before, but I hadn't seen him *do* it. But this time I knew from looking at him that it would never get better. What made it the Great Wave was the trajectory. It was the projection. It was the high line drive on a disgustingly flawed surfboard. It was the validation that every subtlety in his arsenal completely ruled one of the great waves on earth. It was his past decade of sometimes paddling out, sometimes not; sometimes getting ridiculed in the water; sometimes never being seen when a swell happened. If there was ever proof of genius, this was it.

He rode that big, rambling, blue beast of a board, and it was no pretty thing. I think he built it, a backyard special. It had a lot of belly curve, not unlike an early '60s tanker. It was kind of out of place with anything that people were riding there, or in those days. But after having ridden it for so many years, Miki knew that board better than anything.

Joy depends on what board you ride, and being able to discover new, very minor capacities of a familiar surfboard in a classic wave is as rewarding as getting a five- or six-second barrel. You can surprise yourself with small revelations, and as Dora got older I'm sure that's what pleased him. It was the very little bits of magic that he noticed.

That's why I say that what he did in that year, better than he had done in the five or six years before, was just incredible. Dora had been trying to finish his life discourse on what it meant to ride the perfect wave, and I'm sure that's what happened when he rode past me. Something electrifying went through his mind and body. I'm not being overly romantic. He had reached a point where he knew: no more charades. Imagine being a super-veteran and absolutely dominating like you had not done for many a year. Dora was probably twenty-five years past his athletic prime when he rode that wave—yet he performed as well as he'd ever performed at Malibu. He knew point-blank that he could face off a great wave and beat the bloody thing.

He beached the wave. Disappeared. I never saw him surf seriously again. Having bested the force that ruled his life, there was then the question of, What more?

BOKKA DU TOIT: I met Mick when Bruce Gold brought him around. I knew nothing about surfing. Our connection from day one was the spirit. I recognized him immediately as a great healer. He was connected with nature from A to Z. Everything pure. Everything organic. Everything intended by the Great Design.

I'd been working with a Xhoisun traditional healer, one of the last remaining in this area, for more than five years. He and Mick and I went on journeys because it was important for Mick to find his animal guide—and he did. It was the *dassi*, strangely enough, a giant rat. It eats very selectively, and its urine is used in medicine. Dassi are elephant relatives. Tomkulu, the old bushman, confirmed the dassi was Mick's animal. What's great is that Miki recognized the spirit immediately.

Tomkulu also said over and over that Mick was a healer and he should go for training, and that his not dealing with his healer spirit was part of his chronic physical illness. Miki was quite convinced that he had prostate cancer, although, as I understood, he'd already done clinical tests and found nothing. Still, he took many vitamins and supplements and always worried deeply about his health. The other healers said his physical problems were a message for him. Even Credo Mutwa, the senior healer, widely known in Africa and the world, said that. Credo stayed with me a few times, and he and Miki linked.

Mutwa, a widely published author, is, according to his website, "in many ways a national treasure to South Africa. He is over 80 years old and is known worldwide as the Zulu Shaman. A Zulu Sangoma, traditional healer, expert on African Indigenous Knowledge and high sanusi, he epitomizes the African Oral Tradition with his vast knowledge of African beliefs, history, & mythology."

BRUCE GOLD: Miki asked Credo so many questions about life and death. Miki found him fascinating, and he found Miki fascinating. This guy is old now. He's one of the chosen what they call "sanussis": They're not herbalists anymore; they teach other people to be herbalists and beyond herbalism. They've chosen to learn all the tribal traditions, secrets, and history of the whole nation. He's got an ankh that's seven hundred years old. He's got Chaka Zulu's personal jewelry.

Credo loved Scooter Boy and did a miniature drawing of him that Miki carried around. Miki met him the same year Credo did the movie with Bokka du Toit.
BOKKA DU TOIT: When I told Miki about being a healer, he asked me what

it took and meant. He wanted to know about the serious training: five or six years in order to qualify. I said, "Well, you don't need to do that; just accept and apply your qualities in whatever field you're involved in."

At first, Mick seemed suspicious, but he kept coming back to talk, looking for something to connect with. We went on a couple of journeys and participated in a couple of ceremonies where he linked with the traditional healers. They also immediately recognized him as a superior spirit—and they had no idea who *Miki Dora* was. They called him *mhlekaze,* which means "Great Spirit."

On one journey we visited the cave here where the first anatomically modern people emerged. It was like a homecoming. He also did the Sun Path with me: This is the thirty-fourth-degree south parallel equinox from Port Elizabeth to Cape Town, along the southern tip of the continent, a duo-harmonic balanced line. It's seven hundred kilometers long. We climbed various mountains on the line, which have huge markers, human profiles, in stone, facing north-south or interacting with the east-west sunrise-sunset line. We talked a lot about this place beyond the waves, the source, the home of modern human beings.

Miki had a very negative attitude toward Western society, toward the physical aspects that are emphasized, toward the superrational and analytical side. Kept away from people, he was quite happy and content. What he found in Africa was that connection to source, to being—and to happiness. He saw that people who had nothing would still smile and be happy. He liked that. He really liked that.

Then I asked him: "Who are you? Are you happy? Do you know it?"

That's when I got an answer. "No, not happy. Not happy."

I said, "What makes you happy?" He had no answer, but I got the impression that it had to do with being with someone else who could appreciate the basic things in life.

What I kept trying to get out of Miki was this: What is your mission? What do you have to learn? What are you about? Why are you this body and this character and this shape now? He didn't quite want to give an answer. I said, "I think you have a superior spirit. You've applied it in surfing and people recognize you. But I don't think it's *for* the surfing, I think it's for that energy and that spirit."

After our second trip he wasn't cynical. After the third he became quiet and then, after that, got involved in spirit and feeling and seeing. It was almost like a vision quest.

DEREK HYND: Miki's desire to discover simplicity and goodness in people—as well as intensity and majesty—was the spirit of his search from the moment that his stepfather Gard Chapin disappeared. If you look at Los Angeles life before the end of the Second World War and compare it to after the war, you can see that society's gears had changed. It was not as simple as before. It's what led, say, Bob Cooper away from Malibu and to Australia, because he realized that one day he could no longer just leave his board under the pier and expect to find it when he returned.

BOKKA DU TOIT: I experienced his negativism, also. For a time, he kept wanting to talk about the Billabong "Dora" board shorts lawsuit. I said I wasn't interested. He wanted me to read all this stuff. Not interested. He wanted someone to agree with his point of view—and then get into a deep conversation about how bad these people were. Not interested. They, they, they. Some conspiracy theory. The whole big Western thing. I'd say, "Forget it. Live for the here and now. Your being. You. Forget about the rest. We're not gonna save the world. Look at yourself. Are you happy?"

One thing that would have made him happy was permanent residence. He really wanted that. I tried to help. Then a couple issues emerged so that I had to understand his background and the crimes of his past. He said if not South Africa he wanted to go somewhere in South America. It was about running away. I said, "Why do you keep running?"

I got the reply from Home Affairs: an absolute no. There turned out to be dark things in his background. He abandoned that attempt to stay.

Still, I tried to cut off talk about the past because I was much more interested—and he should have been, also—about where we were going.

2

GARY YOSH: Miki and I always watched sports on TV together. In June 1998, [Note: 6/12/98] South Africa was in a World Cup soccer match against France. During a break, Miki went downstairs to his place to check a meal he said he had cooking and saw smoke coming out of his window. He ran upstairs yelling, "Gary, there's a fire!" I rushed down and saw the flames. Miki ran through his sliding door and started grabbing what little he could from the flat. By this time the surfboards had caught and burned like crazy. The heat was so intense from the blazing fiberglass and foam that the plaster just dripped off the wall. I grabbed the hose pipe and sprayed water through the window. My daughter ran down the road and called people living nearby for help. Everyone began shoveling sand.

ABOVE: Riding Supertubes in Jeffreys Bay, 1996. Miki was sixty-two. Frame grab from *In Search of Da Cat*. Courtesy Ovidio Salazar, director.

LEFT: Cristal and Gary Yosh. Miki lived in their guest apartment for years, then carelessly burned it down. Photo: D. Rensin.

RIGHT: Miki's pullover shirt with custom MSD XXV logo, left behind in Jeffreys Bay. Courtesy Bruce Gold collection and Dora Estate.

CRISTAL YOSH: Miki's sliding door led to the kitchen and he only managed to grab a few things. Afterward he was in such shock that he sat on the ground outside and never helped us put out the fire. He just sat there paralyzed while I screamed, "Come on, you jerk! Come on and help us!" He wouldn't move. He couldn't talk.

GARY YOSH: It took almost thirty minutes to put out the flames. The fire brigade—it was just one truck—came after the fire was under control and blasted it all with water. Miki and I were covered in black smoke. But the worst of it was that Scooter Boy had been sleeping in the flat—and didn't come out. Miki wouldn't go inside. Bruce, Cristal, and I did and found Scooter lying on his side. He was in the corner, under some charred papers. He still had all his hair and wasn't burnt, but the room had filled with smoke so quickly that he'd died of smoke inhalation.

Bruce and Cristal buried Scooter next to our dog, Soda. Scooter and Soda were puppies together, and now they're side by side in the garden, just outside the flat, in front of a tree. We had crosses there for many years but they're gone now.

CHERON KRAAK: When Scooter Boy died, it absolutely shattered Miki. I never saw anyone love a dog the way Miki loved Scooter Boy. It was unbelievable.

CHRISTINE LIEPNER: The day of the fire I was at Cheron's, looking after the kids. Miki came in, wearing baggies, covered with soot. He looked in shock. I said, "What is going on?"

Miki's explanations were all over the place. He told some friends that his home had been firebombed. "They burned it down," they being people in town who didn't want him around. To Mike McNeill in France he later said the landlord had started the fire as an insurance scam. Other stories included an electric frying pan in the kitchen, or a broken heater. But the truth: "June is winter here," said Christine Liepner. "He put the hot plate underneath his bed to warm it for later because he was so cold. He'd borrowed the double adapter from me. Sheeesh. 'What do you need the double adapter for, Miki?' 'I need it when I do my washing. I'll bring it back.' Then he used it to put a hot plate under the bed."

CRISTAL YOSH: For seven years he'd had semiprivacy and semifamily here. Maybe that's what he finally realized when I kicked him out. He cried—and it's the only time I'd ever seen him really cry—and said, "Where am I going to go?" I said, "I'm not your mother and you have to go. You nearly killed my kids, my husband, my dog, everything." I really got angry. After I kicked him out, he stayed with Eddie Godfrey on the buchu farm.

As word leaked about the fire, and Scooter Boy's passing, condolences poured in from friends around the world. Steven Taussig wrote what reflected the overall tone: "What can one say when you lose a son, my deepest sympathy . . . We'll be joining Scooter soon. I know you must be devastated over his loss."

One loss Miki did not seem to be devastated over—or care about anymore—was the lawsuit against Billabong. His Australian solicitor, Andrew Cohen, was eager to pursue the case and felt he could reach a significant monetary settlement. He expected Miki to relocate to Australia for a few months to attend the trial, as the law required. Inexplicably, even before the fire, considering his obsession with justice and recompense, Miki refused. After the fire, he wrote to Cohen:

> *Thank you for your fax:*
> *I was fire BOMBED. My home was destroyed. I've lost everything!!!!*
> *I have moved out of Jeffreys Bay for good.*
> *I don't know what to tell you now?*
> *I must start my life over again . . .*

BOKKA DU TOIT: When I heard about the fire, my thought was that nothing happens without purpose or meaning. There are no victims, only volunteers. I felt he had still not listened to his spirit. Only after the fire did he listen. It had to be dealt with. To get him prepared to go to the next level is perhaps why the thing most precious to him had to be taken: Scooter Boy. Scooter Boy was an extension of his emotions. In fact, I think he was a surrogate. I once asked if Scooter Boy had replaced a woman and he said, "No, no, no, not at all." I'm not sure I believed him. Now he had to restart. His place of safety, his hideaway, was suddenly removed.

DEREK HYND: The end of Scooter Boy spelled the end of his time at Jeffreys Bay, and perhaps the beginning of his own end. Dora would have absolutely stayed if Scooter Boy hadn't died. He was still firmly rooted there because he was in peak form. He'd ridden a wave as well as any wave he could have

LEFT: Miki and Scooter in Jeffreys Bay. Miki even made his "child" his own passport. Photographer unknown. Courtesy of Garth Robinson and the Dora Estate.

ABOVE: Scooter Boy's final destination. His playmate, the Yoshes' puppy, Soda, rests with him. "We had crosses there for many years," says Gary Yosh. Photo: D. Rensin.

BELOW: Bruce Gold and "Scooter Girl" at Cape St. Francis, 2005. Photo: D. Rensin.

ridden twenty years earlier, and at sixty-four years old, he'd made a mark that I believe established him as the greatest exponent for his age, by quite a ways.

LESLIE-ANN GERVAIS: In July 1997, after competing in the World Fencing Championships in South Africa, I made a surf trip to Jeffreys Bay. I was nineteen years old, and a semibeginner surfer. I was a bit of an oddity being the only girl out there at the time. Eventually, this guy started to smile and to acknowledge me. I don't know why, but before I knew it, he had taken me under his wing. Later, surfers at Jeffreys Bay would ask me how I knew Miki. The truth is that I had never heard of Miki because I was new to surfing. He said he took me under his wing because he "admired my perseverance." About a year later, his name came up in a conversation with some surfer friends. I told them my story and they told me who he was. I'd had no idea.

I didn't hang with Miki, but I did see him at dinner once or twice as part of a group, and at a couple of barbecues. I remember all the men sitting around him at the table leaning in and asking questions. I also noticed that there was a little dog lying outside in the yard, so I fed it. Later that evening when everyone parted ways I saw Miki walking off into the darkness with the little dog following close behind.

CHAPTER SEVENTEEN

Man Overboard

1

Gary Yosh boxed the remains of Miki's possessions, and Bruce Gold took them for safekeeping. The contents are an eclectic mix, ranging from a polo shirt with MSD XXV and a black cat embroidered on the left breast, to letters and postcards, household items, books, trinkets, some crudely drawn domination porn depicting men in rape fantasies, an old wetsuit, newsletters, and videos. Meanwhile, Miki went to Eddie Godfrey's farm for a few weeks and battled a flu. One night, Miki visited Cheron Kraak and, briefly, Cristal Yosh. They hugged. The next day he left for France, without saying good-bye to anyone else.

On July 10, 1998, Harry Hodge had faxed Bob Simpson to say Miki would arrive in France in two days, to attend the Biarritz Surf Festival. But this time Miki would remain in France, living at first with various friends, then in a flat of his own, courtesy of Simpson and Hodge.

Although Miki had rescued a few valuables from the Jeffreys Bay inferno, no one was really sure what had survived. Occasionally, though, Miki would trot out old pictures or documents supposedly snatched from the conflagration. They were, as expected, slightly burnt around the edges. But friends began to notice something odd: The burn patterns were too uniform, too perfect.

"When he came back, he made photocopies of pictures from LeRoy Grannis's book," said Mike McNeill. "At my house he went through all my old surf magazines. Then he piled up all his pictures—some xeroxed in multiples, some blown up—took them to a local Quiksilver depot, and burned them around the edges with the kind of propane torch used for crème brûlée.

"Why did he do that? Who knows? When I saw him do it, I laughed. He said, 'Don't ask. Don't ask.' It was all part of that mysterious impulse inside that had always been stronger than him."

"After South Africa he was sadder," says Susan McNeill. "Lost. Scooter Boy was only part of it. Something had changed him. But it wasn't all darkness. Maybe it was wisdom."

BOB SIMPSON: It *wasn't* all sadness. I heard Miki tell this story to a girl. "One day I was surfing at Jeffreys Bay. It was the most beautiful, perfect, five-hundred-yard wave. Huge overhead surf. Great tube. Many sections. It just went on and on and on. Finally, the wave petered out right on the sand and I fell, exhausted. Then I looked over, and what did I see lying next to my hand? This incredible shell."

He took a shell ring off his finger and said, "It's brought me luck. Maybe it'll bring you luck, too. It's my gift." The girl was amazed. He seemed to feel quite positive.

Then, one morning over breakfast at the Hotel Madrid, Miki said, "Look in here." He opened a box and I saw about forty of these shells. I said, "Why don't you give one of these to Sophie," my then-wife. Sophie came over a few minutes later, but instead of just giving it to her, he went through the entire story again. Later, Sophie said, "That's really nice of him. I never really thought he was that nice before."

PHILIPPE LAUGA: Miki had been angry at me for talking to the makers of *In Search of Da Cat,* but now he decided he could let bygones be bygones. We played golf at the Arcangues course, where he was a member. We resumed our betting habits: five francs a putt. Miki's short game was strong. He could accurately read the green like he could read the face of a wave. We also bet for the check when playing backgammon at the Patisserie Miremont in Biarritz, overlooking the surf. They served delicious chocolate. Once we played for a meal at Susan McNeill's restaurant, the Surf Hut. He lost, and when he opened his wallet to pay, Susan made fun of him, mimicking the opening of the wallet with the sound of rusted door hinges and of flying moths. Miki didn't think it so funny.

Miki rented a small flat in Guéthary from Bob Simpson overlooking the surf. But the location had its drawbacks. Below was a plaza where cars parked for a popular bar/restaurant. The later the hour, the louder the talk and music. In the summer musicians trained at bongo drums. Miki didn't share their love for this music and he decided to act. Under cover of night he targeted the punks with eggs and spoiled tomatoes and his slingshot. After a short while the lot was littered and started to resemble one of Joe Frazier's opponents.

With no lawsuits to pursue, no book or movie offers pending, Scooter Boy gone, and Miki nearly sixty-five years old, he became an eccentric pensioner-rogue in Guéthary. He kept up his far-flung correspondence, now adding e-mail (his now defunct address: sinkorswim@iname.com; passwords: y2kbug or SOS). He managed some investments and a small account at Banque Nationale de Paris, where Philippe Lauga worked, and lived on the kindness of friends, his small residual checks, and whatever else his father contributed.

MIKLOS DORA SR.: I sent him money for Christmas and birthday presents. I used to give him gold coins, the American Eagle. When I was in my eighties, somebody in France owed me money, around $20,000. I was an old man already so I thought I'd give it to Miki. I told my friend, "You owe Miklos K. Dora $20,000. Why don't you send it to Miklos *S.* Dora." To Miki I said, "I have some money for you now. You don't have to wait until I kick the bucket."

He wrote to me: "Thank you for your letter and the checks. I hope I understand your letter correctly. It sounds like you want to bequest some monies. That's very generous. I am hardly worthy or deserving. I am flabbergasted."

Then, for some reason, the money wasn't available as fast as I thought it would be, so Miki wrote me another letter asking, "Am I getting that money or are you just kidding me?"

HARRY HODGE: Think about it: Given his commitment in life to never settle down, to never have attachments, to live as he chose, how could Miki make money in his later years? He could get $10,000 for a magazine article, but how many could he do a year? He could appear in a surf movie, but again a limited venue. And that's about it. He didn't really want to sell off his best asset—himself—but at times he had to just to make ends meet. He had friends in the Bordeaux wine industry, the tennis community, in Hollywood, in surf industry circles, and he could benefit from the perks, but if he was going to live as long as his father, who is still with us, he had to have the money.

People have said, "If he had only put his brain to productive things. . . ."

Yeah, but then he would never have been Miki Dora as we know him. It's like *Butch Cassidy and the Sundance Kid*: No one did a story about the guy who ran the banks in the towns they robbed.

So . . . when Miki came back from Jeffreys Bay, we created a job for him at Quiksilver. Bob Simpson is probably the one who came up with the idea, and I proposed that Miki become an ambassador at large for our European operation. It wasn't just a charity handout. Miki already liked coming to our functions and contests, so I figured we should make it worth his while. Everyone supported the idea; no one said, "He's going to rip you off and not show up."

When Miki and I talked around the edges of this idea, he asked me, "What do you want me to do?" I said, "Just keep doing what you're doing. Play golf with Kelly Slater. Do face time with people. You spread the good word of the industry and the lifestyle, and come to the surf contests if you want to. Wear our product if you want."

He asked, "Do I have to do interviews and photographs?"

I told him no. We didn't want an old guy telling stories about how it used to be in the *good old days*. That's tragic. The idea was remember the good ol' days, but go into the future. That's what keeps us all young. I wanted to make sure Miki kept his dignity. The last thing we wanted was to have Miki standing there like Joe Louis at Caesar's Palace, posing for photos with every grandmother who came in. I believed the sponsorship deal would take a lot of pressure off Miki. He'd have his dignity, and he wouldn't have to be the antagonist to get by.

In a draft proposal from Harry Hodge to Miki, dated October 6, 1998, Quiksilver agreed to provide Miki with the following (exchange rate at the time was around 5FF per dollar): A base salary of 2,500FF a month. Accommodation valued at 2,000FF a month for Bob Simpson's apartment, paid directly to Simpson. A full membership in the Guéthary Tennis Club, for two people. Access to golf courses in the region. 10,000FF toward a car, including first year of registration and insurance, to be property of M. Dora. A clothing allowance of 10,000FF a year, including wetsuits.

In return, Miki would act as goodwill ambassador for the company; at certain times entertain Quiksilver guests for golf or tennis; attend company functions or trade shows; attend Christophe Reinhardt's surf camp.

An attached revision sheet raised the monthly fee to 4,500FF and noted that while the company would search for a suitable accommodation, the apartment would (now) be at Miki's expense. Quiksilver also agreed to have Miki's new place "painted and carpeted," and expanded his tennis club membership to include an indoor facility in St.-Jean-de-Luz. Miki was also granted a cash advance of no more than 500FF per month for expenses, supported by receipts.

The following year, Miki got a raise to 5,500FF a month, and a round-trip airfare from Biarritz to the United States.

"We also included—though I never told him—a fudge package," says Harry Hodge, "so if he went over a couple hundred bucks a month on expenses, that was fine. We always had more in the budget than we told him he could have."

Bob Simpson says he always had "mixed feelings about the Quiksilver situation. I think Miki did, too. It was a blessing and a purgatory."

Miki's friend Yves Bessas found the whole situation insulting. "For $1,000 a month it was not the value of Miki. It was $20,000 a month for a guy like that."

"I'm sure Miki told people he was forced to do certain things," says Hodge, "because it got him off the hook. Yet I really think he was proud he 'had a job.' But we never used him in one ad, magazine, or brochure. Miki Dora did not sell one bit of clothing for Quiksilver. We did get value out of our association, but not by directly attaching him to our brand. Miki attached himself to us."

JOHN VAN HAMERSVELD: We're in a symbolic society now. Miki was part of a folk culture. But he transcended folk culture and became symbolic—and in a postmodern media world nothing has any more value than a symbology. Today, embryonic folk cultures are not allowed, in the sense that as soon as anything makes itself known, it becomes instantly symbolic. It doesn't have the time to be folk culture.

Dora was anticulture, and that's what most kids coming up through the process are. They can't get accepted in high school so they become part of a gang, and then the gang leads them into skating or surfing and they become a hero at the corner drugstore, and then they get a company's endorsement. If Quiksilver, through its association with Miki, however tangential, could be seen to sell anticulture as symbolic culture, that was the value; that was success.

2

In late 1998, still in an introspective and reevaluative mood, Miki and Mike McNeill traveled to see Greg Noll in Crescent City, California.

MIKE MCNEILL: Driving north from Los Angeles, he went in and out of funks and depressions. He kept looking back on his life, trying to figure out what he could do to make it better and wondering what he'd really accomplished. He never said, "Was it worth it?" but he did ask, "Is it going to make any difference?" He worried that his life wouldn't matter even in his own little surfing world. He said he'd tried to set an example, but he now thought it would have no impact, that surfing had irrevocably gone over the top. Miki wanted to be—not accepted—but just not seen as the bad guy. Of course, he never considered himself a "bad" guy. Only if he knew *you* considered him a bad guy was he a bad guy. He would see your weakness and he would go for the throat.

GREG NOLL: Like most of us, Miki was nonfunctional with everyday shit. Mike took care of everything. We took them fishing. Seeing Miki Dora reel in a fish knocked me out. Laura and I also took him shooting up at the gravel pit. He was very apprehensive, like it was some kind of plot to do him in and I was going to bury him up in the hills.

I sensed a change in him. I live in a pretty neat little spot in the redwoods and I took him hiking. At one point Miki said to Mike, "How about a picture?" I just about fell over. "What do you mean 'a picture'? Are you getting soft in your old age?" He did not allow pictures of any goddamn kind. But he said, "Let's do it" and put his goddamn arm around me. He said, "Well, after all, you are my oldest friend." I thought it was a put-on at the time. Afterward I gave him a bunch of shit. I said, "You're really turning into a pussy in your old age. Getting sentimental."

He said, in all seriousness, "Well, we've known each other a long time."

Makes me want to cry when I think back on it. I knew right then . . . something . . . was up. There were a few cracks in the pillars and maybe he was starting to mellow a little bit. The shield was dropping. In retrospect, maybe he was worried about his health, because otherwise I don't think he'd have made such a point about coming to visit at my house. I said, "Okay, if you promise not to steal the silverware." He promised.

That night we took him to a Mexican restaurant in Brookings, a little town up the road. He had a goatee and looked Mexican himself. During dinner I went into the kitchen and paid these guys to come out and sing "Happy Birthday"—even though it wasn't Dora's birthday. Two guys with guitars came out and got right in his face and sang. His mouth dropped open and he looked goofier than shit, like "What's this all about?"

The minute the song was over, another little Mexican popped up with a Polaroid and goes click! I could see Miki starting to reach for the picture, so I snatched it. He said, "Man, if you ever use this thing, I'll kill ya."

If the word *friendship* is the right one to use, then that's when Miki and I really—finally—became friends. This is important to me, and I'm not trying to make a big deal out of it, because if Miki could hear me, he'd be upset. I don't want him reaching out from beyond and squeezing my balls for anything. But I would say that he dropped a whole bunch of defenses and let me get a little closer.

LAURA NOLL: For years the two of them had gone at each other, circling like two dogs, always putting each other on. They'd bicker and the sarcasm would fly, then they'd settle down. You'd think, "O-kay!" and then they'd laugh. They reminded Mike and me of Ralph and Alice Kramden.

At one point we got out our notebook of ads for the original Da Cat boards. Greg showed them to Miki while Miki looked over his shoulder. They read the copy out loud. Miki would say, "Ah, I never said that," and then he'd chuckle to himself and peek at the ads again.

When Mike and Miki finally got ready to leave, Greg said, "Can I check your bags?" He couldn't help himself.

3

Miki was not only concerned about his personal impact on the surfing world, he was, as Noll suspected, also troubled about his health. According to his father, Miki needed a prostate operation—but declined an offer of help. Instead, he consulted a variety of friends and health professionals, scoured the Internet, and sought any vitamins, supplements, and therapies that would increase his vigor and prolong his youth. Some say he even took human growth hormone.

And, of course, the restlessness that had long ago metastasized in his psyche still obsessed him. "Let's get to Chile before Y2K blows us off the planet!" he wrote to Steven Taussig. "We've got 12 months to set up a new life."

"Miklos, enough of Y2K," Taussig responded. "Chile sounds great if you have contacts as I suspect you do. You must have some 'Nazi friends' still alive down there? Just kidding."

Then, new hope and a familiar focus: Michael McDonnell, a young film producer whose first feature was the well-received and Oscar-rewarded *The Usual Suspects*, got word to Miki that he wanted to make a movie of his life.

"I wanted to do a movie called *Da Cat* and I wanted it to be like *Cool Hand Luke*. I didn't see any other type of biography that made any sense. In this case it would be a Luke-ish antihero. I wanted Miki's blessing. Everyone I spoke to warned me that it would never happen. Through Sam George and the Pezmans, I finally got to Greg Noll, who called Miki, who okayed my getting his fax number. I sent him a note, mentioned *Cool Hand Luke*, Greg Noll, *The Usual Suspects*, and my phone number."

Miki wrote back the next day.

"Greetings from Côte Basque, Guéthary . . . It has come to my attention while in California that there are a couple of unauthorized scripts floating around L.A. trying to get produced. However, there is a writer by the name of Cynthia Applewhite, who claims to have my best interest at heart and seems to like me. A suggestion: perhaps you should contact her . . . I know nothing. I'm completely detached in these matters. If anything is or can be accomplished and you're still interested please fax me back and we can carry on. . . . Thank you for your interest."

McDonnell sent Miki a list of questions about his story rights, wishes, and needs, and asked for information and his opinion of various people, including Greg Noll, Cynthia Applewhite, David Rensin, John Milius, and Bob Simpson. Miki fired off a three-page fax alternately praising and punishing those mentioned, and he also outlined his grand vision for a cinematic portrayal. "This Cinematic Conception must be a rapidly Changing, Beat the Devil life adventure; interjected with Historical implications. The scenes must be logical and realistic! An elaborate plot with a many-sided shrewd and clever-meaningful dialogue; Thus generating the viewers interest to the Boiling Point—at every turn as the plot unravels—Consecrating into a dynamic-climactic conclusion!! If any of the above has intelligent understanding—acceptance—then Lets get started."

Miki also included a plug for his own dependability: "I have friends all over the world who've known me for many many years. If you have questionable suspicious doubts of my trustworthiness, I've got back-ups. Sometimes the confused morons get 'grudgingly jealous' of my lifestyle when they can't figure out 'how I do it???'"

Meanwhile, according to Susan McNeill, as per his new "job," Miki was supposed to stick around Guéthary and be Quiksilver's "Welcome Wagon." Instead, he took a hiatus at a surf camp in Oualidia, Morocco, owned by Laurent Miramon. He was supposed to stay two weeks but languished three months instead, surfing, battling a bronchial infection, befriending Miramon, telling tales of travel and love, and worrying—according to Miramon—that strangers who showed up at the camp were really FBI agents.

"When Miki finally went back to Biarritz, Harry wasn't so happy that he'd stayed so long in Morocco," says Laurent Miramon. "So Miki told Harry that I gave him poison and tried to keep him in the camp because it was good promotion for the camp. It was funny."

He also waited to hear from McDonnell. When he didn't, he got anxious that the producer had suddenly lost interest. He wrote to Cynthia Applewhite, asking her to meet with McDonnell and find out what had happened because his "trip was in shambles," and he had to "plan his life accordingly."

Before Applewhite could set up a meeting, McDonnell wrote Miki, telling him he'd recently played tennis with Johnny Fain, who'd had a hip replacement. "He wants me to do *his* movie," he reported, "but I'm not going to pursue it."

Relieved, Miki replied, "I'm sorry to hear of Johnny's physical problems. I have not had a word from him in 30 years . . . ! He was always a bit confused on the facts of life—along with the rest of his generations. . . . The '60s were audacious times, too bad no one learned anything!"

After Applewhite met with McDonnell, she reported back enthusiastically and advised Miki to rent *Cool Hand Luke*. "When a deal comes about, our agency, CAA, best in Hollywood, will act for you and get you the most money. So just enjoy life and let the wheels move. If it's meant to be, it'll be. Could happen fast, could take forever, could (sigh) all fall apart. We trust not, but we're all in the hands of Destiny."

She also said she'd urged McDonnell to fly Miki to California and put him in a good hotel. Maybe even rent him a car. She included in her letter a page of real estate ads from the *Los Angeles Times*, showing what Miki could buy for $350,000 "if this all works out!" She also urged him to meet with David Rensin—unbeknownst to Rensin—with whom she'd remained friends, and do a book, saying Miki could probably pocket at least $50,000 as his half of an advance.

Miki replied that his earlier anxiety might have been an "overreaction," but he'd become a "wee bit jittery particularly when the guy plays tennis with Johnny Fain."

MICHAEL MCDONNELL: I brought him over in April 1999. I'd only seen Miki in pictures. When I spotted him at the international terminal, he was smaller, older, and grayer than I had imagined, wearing a cravat of some kind, looking pretty dignified in a sports jacket. He was a little ratty but kind of cool.

On the way to my house he told me it had been a very long time since he'd been to Malibu. As we drove up Pacific Coast Highway he pointed out what had changed. Knowing Miki's history with Malibu I was really interested to watch his body language when we went past. Finally, we reached the Malibu pier. I stole a glance to my right to see his face, but Miki just sat there, looking straight ahead. He never looked at the beach or the waves for a second. That was strong.

Later, we talked about Malibu, the crowds, and "localism." He bristled and snapped, "I invented localism." It was a cool quote.

He brought some residual checks with him and wanted me to cash them, so he signed them to me and I gave him a few dollars. When I tried to deposit them, the bank wouldn't take third-party checks. Miklos Dora, Post Restante, Jeffreys Bay, $43, from Sony Pictures. Another for $24 at an address in Costa Mesa, in care of R. Bertram [Miki's mother]. I figured I'd just keep them. Miki Dora's signature, made out to me, on a check from *Gidget Goes Hollywood* or something. I also feel in some way honored that I have sort of bounced Miki Dora checks.

We hung out and talked. I arranged a doubles tennis game with friends. I wanted to do it with Johnny Fain but neither he nor Miki were really that interested. Miki was crafty on the courts. He fought hard. We played nine holes of golf at the Malibu Country Club. We walked on the beach. We had dinner at a little Japanese noodle house, just him and me and my wife. We drank some beers and he got loose and described to both of us the majesty of a six-week swell at Jeffreys Bay. That's the only time I ever felt his passion. He loved waves, not people.

When, finally, Miki and McDonnell talked about the project, Miki turned on a cassette recorder, as was his occasional habit, to preserve the conversation for subsequent redigestion. McDonnell began by saying that however eager he was to do a movie, he was skeptical about finding a story they could agree to tell. Reverse psychology, perhaps, but also true. Miki, however, was ready with his own truths that he'd spent a lifetime refining.

MCDONNELL: Two movies sounded to me like your story—without ever having had the benefit of meeting you or hearing the real story. One was *Cool Hand Luke*, the other was *One Flew Over the Cuckoo's Nest*. Both are stories of a particularly free man incarcerated in a system. In each case, the system is personified by one person. In the case of *Cool Hand Luke*, it's the prison warden . . . In *Cuckoo's Nest*, it's Nurse Ratchet.

MIKI: Unfortunately, both these films wound up in tragedy.

MCDONNELL: Exactly.

MIKI: My life is not tragedy. My life is for living, and going forward, and surviving all this.

MCDONNELL: And that's a significant difference between you and the two movies—

MIKI: And that's the way it's gonna go. . . . In *Cuckoo's Nest*, Nicholson had the chance to get out. Three or four chances—and he kept going back. . . . They deserved everything they got, both of those guys.

MCDONNELL: But both movies celebrate the indomitability of the human spirit. That's why they're commercial movies.

MIKI: That's the death wish of the society, to analyze these films differently. It's a real psychological problem of this country. That you can condition people to look at the worst side of life, the tragic side of life, and think it's something positive, uplifting. It's also done in Shakespeare. Very depressing. Very suicidal. That's why I can't read Shakespeare. I like to go to the stratosphere. I admire somebody who survives it, and comes out ahead, and lives a fantastic, incredible life, despite adversity. That's somebody to admire. He gets through it all, unscathed, with his mind and body intact and does what he wants to do in life. To survive for beauty, and for great excitement, and to have a fulfilled life. That's the person I admire. Not the one who gets his head beaten to hell, and crushed by a system.

MCDONNELL: I agree. But answer me this: Why is it that the more compelling story of the two is the guy who ends up martyred?

MIKI: I'm not a sacrificial lamb for the public. . . . Every love story winds up with someone dying from cancer. [exasperated] Is this the great love story—that they fall in love and have this beautiful thing and one of them dies?

MCDONNELL: It's *Romeo and Juliet* and it's *Love Story*.

MIKI: Life doesn't have to be that way. It can still be packed with adventure and excitement, and go on into the stratosphere. Go on to happiness, not tragedy, and death. . . .

MCDONNELL: But we're not talking about life, we're talking about fiction, in those cases.

MIKI: If you want to have the same goddamn story repeated and re-hashed for generations, for new waves of morons to go look at these films, and identify, in their shallow lives, well fine, I'm not going to be part of this, these tragic heroes. I'm my own hero. I survived it all with dignity, with class, and it all caved in behind me. Everyone's still in prison, I'm a free man. The prison guards are still there, all these crazies are still there. And I'm free. I only spent a year, a couple years. . . . And these people are still back there, rotting their guts out. Since then I've been around the world three times. I don't dwell on this. I have great things in my life, just like I did in the '50s and '60s. My life is convenient. Other people's lives stay in stalemate. Nothing changes. They go to work when it's early, leave when it's late, take orders from the boss. They're twentieth-century slaves.

That's what they identify with: with their death wish in society, and their life, which is dead. Someone like this guy Luke, who dies in the end.

MCDONNELL: Nonetheless, Luke and McMurphy lived on as heroes.

MIKI: Well, if you think people on chain gangs and in the asylums are heroes—most of them are very sick people. Very confused: they wouldn't be in there if they weren't. Unless they were political prisoners, and there's plenty of them. I don't identify with *Dumb and Dumber* or *Forrest Gump*. Making heroes out of half-wits . . . I just don't want to come down to that level of society, do a film for them: the ones who sit by their televisions, drink their beer, their guts fat, vicariously living someone else's life, in a destructive way. I want a positive way.

MCDONNELL: But that's the audience.

MIKI: Well, I don't care about the audience. I want to redeem myself.

Revenge, against them. And the government. And the system. And everyone. That would be my purpose.

MCDONNELL: Mm-hhm. Well, there's a difference between redemption and revenge. Would redemption be your revenge? For you to say revenge implies some sort of malice.

MIKI: Well, I don't say revenge in a derogatory or devious way. Revenge to feel in myself that I did everything right. Redemption: to prove that I survived and they didn't. And that everything that I predicted came true, years ahead of everybody else. And I made it; I made it without being part of the system. Without mortgaging my family, my future, without being on welfare, without having pensions or social security. I traveled around the world without any U.S. dollars in my pocket, without being a drug dealer.

It's a very difficult thing to do. You have to have a brain to put this type of life together. And you don't need all the trappings of the American system to have a happy, successful, simple life, to ride the best waves in the world. And having the enjoyment. The Polynesians did it. The American Indians did it. It might seem corny, but they didn't live with all these social entrapments.

MCDONNELL: Well, they did and they didn't. I mean, they every once in a while would sort of get whimsical and say, "Let's have a war," and then bash each other's brains in.

MIKI: But they didn't have food stamps. They didn't have welfare. That's what I'm talking about. They did things on their own, whether they were warlike or not. They made and created their own lives. Self-sufficient, the way I am.

MCDONNELL: But where's the drama in that?

MIKI: I'm not here to sell myself. I'm here to discuss it, and the way I want to see it. I'd like to portray all these adventures I went through, high drama, which I don't want to discuss at this time. How about a character who didn't depend on overcompromise, the idea that we have to join in, join up, at a certain age, sell out? We can have these great lives without being part of this sellout system where our lives become meaningless.

Someone who sees this film, some poor confused youth who says, "My God, there's no future for me. I've got to pay all these taxes, inflation is eating half my salary and the government takes the other half. What is my future?" And here's someone who twenty years ago saw this whole thing coming, and he did it. And he survived it all, without getting waylaid or murdered, with everyone self-destructing behind him. They all collided, went down the tubes.

That would be the inspiration: You don't have to be part of all this. That's the American spirit, how this country was built. These people did everything on their own, and joined together, and made this a great country. There's a need to have something where there's hope for us. There's no hope where the government owns everything, controls every part of our lives. We work for the government six to eight months out of the year for nothing. With inflation, ten and a half. And we give everything away overseas. We import everything, we don't export anything. We have no more industry. We were supposed to be the exporter of the world. Things have changed. I feel sorry for youth today. They have very little hope. . . . I'm not trying to sell anything. My life is going to go on without this picture. I don't need this picture.

MCDONNELL: Look, we're simply trying to see if there is a middle ground between our conceptions of a possible film—though I am skeptical.

MIKI: Okay. I can accept the prison part of it, and these two scenarios you were discussing, but instead of having the violent ending, the way I got through it all was not putting my head against the unbeatable locomotive that's going to squash you, which is the authoritarian control, but to manipulate that monster. To use, like martial arts, the energy of the other person against themselves. This is the way I survived, and this is the interesting part of the story. When the violence came to me, I turned the violence against them. The tricks of the trade. The ways of survival. Very humorous, the dialogue. Everything working against me, and in a different direction, to my eventual release. And this is the information I'm going to give you. It could be very amusing. It could be educational. The whole thing would be a high adventure if you wanted that type of thing. But it's not going to be the same old story of me getting the shit beaten out of me. Which didn't happen. I used my brain to outsmart the criminals in that system—and their guards. Everyone.

MICHAEL MCDONNELL: Miki's vision of the film was based on *King Rat,* a book by James Clavell. It was meant to star Steve McQueen but it ended up starring George Segal as an American soldier in a tropical Japanese prison camp at the end of World War II, who had managed to elevate himself and survive the prison camp because of a natural capacity to work the system within the system. He was a corporal, but colonels did his bidding. He had lots of money. He was a fixer. But in the end, he went back to being a plain old corporal who rejected the one real friend he'd made—an English lieutenant, I think—and faded into obscurity. He knew the ride was finished. Miki said *King Rat* was one of his favorite books. I thought it was strange that Miki would consider a movie in which the main character is generally incarcerated, because when you talked to him about prison he would reveal next to nothing about what it was like.

Afterward we had dinner with Allan Carter in Malibu. I said, "Clearly it's not gonna work between us, Miki, and that's okay. Let's not even try. Let's just have a good time here. It's been great. We've both been completely honorable about everything we said we were gonna do. Let's let it go."

The break wasn't acrimonious but he didn't want me to drive him to the airport when he left. I called a cab. We said good-bye as the cab pulled up. He planned to head to Hawaii to stay with a friend. Just then my son Cooper, who was then four and a beautiful, white-blond, little Malibu surfer-rat boy, open and loving, came running out. He wanted to say good-bye. "Miki! Miki!" Miki stopped and Cooper jumped into his arms. Cooper threw his arms around Miki's neck and gave him a hug, and said, "I love you. Good-bye." Miki didn't know how to hold him, how to touch him. It was one of the most awkward things I'd ever seen. A grown man and this beautiful little boy giving him love, and Miki had no clue about how to accept it or what to do.

That gave me a really clear vision into who Miki was, his loneliness and separateness, a path he had chosen and committed to. Toward the end of his life, perhaps, he had begun to wonder whether it was the right path. But it was way too late to change anything about it.

A series of letters from Miki to Bob Simpson, Cynthia Applewhite, and others followed, in which Miki claimed he'd blown off the deal. "Being a croaking frog constricted in the digestive juices of the Hollywood slithering snake is not my vision of an acceptable end." He was mostly respectful of McDonnell, with occasional exceptions. As he wrote to Steve Taussig: "I advised Michael McDonnell what he's looking for is a Mary Shelly rip off version starring Johnny Fain and Don Wilson in a chest pounding epic. The M.X. blew itself off the launching pad two minutes into our drive to Malibu from L.A.X. Dangling a home in

Chile and a hundred thousand $$ option is tempting. Delusions versus illusions = seductive SIRENS. Cat-shit at Columbine High School, and football assholes . . . is more like it!!!"

To Applewhite, Miki characterized his meetings in a way that McDonnell would have appreciated, because whatever one might say about Miki's intentions going into the possible deal, clearly he'd been listening closely.

Dear Cynthia,
   . . . Michael McDonnell is a very nice fellow. But there was "a failure to communicate!"
   (There's no motion picture here.)

CHAPTER EIGHTEEN

All for a Few Empty Waves

1

9.11.97 [Letter to Ramona]
 I wish I could repay your love for me when I was a child, when it was so important. I'm an old man now, but that love made me strong to face life. Even though I'm not rich I've made a great life for myself and I owe it all to you. I wish I could start all over, and do it together just you and me. All my love, Miki PS: You could have left me in Budapest. Thank God you brought me back to the US. I'm so lucky.

On August 11, 1999, Harry Hodge invited Miki's friends to the Surf Hut in Guéthary for Miki's sixty-fifth birthday. A huge buffet was served in his honor. Philippe Lauga gave him a book on wine and an old English engraving about golfing. "In the book I wrote: 'Miki is like wine, the older he gets the better he is.'"

Miki's mother, Ramona, however, was moving in the opposite direction. Juanita Kuhn, who'd just visited her sister in California, wrote to Miki that Ramona was ill and living at the Altavista Health Care Center in Riverside. She urged him to get to know his family in the United States and advised him that his unhappiness with California should not stop him from forging family bonds. Juanita also said she understood that Miki didn't want to visit his mother, and that in her condition it might not be more than a "momentary boost to her. Her life has turned out so sad, but I am afraid [it] was mostly her own making."

"Miki said his mother no longer knew who he was," recalls Trudi Forster, "and that the kindest thing to do would be to stick her in a barrel with a straw, so she could just sit there and drink. That was cruel, but he was disgusted. Disappointed. He felt sorry for her."

Juanita's letter also suggested it was a good idea for Miki to give his father power of attorney to settle his affairs if needed. "I assure you there will never be a person who has your interests at heart more than he does."

Miki ignored that advice and wrote to his father that he hoped to relocate to Chile: "Old age is a capricious battle. It's very hard to keep it all going. It's always an inspiration talking with you. It gives me strength that I know I come from good stock. If I live past the eclipse on the 11th I think I can make it to California in November on my way to Chile. Take it easy and good care of yourself. Get well soon, I don't know how you do it! Love, M."

On November 17, 1999, Miki flew from France to Los Angeles, where he visited friends and family before continuing on to Hawaii and, for the New Year, to Fiji, to join an all-expense-paid millennium celebration sponsored by Quiksilver.

He also had some business to settle. Having turned sixty-five, he decided—what the hell—to register with Social Security for retirement benefits. After a brief back-and-forth dispute about not filing the proper forms for someone living outside the country, and with help from his father and Cynthia Applewhite, he got them.

While Miki was in Los Angeles, Ramona took a turn for the worse.

GARDNER CHAPIN JR.: When my mother got sick, I moved her into a private group home in Orange, where a Vietnamese lady took care of her. Then she moved to a Filipino lady's home. Then to my home. She lived in the front bedroom and was fine for a year and a half.

Mother didn't walk very well and one day, going across the living room, she fell and broke her leg. Her foot actually turned around and was facing another way. I almost had a heart attack. I called an ambulance.

The emergency room doctor gave me the facts: She had pretty advanced cancer. I put her in a hospice and visited every day. I also told Miki to come back, that she was going fast. I wanted him there because my mother loved him a lot, a lot more than she loved me. He was the apple of her eye—but I didn't mind too much. Miki said that he didn't want to come because he wanted to remember her the way she was. I thought that was very selfish, but again, I didn't say anything. Aunt Juanita didn't come out, either.

Mother died on December 5, 1999. She was eighty-three. After that, Miki was here in two or three days. Turned out he was already in town. He wanted to get some rolls of film that I'd been keeping for him up at my ex-wife's house. There was an inheritance, too, plus some family heirlooms. There were two rings. Mine was appraised at $6,000; his was just as nice. There were some old English goblets, maybe 150 years old and quite valuable. I gave him everything that my mother wanted him to have.

When Ramona died, she left a family trust in her name worth $69,803.64 at Citibank, with instructions to divide it equally between Miki and Gardner. Coincidentally, the day Ramona died, Miki had himself gone to Riverside Community Hospital complaining again about his prostate. He got treatment, and a bill arrived two weeks later. He didn't pay it.

PHIL JARRATT: In December 1999, my wife, youngest daughter, and I were invited to celebrate the millennium with the Quiksilver hierarchy in Fiji, the first place past the international date line. Harry Hodge booked out Namotu resort while Bob McKnight, the head of the company, took over Tavarua.

HARRY HODGE: Miki also came, and he couldn't believe we had fifty people on the island, ten of us surfing at four or five world-class surf spots. He said, "This is how it should be done."

PHIL JARRATT: Miki cruised around the island like a beachcomber that week, collecting shells, playing table tennis with the Fijian staff, occasionally even surfing—when no one was looking. He happily posed with us in group photographs—once an absolute no-go. He was a delight: wisecracking, laughing, talkative, actually interested in the other person's viewpoint.

HARRY HODGE: On the other hand, he told everyone the world was going to end. "We're lucky we're in Fiji, because we won't even hear it. We'll be the last to know. We're all going to go out." Well . . . why spoil a good story with the truth?

Fiji was the first place on the planet to ring in the new year. Then we watched New Year happen all around the world on television. The celebrations began in Sydney. We ate lunch as the ball dropped in Times Square. Miki kept saying, "Something's gonna happen, something's gonna happen. It's the Big Apple." He expected computers blowing up and rioting in the streets, cops and militia gunning them down like dogs. Chile, he said, might be the only safe place to be. The ball started to descend and suddenly the TV went blank and buzzed. Miki suddenly shrieked: "The bomb went off . . ." Five minutes later, the TV came back and Times Square was covered in confetti. Miki said, "Hey, this wasn't in my script."

And indeed, even though the world didn't end—and he seemed perhaps a bit disappointed—when the party ended, Miki returned to Hawaii and soon lit out for Chile and a potential new life. "Once again," says Harry Hodge, "Miki thought he'd find the Holy Grail."

CHRIS MALLOY: I was at my house, near Pipeline, on the North Shore of Oahu, preparing for a trip to Antarctica. Then I get a call from out of the blue. It's this old guy who clears his throat and goes, "Is this Chris?"

"Yeah."

"I heard you're going south."

"Yeah, actually I am. I'm loading bags right now."

"I'm going south, too, and I could use a little help. I'm getting older and I've got a lot of gear. My goddamn house burned down and I could use a little bit of help."

"Well, who is this?" I heard the guy sigh deeply. "Where are you going?"

"I'm going to Chile."

"Well, uh, I'm actually going to Antarctica."

"Well, that's not where I'm going!"

"I'm sorry. By the way, who is this?"

"My name is Mick, but it seems like we're not going to the same place," and he hung up.

Afterward, it instantly clicked. I went, That was fuckin' Miki Dora. Holy shit. I'd always heard there was good surf in Chile. I pressed *69 and he picked up. I said, "Hey, I'm going to Chile, too. Let's go!"

I met him at a bookstore in Honolulu. I expected to see some old, bloated, bummed-out guy, but he was super-regal. Hair all long and swept back, perfect. The mustache trimmed, perfect. He had a blue-blood air and a thrift store jacket with different colored, resewn buttons. He talked surf stories and history.

I didn't have to pry. We decided to fly to Santiago because he said he knew people and exactly where to go.

Not long after, Miki and I met at LAX. He had an exorbitant amount of gear: suitcases, plastic bags full of vitamins. He even brought a blender. He looked at the pile and said, "I can't do this all by myself." He moaned and groaned a lot about his bones and about getting old. I sensed something nagged at him, but it wasn't just old age. He kept saying how they'd burned down his house and Scooter Boy got killed. Just kind of rambling under his breath. He seemed almost embarrassed, like "Here I am, at this age. . . ."

On the plane he wore a face mask so he didn't get sick. If someone sneezed ten rows away he'd come unglued and get super-agitated. "Is this a goddamn infirmary?!"

Finally, nonchalantly, I asked, "Mick, why Chile?"

"There's this one-eyed sonofabitch who told me there's good waves down here, and he's usually right." He meant Derek Hynd but never said his name. I didn't let on that I knew. I figured if he knew I was a pro surfer he'd probably come unglued. To him I was just a kid recommended by a friend, going south. I was muscle. I brought my boards and all my gear. Of course, when he saw my boards he did a double take, but I made a point not to say anything.

We talked some during the flight, but mostly he slept. We got into some pretty heavy turbulence, and he held on to the little shell necklace he had from J Bay, and rubbed the hell out of it. Later, as we were eating—I think he just pushed his food around—I said, "Hey, what is that?" He said, "I picked it up on the beach the day I got the best wave of my life." I was like, "Where?!" He said J Bay and went on to describe this giant wave. He described it as a "goddamn tornado on its side," coming straight for him, to kill him, and he got it. It was on his sixty-third birthday. He said he rode it all the way through because he had tried to get out of the barrel but the wave wouldn't let him until the very end. Coming back up the beach, he picked up these shells.

In Santiago I hunkered all of his gear and said, "Tell me where we're going and I'll get us a cab." He said, "Tell you where we're going? Where the hell *are* we going?"

Great. I got a cab and said, "Take us to 'la playa' and we'll start there." Luckily, it's a no-brainer. They see your surfboards, there's one place you go: to Pichilemu. Miki had nothing to do with getting us there. He just said, "We're in Chile, aren't we?"

Miki wanted to find a right point break. But in the Southern Hemisphere, and the way Chile is shaped, the chances of finding a right point break is like finding a left point break in Santa Barbara. It's not the way things work. He found out four or five hours later when we pulled up to the coastline and saw these big, bombing, perfect lefts. I was blown away. He was pissed off.

We went to two hotels, but they weren't up to snuff for Miki. A third didn't have hot water in his room and we left. The fourth was the best place in town, but somehow they swindled us for something like sixty bucks a night on the rooms after our three-day stay. I confessed to Miki. "I fucking blew it. We should've been paying eight bucks a night. I'll cover it." He would not let me.

By the time we had our first surf together, I decided not to downplay it. But if he thought I was good, he didn't say. It was just me and him and these overhead three-hundred-yard-long left point breaks. I got the first wave of the set, rode it all the way through, kicked out, watched him take off on the third or fourth wave and ride the thing all the way down the point. His first ride in Chile was amazing. I was so stoked. It was all worth having put up with him to see it. He kicked out right next to me and said, "Goddammit, I hate these lefts. I hate surfing backside." I went, "Oohh," like I was punched in the gut. It was such a beautiful ride. But he stayed out for two or three hours, and we got into a rhythm of riding every day.

At one point, a surfer walked up and said, "Hey, I heard that Miki Dora and Chris Malloy are down here. Have you seen them?" I had my hood on and Miki just stood there. I was like, "Um, no, I haven't seen them."

A few days later we ran into Matt Katz.

MATT KATZ: I got out of the water with this surfboard from Ventura, and Chris, who is from there, made some comment. As we talked, I recognized him from magazines. I grew up in Ventura County and lived in Santa Barbara and Carpinteria for years. He said the guy he was with needed a fin screw for his single fin. I pointed at my house up the hill. "Let's cruise up there and I'll give you a fin screw."

When he first walked in, Malloy's friend asked what I did. I told him I taught English and rented rooms. And he said, "Well, can I stay here?"

I thought it was cool that Malloy was around. We didn't see many pros on our waves. His friend was all decked out in Quiksilver product, from his jacket to his vest to his watch to his sunglasses. He had a camera, and wore a beret, so I assumed he was some dick photographer from France.

Later we went to look at something in my truck and Chris said, "The guy I'm with is Miki Dora." He said he didn't want people to know, so he introduced himself as Michael. I took a second look and was like, "Okay, I suppose so." I thought it was kind of cool, but I'm not a very starstruck person. I've had famous surfers at the house before. It impresses me more how normal and, a lot of the time, uninspiring they are.

I invited them both to stay. Miki had a bunch of crap stuffed in four giant suitcases. He was pretty paranoid about his belongings. He had a portable motion-detector alarm. If you walked into his room, it would ding. He had a shortwave radio. When I went to sleep, I could hear Miki's radio make noises like he was sending off spy signals.

CHRIS MALLOY: In the morning, Miki would make the most vile concoction of vitamins I've ever seen, and chew them—eight or nine vitamins—almost like penance, like he was enjoying the pain.

Sometimes, we'd eat at a horse stable that made pasuella, the Chilean cowboy soup, cooked on a wood-burning stove. They also made fresh bread. Miki loved that. He totally got into this little family. He'd play with the kids and he knew the dog's name. He was happy.

But when we'd go out to the surf spot and other surfers were around he'd turn into this angry, bitter man. Wouldn't talk to anybody, wouldn't tell people his name. A totally different human being.

Each day we'd go into town, by ourselves or with Matt, and buy vegetables and a fresh chicken and a quart of beer and coffee. We'd come back, make a fire outside, cook our chicken. Miki drank a little wine. Sometimes we'd talk politics. Sometimes surf history. Sometimes relationships. He told me about Tom Blake and Pete Peterson and Tommy Zahn. He said they were the last real surfers. When a name like Pat Curren or Greg Noll or Lance Carson or Johnny Fain came up, he referred to them as kids. "Yeah, I remember that kid." He told me about his party-crashing days, the costumes, how he did it. I remember being surprised that he'd admit it.

He also said his mom had just died and I said, "Geez, Mick, I'm sorry about that." He looked at me, startled. After telling this melancholy story, he said, "Well goddammit, she had to die sometime. I don't feel bad for it." Then he went on to complain about how she had never done anything for him.

We slept in the same little room. He had a picture of his mom with a candle next to it, like a little shrine. I realized there were two distinct sides to Miki: He wanted his privacy and would protect it, but he also had a human need to connect and share.

On the day I left, Matt planned to take me to town so I could catch a bus. Miki just said, "Bye." Didn't look at me. Just walked away. I thought, Yeah, that kind of fits.

Matt started the truck, and suddenly Miki walked up and said, "Oh, I've got to get something in town." Maybe it was just me, but I think he wanted to see me off. He also kept saying, "I'm going to find a right point break. We didn't come down here for nothing."

When we got to town, he said, "You're not gonna get waves in Antarctica. You're wasting your time. This is as far south as you can go to get perfect waves." I said, "Well, I've gotta try." He said, "I understand. I understand." He did. When he was young—and still—he went to all these crazy places even if people said he was nuts to do it. He was, to me, the *first* pro surfer. I don't mean being paid. I mean his experience and understanding how precious surfing was because of what he'd been through. Ironically, he not only hated the fact that people could make money off surfing, but that he had helped make that happen. He went through that first. He was far ahead of his time. So whether by that time he'd figured out that I was a pro surfer or that I was a true-blue soul surfer, he could admire that I was going somewhere where no "sane" person would have a reason to go. I also think it was hard for him to know that Chile was as far as *he* could go.

MATT KATZ: Miki didn't speak any Spanish and after Chris Malloy left, he was very dependent on me. Sometimes he'd wake up in the morning and ask me about the waves. "Are they still going left?" Anytime I went to town he wanted to come along. Anything he needed to do, I'd be his guide. I thought, Dude, I rent rooms, go do your own thing! That surprised me: I thought of Dora as a world traveler, get on a bus, take some guidebooks, go check it out. Instead, he very much expected the kindness of strangers, and I think it surprised him a little that I didn't offer it more.

As it turned out, Chile was not the sanctuary Miki had hoped for, and he had very much wanted that; otherwise, why pack your life into four suitcases and drag them—and a blender—halfway around the planet? Perhaps, as Steve Pezman put it, "Miki had come to the realization that the perfect place he sought was, finally, just fiction."

After six weeks, Miki gave up and returned to France.

2

Back in Guéthary, Miki asked Philippe Lauga to teach him French. "That baffled me," Lauga recalls. "Miki had always been the last person in the expatriate community who had any interest in learning French. Nonetheless, we started a little class in the beginning of May at Phil Grace and Trudi Forster's home. I bought recent French grammar books. I talked about clever sayings from Rousseau, and observations made by Sartre. But nothing really caught Miki's attention. It turned out that Miki mainly wished to master some words and ready-to-say sentences, such as *asshole, fuck off, mind your own business, stop staring at me, my heart is broken at the prospect of leaving you."*

A few others found in Miki's notebooks: *Go away, drunk, bad check, hell cat, I have no money, kiss, shut up, you are very beautiful, blind leading the blind, woman, I have won.*

In October 2000, Bob Simpson wanted his apartment back, and Miki, who had left the place in such a state that the interior had to be completely redone, had to find what he called "a new death trap to hang in." He found one on the second floor of Maison "Ustegabea," above the Tabac du Fronton, on Guéthary's little seaside main street. The rent was 2,850 francs per month.

PHIL JARRATT: I lived on the floor above Miki. Both our apartments were in the back of the building and looked out over the surf break. He would often come to my place and I'd ask him in. But at his place, I'd mostly have to stand in the doorway. I only went in two or three times while he was alive. A little bit spooky. He kept the big wooden shutters closed most of the time. He had stuff from his travels. A large cigar collection. Shells. Rocks. Jewelry. Hundreds of pairs of Quiksilver socks. Quite a few pictures of himself on the wall, which surprised me for someone who claimed to be so camera-shy all of his life.

ALAN TIEGEN: I lived across the hall from Miki. We'd have drinks at his place and eat at mine. He'd put on some esoteric music that I didn't know, then talk about some book I'd never heard of. In the middle of my divorce, Miki suddenly said, "Salsa is where it's at, Al." I only felt like hanging out in the corner and moaning, "What's happening to my life?" but he insisted. "Hey, man, you're the most optimistic person I know in the whole world, man. Let's get up and kick it loose. Let's go do it." He had the whole thing organized and dragged me to salsa lessons. We even took some in Spain. He approached salsa as he approached surfing. Miki was naturally graceful and he wanted to get beyond the technique and become instinctive.

We'd take a shot of vodka before we went, to loosen up and get into the spirit.

Lessons in Spain were fun. The Spanish girls were totally into it. The French were much more studious. We didn't understand a word of what the Spanish girls said, but we didn't care. Miki could also be rather timid. He'd practice at home with records. I was all for going and snatching girls off the floor, but sometimes he'd go into a corner and dance by himself rather than ask a woman. He couldn't have been afraid of rejection, because there'd be eight or ten girls dancing, with Miki and me the only guys. I don't think he cared about hustling chicks. His dialectic with women didn't have to include sex. That was nice, but Miki also liked women as a concept. I think he just liked playing hard to get. We'd eventually drag him out, and he'd drop the pretense and dance.

According to Trudi Forster, Miki wanted to learn to salsa because he planned to go to Cuba. "He had dancing footprints on his apartment floor, to learn from. I went with him to classes because he needed a partner. He didn't want to dance with the teacher who was male."

Throughout most of 2000, Miki had cast about for someone to accompany him to Cuba. He asked writer Alain Gardinier, his own brother Gardner, Nat Young—"Let's go to Cuba before the Yanks fuck that over once again"—a Portuguese friend named Goncalo Cadhile whom he'd met in Jeffreys Bay, Steve Taussig, a chiropractor friend from Hawaii named Porter Turnbull, and others. In the end, Miki traveled with his old friend, ski instructor and fellow rogue sportif Jean Yves Robert.

JEAN YVES ROBERT: In Cuba I stayed for three weeks, Miki stayed longer. All Miki wanted was a hotel, a good restaurant, a good shave, and a massage. Well, prostitutes, too. In Cuba the police did not allow you to bring prostitutes back to the hotel, but he did that on the first day, anyway, and got kicked out of the hotel the next morning. He had to rent a flat. Me, I had no problem. I took the girl to the hotel but she didn't stay long and I took care that nobody saw her. He took the girl in for all night. Most of all, Miki wanted to dance. He wasn't very good, but he liked it. We went to the parents' house of a prostitute. She gave lessons there. They are a very poor people, you know.

MICHAEL HALSBAND: He told me he'd met a girl at a salsa club, and later they were on a balcony making out and she said, "I have to go to the bathroom." He said, "Just fucking pee off the edge," so she did, and ended up peeing on some guy. They had to take off quick. He said Cuba was a romantic experience and a crazy adventure that made him feel alive. He told the story with so much excitement. Cuba was like life to him. Every place else seemed sort of tired, and all he wanted to do was get back to Cuba.

Once back in France, Miki, Phil Grace, and Trudi Forster went to Bordeaux to meet Miklos Sr. at the Château Lynch-Bages, home of the world-famous wine.

JEAN-CHARLES CAZES: Miki had met my parents when he came to Bordeaux and the Basque country. His father had set him up with global connections, starting with the Rothschilds. He came to our home looking like a beach bum. He stayed a little bit in our beach house in Cap Ferrat. My mother liked him, but to tell the truth my father, Jean-Michel, didn't like him very much because he looked like an obscure guy who didn't have a day job—which was true. That was not really my father's cup of tea. But my mother had a different eye than my father. She was seduced a little bit by Miki Jr., by the character. He was very charming. He was always very nice to my mother.

TRUDI FORSTER: In the car, on the way to meet his dad, Miki kept saying, "I know you're going to like my father. Everyone I introduce him to likes him. You'll change your mind about me after you've met him. You'll take his side."

Miki often approached situations like an eight-year-old, and even in his sixties was very childlike in front of his father. He was intimidated and wondered if his father would criticize him. Miki's father struck me as someone who couldn't understand why his boy had lived the life he had. He thought Miki was a prima donna and a lot like his mother. He saw Miki as someone with natural ability, intelligence, good looks—a whole show going for him—and yet there was something contrary about him that he couldn't understand and didn't have any patience with. You could see the frustration between them.

MIKLOS DORA SR.: We had champagne and hors d'oeuvres, and somebody brought up the subject of Cuba. Miki said, "I just spent two months in Havana."

Jean-Michel asked, "How could you, an American, go to Cuba?"

Miki reached into his pocket and took out a Hungarian passport. I nearly fainted. I said, "How did you get this passport?"

He said, "Remember when I asked you for my Hungarian birth certificate and you sent it? I went to the Hungarian consulate and said, 'I'm a Hungarian. I need a passport.'"

He was born in Hungary but he was an American citizen automatically. But this was Miki, all his life, little tricks, little tricks.

10/16/98
"Happy Birthday"

LEFT: Miki's "birthday" surprise at a Mexican restaurant in Brookings, California. Miki said afterward, "Man, if you ever use this picture, I'll kill you!" And it wasn't his birthday. Courtesy Noll Family Collection.

BELOW: Miki, by a street artist in Cuba, 2000. Courtesy Dora Estate.

BELOW BOTTOM: Miki riding at Punta Lobos, Chile, 2000. Every morning he asked Matt Katz, "Are they still going left?" Photo: Paul Mills.

3

PHIL JARRATT: In February 2001, Jeff Hakman, Martin Potter, and myself were at the Biarritz airport on a bright, clear morning, to catch a flight to Munich, which, as it turned out, had weather at the other end of the spectrum. With snow blocking the runways, no flights were expected to land all day. Given this reprieve, we reconvened at the bar/tabac below my place at noon for a beer in the sunshine. As we sat drinking, Miki joined us for a coffee.

On a whim, I said to Miki: "How long since you were in Australia?"

"Too long," he said. "I kinda like that place."

"Would you like to come out next month as the guest of a surf festival?" Since 1998 my wife and I and our business partners had been running the annual Noosa Festival of Surfing, a longboard event based at Noosa Heads, our home in Australia.

"There'd have to be a contract," he said. "I'm not a frickin' sideshow."

Since he'd mentioned "contract," I drew up one that required his attendance at several social events and stipulated exactly what we would pay for and what was to be Miki's responsibility. I should have known better.

A month later, I was at the festival when I got a call from Brisbane Airport—"Da Cat has landed."

BOB COOPER: I didn't pay any attention to the Noosa contest until somebody told me Robert August, David Nuuhiwa, Donald Takayama, Miki Dora, and the rest would be there. I called the hotel and said, "Can you connect me to Mr. Dora's room." Ring, ring, ring, ring; finally, somebody answers. I said, "Miki, this is Bob Cooper." As if it hadn't been *years* he went, "Cooper, my friend. Hm. What are you doing?" I said, "I'm not doing anything. What are *you* doing?" He said, "I'm recuperating." I went, "I want to come over and see you." He said, "Well, I'm a little . . . maybe some other time." I said, "I'm coming over."

At the hotel I had reception phone his room. I waited at least a half hour for him to walk fifty paces.

We blabbed and caught up. Miki painted a very rosy picture of his life. "Yes, well. I live in France. I would prefer to live in Africa but people there want to kill me, and I don't want to have to carry a gun. I have a small remuneration from Quiksilver. I don't have a car. I have a radio, not a stereo. I have no television. I live by myself. I go out for dinner. I have good wine. I tour the wineries. In the wintertime, I go skiing with my friends. When I get back from this trip, we're all going to Switzerland." The usual patter.

His hotel was maybe three miles from the surfing action, so I suggested that we go to the beach and look around. Most of the hot young generation had no idea who this old guy was. He sat on a little hill with Nuuhiwa, Takayama, and August. Everybody paid their respects, but nobody snuggled up to him.

We decided to check out a surf spot called T-Tree Bay. Miki asked where he could borrow a board. I said, "I've got plenty of boards. No problem." We got a couple from my house, but he didn't like the one I'd designated for him because it had "too much tail rocker." When we got back to the beach, he exchanged it for a Takayama model that had no tail rocker.

Because the beach was jammed, we parked at a friend's house about a half mile from T-Tree Bay and walked. I noticed Miki lagging behind but I didn't pay much attention. He'd stop every once in a while, and I thought he was checking out the flora and fauna.

We got to the beach and paddled out. If you wanted to catch a lot of waves, you waited inside. I was inside and so was Joel Tudor. Joel said, "Is that Miki with you?" Miki sat outside, waiting for the big ones. Every once in a while, if a really big set came through, he would have a go for it. He caught the biggest waves of that particular session. He'd take off and just straight-line in a full-on speed crouch and just barrel it. He took off in front of whoever else was on that wave, too. What did he care? He was sixty-six years old. Of course, in Australia you don't do that, but we had no etiquette on how to handle his behavior, so they just let him take it.

On Miki's last wave, he was A-lining right in the spot, trimmed to the teeth and in a full crouch. A kneeboarder was paddling out. Miki came so close to the guy that the guy bailed off. Miki rode all the way to the beach.

When I came in later, he said, "Nice surf." Then he said, "Check out my back." He turned around and I saw huge lumps. I poked them and they were soft. I said, "Whoa, man. What happened?" He gave me this song and dance about taking salsa lessons in France and then going to Cuba, dancing there and not being able to keep up with the dancers, they were absolutely incredible. And that somebody had hit him in the back with a beer can, and that's what this lump was. It kind of didn't make sense.

We walked the half mile back to the car, but when I turned to check out Miki's progress he wasn't there. He was way back on the trail, leaning on a rail, trying to catch his breath. I slowed down until he caught up. He was panting and uncomfortable. He said, casually, as if it weren't important at all, "Do you have a good doctor here?" I said, "Yeah, I've got a really good doctor. You want to see him?" He said, "Mm, I'm considering it."

He never did take me up on the doctor.

At my friend's house, my friend took a picture of Miki and me, but the picture never came out.

4

In 2001, Stacy Peralta and his producing partner, Agi Orsi (*Riding Giants*), wanted to follow up their critically acclaimed documentary, *Dogtown and Z-Boys*, with an equally riveting portrait of Miki. He seemed like a perfect subject. Peralta called C. R. Stecyk III, who had been part of the Z-Boy phenomenon. He called publisher Tom Adler, who spoke with Peralta, then acted as a go-between connecting Peralta and Orsi with Miki. Or something like that.

Miki and Orsi exchanged faxes and set up a meeting in France for May 1, 2001. Miki seemed positive, his characteristic paranoia on a back burner. He offered to get Peralta and Orsi from the Biarritz airport and said he planned to spend the six days together "making your trip an enjoyable experience and expediting our adventure." Miki also asked if they might bring him a few items: "a bottle of melatonin lozenges; a bottle of Inter Act, an innovative nutritional formula of ginkgo biloba, Siberian ginseng, flower pollen extras; a box of Triple Power Emergen C with glucosamine. You can order over the Internet or at a good health food store. I need this stuff so I can think straight for our project. I'll pay you in American $ or francs when you arrive." He also wanted a copy of *Topaz* by Alfred Hitchcock, and *Havana*, with Robert Redford.

And although he didn't say it out loud, he seemed finally ready to cooperate with a project about his life.

STACY PERALTA: I told Miki straight out: "You won't get a fictional film made of you in your lifetime. The studio heads don't get you, and they're not going to let you be that involved." I don't think Miki was used to someone from "Hollywood" talking frankly. I said, "We should do a documentary because your surfing ability notwithstanding, the interesting thing about you is what everyone says about you. Everyone who knows you has a story about you. I think *that's* the story." He said, "Well, you're going to have to talk to Harry Hodge about this. Harry does all my business." It was a test: If you pass muster with Harry Hodge, then we can talk.

HARRY HODGE: I organized a function, invited sixty people, got out the big screen, threw on *Dogtown*, and everyone's jaw hit the ground. I went, "Holy hell, this is great." After watching *Dogtown,* I knew Stacy was genuine and I believed he could be trusted.

STACY PERALTA: Miki kept testing me. For instance, he immediately said that he thought people didn't think he was that great a surfer. He acted like a wounded bird. Miki had a very delicate side—but a very manipulative mind. The two were constantly at odds with each other, or compensating for each other, one humidifying, one dehumidifying. And everyone who knew him knew it.

I met with Harry. He said, "I told Miki that this is his final chance. If you don't do this, you are going to blow the one great opportunity you're going to get."

Miki and Agi and I spent almost every day, all day long, with Miki. He took us to Biarritz. We went to Spain one night. We'd have lunch, a walk, a pastry, another walk. He never said, "Well, it's almost four, I gotta drop you guys off because I've got a meeting." He just had ease, as if *he was* the day. I wasn't used to being with an adult who didn't have a schedule or an agenda. We just went with the wind.

We went to his apartment. It was quite small and dark. There were xer-oxed photographs of black women from Africa all over the walls. Not what I'd expected. I couldn't believe he let me and Agi into his home. I didn't go into his bedroom. I didn't use the bathroom. I didn't want to make him feel uncomfortable, like I was invading his space. I felt if I made the wrong move I'd lose him. I knew keeping his trust would be hard. Eventually, before I left for Los Angeles, I said, "Miki, there's going to be this huge geography between us when we go home. And that could inadvertently turn things very sour for this film. You've got to understand that our distance doesn't change anything. But I have to go home and get the financing." And he said, "Go make it happen, go make it happen!"

TRUDI FORSTER: Agi and Stacy were nice people, but they were a little naïve about Miki in the beginning. Things seemed to be going very well, but I told them that no matter how it looks, something negative could happen. After watching *Dogtown*, Miki had said to me, "It's a celebration of concrete and graffiti. These people come from a world that is not where I'm coming from. This is not art. This is not what my surfing was about. They're not going to understand me." Hearing this concern, I thought he might not choose them in the end. Yet Miki could be so charming. And opportunistic. Perhaps he would get a free trip to America out of it, so he'd string them along for a while.

Eventually, Miki asked Phil and me what we thought of Stacy and Agi. We said we thought they were very good. Then Miki became quite irritated because we liked them, and then he started getting very difficult with us.

AGI ORSI: Trudi said, "In some way he's going to screw this up." And it did get screwed up. My lawyer drafted an initial generic deal memo per Harry's suggestion, plugging in some numbers per Harry's suggestion that would be corrected later. Harry said don't send it, hand deliver to him. Knowing Miki so well, Harry wanted to see the structure first. But then Harry went out of town, so he said "fax it directly to my office." Unfortunately, Miki came in to get his faxes, saw the fax to Harry, and read it. Harry had suggested putting in $1.00 for rights and we'd deal with the real amount after getting the rest of the language right. Of course, Miki didn't know that, and thought we were offering a dollar for his rights.

HARRY HODGE: Later I rang them and said, "You didn't send it." So they resent it, and I made all the adjustments. It was one of those standard Hollywood contracts where you sign away your life rights and the universe and everything. I had crossed all that out, spoke to our lawyers, sent it back to Agi, and she said fine. But Miki had the original. He finally told me and said, "This woman stabbed me in the back." I said, "You're taking faxes to *me* off my machine. That's not cool." I also said, "I would never let anyone stab you in the back. That was just a basic contract. I had them make changes." I thought this was his last, best chance, but he wouldn't look at the rewritten version. He said, "Done."

Sigh. DoraWorld.

LEGEND

When the legend becomes fact, print the legend.
—Dialogue from *The Man Who Shot Liberty Valance*

CHAPTER **NINETEEN**

It's a Hell of a Thing

1

Q: Will it be tough for Miki to get old?
Cynthia Applewhite: No. He will always be the way he is. He has a gentle, fatalistic acceptance of his life and the way things are. He appreciates a sunny day, a good wave, a good wine.

PHILIPPE LAUGA: In April 2001, while touring a secluded hamlet in Guipuzcoa, in the southern Basque country, Miki expressed some worries about a lump growing larger in his neck. I already had noticed small lumps on his arms and back, full of fat. He said those were hereditary. But this one was of more concern.

HARRY HODGE: We were at the Bella Gorri restaurant—Phil and Jackie Jarratt, my wife, and about ten others. My assistant, Dominique, sat across from me. She looked like she wanted to say something but couldn't quite get it out. Finally, she said, "Harry, Miki's got this lump on his neck." She said he had been to a doctor and had scheduled a biopsy for the next day. I went straight to the bathroom and started crying. My wife said I was overreacting, but I felt nauseous for the rest of the evening.

TRUDI FORSTER: Apparently the biopsy was in the clear, but the lump still had to go. On June 11 he went to the hospital to remove it. They did an S-shaped incision, took out the lump and some lymph nodes, and sent them off to Bordeaux for analysis.

ABOVE TOP LEFT: Miki and Harry Hodge at the Château de Brindos for Harry and Sandee Hodge's tenth anniversary, 1998. Courtesy Harry Hodge.

ABOVE TOP RIGHT: Resting on a June 2001 trek in Aragon, in the Mascun, in Sierra de Guara Canyon. Photo: Eric Chauché.

ABOVE LEFT: Golfing with Philippe Lauga at Arcangues, Summer 1999. Courtesy Philippe Lauga/Anne Gelos.

ABOVE RIGHT: Miki and Bob Simpson on the Guéthary terrace, 2001. Courtesy Bob Simpson.

LEFT: Miki still smiling, Guéthary, October 2001. Photo by Jan Snyder.

HARRY HODGE: I went to see him afterward in the hospital. He lay on his side, listening to the BBC news on his radio. The back of his gown was open, like Jack Nicholson in *Something's Got to Give.* He was asleep. When I covered him, he woke up. He said, "What? Was my ass sticking out?" We talked for a while and danced around the issue of getting a second opinion if necessary.

After the surgery, Miki experienced complications, including a staph infection and weight loss. He had a CT scan of his abdomen to discover why.

DOMINIQUE TAYLOR: He asked Trudi and me to come with him. He was really scared. You could feel it. Right after the echography, the specialist who did it said, "It's not looking too good," but then she realized maybe she shouldn't have said anything and refused to give a diagnosis. Miki panicked and while waiting for the doctor said, "I'm sure it's cancer. I'm sure it's really bad."

Eventually we were called in to meet the oncologist, Dr. Dominique Larregain-Fournier.

Dr. Larregain could speak only a little English, so I translated. She said, "Well, I don't have very good news. Some doctors don't tell you exactly what's happening, but I'm going to tell you the truth. You have a cancer of the pancreas, and it's spread to your salivary glands, and elsewhere. The cancer is all over your body now, and will come out somewhere else. We don't know where. It's terminal."

I had a hard time to translate that and drew a blank.

Miki said, "Tell me, tell me." And I did. It was really terrible. He said, "Ask her if there is someone in the world I can go and see." Dr. Larregain said, "You can see any doctor in the world and he'll tell you the same thing. If you don't do chemo, you have about six months to live. If you do chemo, you could live three or four months more. But I can't promise your body can handle the chemo, because it will be very strong. So everything's on the table, it's your choice. Do chemo, or live your life and wait."

Miki asked the doctor, "Will I suffer?" She said, "You might live very well for a few months, and then it will come suddenly. But if you feel sick, just come to us and we'll do everything so you won't suffer." She said not to worry. Just that he should make a choice: chemo or not. It was really a shock. Everyone cried, Miki, too.

We sat there for a while. Miki was pale. Stunned. He asked many more questions. "Is there anything I can eat to get better?" To every question the answer was always, "There is nothing else you can do. There is no miracle. The cancer is everywhere in your body."

Afterward, Miki wanted to have a walk in the park next to the hospital instead of go straight to the car. Then we sat for a while without talking. In Guéthary we asked if he wanted to have lunch, but he said no, he wanted to be alone.

HARRY HODGE: When Dominique came back to work, I said, "Where's Miki?" And she said, "He knows. They told him today." Holy hell. I apologized for having put her and Trudi in that position. No one expected that diagnosis.

That afternoon, Miki came to my office. He sat in a chair opposite the desk, where he always sat. It wasn't a long conversation, and I wanted to keep it as to the point as possible. "We're going to get a second opinion," I said. "I run a business, I know you never stop with the first opinion. I've got contacts in California; there are ways of treating this." I figured that's what he wanted to hear. Miki wasn't in denial, but it was like, "Yeah, yeah, yeah." Dull from the shock.

That Saturday, we had a rugby function, a party, about twenty people. I invited him round for lunch. It rained like hell. Most people there knew Miki had real issues, but he came, and he was in a buoyant mood. He was early, dressed well. He made the effort. During lunch I got a call from Greg Noll. I'd tried to keep things upbeat, but Greg was in tears. I said, "He's here having lunch, Greg. I'll put him on." But Greg said, "I can't speak to him now."

DR. KRASSOULIA: Jean Yves Robert introduced me to Miki. My practice is nutritional oncology and antiaging, so he was interested in my job. We also went surfing together, played tennis and Ping-Pong. It was the beginning of a very special relationship. Week after week he came to my office for vitamins and antiaging with natural products. He was also interested in hormones but I'm very careful, and he was, too. I didn't give him any human growth hormone.

After the diagnosis I spoke with Dr. Larregain and she said he had six months. I called Miki and said, "We have to talk." He came, and he said, "Tell me the truth." I didn't tell him six months, just that the cancer was very rapid and aggressive. I said, "You have to fight, and you have two choices: chemotherapy or nothing." Miki understood that if he took treatment he would live longer but the quality of life wouldn't be so good. He said, "I prefer to go home and die alone." He made the choice. He knew what he had and he chose. But he still didn't believe the diagnosis. He would say, "Well, but what if I *don't* have cancer. . . ." He looked for other opinions. That's only human.

PHILIPPE LAUGA: I visited him at home, where he rested and tried to grasp the vastness of the void he had to face. His whole world had collapsed. No longer did World War III, nor Armageddon, the Y2K bug, or anything seem important. Now the disaster was him. For a full week he remained home.

Miki didn't want his father to know about the cancer but Phil Grace called Miklos Sr. anyway, gave him the facts, and told him that Miki hadn't wanted him to make the call. Miklos Sr. immediately called his son's cell phone, a gift from Harry Hodge.

"Miki said, 'Who told you?'" says Miklos. "I said, 'What's the difference? You are sick. I'm a factual man. We have to do something about it. Come home.'"

Later Miki yelled at Trudi and Phil for betraying him.

"Miki didn't believe he was terminal," says his father. "He wanted to cure himself with diet. Harry Hodge and he knew a doctor at the University of San Francisco Hospital, an oncologist who was a surfer. I said, 'Come!' and made all the arrangements."

The doctor was Mark Renneker. He had helped Rell Sun, one of Hawaii's greatest women surfers, before she died. But even Renneker said that if Miki had pancreatic cancer, there was no way he could make a comeback. It would be all downhill.

"Miki also got the name of a German doctor named Scheef, and said he'd made an appointment with him at a clinic in Bonn," says Miklos Sr. "I said, 'I will come and be with you. I speak German.' He said, 'No. I will let you know.' This was Miki: He didn't trust doctors and he thought he could cure himself of anything."

While everyone worried, Miki pursued alternative treatments: diet, vitamins, massages in Bali, and visiting Dr. Scheef, who, at the time, worked at the Robert Janker Clinic in Bonn.

YVES BESSAS: When Miki got sick he called me and asked if I could help him to verify if the doctor in Germany was a good man. I said, "You should go back to California." I didn't live in France anymore but I spent three hours one night in Guéthary with Miki. We also talked about other matters. I said,

"You're like a prostitute for $1,000 a month from Quiksilver." I felt like he was in jail. He couldn't move. He didn't have enough money. He said, "Yes, but Quiksilver will protect me. If I go back to California, all these people are going to sue me. I don't have a friend anymore." I said, "That's stupid. All your best old friends will come. They're waiting for you." I said very tough things to Miki. He said to Bob Simpson that I was very aggressive against him, and he didn't understand why. Miki was pretty depressed and he was lost. When you get lost, maybe you lose judgment. Miki said, "Call Tom Adler. Call Steve Pezman. Verify if I have friends in California." I called Pezman and Adler, and everybody said, "We have a very good surgeon in San Francisco waiting for him."

CYNTHIA GARRIS: Before Miki was diagnosed, my mother, Cynthia Applewhite, died from cancer on February 21, 2001. She was Miki's rock for over forty years. Even though he often lived on the other side of the world, he could always count on her to be at home, where she died, and to be there for him. I think they were tied together. She told me that she had once asked him, "Do you love me?" and he said, "If I ever loved a woman, it was you."

Because of all the information I'd gathered to try and save my mother's life, when I found out Miki had cancer, I asked my father to give me Miklos's phone number. I called and said, "There's a man who's very well known in New York and who specializes in alternative treatments for pancreatic cancer. He has a very good survival rate. He's the only alternative person that the AMA is putting a lot of money into, investigating his techniques."

Miki's father was very excited and said he'd inquire. He called me a few days later. He said, "I told Miki what it entails"—coffee enemas and a pig pancreatic enzyme—"and Miki doesn't want to take 100 pills a day and do coffee enemas." I felt really sad. I guess it was too much humiliation to fight for his life, or maybe he just didn't want to live without my mom being around.

PHILIPPE LAUGA: Soon, Miki wouldn't talk seriously about the cancer; he'd make fun of it. In golf, when you putt very close to the hole but it doesn't go into it—but it would be impossible to miss the next shot—it's a gimme. He would not give shots away to others if he could avoid it, but if he had a ball so close to the hole, he would wait for me to say something. He'd say, "It's not a gimme?" I'd say no. He'd say, "But I'm a dying man!"

HARRY HODGE: I wanted to keep Miki upbeat so on August 11, we threw a surprise sixty-seventh birthday party at the Chez Francois in the village of Biriatou right on the French-Spanish border. Beautiful Basque valley. Susan McNeill organized it.

PHIL JARRATT: It was the kind of social event that Miki had pretended to loathe for much of his life, yet on this warm evening on the terrace overlooking the Bidassoa River, he played the tables like a politician, moving from one group to the next, full of smiles and funny stories. It was a particularly poignant occasion, because all of us there knew that for Miki there would not be many more.

HARRY HODGE: I sat next to Miki. He had just gotten back from Germany, and he said Dr. Scheef had diagnosed his problem as "a family disease from Transylvania. It's just a rare blood disease." He told this story to everyone. Of course it wasn't true; he knew that a simple body scan would have seen the cancer; he just created this beacon of hope to avoid being down and getting everyone else down. Funny, but I wanted to buy it. Somehow I thought, if I'm negative, then he's dead, he's dying. The weird thing, in person and in pictures from the dinner, is that he looked well. Better, in fact. He'd put on weight. It's as if he'd actually convinced himself that this was a rare family blood disease. His father could have had it, he could be treated, it's all going to be good.

For the next six weeks Miki lived a totally normal life. He surfed again, and everyone thought maybe the French doctors had misdiagnosed after all; maybe miracles do happen. I rang Dr. Renneker in San Francisco—Miki had decided not to go there—and he said if he really did have pancreatic cancer, he shouldn't be able to surf, golf, play tennis. Perhaps this was Miki's fait accompli: the final joke that he'd beat it all.

DR. KRASSOULIA: I decided to phone Dr. Scheef about his diagnosis. I said, "Why do you say it's nothing?" He said, "I never saw cancer." Then, "This man, does he have money? What is his job?" I said, "He's a professional surfer. He has no money." I told Miki, "This man is a quack. Don't go back." Miki said, "But I'm not sure that I have cancer."

As news of Miki's health began to trickle to the outside world, friends faxed best wishes and concern. Miki wrote back that he would travel "to Lourdes for the cure." He didn't go, of course, and not too long afterward, his communiqués—none of which went into any detail about his health—began to bear the subtitle "DEAD MAN WALKING." In a fax to Greg Noll he signed himself "Dr. Kevorkian, France." Yet Miki refused to lie down and die.

With friends like photographer Eric Chauché, Philippe Lauga, and François Lartigau, he took walks through the countryside to keep his strength and spirits strong.

"One day we went to a Benedictine monastery," Lartigau recalls. "The monks showed us how they wove carpets and tapestries. Miki told me, 'I could have been a good monk. They've got a good life. Peace. They can do whatever they want, no bothering with the system. It's great.' I agreed, but I could see he was still grinding something in his head. Then he said, 'But you know what? They miss out on all the waves, don't they? They miss out on a lot of great hash, too.' He ground some more. 'I wouldn't mind being a monk if we had good parties with the nuns next door.'"

ERIC CHAUCHÉ: We had shared three years in the Pyrenees Mountains trekking Aragon, the Pyrenees part of Spain. He liked the place very much because it reminded him of South Africa.

I took photos of Miki in the Pyrenees, in September 2001, the last trip we made with Philippe Lauga, to a canyon filled with olive and almond trees. We camped two thousand meters high and went on the river. He liked to swim in the rivers and stayed a long time. It was icy. In one photo his hair is swept back and he is bare-chested. I think he liked it, though with him it was not always so easy to say.

We slept outside. We built a fire. At night, when we lay under the stars, sometimes he would talk about the natural world, the light, the people he'd met in Cuba and Chile and Thailand. He still wanted to go to Ecuador and find some special balsa wood. He never talked to me about politics. We joked a lot. He didn't see life the way most others did.

He liked to be in contact with the elements and natural people: fishermen and farmers, shepherds. He liked waterfalls. He said that when he was young he would get out of the water and take a shower in a waterfall. He was into the good vibrations of life, and sharing food and wine, trekking, surfing. He was very curious.

When I first met Miki, it was difficult for me because I was disturbed by what I'd read about him in the magazines. Then I discovered who he was. And even with the sickness, each second was positive, positive, positive.

I think he just wanted to be with people who live with the ocean, who spoke about the life, on every beach in the world, waiting for the waves.

2

ALAN TIEGEN: Because we lived across the hall from each other, Miki and I would get together a few nights a week. I'd make a pasta and Miki would do the dishes. We'd watch movies; he loved Al Pacino in *Carlito's Way*. As such, we were together when 9/11 happened. Neither of us said anything initially, we were so blown away. It's not like he loved America, and it's not as if he was greatly sensitive to the Arab cause, either. CNN played the tape over and over, and Miki said, as if he knew this would happen one day, "Well, here we go. This is it." To him it was more of a confirmation of his worst fears.

PHIL JARRATT: As the summer faded away, Miki kept on surfing as much as he could, although he no longer really had the strength to push himself onto the wave face at Guéthary. I ran into him panting on the stairs one evening, dripping wet in the gloom, leaning on the railing gasping for air. I asked if I could help. "It's okay, I got oxygen inside," he said, nodding in the direction of his apartment. Oxygen. We were on the last straightaway now.

In late October, Miki spoke with Dr. Adrian Cotton, an oncologist at the Loma Linda Hospital, near San Bernardino, in southern California. They specialized in cancer and offered an advanced proton laser treatment that could destroy tumors without damaging the healthy tissue in the beam's path.

JULIETTE KRASSOULIA: The last times I saw Miki he was very thin. I said, "Miki, you have to eat." He said, "I don't know what to eat." I said I made soup every day for my children, with a lot of vegetables. I said, "I will do a Magic Soup. If you eat it, you will feel much better." He came every evening. He didn't want me to give him a big portion, but it was like he needed to come every day. I said, "Stay with us, Miki, if you want," and sometimes he would. He'd eat the Magic Soup and look at all the children, and say, "Ah! I feel better. I feel better!" I think maybe he didn't eat so well because he was alone. So when he had a table with good food, he enjoyed it. Maybe it was a problem in his life, the lack of good food and company. I was a little bit like a mother for him. I felt that he was very broken inside.

DOMINIQUE TAYLOR: In November, he really started to have pain in his stomach. Suddenly, in two weeks, he looked tired, white. He couldn't eat anymore. Then he got really scared. He said, "Get me a plane ticket; I want to go to my dad's place. I'm starting to get really sick, it might be my cancer. I want to go to where I come from. I want to go back there."

Harry was not in the country at that time. But I called him and told him Miki wanted to go right away. We bought him a round-trip ticket. He came into my office, gave me a kiss, and said, "Thanks for everything, you've been great to me." We cried a bit and he left.

Miki also composed a short document, which Dominique typed out on the same page after he'd written it in longhand. "I, MIKLOS DORA JR., hereby certify that in case of my demise, all my personal effects, surfboards, located in my apartment in Guéthary, France, will belong to Harry Hodge. Guéthary, Nov. 6, 2001."

SUSAN MCNEILL: Miki wanted me to drive him to the Biarritz airport, but I was so upset at his condition that I wouldn't answer the phone. He called me every fucking day leaving messages, saying, "Call me. What are you doing?" I wouldn't call him. I didn't call anyone. So he ended up calling Frances Christopher, a friend I'd introduced him to.

FRANCES CHRISTOPHER: I went to his place around noon. He had decorated his front room with all the pictures he'd taken in Cuba, and there were other pictures everywhere: of beautiful girls, of waves. Shrines with miniature statues. Cigars. It was really beautiful the way he had done it. He left everything up on the walls.

We went into the kitchen and he combed through certain remedies he wanted to take with him. He cleaned out the refrigerator: onions, vegetables, bottles of olive leaf extract and colloidal silver. Carrots. Mainly fruits and vegetables, some of which looked like they'd needed to be thrown away days before. I helped him take out the trash.

I said, "Are you going to take your golf clubs?" He said no. I helped him carry his bag down the stairs. It weighed a ton. He took clothes but no memorabilia. He left everything as if he was coming back. He didn't take his surfboards.

We drank a little sherry before going to Quiksilver and the airport. As we left the apartment, he asked if I wanted a key. He said, "If you ever need a place . . . ," but I said I didn't want his key. He shut the door and said, "I've had a lot of good friends here in France."

That's when I knew he knew he wasn't coming back after all, and maybe that's why he left things that way: so there would be a visual legacy of what he was doing at the end.

We went to Quiksilver. Harry wasn't around.

We talked a little bit on the way to the airport. He was kind of distant. I gave him a hug—Miki wasn't a very physical person in that way—and that was it. That was the last time I saw him.

Miki left for America on November 7, 2001.

He flew first class.

This time friends were waiting.

CHAPTER **TWENTY**

Million Waves to Darkness

1

Please don't bother about my soul
I've got summer . . . in between the cold
Postcards from Hollywood
Enchantment by the sea
Como esta?
Do you still think of me?
Please don't bother about the time
Ain't no hurry . . . when you walk the line
Postcards from Hollywood
They know just what to say
"Wish you were here"
I could be there today
With a fascination . . . bordering on madness
We're born of the blue: me and you . . . me and you . . .

—Ned Doheny, "Postcards from Hollywood"

Miki landed at Los Angeles International. Tom Adler and C. R. Stecyk III picked him up and took him to Loma Linda Hospital, a few miles east of San Bernardino. According to Adler, Miki looked "really healthy. A little cranky and different, but healthy looking."

Adler had arranged, through a doctor friend of Steve Pezman's, to get a suite on the hospital's top floor. In the room, Miki set up his radio and, as always, tuned to the BBC.

DR. COTTON: Tom Adler paged me after he got Miki at the airport. I met him at the hospital sometime between eight and nine at night. I took him upstairs. Miki wanted to be evaluated for proton therapy. Harry Hodge offered to pay for everything, but Miki ended up proving he would get Medicare.

I'm not a surfer. I'm Canadian and we play on frozen water. I looked up Miki on the Internet and found the classic picture of him surfing at Malibu, and talk about his arrogance, his fleeing the country. He sounded like a pretty interesting character.

When I met him, he was sixty-seven years old, had wild hair, bit of a beard, a bit of a French accent. He acted very European. Took things very slow. Loved to talk.

After he got settled, he sent Tom and Craig to the local grocery store to get him bottled water and herbal supplements. Miki also wanted a small refrigerator.

I did a physical exam and asked some medical questions. I also asked, "What do you do for work?" He said, "I'm an environmentalist."

"What do you do as an environmentalist?"

"I go around from place to place and just kind of take care of things."

"Why are you living in France?"

"Most wonderful place in the world to live. I can do what I want when I want. I don't have to worry about anything. Everybody's nice. Everybody's wonderful."

Miki had brought a suitcase or two. During his stay he may have worn the hospital pants, but he always had on a loose, comfortable shirt. He tried to make it look like he wasn't a patient. In the morning he'd wash his face, straighten his hair and beard. I got the impression he was a very proud person and didn't want to feel like he was relying on anybody—me, Tom, his dad. I remember him saying, "I'm sixty-seven: Look at me. I'm a good physical specimen for sixty-seven." And, other than the cancer, yes, he was. He moved his hands all over the place all the time. Talked a lot with his body. He had a good sense of humor. He told me jokes. He took a lot of vitamins and supplements. I had no problem with that.

Miki also talked to me about human growth hormone and said he had used it and that it made him feel younger and healthier and more energetic. I think it can be potentially dangerous. If you think of a cancer as a normal cell gone bad—and, say, it doubles every five minutes, versus a healthy cell that doubles every two days—and then hit both cells with something that makes them stronger and more potent, you could deduce that the bad cell will really tear up. It's possible that HGH could make an existing cancer accelerate, but is HGH going to cause cancer? Probably not.

Pancreatic cancer is called adenocarcinoma. It usually shows up in the head because after you've had it for three, six, nine months, it blocks off either the blood supply or a bile duct, and a patient notices he is turning yellow. Otherwise there are no symptoms. It's not painful. You feel okay. The rest of your pancreas works just fine. You don't see the doctor until you turn yellow.

Miki was a good patient, understandably a little nervous. Anytime he had to have something else done, it took thorough explaining, as opposed to convincing. After the first few days he let me know, "Doc, whatever you want to do, as long as you tell me it's you who wants to do it, I'll have it done." He'd learned to trust me.

For Miki, I came in early and stayed late and spent more time talking with him than any other patient. I just took care of him by myself. He was very curious about knowing what we'd found. He didn't care if it was good news or bad news.

One day he said, "Doc, would you go through treatment for this? Would you look for something else? Would you go to Mexico?" He kept talking about Fiji or Haiti and spending the rest of his days there looking for some magical cure. He asked, "What would you recommend for *your* dad?" I was as honest as I could be, which was, "There are no options. At this point, whatever it is you enjoy doing, go do it."

Once, I asked him about his nickname "The Cat." He said, "Yeah, I was a big-time surfer in Malibu. It was just a bunch of political b.s. Time to leave and get away. I did what I wanted to do."

Then the moment came when the biopsy proved he had cancer. Until the result comes back, it's always like, well, *maybe* it could be something else. I don't know why, but there's always that weird hope. I sat with him and said, "These are the results of your tests." It was just the two of us. He didn't seem surprised. Didn't seem particularly nervous or anxious. I think he had known for six months. I don't think I've ever told a cancer patient that they had cancer when they didn't kind of already know.

2

CHRISTINE DORA: We got Miki from Loma Linda and when we got off the freeway in Montecito, I said, "You're home now, Miki." He said, "Are you quite sure it's all right that I come? You don't want somebody dying in your home."

I said, "It's a good place to go, if you have to go."

We made him as comfortable as we could in his room. Got a television and music—salsa—and all that stuff. He would listen to his radio practically all night long. Then we got hospice involved, and they sent social workers and nurses and masseurs. Monday, Wednesday, Friday the nurse would give him a bath. Tuesday and Thursday he'd get a massage.

In the beginning he was mobile. Every afternoon he walked down to the beach by himself or with C.C. I'd offer to drive him but he said no. If it was a sunny day he would always sunbathe in the backyard—in the nude.

MIKLOS DORA SR.: At first he ate breakfast, lunch, and dinner. It had to be organic, and we would try and entice him with wheatgrass, carrot juice, garlic. Christine got all this for him. In the beginning he could take it, but then he couldn't tolerate it.

C.C. was also fantastic to him. She stayed with him, in his bedroom, for three or four days at a time, from morning 'til night. She knew all his tricks and all his faults. I said, "You are so good to him." She said, "I love him." And he got love from us.

C.C.: Miki had so much mail and so many calls that there was no way Miklos and Christine could have handled all that and stayed sane. He could have used two full-time assistants. Miki was happy to hear from anyone who was interested. He told a lot of people he loved them. He meant it and he truly cared. I would overhear the conversations because I had to hold the phone for him. He would never have said the words if he didn't. No way. He could be as macho as macho gets. He may not have shown it in life, but it showed when he was finally in a vulnerable position: terminally ill.

Eventually, I had to read him his mail because he started losing his vision about six weeks before he died. In order to support your liver and kidneys and keep your heart pumping, your body redirects its resources. Everything starts to shut down.

Miki would always say how thankful he was to have his father and Christine. His father loved him dearly, and Miki loved his father; he just had a hard time showing it. He would always bring gifts to Christine. Once he brought beautiful flowers, and in the middle of one flower was a huge gemstone. He was totally unconventional.

I probably spent more time at the house in Montecito than I spent at my own house. We would just hang out and do whatever he wanted to do. Sometimes he'd come with me to Trader Joe's. I'd buy fresh coconuts and drill them and put in a straw so he could drink the milk. I made sure he'd get a bath with Epsom salts so he wouldn't get dehydrated. He didn't deteriorate like one might think. He was a little bit skinnier, but he still weighed a ton. I couldn't have lifted him.

Miki's attitude was okay—depending on the medication. He did not like being on the morphine. He purposely underdosed himself because he didn't like being out of it. And then he changed to oxycontin and he was pretty much back to normal. He'd make corny jokes.

He knew he was dying, though. Once he told me he was working on a miracle and if I helped him pull out of it, he'd take me on a trip around the world. He meant it.

Miki and I had great conversations. Most of the time they'd be so comical that you couldn't have planned it that well. I had been doing so much medical stuff for him over the phone, talking to doctors all over the country, in a last-ditch effort to help him in any way—and I had to look at his medical records. Ironically, most people don't know their own blood type. One evening I drove him to the beach in Montecito, to look at the sunset. I asked him if he knew his blood type. He said no. I said, "It's B positive." He said, "You're shitting me!" I said, "No." He said, "Maybe my body's trying to tell me something." I said, "Yeah. Take a hint."

HARRY HODGE: On December 16, 2001, I went to Montecito to see Miki. I arrived, forewarned that Miki was in bad shape. This was the first time I'd met Miklos and Christine, and they told me Miki had just been outside, but now he was in bed. All the way to Montecito I had pictured this lunch with Miki—and I was going to make it a great lunch. But they told me he couldn't come to the table. I was like, holy hell. I think the hardest thing was when they said, "When he comes out, you're going to be in shock. He knew you were coming, we took him down to the local barber. He had a haircut, he had his nails done, his ear hairs pulled out. He just wanted to look good."

But Miklos said, "He can't look good."

Miki came out in a robe, shuffling. He had lost almost fifty pounds and had jaundice underneath his suntan. He was gaunt. When our eyes connected, I thought it was a defining moment in our friendship. I don't know what it defined, but it defined something.

We went outside. He sat on a bench. He had the catheter in, because he had incontinence and stuff. Miki opened his robe, and he was naked. It was a little bit undignified, but he didn't care.

I said, "So, Miki, you come out here every day, just sit here?" And he said, "You gotta die with a suntan." We talked for a while, just shooting the shit. He apologized to me, because he wore a pair of Smith's sunglasses—they weren't Quiksilver. I said, "Miki, you know, that's not something to worry about."

We didn't get too philosophical. I think Miki wanted to keep it like that. We didn't talk about death, or that it might be the last time we would see each other. I don't think that anyone in that situation does. I just can't imagine hugging and crying, "Oh, I'm never going to see you again." It's different than going to live in another country for three years, or leaving for a few weeks and hugging my kids good-bye. I think that was a mutual understanding, and we appreciated it. When you're dying, you're dying.

Miklos had asked me to talk to Miki about leaving a will. He was right. I said to Miki, "You've got to write down what you want us to do and sign it." I said I'd take care of everything, don't worry about it. He said, "Yeah, yeah, yeah," but I could tell he was zoning out. After twenty minutes he was pretty tired. As he got up to walk in, his urine bag dropped off his lap. I picked it up. He said, "I bet that pisses you off."

We went inside and he went back to the bedroom. The rest of us had lunch. I *was* pissed off, but at myself. I needed to hold it together and I was coming unglued.

After lunch I knew I had to go say good-bye. I didn't want it to seem contrived or make a speech. So I just went in. And it was great. He was in bed. We had a talk about the guys in France and the surf. On his shelf, framed, was a print of myself and my kids standing in front of a print he'd given me of a surf spot in Chile, that he'd signed "Thanks for this great friendship." We hugged, and he said, "Thanks for everything." I went to the bathroom to recoup. I thought, "I've got to go back in there, because there's so many other things I want to say." But I couldn't.

MIKLOS DORA SR.: Harry was very generous to Miki. He wrote that he wanted to meet me. He offered me money for the expenses for Miki. I said, "Thank you very much, it's very generous of you. But I am his father. This is my duty and my belief." Then we became friends.

HARRY HODGE: The next day I wrote Miki a letter and said many things I couldn't say in person. I also told him how I'd driven down the coast to Los Angeles and stopped at Malibu. The place was a mess. Crap on the beach. No surf, overcast, concrete. But "Dora Lives" was still on the wall.

I emphasized again that he should leave a will beyond the document he'd left for me in France, that he needed to leave instructions for those he left behind, and that by doing so he'd keep the government's hands off his possessions and continue beating the system like he always had. I talked a bit about a memorial ceremony and where his ashes might be scattered. I remembered that Miki had often told me, "I never want to have one of those functions, at the Chart House in Malibu, with all those fat, old guys in corduroy shorts, wearing Hawaiian shirts over beer bellies. I never want it to be like that." I thanked him again for his friendship and wished him the best.

MICKEY MUÑOZ: Through the grapevine, I'd heard that Miki had cancer. I'd seen him six months before in France. Fast-forward to several weeks before Miki passed away. Steve Pezman and I went to visit him. I learned from Steve on the drive up that Dora Sr. had been the first to take Miki surfing. I had always assumed that it was Gard Chapin.

I called Miklos Sr. "Is there anything I can bring him? Is there anything he needs?" He said to bring my sense of humor. "He still has his."

I had this two-foot-high mechanical plastic Santa Claus on a plastic surf-board. You flicked a switch and it played some Beach Boys song and did a hula. I thought it epitomized everything Dora hated. It seemed like a humorous gift, so I put it in a grocery bag and took it.

About fifteen minutes after we arrived, I walked out to see Miki on the patio. I didn't know what to expect. I was shocked: Miki was black as the ace of spades from sitting in the sun. He looked like Gandhi. He'd lost weight. He wore sunglasses, and he was naked except for a little towel over his loins.

I wanted to know from his perspective what dying was like, where his head was at. But I didn't know how to get into it. The first words out of his mouth were, "What are you trying to do? You're trying to kill me! You bring that fucking Pezman? What are you doing?!" I thought he was serious—he wasn't—and it totally disarmed me.

Miki's dad came out once or twice, but Miki said, "Leave us alone, leave us alone! I'm okay." Miklos really doted on him.

Finally, he said, "What's in the bag?" and I said, "A Christmas present." I presented the Santa Claus, pushed the switch, and some stupid Beach Boys surf song came on, and Santa did a hula. There wasn't even a hint of a smile on his face.

Then he said, "Is that . . ." and he said the name of the tune. I said, "Yeah, I think so." I turned it off, put it in the bag. I was afraid I'd really pissed him off. Then Miklos came out and said, "I'm going to bring Steve out." I went in and out came Steve. They spent about five minutes, then we waited in the living room while Miki rested.

About half an hour later, Miki came in. They had to support him walking. He sat on the couch, I sat next to him, and Steve across the way. We talked and Miki specifically apologized for some of his past actions. Not all of it, but some. I don't know whether it was stuff he had written or some of his outbursts, but I could tell he realized there were things in his past that he couldn't justify. For me, the poignant part was when the conversation had big gaps. What do you say? Where do you go? How deep do you go with it?

Miki got tired and it was time to go. I shook Miki's hand a bit, so did Steve. I'd brought the Santa inside, thinking I should just take it away. I grabbed Miki, hugged him, and held him a bit. At first he didn't respond, then I could feel his hands pressing. We broke, and when I grabbed the Santa bag, to go, Miki pushed my hand down. "No," he said. "I want it."

3

MIKLOS DORA SR.: One night at dinner Miki just couldn't swallow anything. He burst out and said, "I don't understand how this happened to me. Why me? Everything was going well for me."

He broke down. Put his head on the table. He really didn't cry, but he was desperate. "Why did it happen to me now, when everything looked so good?"

CHRISTINE DORA: Miki started staying in his room a lot then, too weak to come out. Someone had brought him some fabulous orchids and I told him, "Hallucinate on the orchids, Miki, if it's a really bad time." He made a real effort to tolerate the pain because he didn't want to fog his mind. I made sure he had vials of morphine if the pain was bad. Miki was often difficult to approach, but once, when we were alone in his room, he said, "Just hold my hand."

BOB SIMPSON: In the middle of December, I gave Miki a call. His voice was garbled. He said, "They're giving me all this morphine and stuff. I've got to get off this stuff. Next week they'll give me a new medicine so I can start eating again. I'll be feeling better if I can just get off this shit. It's really terrible." I told Miki that I loved him several times, and I really did. He had just sent me—of all things—a menu from a restaurant that had now become my living room in my apartment at the Residence Gurutzia, in Guéthary. His farewell annotation was: "Thanks for the good times."

They *were* good times. Then I remembered that just after he moved to Guéthary, we got this list that was faxed around, called "What I've Learned."

You're supposed to check off what applies to you. I kept Miki's list. Here's what he checked:

✓ I've learned that it takes years to build up trust, and only seconds to destroy it.

✓ I've learned that you can get by on charm for about fifteen minutes. After that, you'd better know something.

✓ I've learned that no matter how thin you slice it, there are always two sides.

✓ I've learned that money is a lousy way of keeping score.

✓ I've learned that sometimes the people you expect to kick you when you're down will be the ones to help you get back up.

✓ I've learned that maturity has more to do with what types of experiences you've had and what you've learned from them and less to do with how many birthdays you've celebrated.

✓ I've learned that our background and circumstances may have influenced who we are, but we are responsible for who we become.

✓ I've learned that two people can look at the exact same thing and see something totally different.

✓ I've learned that credentials on the wall do not make you a decent human being.

✓ I've learned that it's hard to determine where to draw the line between being nice and not hurting people's feelings and standing up for what you believe.

JOHNNY FAIN: I didn't know he was dying. He'd tried three times to see me—I guess he wanted to make amends—but I wouldn't have anything to do with him. I don't know why; I guess I was unsure of his intentions and thought he wanted to pick a fight. You can't blame me, considering everything. But he supposedly told some people, "Hey, I really liked the guy—where is he?" For him to want to make amends—that's the last thing I thought! Steve Pezman went to see him. That's more guts than I had.

LINDA CUY: When I saw Miki near the end, I said, "Look: You're gonna get well and we're gonna go surfing. You're gonna eat and you're gonna build yourself up. You're gonna take loads of vitamins and you're gonna get out of this." Miki looked at me and he saw that I was really serious. His face went kind of calm and he looked me straight in the eye and he said, "Boy, if I get out of this one we're all gonna take a nice trip together." It was like, "Here's the next game."

ALLAN CARTER: Just after Miki came home, I had dinner with Ned Tannen, who used to run Universal Pictures and Paramount Pictures. He said, "How's Miki doing?" I said, "He's not doing so well. Things are bad." So Ned said, "Why don't we go see him?" and took me to Montecito. We drove in one of his collector Ferraris, a 275 TTB four-cam that at one point was worth about $1.6 million. Miki was in pretty bad shape, sitting in the garden. We'd planned lunch but Miki didn't feel like eating. Instead he just wandered around the living room. I said, "Miki, throw your clothes on"—he just wore a dressing gown—"and Ned will take you out in the Ferrari."

Miki got all hopped up and he got dressed. They disappeared in the Ferrari and Ned took Miki out in the hills, way in the back of Santa Barbara, going 150 miles an hour. They were gone for two hours or so for a really wild last ride.

MARCIA MCMARTIN: Allan and I saw him three or four times. The first time we went for lunch, he actually sat at the table. He didn't eat much, but he had some special soup his father had made. After that, there was always less time to talk because his strength was fading. It was so sad. [cries] He was going to die. He was too young. A great shame. He knew it, but he didn't talk about it. In fact, he talked about a doctor in Hawaii and another diagnosis. He still hoped for something to save him at the last moment. We didn't talk about the past. Instead, we talked about dancing and he made jokes. I remember Christine saying later, "That must have been good, because we heard you laughing."

LOUIS ZAMPERINI: Mick called me and it thrilled my heart. When a person's dying, that's when they know their inner truth. He said, "I feel comfortable in my faith now. I want to thank you for being such a good influence on me."

"Mick," I said, "those are precious words to me."

C.C.: This may surprise everyone, but Miki *was* religious. Or let's say he was spiritual. He had his own ideas and wouldn't often talk about them, but we had some brief conversations. I don't know if he believed in heaven, but he believed in an afterlife. Heaven is a state of mind. Surfing was his religion.

MIKLOS DORA SR.: Miki got Harry's letter about writing a will. We bought a simple one at the stationery store. The hospice people said they had a notary who would come. C.C. and Tom were around. But when the notary came, he still wouldn't do it. C.C. tried. Tom Adler tried. I said, "I'm not going in. I won't ask him because I'm most likely to blow my top."

C.C.: Tom and I and Miklos had all talked to him separately about doing a trust because then his death wouldn't be a matter of public record. He didn't understand that; most people don't. And when you're dying, it's hard to do a lot of critical thinking because you're just worried about surviving. Miki wouldn't do the will, but we kept talking to him gently and finally he dictated something and I just took down his words. At first he mentioned his father only, then he mentioned Harry. I said that would be nice if he paid Harry back. I spelled Miki's name wrong, though. I was thinking of the Greek island Mykonos.

> *29 December 2001*
>
> *I, Myklos [sic] Sandor Dora under the circumstances I find myself, have no alternative but to leave all my personal effects, including film, photographs, and memorabilia to my father, Myklos K. Dora, in conjunction with Harry Hodge, to protect and non-commercialize my life in any manner.*
>
> *I'd like to be cremated as soon as possible after my demise, and have my ashes distributed in the wind in the forest behind my father's house, where he goes hiking every day, without any fanfare.*
>
> *Go in peace. (Signed) Miklos S. Dora*

CHRISTINE DORA: For the last two or three days, Miki couldn't even talk. He could only lie there. The morphine had taken over. At first he resisted because he always wanted to be conscious and aware. But finally he had to for the pain. And then he reached the point where he couldn't swallow the morphine; I had to administer suppositories. I hesitated because it's a very personal thing, but he said it was okay. Then we had to put on the morphine pump that releases the drug into the bloodstream all the time. I stroked his head. Miklos massaged his feet.

MIKLOS DORA SR.: While he could still talk he was very civil. He'd thank me and thank Christine every day, two or three times. I am very happy that he came home and he spent his last few months here. It would have been horrible if he had not. But I tell you what's surprised me most, the honest truth: that Harry Hodge and Tom Adler and others would talk about Miki like he was the greatest individual on this earth. I remember at one lunch that Christine and I looked at each other and I said, "What goes on here? Are we so bad that we don't see it?"

We got telephone calls and e-mails from his friends, from everywhere, who not only thought of Miki as a surfer, but as a good man. I was very happy to hear it. He was a Nureyev on the surfboard. He was fantastic.

But I have to be honest: Beside that, I think he was nothing. This is the father talking. Still, he was my son and *I always loved him*. He always had a place to come.

I think about Miki every day. Sometimes I ask myself, How come we couldn't get a little bit closer? Understand each other more? I really miss him today more than any other time.

Every night I went in to see him. Sometimes he was awake and listening to the radio. I'd say, "Can't you sleep? Can I do something? A cup of tea?" The last night, he was on the pump and he was very bad. I went in around two o'clock in the morning and he was . . . he was alive but he was very. . . . Then I went in around five thirty, and he was gone.

The last picture of Miklos and Miki, "taken in April 2001 in front of Château Lynch-Bages in Pauillac, Bordeaux, when Miki came to join me for a few days of fun and drinking good wine," says Miklos. Courtesy Dora Estate.

CHAPTER TWENTY ONE

The Legend Lives

1

Waves are the ultimate illusion. They come out of nowhere, instantaneously materialize and just as quickly they break and vanish. Chasing after such fleeting mirages is a complete waste of time. That is what I chose to do with my life.

—Miki, from *Dora Lives*

HARRY HODGE: When I got the keys to Miki's apartment in Guéthary, I went in by myself. Funny, it was my first time there. His place was very homey. The shutters were open. His golf clubs stood in the kitchen. The fridge had been cleaned out. He had lots of movie videos and salsa music tapes. I took a few photographs of the apartment but was pissed off when they came out badly. There were no feet on the floor for salsa dancing. The kitchen reminded me of the Mercedes van twenty years before. He had the same frying pan and the same shit everywhere. In the bedroom I saw the oxygen tank and all the pills. He had a double bed. It wasn't made. The room was full of Quiksilver clothing. He never threw anything away. He had more Quiksilver clothing than I do. There were photographs, and photocopies of photographs. Also, books, videos, CDs, pages and pages of jokes e-mailed or faxed to him. A lot of junk: cigars, small artifacts, wooden carvings, hats. In the bathroom were more pills.

I was so emotionally overwrought that I wanted to throw away everything as quickly as I could. Phil Jarratt said, "Harry, you don't touch anything. Everything is valuable."

"Not even the cigars?"

"No. We put it all in boxes."

I stood there and wondered how Miki would finally be remembered. I recalled that Bob Simpson and I and Miki had, since the mid-'80s, always talked about him doing a book. He always said he wanted to. As the two guys who had the most access and influence on him, a lawyer and a businessman, we offered to get the writer, the money. The only thing we couldn't get was to get Miki to cross the line and do it.

Controversy and disagreement will dog Miki's biographical intentions until the oceans run dry. But look at it this way. Blessed—or cursed—with enough advance knowledge of his impending demise, a clue to Miki's desires might be that he had a choice: burn the records and artifacts of his life, or leave them intact and, from the grave, hope for the best.

Miki had famously grumbled that he had no doubt, when he'd passed on, that the vultures would surely pick at his bones. "I've got no life at all left now. I am certain that the horrors of the circus of my corporeal existence will seem placid when compared to the necrophiliatic actions of the greedy vultures who will orchestrate over the carnival of my death."

Truly felt and totally in character, as well as an enduringly creative way to cover his assets, so that even in death Miki's mantra of never having sold out would remain consistent, his mythos unassailable, his permission never directly given.

But here's what happened: no mysterious fires.

He left the evidence.

HARRY HODGE: We'd planned a memorial service in Malibu, and there was logic in that, but Miklos said, "He doesn't want anything." He wanted to be cremated, and the ashes thrown on the path where his dad took the dogs for a walk. Miki thought that was interesting: Every morning his dad would take the dogs out on the path, and the dogs would pee on him.

Later, I suggested we hold a memorial service at Guéthary in April 2002. We had waters from Malibu, Jeffreys Bay, and Guéthary mixed in a bowl by Martin Potter and Jeff Hakman, and then paddled out, and tipped into the sea.

[Greg Noll: Eulogy for Miki excerpt]
I've tried for two days now to write something about Mickey that isn't just a pile of meaningless words and I haven't had much success. I find it impossible to summarize such a complicated individual as Mickey Dora in a few sentences, but then of course, that's always the way it is when anyone has ever tried to conveniently fit Dora into one of society's many categories or molds. The problem is that Mickey just didn't fit into any of their perfect little scenarios to describe the model citizen. Dora was one of a kind, a bit like a wild animal. . . .

I can tell you this: other than a few boards we made together he never, ever, sold out although he had numerous opportunities. His personal integrity was much more important to him than taking money in exchange for endorsing some phony surf product just to make his life easier financially. Look around you, how many other top name surfers can live up to that standard?

The other great quality that the man upheld throughout his life is that he NEVER, EVER, EVER kissed ass to achieve his goals. Never. This cost him dearly on many occasions, but he held the line and refused to give an inch.

It is hard for me to believe that Mickey won't be around to challenge us about what surfing and life is really all about. I halfway expect to see him running across a sand dune with his board under his arm and just before he disappears over the edge, he turns around and gives us all the finger.

PHIL JARRATT: Miklos and Christine came from California and several of Miki's oldest friends came from around the world. Those who couldn't make it, like Greg Noll, sent written tributes. The mayor of Guéthary unveiled a memorial plaque on Miki's favorite bench, on the Guéthary terrace, overlooking the waves, and we all went off and had a few drinks, a few tears, and a lot of laughs.

Two days later I walked down to the terrace to check the surf and discovered that two of the screws holding Miki's plaque in place had been removed in an obvious attempt to convert the memorial to private memorabilia. I replaced the screws but within a week the plaque was gone. Ah, Miki, your memorial a prized trophy on some shithead's wall. Exploited to the end.

Because Miki left no will, Miklos Sr. and Harry Hodge began the probate process.

MIKLOS DORA SR.: I didn't want to do probate because I didn't think Miki had anything. We knew that he'd had a Swiss bank account once, because I sent him money there, but when C.C. asked him about it, his response was, "Why does everyone want to know about my bank accounts? I have nothing."

If anything, I thought he had a dollar, or less than a dollar. I thought it was a waste of time.

Harry talked me into a probate. He said some people would take advantage of Miki's name, and if you don't have a probate, we can't stop them. I said, "As long as you want to do it and you take care of the expenses, fine with me."

We found some things: six bank accounts plus two safety deposit boxes. One safety deposit box was in Vancouver. Christine and I went up and got it; it was full of silver coins, about $4,000 worth. I asked the bank to put me in touch with a coin dealer because I couldn't carry it back. It weighed a ton.

The other deposit box was in Zurich. I went to Europe in April for Miki's memorial and told the attorney that I would like to arrange to take possession. When I got there, the attorney of the bank said, "I am very sorry, but the authorization didn't come through. We have it in fax but we have to have the authorization in an original," and Harry Hodge didn't send that in time. "But," he said, "I'll let you look at it." The safety deposit box was full of silver coins. I found my mother's ring, and I found some money.

Then we sat with a Quiksilver attorney in Huntington Beach. He brought in the probate lawyer. Harry would be the administrator. I said, "Fine. And as long as you're making a probate, I know that Miki had a bank account at Credit Suisse. I don't believe he has a dollar in it, but you might as well check it out."

HARRY HODGE: When we checked the accounts, we found more than $400,000 in cash and investments.

C.C.: I knew he had an account; so did others. I may not have known the exact amount in his account, but he told me he had it in case anything happened to him. After his experience in New Zealand, he became overly cautious and tried to diversify. He was going to use the money to build his retirement home—in Chile, or wherever. He wanted to use it when he found a sanctuary.

MIKLOS DORA SR.: He was amazing. In thirty years, I sent him maybe $50,000. His mother left him almost $40,000. But $400,000? I still don't know where he got his money. However, he was always very frugal. Never even bought me a Coca-Cola—not that I drink Coca-Cola. He let everyone else pay for him, and he always played absolutely poor.

Miki had fooled everyone. According to account statements, he was heavily invested in silver, gold, and platinum. He owned shares of mining companies. He had high-interest-bearing CDs, as well as positions, for a time, in energy companies such as El Paso, Dynergy, Consolidated Energy, and Enron—on which he made healthy profits, selling in advance of the bust. He owned dollars, Deutschmarks, and Swiss francs. He wasn't always a winner, though. According to C.C., he had once bought silver with some money from an inheritance and lost it. "He said he'd have done better if he'd just given the money to me." Still, at one time his worth totaled nearly $500,000. And yet . . . and yet, by having the money but not using the money, Miki had taken to heart Sterling Hayden's maxim: "To be truly challenging, a voyage, like life, must rest on a firm foundation of financial unrest."

HARRY HODGE: I understand why he kept the money secret—security, something to fall back on—but I don't get why Miki didn't spend that money at the end when he knew he was dying, or years before, to have health checkups. He kept saying, "I don't have the money to go to Bali." I'd go, "We'll pay, we'll pay." He was crying poor.

Miklos was concerned about telling people about the accounts and the amount, and I understood. But I also said, "It's going to come out in probate anyway. And it only adds credibility to your son. People thought he was a bum!"

SUSAN MCNEILL: When Harry told me about Miki's money, I was surprised. I knew there was some but I didn't know there was *that* much. It made me laugh really hard. All the things he got someone else to pay for because he never had any money! Hysterical. I loved it. Miki got the last laugh.

LEFT: Miki's apartment in Guéthary, 2002. Photo: Harry Hodge.

BELOW: The view from Miki's first apartment in Guéthary. Photo: Bob Simpson.

BOTTOM LEFT: Miki surfing in Guéthary, 2001. Photo: Bob Simpson.

BOTTOM RIGHT: Plaque in memory of Miki, on his favorite bench overlooking the waves at Guéthary. Quickly stolen, and since replaced. Courtesy Harry Hodge.

2

What is it about surfers that will make them forgive almost anything? Not everyone absolved Miki of his sins, but many, many did. Is it because Miki was, well . . . Miki? Is it the charisma combined with the doggedness not to go along? The element of surprise he always offered? Is it because he did something the rest of surfers, and the rest of us, can only approach, mostly in our dreams? Is it because he could keep a secret? Is it because he understood that the world of men, although it appears solid and rooted in dry land, is in many ways a sham and a mess, and about yoking oneself to debt and people and, really, it's all allusion and crutch and temporal, whereas the ocean is perpetual motion, and one's place in it will always be the same. You can never argue with the ocean and win. The ocean will always be bigger than you. Always.

DEREK HYND: To me, Dora's life is *Cannery Row*. The whole notion of Steinbeck's America runs very strongly through the way he lived. It's not that far from the California of *The Grapes of Wrath* to when Dora was a kid. Look at Miki's bloodlines. You've got a very strange central European madness born of the Transylvanian steppes almost. His forebears traversing rolling plains where there's not meant to be anything around. No wonder something deeply affected Dora about the way California was peppered with more and more progress. He longed for the open spaces. Something in his DNA was twisted by the California postwar madness. That goes aside from all the urchin tricks that he learned. Yet a lot of what Dora is and was and did is viewed by others from this more modern context that assigns judgment. But can you, out of context? Miki was a constant in surfing. Everything else changed. He was a time capsule. Of course, his observations and predictions became more contemporary as time passed, but it was still the same-old same-old. He held firm to the ethos of his times.

Dora never had a real need to connect with anybody to make his way. He might have enjoyed—and occasionally did—an emotional rapport, but he used people not in a partnership sense. To know from a young age that you could blow anybody off because you'd wired the system has to be key in the way someone can last forty or fifty years without bowing to anyone. I believe Dora was the master of all he surveyed, even if he was an asshole. He was aware of who he was.

Dora was not in the mold of. There was no plan to the way he developed. Miki's plan was no plan until, I reckon, he was on that wave.

Then everything was as clear as a bell.

RICK PETERSON: Miki was an artist in the art of living. The moment was not to be wasted. Whether surfing, playing golf, or simply listening to jazz on his Walkman up in his room in my house, while appreciating a fine sunset; being able to find fascination in very simple things, in addition to being a connoisseur of fine irony. He was true to his nature, and therefore a man of great integrity, more so than anyone I have ever known.

He did have a bit of a go at the surfing world, which was a balloon ripe to be pricked, from many angles, and took itself far too seriously, even more so today. One goes to the beach, rides the waves, and goes home and gets a life. Finis. He *did* try to tell us that in the glorious millennium the Pacific Ocean would be, in every sense, the world's largest toilet, which indeed it now is. Even the waves have left.

This was a person who, as the reality of his affliction hit home, would say to me that he felt excruciatingly deeply for the planet, nature, animals . . . earthworms, the Gaia principle—and that the stress of caring and the angst he incurred for this and the flack he endured for being outspoken on the subject, that all of this had somehow contributed to his fatal condition. He *really* bloody cared! Several quack doctors expound on how if one goes through life smiling like an imbecile one can live to be one hundred.

It is too bad that all of the "Walk of Fame" attention he has gotten postmortem wasn't proffered premortem. Thanks, folks, but the train has left the station. He would have shrugged his shoulders and made some light of it—and deep down really appreciated it. He was never beaten down, ever, by anything. Just once, when he died years ago, and he did not go complacently into that dark night.

He was a great and loyal friend, appreciative, funny, trustworthy—my only friend who ever had a key to my home door. He is irreplaceable.

This was the guy who rode in the back of my van, steadying my 150-pound pet sheep who was sick and needed to get to the vet.

Wherever he is now, I hope it is summer at Malibu, winter in the Alps, and Scooter Boy is running along the sand or romping in the snow.

GREG NOLL: I called Miki just before he died. We made some idle chitchat and then I said, "Well, how's the battle going?"

He said, "They gave me a shot of morphine, so you'll have to excuse me if I don't make sense too good. And then they followed that up with an enema, and as soon as I'm through talking to you, I'm seriously considering doing a wall painting."

**Last portraits of Miki,
for *Vogue Hommes
International*, 2001.
Photos: Taki Bibelas.**

That may tell you more about Miki Dora than anything else. He took his sense of humor with him straight to the end.

I said, "Take care of yourself, Miki," and went to hang up the phone, and I don't know why but it just jumped out of my mouth: I said, "I love ya, man." I'd never said anything like that to him.

There was a moment of silence and he said, "I love ya, too, pal."

And then we hung up. It was pretty personal and I didn't think I was going to say it. But it just came out of my mouth.

And I'll be goddamned if my next thought wasn't that I'd spend the rest of my life trying to figure out if he was putting me on or not.

JOHNNY FAIN: After Miki passed, for a moment I thought he'd faked his death, that it wasn't Miki, that it was somebody else. I thought he could pull it off, if anyone could. Then Pezman told me it was for real. I told Greg Noll that Miki had died for our sins. He was the Messiah then. And then I got remorseful about having not wanted to take him up on his invitation to get together. I figured I owed him that. If it wasn't for Miki, I wouldn't be where I was because he always pushed me. He drummed this crazed feeling of "You can always be better," into me. And because I got to be with Miki and see his moves, I tried to make mine better. I never told him that, though. He thought I was just a puppy dog following him, and that's the way he wanted it.

MIKLOS DORA SR.: In 2002, when Miki was inducted in the Walk of Fame, in Huntington Beach, I made a short speech. At the end, I said, "I hope Miki is looking down at us. But knowing Miki he could be giving us the finger."

SAM GEORGE: One night, in the late '80s, in the old Atlantis hotel that used to be on the beach in Jeffreys Bay, I was in the bar—a classic dark bar—and Miki walked over. I'd come to interview him at his request, and we'd seen each other a couple times, but the interview had never happened.

This time he said, "Let's just talk a little bit."

I sat next to Miki. He wore a greatcoat and looked pretty dapper. Scooter Boy was there. I didn't have a tape recorder. This wasn't an interview. We had developed a rapport as surfers, and I didn't want to change that and suddenly become a reporter. Miki talked in what I would like to think was a relatively candid manner about how much he loved to surf and how much he loved the *sensation* of surfing. The actual acute feeling of it. He talked about what he looked for in a wave, and about moments on the wave. He had a song to sing, he did it on a certain kind of wave, and he described that wave—a point break obviously—and he told me how he'd looked for it in many places. At that moment, Jeffreys Bay held it for him.

ABOVE TOP: Dora: always at Malibu, one way or the other. Photo: Matt Katz.

ABOVE: Miki on the nose at Malibu. Painting by Richard Peterson, signed—a rarity—by Miki. Courtesy and copyright Richard Peterson.

We talked for an hour and a half. He prefaced almost everything with, "You've got to understand. . . ."

He said everything he did and everything he became, and all the stuff that people made him out to be, right or wrong, the root of it *all* was this feeling he got when he surfed.

All surfers look for those moments.

I thought, that's all I need to know about Miki Dora.

The legend of Miki Dora is so big.

But underneath is this guy who just loved to surf.

Miki at Malibu, 1960. Courtesy Dora Estate. Photographer unknown.

Paddle Out

All is waves—as far as the mind can see, and where the eye cannot yet see: vibrating fundamental quantum stuff, pure frequency assuming the shape-shifting shape of things. All is waves: matter, energy, light, sound, and even the friction of the wind that compels the ocean, chop and groundswell, into waves within waves, driving each to its inevitable nexus with the rocks and sand and the curious bipeds who, through time, with audacious invention and fearless imagination, come to ride the wild surf.

Who was Miki Dora, and why did he create himself in his way?

Personal freedom, the thrill and challenge of living on the edge, the quest for a better world because the one he lived in just never made sense, and the surfing dream state are reasons as good and true as any— and in the end it's all we get. Is it enough? It's a beginning. This much is certain: Miki was reluctant to solve the puzzle for us. Indeed, he kept tossing in pieces that never seemed to fit, and he answered our questions with questions of his own—if he answered them at all. Perhaps he simply existed beyond our ken: a surf god. Perhaps we saw him all too clearly and could not believe that was all there was: a surf bum. Likely both, and neither, a throwback and the next evolutionary stage—a thing entirely new.

Miki's life is what happens when you don't want to live like everyone else and are willing to do whatever it takes. It's about what happens when all you want to do is blur the boundary between man and wave and sense each moment wide awake. It's about what happens when the ride ends before you're ready and you don't know why.

But what a ride. Man overboard. Sink or swim. It's a hell of a thing.

And now, Miki, like a spent wave, has become a glorious ephemera: windblown, sparkling, ionic, subsumed, recycled, transformed, and ready to be reborn and break again on some future distant shore.

Like light, water, and wind, Miki can't be held; but he's not gone.

Wherever his spirit now resides, surely the desire to paddle out once more and ride the wild surf lives on.

Dora's World

Voices

A few of the major voices of the book identify themselves sufficiently in the main text (and are so noted here), but not all. Therefore, what follows is an alphabetic compendium of those whose words are featured here, in their own words, or mine, or as sourced from Matt Warshaw's *Encyclopedia of Surfing*. Also included are bios of some other important characters. Even though they don't speak directly, their voices (but not thoughts) were unfortunately lost due to space considerations.

DENNY AABERG: Writer, musician, and younger brother of Kemp Aaberg. Cowrote *Big Wednesday* with director John Milius.

KEMP AABERG: "I am probably best known for being in the early Bruce Brown surf movies, as well as John Severson's photo image of me doing an arch-back turn that he used as the logo for *Surfer* magazine for over twenty years. My history with Dora dates back to the *Gidget* era."

BILLY AL BENGSTON: Los Angeles artist and surfer; knew Miki in the '50s. Now lives on Vancouver Island, British Columbia, Canada.

CYNTHIA APPLEWHITE: Painter, novelist, free spirit. Wife of Louis Zamperini. Cynthia arranged the first meeting between Miki and David Rensin. Rensin later wrote her husband's book *Devil at My Heels* (William Morrow, 2003).

CLIVE BARBER: Jeffreys Bay surfer and craftsman. "I used to drink with Miki Dora, and we drank the best. He respected me because I had a good reputation as a board shaper and a good surfer in the '60s."

CAROLINE BARNETT: "I earned a master's and Ph.D. in clinical psych. I worked on staff in a private psychiatric hospital for almost fifteen years and just retired. Now I live on the Olympic Peninsula in Washington."

PETER BARNETT: "I was his go-to guy while he was on the run or in hiding from certain matters. I sent him money when he needed access to his residuals and other incoming assets. I kept his car, which he later sold to me (Lotus X7), his skateboard, surf magazines, passport, driver's license, bank books, and so on."

BOB BEADLE: "I doubled as 'Frankie' Dora and 'Tab' Beadle riding Waimea in 1962 for Hollywood surfkitsch flick *Ride the Wild Surf*. That was followed by four decades of scattershot antics in California, Oahu/Kauai, Costa Rica, and in Brazil, where I've recently returned."

RICK BECK: "I was surfing Rincon in about 1963, the kook of kooks. Miki pushed me off my board. Years later, I'm driving down to Raglan Point in New Zealand, and Miki comes driving up in a beige VW bus, stops window to window, and says, 'How's your memory?' I had a small surfboard shop there. He would park out front, living there."

YVES BESSAS: "I'm a lifetime surfer and doctor of pharmacy (University of Bordeaux). I specialize in nutrition and antiaging. I'm also a researcher-writer and creator of 'Sports de Glisse' concept, a surf and snow films producer."

JIM BEST: "We were teenagers. He was about thirty. I saw him just about every summer weekend from 1962 until 1969."

TAKI BIBELAS: "I'm a photographer, currently filming *The Still Point*, a documentary on the spirit of surf (due Fall 2007). Most of my exhibitions and films have been for galleries or art centers. Published photography includes *Vogue, Vanity Fair, Marie Claire, Elle, Tattler, Glamour, Sleek, Oyster, Surfers Journal*."

GREGG BLUE (MARSH): "In 1971, I was living in Jeffreys Bay when I met Miki in the car park and brought him home for dinner. A year later, in September 1972, Miki and I and a couple other surfers rented an old house in Guéthary that overlooked the ocean. We reconnected a couple years later in Val d'Isère, skiing."

DUKE BOYD: Surf entrepreneur. Founded Hang Ten surfwear in 1960, sold it ten years later. From 1968 to 1970 acted as managing editor for *Petersen's Surfing Magazine*. Boyd now runs Duke Boyd America surfwear. Worked with Greg Noll and Dick Graham to create some ads for "Da Cat" boards in the '60s.

GARTH BULLOCK: Currently an artist and fine arts instructor. 1970s /1980s regional and national award-winning sculptor and ceramist. Founder in 1988 of Pismo Beach Longboarders.

DAVID CALDWELL: "I met Miki in 1959. He gave me a "lesson" on a tandem board at 3' perfect Malibu. Crossed paths, surfing and traveling, 1974 and 1975 in New Zealand, L.A., Biarritz, Australia, and Bridgeport. I'm currently building large-scale animatronics for the special-effects movie trade and the occasional ultracustom surfboard."

CORKY CARROLL: (see main text)

ALLAN CARTER: (see main text)

DOUGLAS CAVANAUGH: "I'm a writer, surfing historian (1950 to 1968) and the only person alive who offered Dora money and was turned down!" Cavanaugh's forthcoming book, about a legendary surfer who died young, is called *Remembering Butch: The Butch Van Artsdalen Story*.

JEAN-CHARLES CAZES: French winemaker, scion of Château Lynch-Bages, maker of fine Paulliac wine. "When Miki learned I wanted to surf—I was eleven— he said, 'You should play golf. Surfing's no good.' I didn't listen."

RUPERT CHADWICK: Well-connected, South African–born entrepreneur. Started the Billabong contest there. Started the Jeffreys Bay Boardriders Club. Founding member of the Supertubes Trust. Helped create and curates the J Bay Surf Museum, a "non-corporate-denominational" establishment, housed in the local Quiksilver premises.

RHONDA CHAGOURIE: (see main text)

GARDNER CHAPIN JR.: Son of Gard Chapin and Ramona Stancliff. Born in Los Angeles, California, on August 4, 1946; passed away August 4, 2006.

C.C.: "Namaste."

ERIC CHAUCHÉ: "I'm a photographer in quest of light, nature, and waves. I live in Anglet, near Guéthary, in the French Basque country. I shared with Miki, during his last four years, trekking in the Basque country and Pyrenees Mountains, looking for wildlife and harmony, skiing, a river bath, or simply a good meal." Chauché's many books include *Perfect Waves: The Endless Allure of the Ocean* (Edition Herm 2004 and Abramsbooks edition 2006) with Tim McKenna and Sylvain Cazenave.

FRANCES CHRISTOPHER: Friend of Susan McNeill's. Married to a marquis.

JACKIE CLEMMONS: Jackie and her husband, Mike Clemmons, "used to belong to a Charismatic church in South Africa. Miki wanted to know why the pastors didn't sell their BMWs and help the poor. He didn't like hypocrisy at all, it freaked him out."

STEVEN CONNERS: Mormon missionary on Mahia Penisula in 1975. Worked to convert Miki to the Church of Latter Day Saints.

BOB COOPER: "Regarded as the original surfing beatnik," says the *Encyclopedia of Surfing*. Surfed Malibu in 1952, at age fifteen, and "eight years later was one of the first American surfers to visit Australia, where he has lived since 1969."

ADRIAN COTTON, MD: Miki's physician at Loma Linda University Medical Center.

LINDA CUY: (see main text)

PETER DAY: Producer, with Grant Keir, of the documentary *In Search of Da Cat* for Faction Films.

BILL DELANEY: Did the '70s surf film *Free Ride* featuring Shaun Tomson, Rabbit Bartholomew, and Mark Richards, then the 1990 film *Surfers: The Movie*.

ROBBIE DICK: "From 1962 through 1966, I was a member of the Hansen, Harbour, and Hobie surf teams. In 1967, I landed a job with Wilken Surfboards. I helped Mickey rough out some radical 8'10" pintails that were part of the shortboard revolution. I started Natural Progression with Skip Smith and Terry Lucoff in 1968. I left the company in 1985 and started shaping my own label, R. Dick Custom Surfdesign. I now live in Oregon."

WILLIE DIX: Owned the Freedom Surf Shop in Biarritz when Miki lived in the area from 1975 to 1981.

PETER DIXON: Wrote four books on surfing in the '60s, including *Men Who Ride Mountains* (1969).

TONI DONOVAN COLVIN: "I'm enjoying life in Topanga Canyon as an aging hippie, passing time with good friends and my animals, and traveling to exotic islands. I can still be seen on the beach at Malibu and Topanga."

MIKLOS AND CHRISTINE DORA: (see main text)

MIKE DOYLE: "Arguably the 1960s best all-around surfer," according to the *Encyclopedia of Surfing*. "Everyone wanted to look like him, dress like him, surf like him." He sold Kathy "Gidget" Kohner her first surfboard in 1956, for $35. His autobiography, *Morning Glass: The Adventures of a Legendary Waterman*, was published in 1993, and copies today sell for collector's prices. He moved to Baja in 1980, where he paints.

JIM "BURRHEAD" DREVER: According to Steve Pezman, "One of the best surfers on the coast in the '40s and early '50s." Contemporary of Gard Chapin.

BOKKA DU TOIT: Filmmaker, producer, herbalist, and Renaissance man from Jeffreys Bay. Befriended Miki, tried to help him forget the past, focus on the future, and live a happier life.

WOODY EKSTROM: Legendary surfer from the Tijuana Sloughs to San Onofre. Helped build the original Windansea Shack.

BRIAN EDDY: Owner/auctioneer/partner at Barwicks in Gisborne, New Zealand. Eddy still has a plated ewer given to Miki by his father. It's a family heirloom and part of a set (with a bowl) in which Miki was bathed as a baby. Miklos, now ninety-five, would really like it returned and is willing to pay a fair price.

PHIL EDWARDS: "During my life, I've seen a few special people who made me think, there's no prior art there. This is true creativity. Miki was one."

JOHN ELWELL: "I am a retired educator who began surfing in 1947. My era includes Bob Simmons, about whom I have written biographical stories."

SKIP ENGBLOM: Native Californian born in Hollywood in 1948. Began surfing 1959 at Venice, California. Cofounder of Zephyr Surf Shop and skateboard team. Founder SMA skateboard label. Published poet. Original member of Surfrider Foundation.

JOHNNY FAIN: *The Surfer's Journal* called Fain "one of the four aces of Malibu." The others were Dewey Weber, Lance Carson, and, naturally, Miki. Questions lingered long about whether their feud was real or staged, but the facts suggest that it was, at least at the end, authentic.

BOB FEIGEL: "I grew up in Santa Monica and Malibu, started surfing in the late 1950s. I write for surfing and lifestyle magazines and have been living in Aotearoa, New Zealand, since the mid-'70s. Miki's and my paths crossed several times over the years—both in and out of the water—and each encounter was unforgettable."

JIM FISHER: Surfer and body surfer from the early days of Malibu and Hawaii. Lifeguarded at San Clemente, hiring Miki one summer. Wild at heart and sometimes referred to as "Klepto-Jim."

VICKI FLAXMAN: Early Malibu surfer. Met Miki in 1950, in San Onofre, when he was still named Chapin.

HENRY FORD: Surfed in all the Bruce Brown films and was manager of the Jacobs Surf Team. "I was lifeguard from 1963 to 1969 at Malibu Point. Currently I have a clothing company, Koko Island, and have model surfboards with Hobie and Surf Tech."

TRUDI FORSTER: "I met Miki through my partner, Phil Grace. He played tennis and golf with Phil and came very often to dinner or just to hang out and watch movies. Miki poached me from Phil, who doesn't dance, as one of his salsa partners."

KIM FOWLEY: What can one say about Kim Fowley that hasn't already been said, whispered, or screamed? According to the website www.rocksbackpages.com, Fowley is, "the greatest hustler in the history of rock 'n' roll. . . ." If you go to www.kimfowley.com, he'll be glad to tell you all about himself. His forthcoming authorized and uncensored memoir is titled *Vampire from Outer Space*.

MARK FRAGALE: Surf journalist, archivist, and collector of historic surfing artifacts. Mark is a founding member of the Surfing Heritage Foundation and has been actively surfing for more than forty-five years; he lives in Kailua, Hawaii.

BILL FREY-MCLEAN: Screenwriter, living in the Okanagan Valley, in B.C. Canada and nowhere near the surf. "Miki recommended that I read *How to Be Free in an Unfree World*, one of his bibles."

ANTHONY FRIEDKIN: Photographer who, according to *The Surfer's Journal*, picked up a brownie "at age eight and aimed it seaward." He started surfing three years later—and still does. His first published photo appeared in *Surf Guide* in 1963. Friedkin works often for the movies as a unit still photographer (*Titanic, Dogtown and Z-Boys*—in which he was also interviewed—*Stand and Deliver, Riding Giants*), and recently published *Timekeeper*, a collection of his work.

JIM GANZER: Aka JimmyZ. "I'm an artist. I met Miki in 1959–60. I was about fifteen. We watched him work Malibu, State Beach, Topanga, Pop Pier, Rincon, parties, movies, contests, filmmakers, chicks, surfboard makers, surf mags, skateboards, Africa, Europe, golf, lunch, dinner, plane rides."

ED GARNER: Friend of the "House of Suede" Wilsons: Tony, Brian, Jeff, and matriarch Eugenia. Ed went to Beverly Hills High and hung out with Duane King, Mike Nader, and others and started going to Malibu. Appeared in the beach party movies, got into the music business, then moved to Santa Barbara in the mid-'70s.

GEORGE GEORGE: Schoolmate of Miki's at St. John's Military Academy. This really is his name.

MYSTO GEORGE (CARR): Retired schoolteacher, Malibu regular still, in his seventies.

SAM GEORGE: A former professional competitor, magazine editor, surf journalist and filmmaker, Sam, fifty, is also one of the sport's premier surf explorers, having traveled to over forty different countries in search of waves.

LESLIE-ANN GERVAIS: Full-time athlete. "In 1997, while in South Africa for the World Fencing Championships, I made a side trip to surf at Jeffreys Bay. At that time, I was a die-hard beginner surfer, so I am very thankful to Miki who took me under his wing."

EDWARD GODFREY: "I am still living on Cape St. Francis, surfing, as well as making buchu oil. Miki was a family friend who participated in the lives of our children and ourselves for many months when he lived with us on our buchu farm in Paarl, near Cape Town, and at our home at the Cape. We surfed together many times."

BRUCE GOLD: According to his friend Dr. Kurt Mariano, Gold is "a living legend in Jeffreys Bay. A free spirit with wit and tenacity . . . surfs every day, more than once if possible." Formerly an Afrikaans police officer and Durban taxi driver. Now, occasionally, a skilled and talented massage therapist.

Says Gold himself, exactly as written: "Can you Adam and Eve it? SIX 0 years old & now heavily dreadlocked by Danish beauty in Tofu, Mozambique while shooting a surfing doccy. Caught biggest wave & longest this year at Supers, separately. Met MIKI & Scooter on the Main St. of Jeffreys after studiously avoiding him for a month . . . He thought I was the last of the Purists. I wasn't so sure . . . 'Don't Sell Me OUT,' his last words after leaving me all his stuff. Maybe, maybe not MIKI."

PHIL GRACE: "I met Miki around 1975 in Pippi Beach near Angourie. I saw him again in Jeffreys Bay in the late '80s and in France in the '90s, for tennis, golfing, surfing, skiing, and at any event where they served free food and drinks. Good old Miki was one of the funniest/caustic buggers I have ever known. When he went home for the last time, he said, 'Stick a fork in me, I'm done.'"

LEROY GRANNIS: Born in 1917 in Hermosa Beach, when the Pacific Coast Highway was just a dirt road, Grannis began surfing in 1931 and eventually became one of the sport's premier photographers. His book of 1960s photos, entitled *Photo: Grannis*, was published in 1998 by *The Surfer's Journal*. His latest book is *LeRoy Grannis, Surf Photography of the 1960s and 1970s*.

RICK GRIGG: "Supremely confident surfer from Honolulu, Hawaii, winner of the 1966 Duke Kahanamoku Invitational, and sometimes referred to as the first big wave hotdogger," according to the *Encyclopedia of Surfing*. Grigg, who earned a bachelor's in biology, a master's in zoology, and a Ph.D. in oceanography, is now a professor in the Oceanography Department at the University of Hawaii. His autobiography, *Big Surf, Deep Dives and the Islands: My Life in the Ocean*, was published in 1998. Six months before Miki died, he faxed Grigg, praising the book.

SHANE GRIMES: New Zealand surfer, friend of producer Peter Day.

MICHAEL HALSBAND: Portrait photographer/filmmaker. "I was the tour photographer for the Rolling Stones 1981 *Tattoo You* Tour. I made the well-known photograph of Andy Warhol and Jean-Michel Basquiat with boxing gloves. Currently directing a documentary on the life story of Sri K. Pattabhi Jois, guru of Ashtanga yoga. I met Miki in Australia in 2001. We surfed together, spent a lot of time talking about Cuba. I made a portrait of him alone for *Surf Book*, and one with Donald Takayama."

JAN HANDZLIK: A partner in the Securities Litigation, Government Enforcement and White Collar Defense Practice Group in the Los Angeles office of Howrey LLP.

GLENN HENING: "I'm currently a consultant doing research into environmental issues at former military sites. I was recently named Regents Lecturer at UCSB based on my reputation of "asking the hard questions" about modern surfing as founder of the Surfrider Foundation and cofounder of the Groundswell Society. I grew up surfing State Beach in Santa Monica and saw Dora's act in the water—and on the beach—for years. To him, I was just another gremmie at State. To me he was just enough of a role model to help me always recognize bullshit wherever I've found it—including, in the end, his."

FRAYNE HIGGASON: Born in 1934, moved to Malibu 1949, and started surfing there regularly from 1951 to 1963. Recently won the 70-and-over division at the 2006 Malibu Classic. "I'm a landlord with properties in West Los Angeles and Santa Barbara."

ANDY HILL: "Surfing for almost thirty years. I started in 1979, in Ireland, aged ten. I'm six times Irish National Surfing Champion, and owner of Troggs Surf Shop in Portrush since 1991. I met Miki in Ireland in 1985."

MIKE HISCHIER: Owner of Wavelengths Surf shop in Morro Bay, California, since 1980. Collector of surfboards and skateboards.

HARRY HODGE: Harry Hodge started surfing at fifteen in Melbourne. He began his professional life in the mail room and became a journalist. In the '70s, he produced and directed the surf film *Band on the Run* with the title track by Paul McCartney and Wings. In 1982, he became Quiksilver Australia's first marketing director and, in 1984, founded Quiksilver Europe with Jeff Hakman. He is currently an executive adviser to Quiksilver Inc.; director of the Quiksilver Foundation; chairman emeritus of Quiksilver Europe; director of SAI (SurfAID International), and chairman of Better Energy Systems Inc. After retiring from his positions as CEO and chairman of Quiksilver Europe in 2003, Harry relocated back to Australia with his wife, Sandee, and three boys: Mat, Tom, and Ben. He just recently acquired a significant stake in the Sydney-based jeanswear label, ksubi (pronounced subi), and is executive chairman of the company.

RICK HODGSON: "Three things come to mind when I think of Miki. First, he knew me as the Phantom of Topanga Beach when I returned to him some of his possessions from the Gisborne, New Zealand, auction. Second, as a surfer, I learned style from him—but not method. Third, when I correctly predicted a coming swell—and no one else believed me—Miki said, "You lead a charmed life." Ever since then I have. As for what I do, I think being the Phantom says it all. I'd rather no one know; I'm having too much fun and I'm very lucky."

PAUL HOLMES: Surfboard shaper, surf journalist, surf contest director, and surfwear marketing executive. "I'm a former editor-in-chief of *Surfer* magazine and the author of *Dale Velzy is Hawk*, the story of the legendary Californian surfboard shaper, cowboy, and hot-rodder, published in 2006."

KIT HORN: "I was at Malibu before Gidget. I went with Chuck King in 1942 or 1943. Most of the time you had Malibu to yourself, or with a buddy."

WILLIE HOUSE: Surfed with Miki at Malibu but had to quit because of family issues. Miki thought House's exit was a tragedy. Currently lives in Switzerland.

ROD HUGHES: Mormon missionary in New Zealand's Mahia Peninsula in 1975 who performed Miki's conversion.

SCOTT HULET: The editor of *The Surfer's Journal* for nearly a decade. "My interactions with Miki were brief, collegial, and engaging."

DEREK HYND: Australian surfer and writer, who lived for a time on Supertubes in Jeffreys Bay.

MIKE HYNSON: Costar, with Robert August, of Bruce Brown's *Endless Summer*. Hynson created the "red fin" model for the Gordon & Smith label, as well as other board design improvements.

HAP JACOBS: Quiet and thoughtful surfboard shaper from Hermosa Beach, California. Partnered with Dale Velzy for four years before starting his own brand and, by the mid-'60s, producing 125 boards a week. Jacobs quit to become a commercial fisherman for fifteen years but returned to shaping in the early '90s.

PHIL JARRATT: "I've been writing about surfing for almost forty years and my most recent work, *The Mountain and The Wave: The Quiksilver Story*, was published late in 2006. I first met Miki in Bali in 1975, spent twenty years on his shit-list for writing about a conversation we had, and twenty-five years later we were friends and next-door neighbors in Guéthary, France."

BILL JENSEN: Malibu regular in *Gidget* era and object of a Kathy Kohner crush. The real Moondoggie.

RICHARD "SPIDER" JOSEPHSON: "I became a Buddhist monk and ran the Chan (meditation hall) for ten years, returned to lay life, went to Nepal and married a Nepalese, and lived there ten years. I very, very rarely surf because of the crowds. My website www.buddhadharma.com pretty much covers my days. I now live on Maui."

DREW KAMPION: Self-described "hodad from Buffalo, New York, who rode his first wave at Malibu in 1962." John Severson made him editor of *Surfer* magazine in June of 1968. He enjoyed the job and eventually parlayed it into an extended feature-writing arrangement with *Surfing* magazine in the 1970s. Now it's forty years and about nine books later, including *The Way of the Surfer, Stoked: A History of Surf Culture, The Lost Coast, The Book of Waves,* and *Greg Noll: The Art of the Surfboard*. He's currently the U.S. editor of *The Surfer's Path*, the only 100 percent green surf magazine.

GERRY KANTOR: "I am the owner of Leucadia Surf School (www.leucadiasurfschool.com) in north San Diego, California."

MATT KATZ: While living in Chile, writer/surfer Matt Katz opened his doors to a mixed bag of idiosyncratic travelers, most notably Miki Dora. A native of Ventura County, California, Matt moved to Chile in 1995. He now lives in Carpinteria, California. Matt edits the *Broughton Quarterly* travel magazine. In 2004, *The Surfer's Journal* published "Full Circle California," his account of six weeks in Chile with Miki Dora.

JIM KEMPTON: Jim Kempton met Miki in 1974 in Biarritz, France. For the next six years they shared surfing, Ping-Pong, tennis, a lover, numerous French feasts, and uncountable stories. Kempton became the editor and then publisher of *Surfer* magazine, was a publisher at TransWorld Publications, traveled through several continents on the Indies Trader Crossing Boat, and now works at Billabong as the media director.

DUANE KING: "I met Miki at Malibu when I was fourteen, in 1959. I watched as Miki gained insight and perception into all of the forces working to destroy the pristine Malibu at the center of his universe. I now work in Santa Monica, financing commercial construction."

MATT KIVLIN: Accurately described by the *Encyclopedia of Surfing* as "elegant," Kivlin, born in 1929, and an architect since 1971, set the stylish trim pose at Malibu that Miki copied; it helped that they bore a resemblance to each other in hair color and body type. They did not share temperament. "Matt invented what I call 'performance cruising,'" said Kemp Aaberg. "He was gentlemanly and rode that way."

KATHY KOHNER ZUCKERMAN: "I surfed Malibu from 1956 to my last wave there in 1960. Did it again in the mid-'90s. Call it a lull. I was called Gidget at the "Bu"; Miki was called Chapin."

CHERON KRAAK: (see text)

KRIS KRUSESKI: "I was vacationing in Biarritz in 1985 when I was introduced to Miki by a dear friend. We had an eight-month relationship, which included four days of togetherness and lots of love letters. I still live in the San Diego area where I have a garden design business."

JUANITA STANCLIFF KUHN: Ramona's younger sister, Miki's aunt.

FRANÇOIS LARTIGAU: An artist for Quiksilver for more than twenty years. "I have been surfing since 1961, one of the first French grommets, and I am still doing it as much as I can. I met Miki in 1968. He was older but his 'aura' was very strong in the surfing community. At the end of his life I got closer to him and it really hurt me to see the old Cat fading away."

PHILIPPE LAUGA: A native from a fishing village in Euskal Herria (the land of the Basque). "I met Miki as a young man, in the mid-'70s. I worked then in a financial institution. We shared friendship and angst, numerous and various activities, throughout most stages of his life in Europe. Miki was always ready on the spur of the moment, questioned my intellect, induced me to look on the other side of the mirror, taught me that the word *compromise* contains the word *promise*."

JOEL LAYKIN: School and running mate of Miki's in the late '40s and beyond. Joel's father owned Laykin et Cie jewelers. He currently lives in Hong Kong.

CRAIG LEONARD: "My twin brother, Keith, and I used to go to State Beach. I used to play tennis with Miki a couple times a week."

CHRISTINE LIEPNER: Sister of Jessica Naude. Works for Cheron Kraak at Billabong, in Jeffreys Bay. Her relationship with Miki was instinctive and needed few words.

TERRY LUCOFF: Onetime owner and manufacturer of Natural Progression surfboards from 1966 to 1990. Surf shop located across the street from the Malibu Pier—the only one during the golden era of Malibu. "Miki could come into our factory in Santa Monica and create whatever he wanted without any strings attached. He rode our boards. We never exploited it."

CHRIS MALLOY: Oldest of the three Malloy brothers, from Ventura, California. Seen in front of the camera (*Momentum* and other surf videos), and now behind the camera, making independent surf films through the brothers' Moonshine Conspiracy collective: *Thicker Than Water, September Sessions, Shelter,* and *A Brokedown Melody.* Malloy's direct connection to surfing's soul is apparent in the respect he gets from surfing's greatest generation. He's always headed somewhere to film and ride.

THE MASOCHIST: Miki's designated nemesis at Malibu. Miki did everything he could to irritate him or frame him for mischief. "The result was a hate/love relationship."

JAN MAYER: Surfer-skier friend of Miki's in the mid 1970s in Biarritz, Chamonix, Val d'Isère, and Innsbruck. "I was a ski instructor and beginning leather worker when I met Miki, and now own a fiber arts studio (Kriska Painting on Silk) and live in Salt Lake City, Utah. I still love to ski the steep and deep." Cofounder of Valley Longboarder Surfing Association.

ANNABELLE MCBRIDE: Known as Terry. Her mother was Rebecca Harkness, of the Standard Oil family. Rebecca founded the Harkness Ballet, as well as Harkness Pavilion in the Columbia University Medical Center. Annabelle was briefly married to Tony McBride, son of Miklos Sr.'s second wife, Lorraine (mother of Miki's half-sister Pauline). She died in 2005.

MICHAEL MCDONNELL: Currently a film producer. Credits include *The Usual Suspects* and *The Replacement Killers.*

MARCIA MCMARTIN: Born into a wealthy family with mining interests, Marcia's life has been filled with many pursuits, including interior decorating, photography, and a job as a meter maid. Growing up she spent summers with her father, an avid hunter, in Bermuda at his palatial home, Elephant Walk. She has traveled most of her life, circling the globe, and was Miki's traveling companion from 1970 to 1974, and friend until the end.

MIKE MCNEILL: Former husband of Susan, below. Expat American living in France for almost thirty years. Surfboard maker then, now working for Quiksilver Europe. Had the pleasure to share voyages with Miki and to be his friend.

SUSAN MCNEILL: Miki's longtime confidante, former lover, spiritual supporter, keeper of many secrets. Co-owned the Surf Hut in Guéthary. "He changed my life. He was an intelligent, loving, and beautiful person with a wicked sense of humor. I now live in California and sell art. He once told me life was too short to waste it working. I look for joy in what I do and I have found it. I miss him every day."

GREG MEISENHOLDER: One of the four horsemen of the Apocalypse, traveled with Miki, Allan Carter, and Don Wilson to Acapulco and Rio in 1969 and 1970. Now deceased.

MIKEY MEYER: "Although I live in Jeffreys Bay and knew him there, I met Miki in France in 1985 in Seignosse, which is north of Anglet and Hossegor in the Côte D'Argent, which itself is just north of the Côte Basque. He was like a mentor."

JOHN MILIUS: Hollywood's ultimate insider/outsider. Directed *Big Wednesday, Conan the Barbarian, Red Dawn, Farewell to the King, The Wind and the Lion, Dillinger.* His writing credits are stellar: *Dirty Harry, The Life and Times of Judge*

Roy Bean, Magnum Force, Jeremiah Johnson, Apocalypse Now, Clear and Present Danger, Rough Riders. Created Dirty Harry's famous speech: "Do you feel lucky, punk? . . . Go ahead, make my day." Also wrote the line "Charlie don't surf!" uttered by Robert Duvall in *Apocalypse Now.* Milius surfed Malibu in the '50s and '60s with friends Shelly Riskin and Jack Barth, both of whom are pictured with him under the director's credit on *Big Wednesday.*

TOM MOREY: "Mickey Chapin was the kid I knew, a year older and well seated at Malibu, which I'd just discovered in 1953. Naturally, he was the guy not only to learn from, but to then try and best. At times I did. 'They say you're seven times as good as me, Morey,' he would always say to me."

BOB MORRIS: Los Angeles restauranteur. Built Gladstone's 4 Fish, R.J.'s Rib Joint, and "twenty-six other restaurants in the Los Angeles area." Currently runs Paradise Cove Cafe, on land originally owned—and sold—by his father. "I never hung out with Miki like Joel Laykin did, but he would float in and out of my life. He'd show up and always try to get a free dinner. We'd end up giving him one."

MICKEY MUÑOZ: One of the world's most durable surfers. In 1957 was one of the first to ride Waimea Bay. "He was highly regarded as a snappy and playful small-wave expert," says the *Encyclopedia of Surfing.* Muñoz continues to shape boards and recently appeared in *Chasing Dora*, a documentary based on Miki's posthumous article (and original environmental concept)—"The Aquatic Ape"—in *The Surfer's Journal.* Muñoz rode at Jeffreys Bay on a board, and wearing a wetsuit, both made of biodegradable material. He had the longest ride.

MIKE NADER: Beverly Hills High graduate, friend of Duane King and the Wilsons. Best known as character Dex Dexter on *Dynasty*, but also appeared in the beach party movies, in *The Trip*, and an assortment of daytime soaps.

JESSICA NAUDE: Still living in Jeffreys Bay. "Miki was the best ballroom dance partner I had and I sure miss our lessons together filled with laughter and fun."

CLIVE NEESON: "I'm a consultant physicist and grew up in Raglan whilst Miki was there in the 1970s. Miki's conversations, photo albums, and advice influenced me to capture the '70s era and the planet's unspoilt surf paradises with a movie camera before they were swallowed by the pending commercialism he warned of. As Miki's prophecy has come to pass the time is now ripe and work on the movie is under way."

GREG AND LAURA NOLL: Nicknamed "Da Bull," Noll coauthored a 1989 biography with Andrea Gabbard, *Da Bull: Life Over the Edge.* Originally from Manhattan Beach, California, Noll is generally regarded as the first person to ride Hawaii's Waimea Bay, in 1957. A hotdogger in his youth, he visited Hawaii in 1954 and lived in a Quonset hut at Makaha for seven months. Noll made five surf movies and became a premiere board maker, opening a twenty-thousand-square-foot operation. Laura Noll is Greg's second wife, and although diminutive in comparison to her sizeable husband, she has always been more than capable of keeping him in line.

AGI ORSI: Film producer. When Orsi teamed up with director Stacy Peralta on the skateboard culture documentary *Dogtown and Z-Boys*, they went on to win both the Audience and Directors Award at Sundance Film Festival and a worldwide theatrical distribution. Orsi next produced Peralta's big surf documentary, *Riding Giants*, which was the first documentary ever to open the Sundance Film Festival.

E. J. OSHIER: E. J. met Gard Chapin at the Palos Verdes Cove before World War II. Member of the Palos Verdes Surf Club and San Onofre Surf Club. A mainstay at San Onofre from the '30s until he died in March 2007.

PEACHES: Met Miki on the beach in 1966 when she was seventeen. Their on-and-off three-year relationship went badly, and even today she profoundly regrets having known him at all.

STACY PERALTA: A founding father of modern skateboarding in the '70s and former action-sports entrepreneur. Peralta directed and cowrote the award-winning 2001 documentary *Dogtown and Z-boys*. In 2004, he directed and cowrote *Riding Giants* with Sam George. He also directed *The Baron Davis Project*, an L.A. gang documentary, and is slated to direct the screen version of Allen Weisbecker's surfing adventure novel, *In Search of Captain Zero*.

DORIAN "DOC" PASKOWITZ: One of the most fascinating characters in surfing. He grew up surfing San Onofre, currently lives in Hawaii with his wife, Juliette. "My connection with Miki Dora is hooked to three mental images: One, a feisty little boy, maybe twelve years old running across the coarse gray sand of San Onofre beach. Miki is laughing. Two: A thin, tanned young man, eighteen or nineteen, dancing on the waves, elegant, bold, maybe even arrogant. Three: a man in a trench coat stops at the top of the old wooden stairs at Malibu to say hello. 'Hi Paskowitz,' 'Hi Miki.' And off he goes, heading for the burger stand. He's not smiling."

GREG PERSON: Newport Beach surfer, friend of Joe Quigg and Joey Cabell. Met Miki in 1965 at Malibu and then again in Costa Rica in 1991 at Greg Noll's first Legends event. Currently a manager at Morningside Recovery Center in Newport Beach.

RICK PETERSON: Longtime friend of Miki, partner in both the water and worldview. According to his website, www.richardpetersongallery.com, "that he is not a 'household name' is merely an attribute of creating works that are decidedly not 'commercial,' being created in a very limited number for a very discerning clientele all over the world."

STEVE PEZMAN: Steve started surfing in the late '50s and explored California, Mexico, and Hawaii. "I did six months in the merchant marines hauling stale beer to Vietnam in 1965. Came back and started making surfboards, then writing about it. Ended up at *Surfing* then *Surfer*, where with less than a year's experience I fell into the publisher's chair. I stayed seated for twenty-one years, and then founded *The Surfer's Journal* with my wife, Deb. That's what we do now, along with parenting three great boys at varying stages of life, from San Clemente, California."

JOE QUIGG: According to the *Encyclopedia of Surfing*, Quigg is a "virtuoso surf-board designer and craftsman . . . co-founder of the modern longboard and the specialized big-wave board, and credited by many as the most influential mid-century board maker."

RANDY RARICK: According to the *Encyclopedia of Surfing*, Rarick is "an authoritative surf traveler/organizer/board-maker from Sunset Beach, Hawaii." A 1998 profile in *The Surfer's Journal* referred to Rarick as "Mr. Clean." Among his many accomplishments was being location scout for Bruce Brown's *Endless Summer II*. "As a kid, I repaired Miki's board that he rode in *Ride the Wild Surf* and then spent the next forty years waiting for him to thank me!"

DOUGLAS RISHWORTH: Miki's lawyer in New Zealand. Kept some artifacts from the 1984 Barwicks auction and, after not being able to hand them over in person, sent them to Miki in Montecito before he died.

ARMAND RIZA: State Beach habitué, volleyball player, and member of the party-crashing club. Lives on the beach.

JEAN YVES ROBERT: Ski instructor, friend, and traveling companion (Cuba) of Miki's for many years. Based in Guéthary.

OVIDIO (ANDY) SALAZAR: A Dogtown local and impressionable teenager inspired by Miki during the '60s. An interest in Sufism led to his self-imposed exile from California and to a career in documentary films in Europe and the Middle East. *In Search of Da Cat* was his eulogy for Miki and to the "Golden Age" of Malibu. He continues to make films and to ride waves whenever he can. www.matmedia.org.

JOHN SEVERSON: Currently surfing and painting in Hawaii. Made surf films in '60s and '70s, started *Surfer* magazine, inducted into Hall of Fame and received assorted awards. Living full life, close to nature and thankful of surfing influence, friends, and family. "Surfed with Miki—what a trip!"

BARBARA SIEVERS: I'm an artist, psychotherapist, and currently work with my son, Teal, at his company, Living Dream Films. Miki was one of my first true loves and a great friend.

BOB SIMPSON: An American international lawyer in Paris and a lifetime surfer. Miki lived at Bob's place in Guéthary, during the 1990s, and the two surfed, played tennis, golfed, partied, and enjoyed fine meals and wines together. Bob also doubled as Miki's personal lawyer in negotiations for media deals.

DR. DON SMALL: I started surfing when I was a state lifeguard at San Clemente in about 1951. I had seen Miki Dora surf, but I only met him in the brig of the SS *Lurline* when we both were caught trying to stow away to get free passage from Honolulu to Hilo, Hawaii. For the last fifty years I have been a medical scientist studying cholesterol, gallstones, and heart disease.

JACKIE SMITH: From Long Beach, California. Left the United States in 1969 with four sons: Mike, 15; Steve, 13; Jeff, 11; Joe, 9. "We went around the world looking for the perfect surf spot, which included Portugal, South Africa, Australia, and New Zealand. Crossed paths with Miki over the years and always enjoyed his company."

WAYNE SPEEDS: Veteran waterman, "graphic arts visionary," and Dora's neighbor in the late '60s and early '70s. "Mickey was one of my few role models in my teenage years. He was good for rides to the beach and wildly outrageous commentary on life and times, keeping me rolling with laughter."

DOUGLAS STANCLIFF: "I currently own a company that makes in-store merchandising displays for manufacturers of extreme sports, and food and hardware products. Miki is my first cousin and had a positive influence on my life."

MERRITT STANFIELD: Got his degree and teaching credential from UCLA and coached football and track at Palisades High School.

DARRYL STOLPER: "I'm a real Californio, born in Ventura (1942) and raised on State Beach and Malibu, where I started surfing in the mid-1950s. I first met Mickey Dora (aka Chapin) in the late '50s, when I brought my brand-new Dave Sweet foam board. Mickey asked if he could try it out and that was the beginning of a friendship."

PAUL STRAUCH: Gentleman surfer from Hawaii who invented the "cheater five" nose ride. Always a strong competitor. Won the Peru International contest in 1963. "When I got out of high school, my graduation gift was to spend the summer in California. I met Miki at Malibu in August 1961."

MARTIN SUGARMAN: "Dora and I were very close surfing companions. We surfed Will Rogers State Beach together for years. We surfed Old Joe's, Zeros, the Overhead, Hammonds Reef, and Rincon." Sugarman publishes H_2O magazine.

DIANE SWANSON OOSTERVEEN: "I've been happily married for thirty-seven years and now live in the Islands. Miki was my first love. My Svengali of life. He taught me the good and the bad. I lived in secret with Da Cat for a couple years."

MIKE TABELING: "In the '60s I broke the 'East Coasters are kooks' mold to become the first 'Right Coaster' to win contests in California and internationally. In the '70s, I dropped out to travel the world searching for perfect waves. In 1988, I bought a piece of property at Supertubes in Jeffreys Bay and moved there. I'm currently living in California and working as the West Coast sales director for Global Surf Industries."

STEVEN TAUSSIG: World observer, living on the side of Haleakala volcano. Owner-operator of Royal Hawaiian Cigars. Still enjoying the ocean and company of Cavalier King Charles spaniels. "I knew Miki over forty years."

DOMINIQUE TAYLOR: "I met Miki during a very tough winter when he was living in his van in France, in the mid-'80s. I offered him to stay in a studio apartment attached to my house for a few weeks. I then got to meet him again when I worked at Quiksilver as Harry Hodge's assistant. I used to help him in his general life (flat, car, administration documents, trips) and we had a friendly relationship. This relationship got closer with his illness as I got to be the intermediary between him and his doctors. I have now stopped working for Quiksilver and am taking care of my family."

ALAN TIEGEN: In the late '70s, Tiegen got involved with Rip Curl and Quiksilver and did films with Yves Bessas in Europe. Former executive director of EuroSIMA (Surf Industry Manufacturers Association). Now lives in Encinitas, surfing and enjoying life.

TUBESTEAK/MALIBU: "(I'm a) legendary figure from Malibu's olden days. Friend of all, hated by none. Having gone from Malibu's outhouse to the penthouse back to the outhouse, I'm now a recluse residing near the ocean in San Clemente, California. Real name: Terry Tracy."

BILL VAN DORN: "I went to Stanford and studied engineering and physics. I came to work at Scripps in 1947, thanks to Walter Munk, who had married Martha Chapin."

"Bill became an oceanographer, a big shot at Scripps Institute of Oceanography," said Doc Paskowitz. "He traveled all over the Pacific and was the father of the buoys that predict wave heights in tsunamis. He was also an avid surfer."

JOHN VAN HAMERSVELD: "I created a new *Surf Guide* magazine in 1964 as the famous 'Malibu Issue' for a September release. I developed the cover with Doctor Don James involving Dora, Kemp Aaberg, Mary Sturdevant, and Lance Carson. Bill Cleary and I thought up the article and interviewed Dora to fit into the piece. I designed the *Endless Summer* poster in 1964, too, as well as the Rolling Stones' *Exile on Main Street* and the Beatles' *Magical Mystery Tour* album covers." An iconist and artist of the first caliber, Van Hamersveld continues to create and is currently working on his autobiography in words and images, *Existential Monkey*.

DALE VELZY: Nicknamed "The Hawk." "Swaggering, innovative surfboard designer, builder and retailer from Hermosa Beach, CA," says the *Encyclopedia of Surfing*. "'Dale could out-drink, out-shoot, out-ride, out-shape, out-sell, and out-finesse all comers,' *The Surfer's Journal* magazine said in 1994." Velzy died in May 2005, but not before completing an autobiography, *Dale Velzy is Hawk*, with Paul Holmes.

DON WILSON: (see main text) Deceased.

BILL WISE: The Maryland/Delaware surf pioneer who became a quadraplegic in 1965 after a surfing accident, died February 23, 2007, after living a life inspirational to all who knew him.

PETER WOOLEY: Former assistant headmaster at St. John's Military Academy about ten years after Miki's time there. Later became an art director and production designer on many movies.

REYNOLDS YATER: Reynolds "Renny" Yater was one of the first real commercial surfboard builders of the 1950s. Glasssed for Hobie, then, in 1957, he moved over to Dale Velzy's shop in San Clemente where he began to shape balsa boards. During the 1960s, Yater's two most popular models were created: the Yater Spoon, one of the most innovative surfboard designs of the time, and the Pocket Rocket, a surfboard designed with Hawaiian surfing in mind. In the 1960s, Yater's customers included surfing legends such as Joey Cabell, Gordon Clark, Miki Dora, Philipe Pomar, Kemp Aaberg, Bob Cooper, Bruce Brown, and John Severson. (from www. yater.com)

CRISTAL YOSH: Co-owns, with husband, Gary, Cristal Cove guest house in Jeffreys Bay, right on Supertubes. Remarkable woman with a fierce mind; a force of nature, really.

GARY YOSH: Jeffreys Bay surfer and craftsman. Miki lived in the apartment beneath the Yosh home, on the hillside overlooking Supertubes, for seven years—until the accommodation was destroyed by fire in 1998.

NAT YOUNG: From Young's *The History of Surfing*, "Nat Young is recognized as one of the great surfers in the history of the sport. Grew up in Collaroy on Sydney Australia's northern beaches, and won the World Championship in 1966, in California . . . was several times Australian junior and open champion. In the late 1960s he and a handful of others ushered in the 'new era' in surfboard riding, a power-oriented style which forms the basis of contemporary surfing . . . he was World Longboard Champion in 1988, '89, and '90. He is the author of several books." These include his autobiography, *Nat's Nat and That's That*.

LOUIS ZAMPERINI: Juvenile delinquent from Torrance, California, who turned his life around and became a championship runner. Crashed at sea in World War II, but Zamperini survived and spent forty-seven days drifting two thousand miles on a raft before being captured by the Japanese in the Marshall Islands. He spent two years in a variety of prison camps, but survived. Born again in 1949, started Victory Boys Camp for delinquent boys, active in military, religious, and sports circles. Coauthored his biography, *Devil at My Heels* (William Morrow), with David Rensin in 2003. Now ninety-one years old, Zamperini had to quit skateboarding at eighty-five—but still skis and travels regularly as a motivational speaker.

Acknowledgments

To start in early 2003 and take four years to pull together hundreds of voices from Miki Dora's life and let a portrait emerge of a man who told everyone not to talk about him ("Don't sell me out"), who didn't want to be known on any but his own terms, and who was blessed and cursed by becoming a legend in his own time, is, like riding a wave, a transaction between all one's skill, the ability to live completely in the moment, and the great gaping jaws of the unknown.

When I began—in 1982, actually, when I first wondered what had become of this surf hero of my youth and wrote about Miki for *California* magazine—like the nonsurfing readers of this book, I, too, had to learn the shape and form of Miki's life from anyone willing to share. Not an easy task then with Miki ever looming in the background, disapproving, calculating the advantages and disadvantages of cooperation.

Twenty-one years later, when I decided to write this book, his depths seemed even less fathomable. I had more years to account for, filled with layers of attitude and ocean romance, and plenty of Miki stories—but the thread that might pull it all together was still as elusive as ever.

That thread, I now believe, was the intertwining of three threads: Miki's artistic temperament and emotional inner life, his addiction to the sensations of surfing, and his never-ending quest for personal freedom.

My own reasons for wanting to step back into DoraWorld were also at first inchoate. I knew I had only scratched the surface earlier, and I believed that the part of Miki's life that I knew, which already contained all the elements of classic myth, was only an outside swell, a potential wave that beckoned, but may or may not have been suitable for riding. Although there already were, in the surf genre magazines, excellent ponderings about, playful interviews with, and far-out meditations by Miki, as well as appreciations by others of his style and deeper meaning, Miki's way of being in the world contained, at least to me, a universal resonance that went beyond the beaches and waves.

Even Miki, who always wanted to be acknowledged as more than some surfer from Malibu, seemed to think so.

And who can resist a mystery? I saw a limiting curtain of conventional wisdom about Miki—a man who could not be accurately pigeonholed as a single personality type—begging to be lifted. That's always an exciting challenge for a writer. Everyone's long-standing apprehension at talking about Miki was also a tip-off. I realized that those closest to him were afraid that any biographer would take the easy way out and focus only on the darker aspects of their love/loathed antihero, and paint him as a surfer gone bad, a common criminal.

I had to work hard to convince almost everyone I spoke with otherwise. I had to encounter again Miki's own conflicted reaction to my *California* magazine piece, filtered through his friends. (I was gratified that so many remembered the story positively.) I had to explain to everyone who said that Miki would never approve or cooperate with this book that they were, in one sense, right—but that I had ample evidence to show that he wanted to leave a written legacy nonetheless and had, in his own way, tried many times with many potential writers. And not only for the sake of the game.

I had to assure his most ardent protectors and disciples that I could be both nonjudgmental and do a compelling book—and then prove it.

I sincerely hope that this book makes good on the promise to be authentic, bar no holds, remain above sensationalism, and present enough of Miki's life to let readers reach their own reasonable conclusions. I couldn't cover everything; there is much left out (a first draft of this book was about three times as long), or simply undiscovered—as Miki intended—but there is also much to sift through. I didn't write this book to make Miki happy, but I believe I've honored his wish to be remembered as more than a surf relic who, for a moment frozen in time, ruled at Malibu. I saw also a rebel spirit who explored the world, modes of thought, human nature, and nature itself.

Still, I realize that in biographies, some judgment—call it an authoritative assessment—of the subject is expected. Like Miki, I couldn't make it easy for you, but not because I know some secret that I'm withholding. I play no coy game here. I, too, circled Miki's event horizon, hoping only to come closer to the singularity than most before being frozen in place.

For the record, my own view of Miki is romantic, sober, and certain that no one like him will ever pass this way again.

Fast-forward five years—from inception to publication—and it's obvious that many, many of those who knew Miki with various levels of intimacy, despite any initial reluctance, gracefully cooperated. Believe me: This book is all about the cooperation. One reason, of course, is that although Miki had passed away, his legacy had only grown. Miki's name continued to come up in conversations; movies were planned and abandoned; books, too, because memories of Miki are always good for an amazing story. My contributors not only wanted to finally share their part of the adventure, but realized that the time to participate was now, before too many who knew the tales were themselves gone.

And so, I gratefully acknowledge everyone who spoke to me, on the record—and, rarely, off; those whose voices appear in the book, and those whose voices should have, but don't. It wasn't lack of good material, just too much of it.

To those already in the know about Miki, there might seem to be some voices missing. There are reasons: the person in question was dead or died during the project and I did not get to him in time; I did not know of her existence or part in Miki's story, and when I did—if I ever did—it was too late to include her; he had nothing new to add; there was simply no more room; or he chose not to cooperate. The latter, a very few, had their reasons. I can live with that; they will have to as well. Of course, as you know by now, no one knew Miki completely, not even his closest comrades. Miki showed only facets. Most were left to wonder at the jewel's beautifully cut surface. Others were allowed to see deeper, into the gem's fire. For them it might have been both impossible to look, and to look away.

Of those who freely revealed Miki's multichromatic heart, I am eternally grateful to Miklos and Christine Dora; Harry Hodge (for the constant faith and the means); Greg and Laura Noll; Bob Simpson, Allan Carter; Steven Taussig; Derek Hynd; Steve Pezman; Susan McNeill; Marcia McMartin; Linda Cuy; Jan Mayer; Philippe Lauga; and the late Gardner Chapin Jr. who, sadly, just as this book was finished, died on his sixtieth birthday. Each were key participants who gave their time willingly, again and again, asking nothing in return, and paired their words with emotion and insight, which are to writers what perfect waves are to surfers. Without their faith, trust, and understanding that the time had come to tell the story, there would be no book. Although each saw Miki in his or her own way, I am honored by their willingness to contribute their viewpoint but not impose it, and instead let the information I accumulated evolve into a picture uniquely its own.

A special word about Miki's dad. When I brought the manuscript to Miklos to review for accuracy and to listen to any suggestions he had, it sat on the table between us as we drank green tea and ate a delicious blueberry torte his wife, Christine, had made. Miklos stole glances at the pile of paper as we spoke about his Hungarian youth, and the depressing world situation. Finally, he said he knew the read would be difficult and emotional; understandable, since no man should have his child die before him. And his child was like no other.

A week later, we met again. As expected, Miklos had responded with tears and laughter, pride and anger, and finally acceptance. His son was his son, he said, and he loved him no matter what.

"It's a good book," he added. "Well written." He agreed that I'd been fair and honest and hadn't sensationalized. "You captured Miki's character," he said. Then, and this still resonates: "But I would have liked it more if it had been about someone else's son."

I get it. Thank you, Miklos.

Extra special thanks to the great Phil Edwards for his trust, and to the irrepressible Mickey Muñoz for his generous insights. The same to: Tom Adler, Bob Beadle, Bob Feigel, Drew Kampion, Gerry Kantor, Phil Jarratt, Ben Marcus, Stacy Peralta, Agi Orsi, Alan Somers, Matt Warshaw, Scott Hulet, Terry "Tubesteak" Tracy, Dale Velzy, Johnny Fain, Matt Katz, Jim Kempton, Bruce Gold, Cheron Kraak, Gary and Cristal Yosh, Jessica Naude, and Christine Liepner. Doug Cavanaugh, Lee Nicholl, and Mark Fragale also went the extra mile behind the scenes to make this book worth reading.

I'm forever indebted to the many around the world who provided copies of Miki's letters, faxes, drawings, photos, and hand-scrawled notes, particularly Miklos Dora Sr., who graciously told me to "use whatever I need to make a good book"—and meant it.

My steadfast and wise literary agent, Brian DeFiore, traveled the twisty and taxing road through DoraWorld with me to get this book written. His calm counsel and sense of humor were bulwarks against the madness. Laurie Abkemeier was always there with moral support, focus, and enthusiasm. Kate Garrick knows the international taxation system like nobody's business, and still manages to remain cheerful. William Morris Agency honcho, Rob Carlson—who has believed in the Dora story since I told him about it in 1990—strategized the Hollywood angle and kept me excited and afloat. Thanks also to Mike Esola, Rick Yorn, Brad Simpson, Franklin Leonard, the DiCaprios, and everyone then and now at Appian Way for their enthusiasm, and D. V. DeVincentes for the reading list and knowing the essence is the essence.

Cynthia Price, who has been invaluable to just about every book I've done, and Sara Grace Rimensnyder, who was priceless here, not only brought over a million words of transcript to life, but listened patiently every step of the way, providing all manner of mental and editorial CPR. Any superlatives I trot out here will do them no justice. Let's just say I couldn't have done the book without them.

Nancy Rommelmann, a writer with the right stuff, not only bravely stepped up, read the first huge manuscript, and gave me indispensable guidance and the right words at the right time, but she let me steal and add to a stunning paragraph she tossed off in her comments. It opens Chapter 20. She gets the credit. For some reason she just gets what I do better than most—and says I get her in return. I'm grateful for her generosity.

Mauro DiPreta at William Morrow and Co. is the best editor anyone can have. He listened to me talk about Dora for nearly ten years, then when I was ready, he said yes. When he got the manuscript, his wise editorial eye saw ways everyone else—including myself—had missed to coax the statue out of the stone. Then he tossed me the hammers and chisels and said, "cut!" He was right. Also, at William Morrow: Joelle Yudin, Jennifer Schulkind, Laurie McGee, and Joyce Wong.

Thanks to Scott Kaufer and Janet Duckworth, former editor-in-chief and editor at *California* magazine, for the original assignment and their help then in making a difficult story happen, as well as their unstinting support twenty years later when I told them about this book. Author Steve Oney has also been unrestrained in his enthusiasm for the project. Thanks also to Allan and Jody Marcil for being early believers.

Jean Stein and George Plimpton's *Edie: An American Biography* (Knopf, 1982), is the ultimate oral biography, the original inspiration, and constant spiritual adviser to this endeavor.

Dennis Klein has always been a great friend and mentor. He was the first to tell me to get into the David Rensin business. He was right. This book is that. All satisfaction lives there.

No book is possible without one's friends, peers, and betters to cheer you on. They are my brother-in-words Bill Zehme, Bernie and Carrie Brillstein, Amy Alkon, Jane Ayer, Steven Baker, George S. Clinton and Charlotte Blunt, Suzette Clover and Leonard Pape, Darcy Cosper, Catherine Crier, Cameron Crowe, Meghan Daum, Veronique de Turenne, Carl Fisher, Luke Ford, Jennifer Gates, Ron Hamady, Laura Hillenbrand, Barry Huan, Peter Kaufman, Judd Klinger, Lisa Kusel, Jennifer Laurie, Joshua Marquis, Greg McClave, Neal Preston, Steve Randall, Jody Rein, John Rezek, Emmanuelle Richard, Kevin Roderick, Cathy Seipp, Congressman Brad Sherman, Loni and Julie Specter, Richard Thompson (of counsel), Linda Thompson, Irena Vidulovich, Matt Welch, First Friday at Yamashiro, the Campbell Hall School library staff, and the friendly folks at the FBI. Carrie Ann Neeson gets long overdue thanks, a long overdue dinner, and a long overdue hug for clearing up one mystery so I could focus on another.

Thanks to Freddie Fields and Gil Cates for being good sports, to Tom Cruise and Kathy Anderson for taking the meeting, and to Craig Stecyk; he knows what for.

Michael G. Newman, Wally Oetzell, Doug Pace, Robert Rauch, Daniel Dunham, Kip Gray, David Youngs, Mark Christensen, Rob Schapper, Bill Haas, and other Granada Hills High School and neighborhood pals—including some now forgotten—were my original surfing buddies, and I am grateful they put up with my nearsighted attempts to catch close-out waves and mostly stay out of their way. Thanks also to Garry Ross (not the director) for loaning me his concave bottom Yater, as well as Cindy Christensen, the Bess girls, the Lewis brothers, John Abercrombie, the Haberers, Steve Marsilio, Richard Gomez, Gordon Brown, and the rest of the Oak Park Avenue gang for making growing up unforgettable.

Lainey O'Connell made my travels possible—and comfortable. Thanks to the Villa Catarie in Guéthary for the wonderful accommodations, and the Yosh family in Jeffreys Bay for a home away from home. A tip of the hat also to Best Western for an always dependable bed, and to Starbucks for an oasis and a comfy chair.

Without the unprecedented participation of the following . . . well, there would be no book in which to publish this list. Not everyone's voice appears, but all had something to say, and said it well.

Kemp Aaberg, Denny Aaberg, Chris Anderson, Cynthia Applewhite, Les Arndt, William Asher, Sam August, Robert August, Clive Barber, Peter Barnett, Peggy Barr, Caroline Barrett, Brad Barrett, Rabbit Bartholomew, Rick Beck, Brad Bemis, Billy Al Bengston, Yves Bessas, Jim Best, Taki Bibelas, Gregg Blue, Estaban Bojorquez, Peaches Booke, Paul Botha, Duke Boyd, Gary Boyle, Jeff Bradburn,

Shorty Bronkhurst, Scott Bryson, Garth Bullock, Joey Cabell, David Caldwell, Marge Calhoun, Tom Canterbury, George Carr, Corky Carroll, Lance Carson, Jean-Charles Cazes, Rupert Chadwick, Eric Chauché, Frances Christopher, Barbara Cleary, Mike Clemmons, Cecilia Clouse, Corny Cole, Peter Cole, Steve Conner, Terrence Cooney, Bob Cooper, Ricardo Correia, Dr. Adrian Cotton, Carin Crawford, Spencer Croul, Dennis Daly, Peter Dane, Christian Darren, James Darren, Maritxu Darrigrand, Pat Darrin, Peter Day, Bill Delaney, N. Edward Denton, Roger Diamond, Robbie Dick, Willie Dix, Peter Dixon, Joe Donnelly, Corb Donohue, Toni Donovan Colvin, Mike Doyle, Jim Drever, Joel Drucker, Jacky Dupin, Mike Eaton, Jon Ebling, Ned Eckert, Carl Eckstrom, Brian Eddy, Dean Edwards, Woody Ekstrom, John Elwell, Skip Engblom, Paul Fegen, Lee Fineman, Jim Fisher, Jimmy Fitzpatrick, Vicki Flaxman, Herbie Fletcher, Henry Ford, Trudi Forster, Kim Fowley, Bill Frey-McLean, Anthony Friedkin, Charlie Galanto, Jim Ganzer, Alain Gardinier, Ed Garner, Malcolm Gault-Williams, George George, Sam George, Colin Gilbert, Robert Gilbert, Edward Godfrey, Juliette Godfrey, Peter Gowland, Phil Grace, Jim Graham, LeRoy Grannis, Ricky Grigg, Shane Grimes, Jeff Hakman, Michael Halsband, Michael Hamilburg, Craig Hamlin, Jan Handzlik, Barry Haun, Gregg Henderson, Glenn Hening, Dale Herd, Frayne Higgason, Nile Hight, Andy Hill, Steve Hilton, Mike Hischier, Sandee Hodge, Rick Hodgson, Joyce Hoffman, Walter Hoffman, Tom Holbrook, Paul Holmes, Mike Holmquist, Dick Hoole, Kit Horn, Gwen Horne, Willie House, Mary Hughes, Rod Hughes, Mike Hynson, Hap Jacobs, Madame Jardine, Bill Jensen, Hal Jepsen, Richard Josephson, Prosper Keating, Duane King, Matt Kivlin, Kathy Kohner, Ari Kraak, Dr. Alexandre Krassoulia, Kris Kruseski, Harvey Kubernik, Ray Kunze, François Lartigau, Erik Laykin, Joel Laykin, Michael Laykin, Craig Leonard, Alison Leopold, Larry Lindberg, Gerry Lopez, Terry Lucoff, MJ Luten, Paul Luten, Steve Lyons, Tim Lyons, Dr. Kurt Mariano, Peter Masica, The Masochist, Annabelle McBride, Tom McBride, Tim McCollough, Ian McCormack, Jack McCoy, Jenny McDonald, Michael McDonnell, Barry McGrath, Roger McGrath, Mary McGuiness, Kristine McKenna, Mick McMahon, Mike McNeill, Peggy McGuinness, Greg Meisenholder, Jim Mellor, John Melton, Melinda Merryweather, Dick Metz, Mikey Meyer, John Milius, Rusty Miller, Laurent Miramon, Virginie Miramon, Jenny Moore, Tom Morey, Bev Morgan, Bob Morris, Shafiq Morton, Brendan Muldoon, Mike Nader, Clive Neeson, George Van Noy, Kem Nunn, Diane Swanson Oosterveen, Ira Opper, E. J. Oshier, Faye Parker, Dorian Paskowitz, Tom Payne, John Peck, Greg Person, Thomas Petersen, Rick Peterson, Christine Petrucci, Peter Piper, Gene Poole, Jericho Poppler, Ken Price, Jon Price, Joe Quigg, The Surfing Rabbi, Gerald Rafferty, Patti Rane-Green, Jim Rapheld, Randy Rarick, Paul Reader, John Reilly, Walter Reinhold, LJ Richards, John Richilano, Douglas Rishworth, Armand Riza, Jean Yves Robert, Garth Robinson, Pua Rochlen, Grant Rohloff, Chris Rohloff, Judy Rohloff, Don Rohrer, Ovidio Salazar, Susan Samama, John Severson, Richard Shivetts, Barbara Sievers, Richard Slade, Dr. Don Small, Ron Smerling, Mike Smith, Ruby Smith, Jackie Smith, Bill Sobel, Gibus de Soultrait, Wayne Speeds, Douglas Stancliff, Elwood Stancliff, Juanita Stancliff, Baron Stander, Merritt Stanfield, David Stern, Deanne Stillman, Kathy Stolkin, Darryl Stolper, Linda Stolper, Paul Strauch, Martin Sugarman, David Sumpter, Jock Sutherland, Dave Sweet, Mike Tabeling,

Dominique Taylor, Alan Tiegen, Dave Timbs, Bokka du Toit, Porter Turnbull, Bill Van Dorn, Fred Van Dyke, John Van Hamersveld, Peter Viertel, Dusty Waddell, Sheila Weller, Les Williams, Don Wilson, Tony Wilson, Bill Wise, Anthony Wolff, Peter Wooley, Bank Wright, Reynolds Yater, Nat Young, Louis Zamperini.

I've probably forgotten more than a few. Apologies. My memory isn't what it used to be, my handwriting an abysmal scrawl. I know I took a few phone numbers and never got around to calling, and a few offered to speak and never called back (c'est la vie). Many thanks all around.

Thanks, Mom and Joe. I miss you, Pop. I wish you'd been here for it all.

First and last and forever, without the understanding, wisdom, patience, insight, and love of my wife, Suzie Peterson, and son, Emmett Rensin, what would be the point? People may tell me everything, but you both mean everything to me.

Want to reach the author, comment on *All for a Few Perfect Waves*, keep up with media coverage, read more about Miki Dora—including material that for reasons of length didn't make it into the book—and even tell *your* story about Miki? Go to www.tellmeeverything.com.

Excerpts of Ben Marcus's thoughts and words, courtesy Ben Marcus.

Dialogue from *Surfers: The Movie*, as well as interview outtakes, courtesy of Bill Delaney.

Repurposed excerpts from Phil Jarratt's "The Last Days of Miki Dora," courtesy of Phil Jarratt.

Selections from the diaries of Steve Conner and Rod Hughes, courtesy Conner and Hughes.

Photos and selections from Kathy Kohner's diary courtesy Kathy Kohner.

Painting of Miki on the nose at Malibu, copyright and courtesy of Rick Peterson. Limited edition prints available at www.RichardPetersonGallery.com.

Quotation from Sterling Hayden's "Wanderer" (Bantam, 1964), reprinted by permission of SLL/Sterling Lord Literistic, Inc. Copyright by Sterling Hayden.

In 1969, John Severson interviewed Miki Dora for his film *Pacific Vibrations*. The film is scheduled to be re-released by Severson and *Surfer* magazine. Dialogue excerpt, as an epigraph, courtesy John Severson.

Selections from "Nine Lives of the Cat," from the unpublished papers of Bill Cleary, courtesy of Barbara Denzel Cleary.

Ramona Stancliff Dora's 1934 letter to her friend Yolande, and letters from Miki to Ramona, and photos, courtesy of the late Gard Chapin Jr.

Thanks to Malcolm Gault-Williams for continuing to capture the history of surfing on his "Legendary Surfers" website at www.legendarysurfers.com. The material was invaluable as research, and I recommend it highly. Quotes from the site attributed. Gault-Williams is now issuing his material in book form.

Thanks to Matt Warshaw for good cheer, early groundwork, and his ultimate resource, the unparalleled *Encyclopedia of Surfing* (Harcourt, 2003).

Thanks to everyone who keeps the surfing flame alive on websites worldwide. Some I have quoted directly. Others provided research nuggets that enhanced the book. Your spirit informs this biography.

Thanks to Paul Reader for his description of the surfing dream state.

Miki's FBI file courtesy of the Freedom of Information Act. Various court records, police and prison records, courtesy of same. My congressman, Brad Sherman, and his aide, Irena Vidulovich, and the staff never let up for a moment of the two years it took to get these documents.

History of the Diners Club card, courtesy of the Diners Club International website, www.dinersclubnewsroom.com/anniversary.cfm.

Lyrics from "Postcards from Hollywood," used by gracious permission of singer/songwriter Ned Doheny.

Some C. R. Stecyk info and interview excerpts from the transcripts of film, *In ⸮ of Da Cat*, courtesy Ovidio Salazar and Peter Day.

⸮-lost Dora collectibles, photos, descriptions, courtesy of the Refrigerator

⸮nd auction photos, courtesy of Rick Hodgson; excerpts from "A ⸮ Story" on www.atomicbride.com, and in Glenn Hening's "The ⸮e End of an Era," from the Groundswell Society publication, ⸮rmission of Hodgson.

1970–1974 "World Tour" photos, courtesy of Marcia McMartin.

All Greg and Laura Noll photos, courtesy of the Noll Family Collection.

Photos by Peter Gowland, courtesy of Peter Gowland.

Photo of Miki standing by his van in France, courtesy of Chris Clements.

Early photos of Miki and Gard Chapin Sr., courtesy of Bill Van Dorn.

Photos of Miki, Johnny Fain, and Deetsie at Malibu in the '60s, by and courtesy of Toni Donovan Colvin.

Photo of Philippe Lauga and Miki on the golf course, courtesy of Philippe Lauga.

Photo of the Four Horsemen on the tarmac in Rio, courtesy of the late Greg Meisenholder.

Permission to quote and repurpose Jan Mayer's thoughts and words about Miki, courtesy of Jan Mayer.

Photo of Miki (en mask) and Greg Noll, courtesy of Tom Servais.

Photo of Miki at Punta Lobos, courtesy of Paul Mills.

Excerpts and repurposing of Derek Hynd's elegy to Miki Dora, "The King Is Dead," first printed in *Surfer* magazine, May 2002, used with permission of Derek Hynd.

Photo of "Dora" on the Malibu Wall, courtesy of Matt Katz.

Frame grab of Miki surfing at Jeffreys Bay in 1996, from *In Search of Da Cat.* Courtesy of Ovidio Salazar, director.

Photo of Miki grinning in Guéthary a few months before his death, courtesy of Jan Snyder.

A few of the voices interviewed here supplemented their contribution by offering to "write it down" in essay or e-mail, or grant permission to use something previously written, as well as speak on tape. Thanks to Clive Neeson, Philippe Lauga, Darryl Stolper, and anyone else not elsewhere thanked who corresponded with additional thoughts and recollections.